Windows Sources Microsoft Excel 97 for Windows SuperGuide

Windows Sources Microsoft Excel 97 for Windows SuperGuide

Bruce Hallberg

Ziff-Davis Press
an imprint of Macmillan Computer Publishing USA
Emeryville, California

Publisher	Joe Wikert
Associate Publisher	Juliet Langley
Acquisitions Editor	Lysa Lewallen
Development Editor	Nancy Warner
Copy Editor	Mitzi Waltz
Technical Reviewer	Leigh Yafa
Proofreader	Jeff Barash
Cover Illustration, Design	Megan Gandt
Book Design	Bruce Lundquist
Page Layout	M. D. Barrera
Indexer	Carol Burbo

Ziff-Davis Press, ZD Press, the Ziff-Davis Press logo are trademarks or registered trademarks of, and are licensed to Macmillan Computer Publishing USA by Ziff-Davis Publishing Company, New York, New York.

Ziff-Davis Press imprint books are produced on a Macintosh computer system with the following applications: FrameMaker®, Microsoft® Word, Quark XPress®, Adobe Illustrator®, Adobe Photoshop®, Adobe Streamline™, MacLink®*Plus*, Aldus® FreeHand™, Collage Plus™.

Ziff-Davis Press, an imprint of
Macmillan Computer Publishing USA
5903 Christie Avenue
Emeryville, CA 94608

ISBN 1-56276-507-8

Manufactured in the United States of America
10 9 8 7 6 5 4 3 2 1

■ About the Authors

Bruce Hallberg

Bruce Hallberg, with more than 15 years experience in the computer industry, heads the Information Systems group for a biotechnology company located in California. His background includes consulting nationally with Fortune 1000 companies on accounting and management information systems. He is the author and/or co-author of more than 15 books, including *Inside Windows NT Workstation 4, Inside Microsoft Exchange,* and *Windows Sources Microsoft Office 97 for Windows SuperGuide.*

Victor Wright

Victor Wright is a popular lecturer at the School of Engineering and Computer Science at California State University, Fullerton. For the past seven years he has taught PC courses for the University's Department of Extended Education. Also employed with Hughes Aircraft Company, Wright serves as training coordinator for the Systems and Software Engineering Council. He is the author *of How to Use Microsoft Works for Windows 95*, published by Ziff-Davis Press.

For my brothers, Brad and Brian, with love.

■ Contents at a Glance

■ Table of Contents

Chapter 13: Drawing and Adding Graphics to Documents   481

■ Acknowledgments

Combine the patience of Job, the toughness of Schwarzenegger, the diplomacy of Kissinger, and the business sense of Bill Gates, and you have the recipe for a great acquisitions editor. Lysa Lewallen is just such an acquisitions editor. She is responsible for Ziff-Davis Press's publication of this book, and for guiding it through from initial concept to the final product you see in your hands. She has also put up with working with me over the past six months, which is worth major accolades no matter how you look at it.

Nancy Warner saw each chapter as it was submitted before anyone else, and performed what is called the developmental edit on the book. In this role, she examined each chapter for overall content, for how well it stayed on track, and for its relevance. When she saw something that was amiss, she pointed out the problem and recommended solutions. Her comments were always useful, and invariably improved the book.

I seem to have run out of superlatives to describe Mitzi Waltz, the copy editor of this book, from my acknowledgment of her in my *Windows Sources Microsoft Office 97 SuperGuide*. I can't count the number of different copy editors that I've worked with over the years. Generally, my copy editors annoy me, because they often serve to make these books duller and more lifeless than otherwise. (And remember, we're talking about books on computer software here!) Not so with Mitzi's work. Heck, I don't even look at her improvements to my writing any more, because they're always perfect, always improve on how I wrote something, always make it more readable and understandable, and I never need to ask to have them changed. Not ever. It's remarkably satisfying to work with someone of Mitzi's caliber, and I really can't go on enough about her.

Leigh Yafa performed the technical editing on most of this book, where she checked every fact and made suggestions throughout that improved both its technical accuracy and its ability to communicate what you need to know about Excel 97. Leigh knows Excel like the back of her hand, so she performed meticulous fact-checking and made literally hundreds of suggestions throughout. Leigh really threw herself into helping make this book the best, most accurate volume available on Excel 97, and she has my deepest gratitude for the fine, thorough work she did.

Sally Neuman also did some of the technical edits on the book. Sally actually worked on an earlier incarnation of this book as an author, and it was gratifying to have her involved again, albeit in a different role. She came through at the last minute to make sure several of the chapters were ready in time for our publication deadline, and so her contribution is magnified because of the importance of meeting such deadlines. In other words, Sally can be counted on to come through in a pinch, and did so in spades.

■ Introduction

Welcome to *Windows Sources Excel 97 SuperGuide*!

This book is the most complete guide to Excel 97 available, with extensive information about using Excel, linking Excel to other applications, and developing your own custom spreadsheet projects with Excel.

■ Microsoft Excel 97

Excel 97 is an important upgrade. It adds impressive features to an already feature-packed product. The most notable enhancements to Excel 97 for Windows include the following:

- The new Office Advisor, an on-screen assistant that helps you with Excel 97, which offers important tips and advice.

- Integration with Microsoft's new Intellimouse, which lets you pan and zoom within your worksheets quickly and easily.

- Multiple-level undo, which lets you undo any number of actions since the last time you saved your workbook.

- Increased capacities! Excel 97 now supports 65,535 rows of data, up from 16,384 — and more importantly, each cell can have up to 32,767 characters worth of data, which is a vast increase from the old limit of 255 characters. Charts can also have more data points: 32,000 versus the 4,000 that were possible with earlier versions of Excel.

- Shared Workbooks, an upgrade of the older Shared Lists feature, now let you consolidate information from multiple users at intervals that you specify, and also store View and Print layout information for each user.

- Improved comments, with many more capabilities than Excel for Windows 95's "note" feature. Comments attached to cells can now be viewed by merely resting your mouse pointer for a moment over the cell.

- Formula AutoCorrect, similar to Word's AutoCorrect feature, now corrects 15 of the most common typing errors in formulas, such as double operators, extra parentheses, and transposed cell references.

- You can now use Natural Language Formulas. In Excel 95, you could enter formulas like **=SquareFootage*RentalRate** only when you had properly defined the names of the cell ranges. Excel 97 is much more intelligent in this regard, so you can now use such formulas automatically. As long as the column and row headings are in the proper place in relationship to the data, Excel will automatically understand formulas based on those row and column headings.

- A new Data Validation dialog box makes validating cell data quick and easy.

- For Shared Workbooks, you can now track changes made by users, highlighting insertions and deletions that each one makes. You can view the changes for a selectable number of days, and can even create a summary worksheet that details all of the changes made.

- Collapse/Expand Dialog Boxes: There are many dialog boxes in Excel that let you use your mouse to select the range of cells that should be input into a particular field. In Excel 95, it was often difficult to move the dialog box away so that you could select the range of cells you were interested in. In Excel 97, such dialog-box fields have a Collapse/Expand Dialog Box button to the immediate right of the field. This button lets you move the dialog box completely out of your way while you select a range. Click the button again, and the dialog box will reappear.

- A new Range Finder makes it easy to see what cells a particular formula uses. When you edit a formula or double-click on a cell, the source cells will be highlighted for you while you work. This makes it easy to ensure that you're referencing the correct cells in your formulas.

- A new Page Break Preview feature with draggable page breaks makes it much easier to correctly position page breaks in Excel 97 than it was in earlier versions of the program.

- A new Conditional Formatting dialog box lets you choose custom cell formats for cells, based on their content. Using the Conditional Formatting feature is easier than defining custom formatting codes, as you had to do in earlier versions of Excel.

- A new Formula Palette makes it even simpler to create formulas in your worksheets.

- The charting function has really been upgraded! The new Chart Wizard is both easier to use and more powerful than previous versions. Also, new chart types have been added: 3D variants of the column chart, Bar of Pie, and Pie of Pie, as well as a few others that simplify representing your data as you wish.

- Excel 97 now integrates with the Internet! You can query Web pages directly from within Excel to retrieving stock quotes, for instance, without ever firing up your Web browser. You can also use the Query Wizard to query Internet sites.

- You can create Web pages with Excel 97. You can create standalone pages, or you can generate tables and graphic images from your charts for inclusion on existing Web pages.

Windows Sources Excel 97 SuperGuide shows you all these new features in detail, while also providing extensive coverage of every other Excel feature, complete with examples and step-by-step instructions.

■ How This Book is Organized

To keep the book organized, *Windows Sources Excel 97 SuperGuide* has been divided into eight main sections, each one of which details a particular area of Excel.

Part 1: Worksheets

Chapter 1, "Introducing Excel," is for those readers who are completely new to Excel. In this chapter, you'll walk through all of the steps necessary to create a simple worksheet, format the worksheet, create a chart from the worksheet data, and then save your work. Along the way, you will learn about the key parts of the Excel screen, how to manipulate data in Excel, and how to perform other basic spreadsheet functions. If you have used Excel before, you can skip this chapter, or just browse it briefly.

Chapter 2, "Working with Worksheet Data," is devoted to teaching you how to work with data on worksheets. This chapter shows you all the ways to enter and manage data on an Excel worksheet. You'll learn about data-entry techniques, a variety of ways to address cells, moving data around the worksheet, working with named ranges on an Excel worksheet, and using Excel's AutoFill feature.

Chapter 3, "Worksheet Formatting," shows you ways to format your worksheets to make them more attractive. You'll learn to format numbers, dates, times, and text. You will also learn how to apply fonts, underlining and shading, cell borders, format styles, and more.

Chapter 4, "Printing Documents," shows you all of the tricks you'll need to print your worksheets and charts. You'll learn about previewing printouts, how different fonts work with Excel, how to get the most from your printer, and so on.

Chapter 5, "Working with Multiple Windows," covers all the ways that Excel can work with different views of your workbooks. You'll learn about 3D cell references that let you build complex workbooks, how to link pictures between documents, and how to set up workbook templates.

Chapter 6, "Advanced Worksheet Features," explains all of the advanced features you may need to use with your worksheets, such as outlining, auditing tools, and PivotTables.

Chapter 7, "Mastering Functions," teaches you how to use Excel functions, which give you the ability to really master Excel. You will learn about entering functions, using parameters, and dealing with function error messages.

Chapter 8, "Complete Guide to Excel Functions," is a reference guide to all of the Excel functions. Look here for detailed information about each of the program's functions.

Chapter 9, "Mastering Excel Analytical Tools," shows you how to use the more-advanced analysis features in Excel's optional Analysis ToolPak add-in. The Analysis ToolPak add-in includes highly technical tools that are not part of the base Excel package. These tools include functions for engineering and statistical analysis of your data.

Part 2: Databases

The second part of *Windows Sources' Excel 97 SuperGuide* takes a detailed look at the database features in Excel.

Chapter 10, "Excel Database Basics," explains the process of creating databases, setting up fields, entering data, and editing data.

Chapter 11, "Using Microsoft Query," teaches you how to find query data in your Excel databases, how to use Microsoft Query to access other databases, and how to set up database reports.

Part 3: Charts

Part 3 provides the low-down on creating charts and graphics. It includes a complete guide to Excel charts, an advanced charting chapter, and a chapter on using the Excel drawing tools on worksheets and charts.

Chapter 12, "Complete Guide to Charts," takes you through all of the details of creating and changing charts. You'll learn to use the ChartWizard, and to format and rearrange your charts. This chapter also includes a guide to all of the Excel chart types, along with notes about each type of chart and how it is best used.

Chapter 13, "Drawing and Adding Graphics to Documents," educates you on using the drawing tools in Excel to annotate your worksheets and charts. The drawing tools in Excel are even good enough to use for general drawing purposes, and might just replace a dedicated drawing program in your software repertoire. This chapter also shows you how to import drawings from other programs, and gives you some ideas about how these drawings might be used in your Excel documents.

Chapter 14, "Advanced Charts for Business and Science," covers more-advanced charting needs. You'll learn about stock charts and technical charting features, such as regression trend lines and error bars. You will also learn about dual Y-axis charts, adding new data to an existing chart, and dealing with missing data.

Part 4: Programming Excel

Chapter 15, "Understanding and Using Macros," shows you how to record and use recorded VBA macros in Excel.

Part 5: Excel and the Internet

In Part 5 you will learn about Excel and the Internet. Chapter 16, "Browsing Web Pages with Excel" shows you how to use the Web toolbar in Excel, and how to perform Web queries from within Excel. Chapter 17, "Creating Web Pages," shows you how to create and manage hyperlinks in Excel, and how to create simple Web pages with Excel 97.

Part 6: Excel Tools

Chapter 18, "Using Excel Add-Ins," instructs you in the use of the Excel add-in programs — features that are not considered part of the main Excel program, but that are included with Excel and that can be added to your toolkit at your discretion. These tools include an AutoSave feature that automatically saves your work at regular intervals; a report manager for generating recurring reports based on your Excel worksheets; and an advanced Solver program, which finds optimal solutions to those challenging problems that would otherwise require programming expertise to solve.

Chapter 19, "Excel in Workgroups," covers all of the features that let you take advantage of Excel when you share files with many people. You'll learn about shared workbooks, how file-sharing works in Excel, and how to send people copies of your workbooks. You will also learn about the new Track Changes feature.

Appendixes

Appendix A, "Getting Excel Help," details your options when you need to seek additional help to use Excel. The choices include the program's built-in tutorials, Microsoft's technical-support phone numbers, Internet resources, and a complete guide to the CompuServe support areas for Excel, so be sure to turn to this appendix when you are stumped with an Excel problem.

Appendix B, "Keyboard Shortcuts," puts all the Excel shortcut keys and their definitions in one convenient place to help make you more productive.

■ Conventions Used in This Book

To make this book easier to read, a number of type conventions have been established. Table I.1 explains these conventions.

Table I.1

Windows
Sources Excel
97 SuperGuide
Type Conventions

EXAMPLE	DESCRIPTION
Bold	Boldface type represents something that you should actually type. For example: Type **=(A5*100)/2.34** and press Enter.
Italic	Italic type is used to draw your attention to new terms as they are defined. Occasionally, italic type is also used for *emphasis*.
Key1,Key2	When you are supposed to press two keys in succession, the keys are separated by a comma, as in this example: Press Alt,Tab and then press Enter. You will also see commas used when referring to menus in a shorthand way. For instance, you may see an instruction to access the Tools, Language, Set Language command. This means pull down the Tools menu, click on Language, and then click on Set Language from the submenu that appears.
Key1+Key2	When you are to press two keys at the same time, the keys will be separated by the plus sign. When you see this, hold down the first key and then press the second key while the first key is still held down. Then release both keys. For example, you might see something like this: Press Ctrl+Enter to create a new line.

NOTE *Excel 97 for Windows is a very flexible program. Don't worry if your screen does not look exactly the same as what you see in the figures. The author might have used a customized setup or rearranged some of the elements on his or her machine, or you may be using a customized setup.*

■ Icons

Windows Sources Excel 97 SuperGuide includes a number of different icon sections, which cover material that isn't part of the normal text.

NOTE *A note is an aside that contains information — sometimes background information — about the current subject. Notes are not critical to the discussion, but often contain helpful data.*

TIP *Tips contain shortcuts that can speedup your use of Excel. Tips also contain practical advice that makes Excel easier to use.*

WARNING *If the book is covering material that might be dangerous to your data or your computer if misused or performed improperly, a* warning *will appear in* *the text. Warnings tell you to be especially careful about something. Pay very close attention to them!*

■ Author's Note

A lot of people—authors, developers, editors, and production people—have worked very hard to bring *Windows Sources Excel 97 SuperGuide 97 for Windows* to you. I am extremely excited about the book and the impact it will have on the Excel user community. If you have any problems or suggestions regarding this book, I would love to hear from you directly, and might even be able to incorporate your comments into the next edition. Write to me in care of Ziff-Davis Publishing, or e-mail me directly at 76376.515@compuserve.com.

Enjoy the book!

Bruce Hallberg

P A R T

1

Worksheets

- *Starting Excel*

- *Understanding the Excel Screen*

- *Using Menus*

- *Introducing the Toolbar*

- *Using the Control Menu*

- *Using Control Commands Shortcuts*

- *Understanding the Workbook*

- *Understanding the Document Control Menu*

- *Exploring Other Document Controls*

- *Moving Around the Worksheet*

- *Moving Around the Document Using the Keyboard*

- *Creating a Worksheet*

- *Creating a Graph*

- *Printing*

- *Saving Your Workbook*

- *Using and Customizing the Office Assistant*

1

An Introduction to Excel 97 for Windows

In this chapter, you'll learn the basics of working with Microsoft Windows 95 and Microsoft Excel 97 for Windows. Using what you have learned here, you will be able to set up simple worksheets that contain numbers and formulas, create charts, and print your results. Most of this chapter covers topics of interest to beginning users of Excel. However, experienced users will want to read the section that discusses new features in Excel 97.

The following topics are covered:

- New Features in Excel 97

- Starting Excel

- The parts of the Excel screen

- The parts of the worksheet

- Moving around the worksheet

- Creating a simple spreadsheet

- Creating a simple graph

- Printing worksheets and graphs

- Saving your work

Although these operations are just the basics, you'll get some idea of how easy the program is to use, and you'll be introduced to the power of Excel 97.

With most software products, you use 10 percent of the features 90 percent of the time. Excel is no different in this regard. If you want to get going easily with Excel, learn to use the most fundamental features and functions, and achieve quick success with the product, then this chapter is for you. After learning these basics, you'll be able to perform the most common tasks yourself, and you can use the rest of this book as a guide to the more advanced features of Excel. If you are an experienced Excel user, you can skim most of this chapter.

Excel 97 for Windows adds some terrific functions to Excel. Key among these new features are the following:

- **Office Assistant**. Excel 97 for Windows' newest Wizard lets you ask questions in plain English and then receive visual, interactive, or step-by-step answers from the Office Assistant for the feature, function, or procedure you're using. The Office Assistant can be set to be active only at certain times, or you can leave it on your screen to offer tips and advice as you perform actions. You'll learn more about the Office Assistant later in this chapter.

- **Increased Capacity**. The number of rows allowed in worksheets has been increased from 16,384 to 65,535. Individual cells can now hold up to 32,767 characters: a vast increase from the former limit of 255 characters. Finally, charts can now be created with up to 32,000 data points, up from 4,000 data points in Excel 95.

- **Formula AutoCorrect**. The AutoCorrect feature has been improved in Excel 97. Not only will it perform automatic corrections within your worksheet as you type, but AutoCorrect will now fix 15 of the most common typos in formulas, such as double operators or certain cases of mismatched parentheses.

- **Shared Workbooks**. Excel 95 let you create Shared Lists, which were simple list-oriented workbooks that could be shared among several people simultaneously. Excel 97 addresses some important limitations of Shared Lists (now called Shared Workbooks) so that formatting for each user can be tracked and saved, changes from each user can be consolidated into the master workbook at specified intervals, and changes by users can be tracked. Chapter 19 discusses Shared Workbooks in more detail.

- **Multiple Level Undo**. Excel 95 only let you undo the most recent action. Excel 97 now has the ability to undo multiple actions, and you can even pull down an Undo list to undo multiple actions at once (click the down arrow next to the Undo button in the Standard Toolbar).

- **Natural Language Formulas**. In previous versions of Excel, you could use formulas like =Cost*Quantity only when you had applied the names to the cell ranges you wanted to reference in that way. Excel 97 now lets you enter such formulas without defining the range names: so long as the titles are in the right place in relationship to the data, you can use the title names in your formulas automatically. Chapter 2 will show you how this works. It also covers working with range names, which you will sometimes still need to do.

- **New Data Validation Tool**. Excel 97 now lets you easily apply data-validation rules to your worksheets, such that you can define valid ranges or data types for any cell in the worksheet. These rules can also specify warning or error messages to be displayed if someone enters invalid data into a cell. You can learn about using this tool in Chapter 3.

- **Track Changes**. A very welcome change to Excel 97 lets you track changes in worksheets, much as Word allows you to track changes made to documents. When you enable this option, any changes made to a workbook are tracked and highlighted, and you can review the changes one-by-one, then accept or reject them accordingly. Each change will be marked to show who made the change, and when they did so. Track Changes is covered in detail in Chapter 19.

- **Collapse/Expand Dialog Boxes**. When working with previous versions of Excel that let you directly select cells for use in a dialog-box field, the dialog box itself was often in your way when you tried to select the cells, and could not be moved. Now such dialog boxes have a Collapse/Expand button to the right of their fields. Click on this button to reduce the dialog box to the smallest possible size, select the range you want, and then click on the button again to restore the dialog box to its full size.

- **Range Finder**. A nice new visual enhancement to Excel 97, the Range Finder feature automatically highlights cells referenced by a formula when you double-click the cell that contains that formula.

- **Cell Formatting Enhancements**. A number of improvements have been made that let you format cells more effectively. You can now rotate text within a cell to any angle that you want, you can indent text within a cell, you can merge cells together, and you can automatically fit text within a cell—Excel will choose the optimum font size, given the cell's dimensions. You will learn more about these features in Chapter 3.

- **Visual Printing**. Excel 97 greatly improves your ability to preview how worksheets will print, and to adjust the page breaks within a worksheet. You can now drag page breaks and print area borders to adjust how they will appear on the printed page. You'll learn about these enhancements in Chapter 4, "Printing Documents."

- **Conditional Formatting**. Previous versions of Excel let you perform rudimentary conditional formatting of cells using cumbersome custom formatting codes. Excel 97 includes a new Conditional Formatting dialog box that lets you easily set special formatting specifications to be applied when the cell's contents meet criteria that you define. Chapter 3, "Worksheet Formatting," discusses this in more detail.

- **Formula Palette**. Excel 97 now incorporates a tool called the Formula Palette in place of the Formula Wizard in Excel 95. The Formula Palette is easier to use, and gives you more help with functions than it did before.

- **New PivotTable Features.** PivotTables have been improved dramatically in Excel 97. Formatting is now retained as you manipulate PivotTables. They can also be automatically sorted; a feature called AutoShow lets you restrict your view of data to the most important items, and the memory requirements for PivotTables has been reduced.

- **Web Publishing.** Excel 97 now lets you save your worksheets as HTML pages that can be viewed on the Internet. Also, Excel can open Excel workbook files over the Web, and can even save workbooks to Internet FTP sites directly from the Save As dialog box.

- **Support for Intellimouse.** Like all of Office 97, Excel 97 now supports Microsoft's new Intellimouse, which resides on the Formula bar and includes support for the third roller button. Using the Intellimouse in Excel makes browsing worksheets easier than ever: you can quickly zoom in and out of your worksheet, and you can pan across the sheets using the Intellimouse.

- **Query Improvements**. The ability to query other data sources is much improved in Excel 97. You can directly query Web pages and incorporate their tablular data (stock quotes, etc.) into your workbooks automatically, a new Query Wizard makes writing queries easier, you can distribute queries you've designed to other users, and you can design parameterized queries that prompt the user of the workbook for information on which to run the query.

- **Charting Improvements**. Aside from increasing the number of data points allowed in charts, Excel 97 also includes quite a few other enhanced charting capabilities. There are new chart types, and the Chart Wizard has been simplified to reduce the number of steps you go through. You'll find out about these changes, as well as some other improvements, in Chapter 12, "Complete Guide to Charts."

As you can see, Excel 97 is a significant advance over previous versions of Excel, making it easier to use *and* more powerful.

■ Starting Excel

When you first start Excel by clicking on its command in the Programs group of your Start menu, it opens and loads a blank worksheet, as shown in Figure 1.1. You can see the new Office Assistant in the lower-right corner of the Excel screen.

■ Understanding the Excel Screen

Excel makes extensive use of the graphical user interface with menus, buttons, icons, and many different mouse pointers. The main elements of the Excel screen control the program itself, as displayed in Figure 1.2.

■ Using Menus

Each menu item in the menu bar contains many choices, most of them grouped logically. The File menu, for instance, shows commands that deal with files, the Edit menu shows editing commands, and so on.

You can access menus in Excel with your mouse by clicking on the menu item to activate it, sliding your mouse pointer through the menu to the command you want to activate, and then clicking to activate that command. Where a menu item has more than one command available, a right-pointing arrow will appear on the right side of the menu opposite the command name that's selected.

Figure 1.1

The Excel opening screen

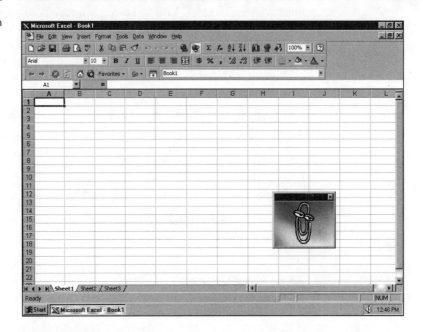

Figure 1.2

Excel program screen elements

Standard toolbar

Formatting toolbar

Menus

Worksheet

Scroll bars

Sheet tabs

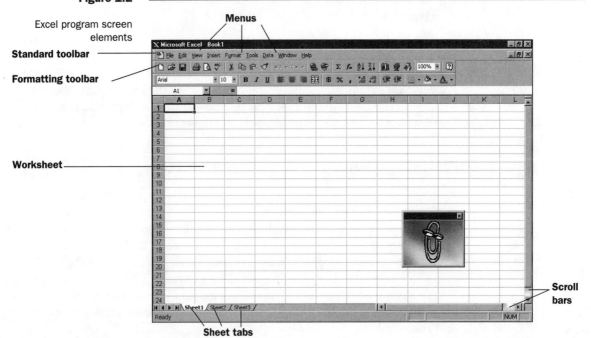

This method is nearly the same as that for Macintosh computers; however, the Macintosh requires that the mouse button be constantly depressed when sliding through menu options, whereas Windows 95 lets you use menus either way.

All menus can also be accessed using keyboard shortcuts. To pull down a menu using only keystrokes, follow these steps:

1. Strike the Alt key and then press the letter on the keyboard that corresponds to the underlined letter in the menu. To activate the File menu, for example, strike Alt and then press the F key on your keyboard.

NOTE. *The underlined letter of a menu option is commonly called a "hot key."*

2. After the menu appears, choose the option you want and press the letter on your keyboard that corresponds to the menu's hot key. Don't hold the Alt key down for this, or even strike it: you can just press the underlined letter to select a command within a menu.

While the mouse is easy to use, if you want to become a lightning-fast Excel user, you'll find that learning the keyboard commands for accessing menus (including the shortcut keys built into Excel) will improve your ability to get work done faster.

■ Introducing the Toolbar

Excel makes wide use of *toolbars*, those little rows of buttons that appear on your screen below the menu bar. These buttons typically show small icons; the icons represent shortcuts to the most common Excel commands. To print, for example, you simply click on the small button that looks like a printer.

The buttons in the toolbar are designed to provide you with quick access to the functions you use most often. Mastering the use of the Excel toolbars can dramatically increase the speed at which you can work with Excel (and other Windows programs, for that matter).

When you open Excel for the first time, the Standard toolbar appears across the top of the window just below the menu bar, as shown in Figure 1.2. The function of each button on the Standard toolbar is described in Table 1.1.

■ Using the Control Menu

The Control menu can be accessed via the graphic icon in the upper-left corner of the Excel window. It functions the same in Excel as in most other Windows programs, although each program's icon will be different. The Control menu is shown pulled down in Figure 1.3.

Table 1.1

Standard Toolbar Icons

ICON	NAME	DESCRIPTION
	New	Opens a new workbook.
	Open	Opens an existing workbook on your disk.
	Save	Saves the workbook document to your disk.
	Print	Prints the active document.
	Print Preview	Shows the document as it will look on the printed page.
	Spelling	Checks for spelling errors in the active worksheet.
	Cut	Cuts the currently selected area into the Windows Clipboard.
	Copy	Copies the contents of the active or marked cells into the Windows Clipboard.
	Paste	Pastes the contents of the Windows Clipboard, beginning at the current cell location.
	Format Painter	Enables you to quickly copy the formatting of one cell to other cells.
	Undo	Reverses the last action you took.
	Redo	Reverses the last Undo command.
	Insert Hyperlink	Inserts or edits a hyperlink code. Hyperlink codes allow you to jump to specified documents or Web locations.

**Table 1.1
(Continued)**

Standard Toolbar Icons

ICON	NAME	DESCRIPTION
	Web Toolbar	Displays or hides the Web toolbar. The buttons on this toolbar allow you to quickly access favorite Web locations and search for new Web locations.
Σ	AutoSum	Automatically determines which cells to sum, depending on the location of the active cell. Proposes a summation range that you can modify before you press Enter. When you press Enter, Excel automatically enters the SUM formula for you into the active cell.
*f*ₓ	Paste Function	Helps you use Excel functions and inserts the result into the current cell.
A↓Z	Sort Ascending	Sorts the contents of the selected cells in ascending order (lowest to highest).
Z↓A	Sort Descending	Sorts the contents of the selected cells in descending order (highest to lowest).
	Chart Wizard	Automatically walks you through the process of creating a chart.
	Map	Inserts a map object into your worksheet.
	Drawing	Brings up the Drawing toolbar, which contains the tools you use to draw in your current document.
100% ▾	Zoom	Allows you to quickly zoom in and out of your document.
?	Office Assistant	Activates (or deactivates) the Office Assistant.

Table 1.2 explains the functions of each Control menu option. On your system, some options might be grayed-out (not selectable), depending on whether they are appropriate options for the present context. Table 1.2 includes notes about grayed-out options.

Figure 1.3

The Control menu lets
you control Excel's
window.

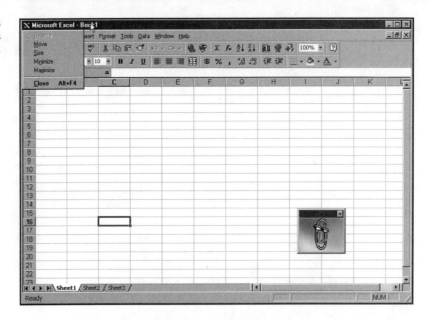

Table 1.2

Excel Control Menu

MENU NAME	DESCRIPTION
Restore	Restores the Excel window to the size it was before the Maximize command was issued. This option is grayed-out when Excel is not maximized.
Move	When Excel is *windowed,* or not maximized to take over the entire screen, you can select the Move option, then use the arrow keys to reposition the Excel window on the screen.
Size	To resize the Excel screen using the keyboard, choose Size from the Control menu, then press the arrow key for the edge that you want to change (up arrow to adjust the upper edge of the Excel window, right arrow to adjust the right edge, and so on). After you select the edge you want to change, use the arrow keys to shrink or enlarge the Excel window.
Minimize	Choose Minimize to shrink Excel to an icon on the desktop. Excel continues to run and process data while it is minimized.
Maximize	Maximize causes Excel to grow to take up the entire screen area.
Close	Choose Close to exit Excel.

■ Using Control Commands Shortcuts

Using the mouse or a keyboard shortcut is often a more convenient method of executing Control menu commands. This section teaches you how to accomplish similar tasks using a mouse or keyboard shortcut. Figure 1.4 displays a few instructions on using these shortcuts.

Figure 1.4

Control menu shortcuts

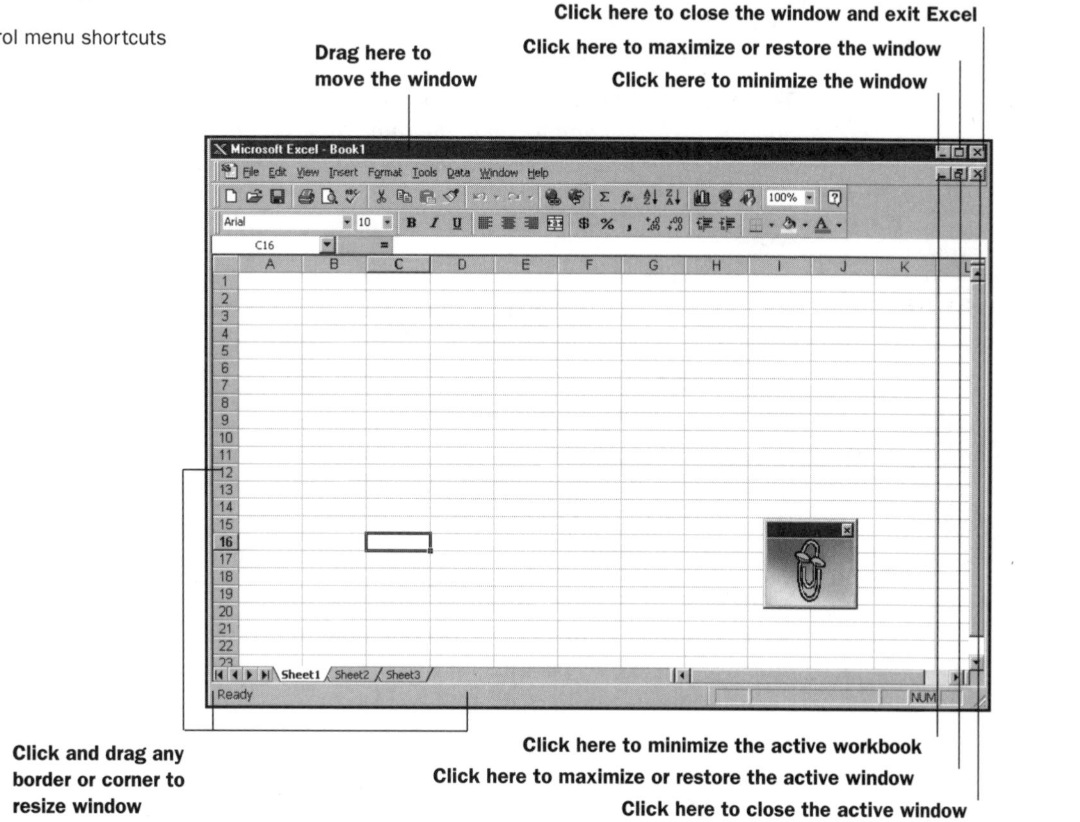

Restore

To restore the Excel window to its windowed state so that it does not take up the entire screen, click once on the Restore button in the upper inside right corner of the Excel window. When Excel is in its windowed state, this button becomes a single windowpane, which indicates that you can maximize Excel.

Move

To move the Excel window around on the desktop, click and hold on the Excel title bar, then drag your mouse to reposition the window.

Size

Resize the Excel window by carefully moving your mouse pointer to an edge of the Excel window. When the pointer is precisely over the edge, it changes shape and becomes a double-headed arrow. At this point, press the left mouse button and drag the mouse to resize that edge of the window.

TIP. *Position the mouse pointer over the corner of the Excel window to control the height and width at the same time. When your mouse is in the right place, the pointer changes to a double-headed arrow oriented diagonally.*

Minimize

The Minimize button is located immediately to the left of the Maximize/Restore button. Click on it to immediately minimize Excel.

Maximize

The Maximize button is in the upper inside right corner of the Excel screen. When Excel is windowed, you can choose this button to cause Excel to take up the entire screen. When Excel is maximized, this button becomes the Restore button, and the icon changes to reflect two cascaded screens.

Close

Although you can use the Excel command to exit the program (File, Exit), you also can exit by clicking on the close button, or by double-clicking on the Control Menu. Another alternative is to press Alt+F4 on the keyboard.

■ Understanding the Workbook

Excel 97 for Windows uses the metaphor of workbooks, just as Excel 95 did. A *workbook* is a collection of different sheets all grouped together. An Excel workbook can contain any of the different sheet types described below:

- **Worksheets**. Contain data and formulas. Worksheets can also contain other embedded objects, such as charts and pictures.

- **Charts**. Contain graphs that you create using Excel. A chart can be its own document or embedded in a worksheet.

- **Excel 95 Dialog Sheets**. Contain dialog boxes you can use in your Excel 95 application. You can draw dialog boxes using dialog sheets, and attach program code for each button and field.

- **Excel 4 Macro Sheets.** Contain macros from Version 4 of Excel.

Each workbook shares certain controls for managing the workbook itself. These controls are used to scroll around the current sheet of the workbook, to minimize and maximize the workbook within the Excel window, and so on. This section discusses these workbook controls. Figure 1.5 shows the controls and key parts of a worksheet.

Figure 1.5

Excel document controls

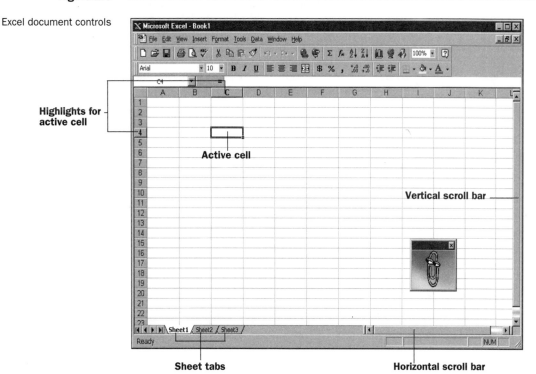

Highlights for active cell

Active cell

Vertical scroll bar

Sheet tabs

Horizontal scroll bar

■ Understanding the Document Control Menu

The Document Control menu duplicates the functions of the Excel Control menu, but its commands affect only the current document itself, and not the overall Excel program. It contains the familiar commands Restore, Move, Size, Minimize, Maximize, and Close.

TIP. *Some other ways to move between sheets are as follows:*

You can quickly scroll through worksheet tabs by pressing Ctrl+PgUp and Ctrl+PgDn. You can also right-click on the buttons to the left of the Sheet1 tab shown in Figure 1.5 to show a menu of sheets from which to pick.

■ Exploring Other Document Controls

Excel offers several other document controls. You already learned to use these controls for the Excel program itself; this section shows you how to use them in a workbook:

- Each workbook has its own Maximize/Restore, Minimize, and Close buttons, which are located at the upper right corner of the document screen. These buttons maximize, restore, minimize, or close the workbook within the Excel window.

- You can resize workbooks by positioning the mouse pointer over the edge of the workbook, then dragging the edge. You can do this only when the workbook is not maximized.

- You can close the current workbook by double-clicking on the workbook's Control menu (as opposed to double-clicking on the Excel Control menu, which exits Excel) or by clicking on the X in the top right corner of the workbook window.

- Reposition—or move—the workbook by dragging on the workbook's title bar. You can do this only when the workbook is not maximized.

TIP. *Double-click on the title bar of the workbook or the Excel window to maximize or restore it. Right-click on the title bar of the workbook or the Excel window to minimize, maximize, restore, or close it.*

■ Moving Around the Worksheet

During a typical Excel session, you move within one of the worksheets in your workbook, enter data in different places, view results in other places, and so on. Excel provides many ways to move around within the active workbook.

TIP. *Some navigation techniques change the portion of the worksheet you are viewing without affecting the position of the active cell. This feature can be used to your advantage. If, for example, you want to view a different part of the spreadsheet before you enter some data, you can use the scroll bars to look at the information you want to see. Because using the scroll bars doesn't* *change the position of your active cell, you can just start entering data to immediately return to the active cell. You can also move the active cell simply by clicking on a cell after you have scrolled to the desired place on the worksheet.*

Identifying the Active Cell

The *active cell* is shown in Figure 1.5. This cell is the one affected by whatever you type or whatever commands you execute (such as formatting commands).

Using Scroll Bars

Very few worksheets can be viewed entirely on a single screen, and they often take many, many screens of space to display. Given this fact, Excel allows you to scroll around the current document and view different parts of it at will.

You can use scroll bars in a number of ways:

- Drag the scroll-box to a different position to change the area you are viewing. If you drag the vertical scroll bar to the bottom or the horizontal scroll bar to the far right, you'll see the bottommost or rightmost part of the active area of your current worksheet. Also, you can hold down the Shift key when dragging to scroll through the entire worksheet.

TIP. *In the upper left corner of the document, Excel shows you the row or column name that will appear after you release the scroll button. This "sneak preview" helps you avoid making guesses as to what will appear after you release the mouse button.*

- Click on the arrows at either end of the scroll bar to move one cell in the direction of the arrow.

- Click on the blank area of the scroll bar (the area between the button and the arrow) to move an entire "screenful" at a time. Move in the direction away from the position of the scroll-bar button. For example, if the vertical scroll-bar button is in the middle of the vertical scroll bar, click once above the button to move your display up by one full screen.

TIP. *Excel's scroll boxes are proportional to the area you are viewing on the screen. In other words, the scroll box itself will change size (larger or smaller) to more accurately reflect the size of the area you are viewing relative to the current size of the worksheet.*

■ Moving Around the Document Using the Keyboard

The keys and key combinations listed in Table 1.3 provide alternative ways to move around within the worksheet. Unlike using the scroll bars, these techniques change the active cell.

Table 1.3

Keyboard Movement Keys

KEY	ACTION
Arrow keys	Moves the active cell in the direction of the arrow key, one cell at a time.
PgUp/PgDn	Moves the display one full screen up or down. The active cell moves with the display, but stays in the same relative position on the screen.
Ctrl+arrow	Hold down the Ctrl key while you press an arrow key to move the active cell in that direction until it encounters a cell that contains data. If no cells contain data in that direction, Excel moves the active cell all the way to the boundary of the worksheet.
	When editing the contents of a cell, Ctrl+arrow moves the insertion to the next word in the direction of the arrow pressed.
F5	Press F5 to open a dialog box in which you can enter the cell reference you want to jump to. This dialog box also displays all your *named ranges* (areas of the worksheet to which you have assigned a name) so that you can just choose a named area. Otherwise, simply enter a cell reference (like AB255 or B5) and press Enter to immediately move the active cell there, and view that portion of the worksheet. This is also referred to as the "Goto" key.
Ctrl+PgUp and Ctrl+PgDn	Changes the active sheet left or right.
Alt+PgUp and Alt+PgDn	Shifts one screen at a time left or right.
Ctrl+Home	Moves you to cell A1 of the current worksheet.
Ctrl+End	Moves you to the last occupied row and column of the current worksheet. If no data exists, it moves you to cell A1.

■ Creating a Worksheet

Now that you know the fundamentals of working with the Excel screen and of moving around the worksheet, it's time to set up a sample worksheet so that you can put these steps into practice.

In the following sections, you create a worksheet that shows sales projections for the ACME Corporation. As you create the worksheet, you will learn more about working with Excel.

Before you begin this exercise, start with a new workbook. Pull down the File menu and choose New. Icons representing the templates upon which you may base your new workbook appear in the New dialog box. Click on Workbook and then click on the OK button.

Entering Text

The first order of business in creating your sample worksheet is to create the title and headings for the worksheet. Follow these steps:

1. Move your pointer to cell A1 (if you started a new worksheet, A1 should already be your active cell). To quickly move to cell A1, press Ctrl+Home.

2. Type **ACME Corporation Sales Projections** and press Enter.

As you type, you will see the text appear in the active cell on the worksheet, as well as in the Formula bar above the worksheet cells, as shown in Figure 1.6.

Figure 1.6

The Formula bar and its buttons

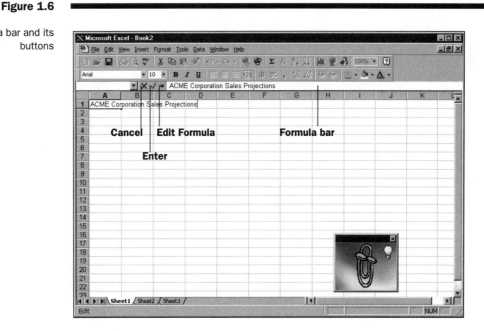

Formula Bar

The Formula bar shows you the reference of the active cell or cells, the data that you are typing, and the Cancel, Enter, and Edit Formula buttons (see Figure 1.6).

When you are entering data in the Formula bar, you can use the normal editing keys (arrow keys, Backspace, Del, Ins, Ctrl+left arrow, Ctrl+right arrow, etc.) to change the data until you are satisfied with it. When you are finished typing or editing the data, click on the Enter button (the check mark), or simply press the Enter key. To cancel your changes, click on the Cancel button (the X) or press Esc.

Centering Text

You can center text across a selection of cells by using the Merge and Center button, as follows:

1. Click on cell A1, hold down the mouse button, and drag the cursor to the right until the cells from A1 to H1 are highlighted (substitute column H for the rightmost column visible on your screen: it varies depending on the resolution of your Windows desktop). Release the mouse button.

2. Click on the Merge and Center button on the Formatting toolbar (see Figure 1.7).

Figure 1.7

The Merge and Center button on the Formatting toolbar

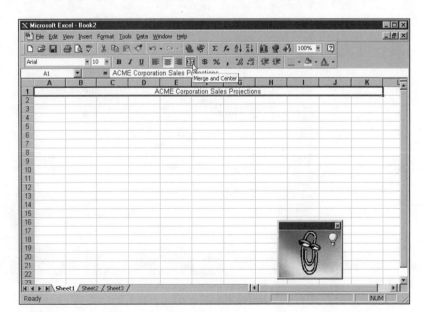

Continue entering the text labels for the exercise worksheet by entering the subtitle and two more labels, as follows:

1. Move to cell A2, type **By Region**, and press Enter.

2. Center the text using the Merge and Center method described earlier.

3. Move to cell B4, type **Region**, and press Tab to move to cell C4.

4. Move to cell C4, type **Q1**, and press Enter.

AutoFill

Excel has a powerful feature that can automatically enter sequential labels. In the example you are creating, you want the labels Q2 through Q4 to appear in cells D4 through F4. You could type each label into each cell or, better yet, you could use AutoFill.

In the lower-right corner of your active cell, you can see a small square. This square is the *fill handle* (see Figure 2.16 in Chapter 2 for an enlarged picture of this handle). You can use this feature to fill in the rest of the titles for you:

1. Move to cell C4. Click once on that cell, or use the arrow keys to make it the active cell.

2. Position the mouse pointer immediately over the fill handle. When it is positioned correctly, the mouse pointer changes to a small cross.

3. Press and hold down the left mouse button, and then drag the mouse to the right of the cell and release the mouse button.

Excel intelligently interprets what you're trying to fill, and correctly places each successive label into the correct cell. The AutoFill feature also works with month names or other types of labels.

TIP. *If you drag the fill handle too far to the right, or not far enough, just grab it again and drag it to the correct position. Excel will refill the region correctly.*

Continue with the following steps to finish entering labels into the worksheet:

1. Enter **Total** into cell G4.

2. Move to cell B5 and enter **North** and press Enter.

3. Repeat step 2 for the other three regions, as follows:

   - Enter **East** into cell B6

   - Enter **West** into cell B7

   - Enter **South** into cell B8

4. In cell B9, enter **Total**.

At this point, you have entered all the labels for the worksheet. Your screen should look like Figure 1.8.

Figure 1.8

The sample worksheet you're building with labels added

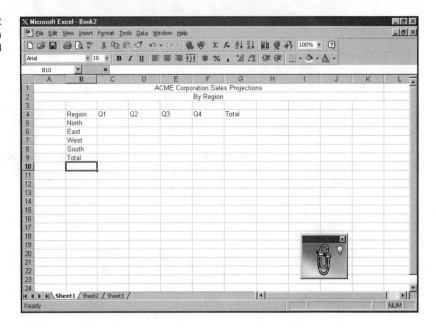

Entering Numbers

For this example, assume that you already know the actual results for the first quarter, and you want to calculate the projections for the following three quarters, as well as the yearly total. Enter these values into each of the first-quarter cells:

*   **25292** in cell C5

*   **13510** in cell C6

*   **8900** in cell C7

*   **43250** in cell C8

When you enter numbers into Excel, notice that they are automatically aligned to the right edge of the cell. This alignment is Excel's default, because numbers are most commonly aligned by their right edges. It also serves as a useful way to find out whether Excel is interpreting what you type as a number or as text.

NOTE. *Normally, Excel correctly determines if data should be treated as a number or as text. Occasionally, however, you may want a number to be treated as text. Perhaps you are preparing a table in which each line is labeled 1, 2, 3, and so on. Or perhaps you are entering inventory labels that begin with a zero: if Excel accepts those numbers as numbers, the leading zero will be removed, because it is irrelevant. In cases like these, where you want to force Excel to treat numbers as text, you must enter the numbers with a leading apostrophe.*

*To force the number 145 to appear as text, for example, enter '**145** into the cell in question. The apostrophe will not appear in the cell once you've pressed Enter—only the number.*

The same holds true for fractions like ¹/₂. You will get the text instead of the default date 2-Jan, when you enter ¹/₂.

Entering Formulas

Continuing with your sample worksheet, assume that each region is experiencing a 5 percent quarterly growth rate. You want Excel to calculate the remaining quarterly sales based on the sales of the first quarter, plus a 5 percent increase. Follow these steps:

1. Move to cell D5. Enter the formula **=C5*1.05** and press the Enter key. Excel immediately calculates the result and displays the answer.

NOTE. *Excel, like most computer programs, uses the asterisk (*) to represent multiplication, and the forward slash (/) to represent division. Addition and subtraction are represented with a plus sign (+) and a hyphen (-), respectively.*

2. You now need to enter the formulas for the remaining calculated cells. You can enter the remaining formulas by hand, but why not let Excel's AutoFill feature do it for you? Grab the fill handle for cell D5, and drag it down so that the highlighted area extends from cell D5 to cell D8. Release the mouse button.

   Each cell now shows the correct amount: the cell to the left plus 5 percent of that amount. This calculation works correctly when you use AutoFill, because Excel automatically adjusts any cell references so that they are *relative* to the cell that contains the formula. (In Chapter 2, "Working with Worksheet Data," you will learn to use formulas that prevent cell references from being adjusted in this way.)

3. Finally, use the Fill Handle to copy the entire column of formulas (cells D5 to D8) two columns to the right, so that all the quarterly sales projections are correct, as shown in Figure 1.9.

NOTE. *You can use the keyboard to quickly select multiple cells. Use the arrow keys to move to the starting cell. Hold down the Shift key, then use the arrow keys to move the ending cell. You also can click on the starting cell, hold down the Shift key, and then click on the ending cell to select the entire range of cells.*

Figure 1.9

Completed sales figures

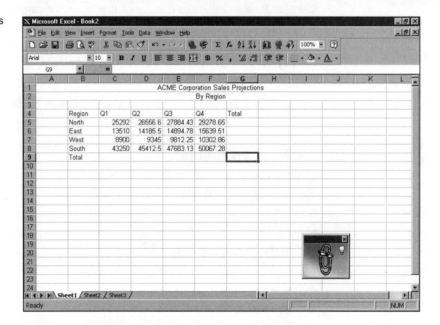

Using AutoSum

To finish building the data for the worksheet, you will need to calculate the totals for both the columns and the rows. To enter the total for cell G5, you have the following three choices:

- You can enter the formula to add up all the cells. Using this method, you enter **=C5+D5+E5+F5** into cell G5 and then press Enter.

- You can use one of the Excel math functions. You can type the formula =SUM(C5:F5) and press Enter. Notice the way the range of cells is given in the formula. The first cell of the range to be summed is separated with a colon from the last cell. The colon tells Excel to sum the values in that range.

- You can use the Excel AutoSum tool, the fastest way to get totals of rows or columns of numbers. To use AutoSum, make G5 your active cell and click on the AutoSum button in the toolbar—the one that shows the Greek Sigma (Σ) icon. Excel automatically enters the SUM function, then determines which cells you most likely want to total, surrounding the suggested cells with a flashing marquee. If the range of cells Excel has guessed is correct, just press the Enter key. If the range isn't correct, use your mouse to select the correct cells, and then press Enter.

After you have entered the formula in cell G5 to total row 5, select cell G5 again and use the fill handle to copy the formula down to cell G9. When you are finished, move to cell C9 and use the AutoSum button again to total up the sales for the first quarter. Then, use the fill handle to copy that formula across to cell F9. When you are finished, your worksheet should look like Figure 1.10.

TIP. *Excel smartly handles AutoSum for you by entering the beginning of the formula (=SUM( ), leaving you to enter or edit the rest of the formula. If you enter the cells you want to have summed and forget to enter the closing parentheses, Excel will also finish the sum for you.*

Figure 1.10

The completed, but unformatted, worksheet

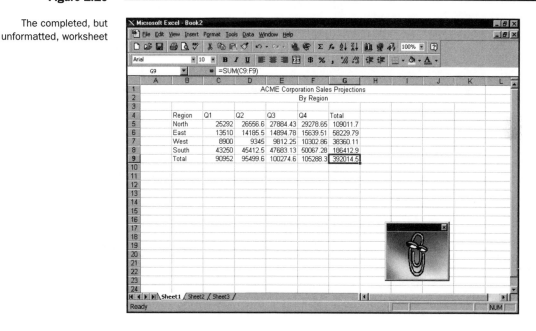

Using AutoFormat

Although all the numbers in your spreadsheet are correct, the document is not quite presentable yet. Excel has many commands that allow you to control the way your worksheet is formatted. One of the most convenient of these is the AutoFormat tool, which automatically applies one of a number of predesigned formats to a table.

To use AutoFormat, make sure that the active cell is anywhere within the table (for example, cell C5). Then, pull down the Format menu and choose AutoFormat. The AutoFormat dialog box will appear, as shown in Figure 1.11.

Figure 1.11

The AutoFormat dialog box

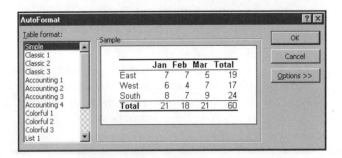

The Table Format list box contains many different predefined table formats for you to choose from. For this example, choose Accounting 1 and click on the OK button. The result of this operation is shown in Figure 1.12.

Figure 1.12

The formatted worksheet

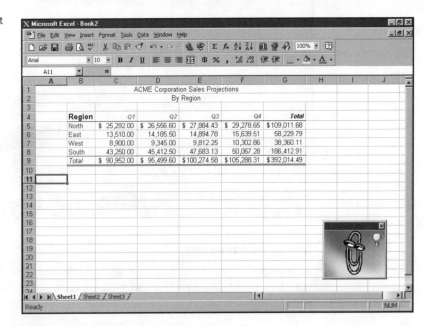

◼ Creating a Graph

Excel contains one of the most powerful graphing functions found in any software program. Part of its power comes from the simple, easy-to-use tool called the ChartWizard.

In this example, you want to graph the regional sales data for each quarter. Later in the book, you will learn to do this manually. For this introduction to Excel, however, use the easy ChartWizard. Follow these steps:

1. Select B4 to F8 as the range to chart. You do not want to graph the totals for this chart.

2. Click on the ChartWizard button in the toolbar. You will see the dialog box for Step 1 of four in the Chart Wizard process.

Excel will now walk you through the four necessary steps required to create a chart. At any point, you can cancel the process by clicking on the Cancel button or by pressing Esc. You can also go backward or forward in the process by clicking on the Back or Next buttons.

1. The first step, shown in Figure 1.13, lets you select the type of chart you want to create. Click on Column and then choose the upper-left subtype. Click on the Next button to proceed.

Figure 1.13

Step 1 of the ChartWizard, in which you choose your chart type

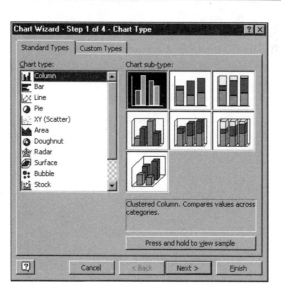

2. The second step, shown in Figure 1.14, lets you select or reselect the range of data on which to base your chart. Since you selected the correct data before beginning, no action is required here. Click Next.

Figure 1.14

Step 2 of the ChartWizard, in which you can select the range of data to be charted

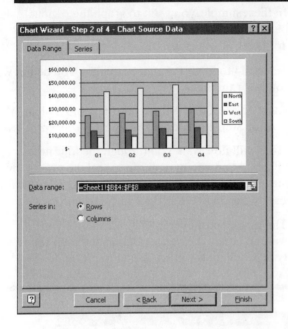

3. The third step brings up a tabbed dialog box, in which you can make a number of different choices about your chart. Figure 1.15 shows this dialog box. For this example, the default choices are fine, so click the Next button to proceed.

4. The fourth step, shown in Figure 1.16, asks you to select where the newly created chart should be placed. You can choose to place it into a new sheet in your workbook, or you can place it as an object on top of the current sheet. Choose As object in Sheet1 and click on the Finish button to complete the chart.

5. If necessary, point to the middle of the chart and drag it to an appropriate location on the sheet. (If you are using a low screen resolution, such as 640x480, the chart may be floating on top of your data!)

NOTE. *The chart you see is compressed—you cannot see much detail because it is fairly small. To see the chart in more detail, click once on the chart to activate it, then drag up the upper handle (the small box in the middle of the top line). To return the chart to its original size, drag the handle back down. You can also use the handles in the corner of the window to stretch or shrink*

Figure 1.15

Step 3 of the
ChartWizard lets you set
a number of parameters
for your chart

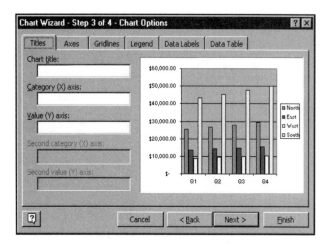

Figure 1.16

Step 4 of the
ChartWizard selects the
destination for the chart

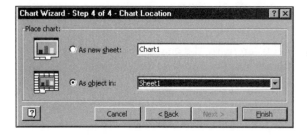

*the chart in two dimensions, and can even hold down the Ctrl key while you
do this to maintain the proportions of the chart if you wish.*

When a chart is embedded into a worksheet, it is "floating" on top of the
cells beneath it (see Figure 1.17). If there was text in the cells behind the
chart, that text would still be there—it simply would be covered by the chart.

Although charts are covered in detail elsewhere in this book, the following tips might help until you go through that information:

•   If you need to delete a chart, click on the chart to select it. You will
    know it's selected when the small squares, called *handles*, appear at the
    corners and edges of the chart. When the chart is selected, press Del to
    get rid of it.

•   You can move the chart within the worksheet by selecting the chart and
    dragging it to a new location.

Figure 1.17

The completed chart
embedded as an object
on your data sheet

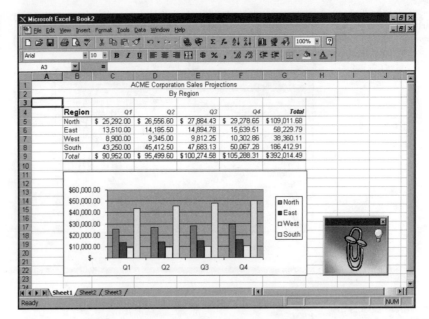

- You can resize the chart. To do so, select it, then drag one of the small handles at the perimeter of the chart.

- When you select an embedded chart, Range Finder will show you the data upon which the chart is based. Figure 1.18 shows you this feature.

TIP. *Range Finder can also quickly show you which cells factor into a cell with a formula—just double-click on a cell containing a formula to see the source cells highlighted.*

■ Printing

To print the worksheet, pull down the File menu and choose Print. This step brings up the Print dialog box, as shown in Figure 1.19.

In the dialog box, click on the option button marked Selection. This option tells Excel to print only the selected area of the worksheet rather than the entire document. Finally, click on the button marked OK to print the document.

Figure 1.18

Selecting a chart
activates the Range
Finder feature to show
you the data upon which
the chart is based.

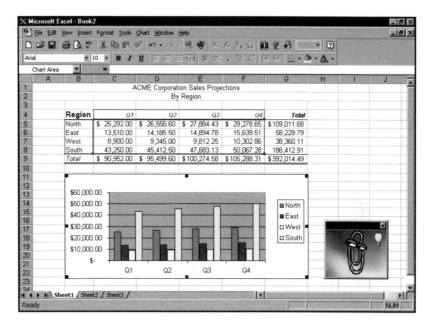

Figure 1.19

The Print dialog box

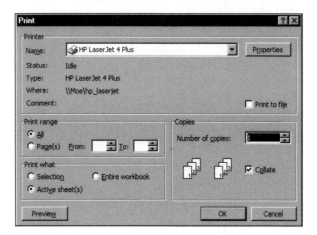

■ Saving Your Workbook

To save the completed workbook, pull down the File menu and choose Save
As. This action opens the dialog box shown in Figure 1.20.

Figure 1.20

The Save As dialog box

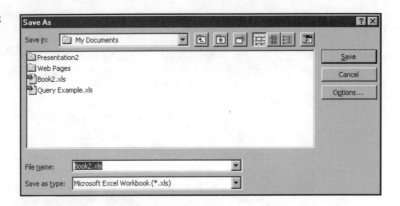

Enter the name of your workbook in the File Name field and click on the Save button to save the workbook. If you need to change the directory in which the workbook is saved, use the Save command in drop-down list box to navigate to the location where you want to store your file.

After you have assigned a name to a workbook, you can save more quickly by choosing Save from the File menu (of the Save button on the toolbar).

NOTE. *Saving frequently is very important. Many people lose time by forgetting to save their work, because if they lose power or their computer crashes, all the work done since the last time they saved the file disappears. Excel also includes an AutoSave feature. You will learn about AutoSave in Chapter 18, "Using Excel Add-Ins." Even if you don't install AutoSave, you should get in the habit of either clicking the Save button on the toolbar frequently, or of pressing Ctrl+S often. Either action will save your work up to that point.*

■ Using and Customizing the Office Assistant

During the course of these examples, the screen shots have shown the Office Assistant in the lower-right corner of the screen. The Office Assistant is a helper that watches what you do, and offers tips when it notices that there are faster ways for you to accomplish your work. You can also use the Office Assistant to search for help on a topic.

When the Office Assistant displays a light bulb, you can click on the light bulb to see a tip. The tips you've seen are remembered by the Assistant, so it will not show you the same tips over and over again. Figure 1.21 shows you a tip displayed by the Office Assistant.

Figure 1.21

A helpful tip, courtesy of
the Office Assistant

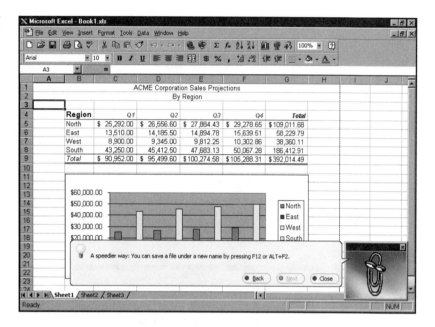

TIP. *When the Tip window is displayed, you can use the Back and Next buttons to scroll through all of the tips offered by the Assistant, based on how you work with Excel.*

Customizing the Office Assistant is easy. Right-click on the Assistant to display a shortcut menu, and choose Options from the menu. You will see the dialog box shown in Figure 1.22, while Table 1.4 summarizes the options available to you on the Options tab of this dialog box.

One neat feature of the Office Assistant is that you can choose the animated cartoon character that it uses. You do this with the Gallery tab of the Office Assistant dialog box, shown in Figure 1.23. Scroll through the different Assistants available until you find one that suits your tastes. Then, click the OK button to select that Assistant. You may be prompted for your Office or Excel CD-ROM or diskettes to finish installing the Assistant you've chosen.

TIP. *Some Assistants are more or less animated than others. An active Assistant may be too distracting for you, or may animate too slowly on an older computer system. The Office Logo assistant is the least active, while Dot and PowerPup are the most active.*

Figure 1.22

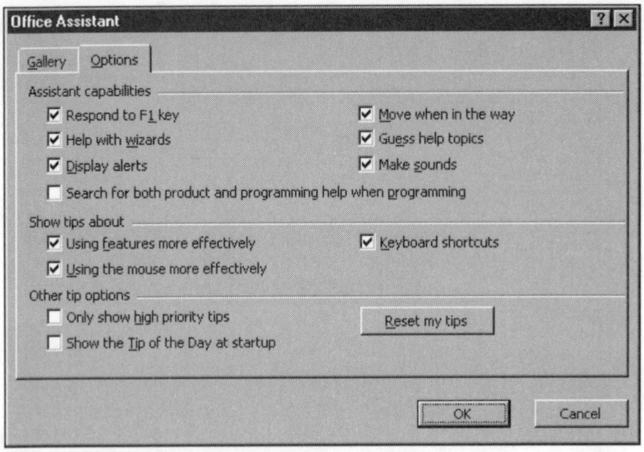

The Office Assistant
dialog box

Table 1.4

Office Assistant Options

SETTING	ACTION
Respond to F1 key	When selected, the Office Assistant responds to the F1 key. When cleared, the normal Excel help appears when you press F1.
Help with Wizards	Causes the Assistant to appear automatically when you use Wizards in Excel.
Display Alerts	Excel warning or information messages are displayed using the Assistant when this option is set.
Move when in the way	When selected, the Assistant window automatically moves when it's in the way of a dialog box you're using. Also, if you don't use the Assistant for five minutes and this option is set, the Assistant window will shrink to roughly half its original size.
Guess help topics	When you activate the Assistant and this option is selected, the Assistant will try to guess what you want help with, based on the actions you took prior to activating the Assistant.
Make sounds	Adds sounds to the Office Assistant animation. This only works when your computer has sound capabilities.
Search for both product and programming help when programming	Displays both programming assistance and help on using the programming tools when you work with Visual Basic for Applications in Excel.

**Table 1.4
(Continued)**

Office Assistant Options

SETTING	ACTION
Show tips about	These three settings let you control the types of tips that the Office Assistant offers. Choose from these options: Using features more effectively, Using the mouse more effectively, and Keyboard shortcuts.
Only show high-priority tips	Restricts the tips that the Office Assistant shows you to only those that can make marked impacts in your productivity with Excel.
Show the Tip of the Day at startup	When this is selected, the Office Assistant will show you a tip of the day when you start an Excel session.
Reset my tips	Normally the Assistant remembers the tips it has shown you, and does not show them to you again. Clicking this button resets the tips that the Office Assistant is tracking, so that all relevant tips are shown again if necessary.

Figure 1.23

You can choose an Assistant that suits your personal tastes.

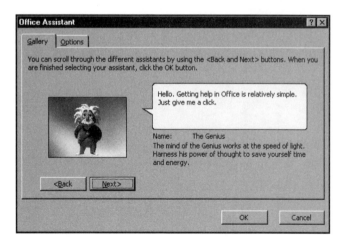

- *Entering Data*
- *Performing Data Entry*
- *Working with Formulas*
- *Understanding Relative and Absolute References*
- *Understanding A1 and R1C1 Cell Addressing*
- *Understanding the Importance of Names*
- *Working with Comments in Cells*

- *Rearranging Data*
- *Filling Ranges of Cells*
- *Inserting and Deleting Data*

2

Working with
Worksheet Data

NEARLY ALL THE TIME YOU SPEND WORKING WITH EXCEL WILL include manipulating the data in your worksheets. Entering data, moving it, cutting and pasting it, and even transforming it, are all functions you will expend significant amounts of effort performing.

This chapter teaches you how to accomplish the following tasks:

- Entering different types of data into an Excel worksheet

- Taking advantage of some large-scale data-entry shortcuts

- Building simple formulas

- Referencing other cells—including combinations of cells—in your formulas

- Taking advantage of absolute versus relative cell addresses

- Understanding the difference between R1C1 cell addressing and A1 cell addressing

- Naming portions of your spreadsheet for better control and accountability

- Including detailed comments in individual cells

- Rearranging the data in your worksheet

As you master the techniques presented in this chapter, you will learn to work with your worksheet data and to use Excel as efficiently as possible.

This chapter covers the basics of working with data—text, numbers, and formulas—on an Excel worksheet. You need to be able to enter and manipulate data with Excel in order to be productive with the program.

■ Entering Data

The first thing you have to do when you build a spreadsheet is enter data. You must also know how to enter labels for different parts of your worksheet, and of course you'll need to enter numbers and dates for calculations, as well as other information.

This section discusses entering text and numbers, and explains how to make Excel treat a number as text when you need to do so. Through examples in the chapter, you will learn how to enter and manipulate text so that you can do an inventory spreadsheet in Excel. You'll enter inventory items, and then enter the quantity and price of each. Finally, you'll use Excel to calculate the inventory value.

Entering Text

To enter text, position the active cell where you want the text to appear, and begin typing. When you type the first letter, the text will appear in the active cell *and* in the formula bar.

TIP. *If editing in the cell is not something you want to do, you can turn off this feature by accessing Options from the Tools menu, clicking on the Edit tab in* *the Options Notebook, and clicking on the line "Edit directly in cell" to remove the check mark.*

The following steps will lead you through the process of entering a title and headings for the different parts of the inventory spreadsheet:

1. Type **ACME Company Inventory** in cell C2. Then click once on the Checkmark button next to the formula bar, or simply press Enter, to store your entry. If you want to cancel what you have typed, click on the X button in the formula bar or press Esc.

2. In cell A4, type **Quantity** and press Tab.

3. In cell B4, type **Description** and press Tab. *Description* spans two cells, with the last part of the word covering part of cell C4. When no text or numbers are in an adjacent cell, Excel allows the text of one cell to continue and display to the right.

4. In cell C4, type **Model #** and press Tab. When you enter the text, the final part of the word *Description* will be obscured. Because of the label in C4, Excel cannot display the complete word, so it will show the contents of cell C4 rather than the final portion of the preceding cell.

5. In cell D4, type **Price** and press Enter.

Compare your spreadsheet to Figure 2.1.

Figure 2.1

The spreadsheet with title and labels

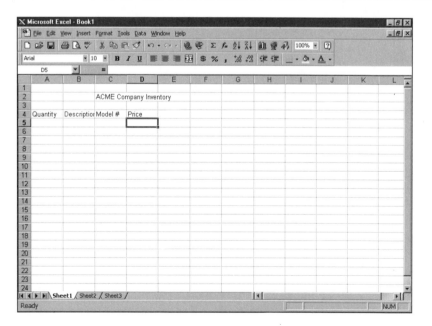

Before you continue, you should widen column B in the spreadsheet. Not only does the text *Description* not fit, but the actual inventory descriptions you will enter are unlikely to fit, either. Use the following procedure to widen column B:

1. Position your pointer directly on top of the line that separates column headings B and C (the gray buttons with the letters B and C on them) at the top of the spreadsheet. When positioned correctly, the pointer will change to a vertical bar with two horizontal arrows.

2. When this vertical bar appears, click and hold the left mouse button and drag the mouse to the right until the column is close to twice the original size. You can watch the ScreenTip as you drag to see the new width.

TIP. *When the pointer has changed to a vertical bar with two horizontal arrows, you can simply double-click to resize the column to accommodate the widest entry in the column.*

3. Release the mouse button to finish the change (see Figure 2.2).

Figure 2.2

The spreadsheet with column B widened

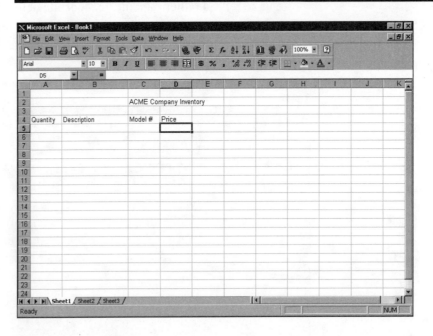

Entering Numbers

Move to cell A5, type **5**, and press Tab. The number immediately springs to the right of the cell after you press Tab instead of aligning to the left of the cell. Excel's default setting assumes that you want text to be left-aligned and numbers to be right-aligned.

In cell B5 type the following description entry: **Paper Clips**.

Entering Numbers as Text

Type the model number **00587** for this item in cell C5, and press Enter. Excel will display *587*, rather than *00587*.

Normally, Excel correctly anticipates whether you want an entry to be treated as text or as a number. In this case, it interprets your entry as a number and eliminates the unnecessary leading zeros. You want this entry to be treated as text, however, for two reasons: you need to preserve the leading zeros for the model number to be accurate, and you want all the model numbers to be similarly aligned. Some are pure text. If you mix numbers and text, by default some entries will be right-aligned, while others will be left-aligned.

To make Excel treat a number as text, you need to enter the number differently. In cell C5, type **'00587** (note the leading single quote mark) and press Enter. Now Excel will know that you want the entry to be treated as text, and it will display it accordingly. The single quote mark is all it takes.

TIP. *If you know you'll be entering a range of cells as text, you can first format those cells using the Text format (access the Format Cells command). When you do this, you no longer need to enter in the leading apostrophe: Excel will assume you mean to enter text in cells formatted as text.*

To finish the first line of data, move to the Price column and enter **.75** to represent 75 cents.

Entering Times and Dates

Before you continue with the exercise, you should learn to enter times and dates into Excel.

Excel does not store times and dates the same way it displays them. When you enter a time, Excel records two things: a number that represents a decimal fraction of a 24-hour day, and a formatting command that tells Excel to display that number as a time rather than as a simple number. In Excel, you can enter times in the following formats:

- 21:45
- 21:45:50 (hours:minutes:seconds)
- 9:45 PM
- 9:45:50 PM
- 5/6/97 9:45 PM

In the last example, you also can combine dates and times in the same cell entry. Any valid date combinations can be used that follow with any of the valid time combinations.

You can enter dates in a variety of ways, as follows:

- 5/6/97

- 5-6

- 6-May-97

- 6/May/97

- May-97 (uses your computer's day)

- May 6 (uses your computer's year)

You can use /, -, or a space to separate the elements of a date. If Excel does not recognize your entry as a date, it will treat it as a normal text entry and display it accordingly.

NOTE. *No matter how the date appears in the spreadsheet, it always appears with the format mm/dd/yyyy in the Formula bar. For example, if you enter **6 May** into a cell, you will see 5/6/1997 in the Formula bar. Seeing the way the date appears in the Formula bar lets you know whether Excel correctly recognized your entry as a date or displayed it as normal text.*

Excel stores a special number called a *serial number* when you enter a date. The serial number counts the number of days from the beginning of the century up to the date entered in the cell. For example, if you view the serial number for the date 1/1/2000, you'll see the number 36526. This number represents 365 days per year multiplied by 100 years (36500), plus the number of days added by leap years (25), plus one additional day (the first of January).

NOTE. *To see the serial number for a particular date, enter the date and press Ctrl+Shift+~, the shortcut key to force a cell to assume a numeric format (also called Normal formatting).*

To return the cell to a date format, press Ctrl+Shift+#, which is the shortcut key for the standard date format.

■ Performing Data Entry

Entering large amounts of data is extremely boring, making it rife with the potential for error. By using some of Excel's data-entry shortcuts, however, you can reduce the chance of errors, and complete the task more easily and quickly.

Selecting the Data-Entry Range

Normally, you need many extra keystrokes to move from the end of one line to the beginning of the next when you enter several records. Fortunately, you can automate this process with Excel.

If you use the mouse to select the range of cells into which data should be entered before you type the data, Excel will move between cells for you automatically. After you choose your data-entry area, use the keys listed in Table 2.1 to move your active cell in an efficient manner for data entry.

Table 2.1

Data-Entry Key Actions

KEY	MOVEMENT
Tab	Stores your entry and moves one cell to the right in the selected area. If you are at the right border of the selected area when you press Tab, the active cell moves to the beginning of the next row down.
Shift+Tab	Stores your entry and moves one cell to the left in the selected area. If you are at the left border of the selected area, the active cell moves to the right end of the next row up.
Enter	Stores your entry and moves one cell down in the selected area. If you are at the bottom row of the selected area, the active cell moves to the top row, one column to the right.
Shift+Enter	Stores your entry and moves one cell up in the selected area. If you are at the top row, the active cell moves to the bottom row, one column to the left.

TIP. *Excel 97 can use Intellisense to help you with data entry. When you're entering a block of data, use the Tab key to record each cell's data and move one cell to the right. When you type the data in the last column, press Enter instead of Tab. Excel will realize that you're performing data entry, and it will move the active cell to the next logical place. Usually that place will be one row down and left from the beginning of the row. You do not need to preselect a range of cells to use this feature.*

Using the Numeric Keypad

If you are used to entering numbers with a 10-key calculator that automatically places the decimal point in the number, you will be pleased to know that Excel can emulate that functionality. To activate this feature, follow these steps:

1. Pull down the Tools menu, then choose Options.

2. The Options dialog box will appear, allowing you to change many global characteristics of Excel. In this dialog box, first click on the Edit tab. Click on the Fixed decimal check box. The field below the check box should already have 2 in it, which indicates that two decimal points will be entered automatically.

3. Click on the OK button to close the dialog box.

After you activate this option, all numbers have a decimal point automatically inserted two places from the right. So, if you enter <u>12345</u>, Excel stores it as text 123.45. If you enter the number **5**, Excel stores it as .05, and so on. You can override this format in an individual cell by entering the decimal point by hand (for example, if you enter **5.**, you get 5). Excel uses the automatic decimal places until you uncheck the Fixed Decimal check box.

Special Data-Entry Keys

When you enter a large amount of data, certain parts of each line are often repeated in the following line. For example, when you enter inventory locations in your inventory spreadsheet, you may notice that many adjacent records share the same location. Also, sometimes you want to copy the formula in a cell, or automatically enter the date or the time into a cell.

The keys in Table 2.2 perform such actions.

Table 2.2

Special Data-Entry Key Actions

KEY	EFFECT
Ctrl+; (Semi-colon)	Enters the present date
Ctrl+: (Colon)	Enters the present time
Ctrl+' (Apostrophe)	Copies the formula from the cell above without adjusting the cell references
Ctrl+" (Quotation mark)	Copies the value (text or number) from the cell above

TIP. *Excel 97 includes AutoComplete, which can make entering data faster. For instance, if you type "Windows Sources" in cell B1 and press Enter to move to cell B2, and then type just the letter W, Excel will immediately offer an AutoComplete entry that types "Windows Sources" for you. The valid AutoComplete entries appear automatically in the cell as you type: just press Enter or Tab to accept them, or continue typing to ignore them.*

Completing Data Entry

Using the preceding tools, enter the remainder of the inventory information into your worksheet. Table 2.3 shows all the records, including the one you already entered. As you enter the data, remember the following points:

- Select cells A5 through D9 before you begin. Then, use the Tab key to move between cells.

- When you enter model numbers, remember to enter the number-only entries as 'nnn, where nnn is the number you want to enter. The single quote mark forces the numbers to be treated as text.

- If you use the Fixed Decimal feature, remember to enter the numbers correctly. For example, to enter the number 31, you can enter 3100 or 31. (with a decimal).

Table 2.3

Inventory Records

QTY	DESCRIPTION	MODEL #	PRICE
5	Paper clips	00587	.75
31	Faber #2 Pencils	2002	.05
12	Office Calendars	OCTZAB	12.95
93	Cs. Manila Folders	12MAN	6.95
12	Rm. #20 Copy Paper	20#500	5.35

TIP. *You can make entering this data easier by pre-formatting the appropriate columns using the Format Cells command. You can format the Model # column as text to avoid entering the leading apostrophes, and you can format the Price column using Currency or Fixed Decimal formats.*

After you finish entering the data from Table 2.3, your screen should look like Figure 2.3.

■ Working with Formulas

To add to your inventory spreadsheet, you might want to add a column that shows the value of the goods on hand, as well as a total amount for all of the inventory items. You can do this work by using a few simple formulas.

To begin, create a new column called Value in column E. Move to cell E4, type **Value** and press Enter.

Figure 2.3

The completed
inventory worksheet

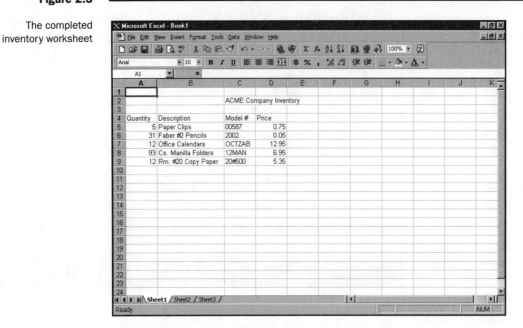

Using Cell References

Now, you must enter the formula. In this case, all you want to do is take the price in column D and multiply it by the quantity in column A—it's far from difficult, as you shall soon discover.

Keyboard

You can enter this formula in two ways using the keyboard. Both methods are depicted in the following two examples. Use E5 as your active cell.

The first method is merely a matter of typing in the formula. In cell E5, type **=D5*A5** and press Enter. The result appears in your active cell. Notice, however, that the formula appears in the formula bar when a cell containing a formula is selected. This display lets you see the basis for the result as you work in your spreadsheets.

The second method involves "pointing" with the arrow keys. Follow these steps, again using cell E5:

1. Type an equal sign.

2. Press the left arrow once. The cell reference D5 appears in the formula bar, and a dashed line appears in cell D5, showing the cell to which you are pointing.

3. Type an asterisk (*) for multiplication. The dashed box (called a *marquee*) disappears, and =D5* appears in the formula bar.

4. Press the left arrow four times. The marquee moves one cell at a time to the left, until it rests on cell A5.

5. Press Enter to complete the formula.

Both methods produce the same result. The method you use is up to you. Sometimes the pointing method works better because your spreadsheet is too big for you to know which cell you want. In that case, you can quickly point an arrow to the cell you want as you build your formula, without having to know the cell reference. However, in a small worksheet like the one used in this example, you might find it faster to use the first method and directly type the formula.

Mouse

You also can enter the formula using the mouse by following these steps:

6. In cell E5, type an equal sign.

7. Click on cell D5. The marquee will appear, and D5 will appear in the Formula bar.

8. Type an asterisk (*).

9. Click on cell A5. A5 will appear in the formula bar. You can press Enter to store the formula.

In a variation on this procedure, you use the scroll bars to locate the cell to which you want to point with the mouse. After you find the cell you want, click on it with the left mouse button. Enter an appropriate math symbol, and your display automatically returns to the cell into which you are entering the formula. However, in a small worksheet like the one used in this example, you might find it faster to use the first keyboard method and directly type the formula.

Working with Ranges of Cells

Finish the column of formulas. If you want to practice the methods you just learned, do so until each row has the inventory value in column E. If, however, you see that as drudgery and would prefer to circumvent the task, copy the formula to the other cells automatically using the following steps:

1. Select the range of cells from E5 to E9.

2. Pull down the Edit menu, and select Fill, then Down.

After you execute the Fill Down command, the formula you entered is copied automatically to all the cells below E5. Those cells should all display the calculated values, as shown in Figure 2.4.

TIP. *You also can press Ctrl+D instead of choosing Fill, Down from the Edit menu.*

Figure 2.4

The completed Value column

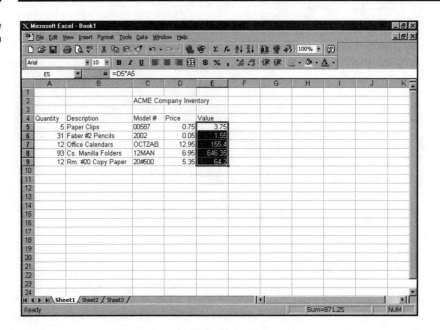

Referring to Multiple Ranges

Next, you want to total the Value column. You already know how to total it by entering a formula, **=E5+E6+E7+E8+E9**, in cell E10. If you have a worksheet that has a large table (one that contains hundreds or thousands of rows), however, entering that formula takes much too long. Furthermore, Excel cells are limited to a bit more than 32,000 characters, which is hardly enough if you enter formulas for thousands of cells in such a manner.

Fortunately, Excel includes a function called SUM that can add a range of cells and display the result. To use SUM, enter **=SUM(E5:E9)** in cell E10 and press Enter. The result of the formula should be 871.25.

TIP. *You can enter the SUM function in several ways. You can type **=SUM (** and use the keyboard arrow keys to indicate the range. (When you use the keyboard, you move the marquee to the first cell, hold down Shift, and then arrow to the last cell.) After you indicate the range, you can, if you wish, enter* *the closing parenthesis to complete the formula, or you can press Enter and let Excel complete the formula for you.*

You can also use the mouse. Type =SUM(and select a range of cells, then type) or just press Enter to complete the formula.

Lastly, you can use the AutoSum tool on the Standard toolbar, as discussed in Chapter 1, "Introducing Excel."

The shorthand notation in the preceding SUM formula is important. In Excel, you can refer to a range of cells by indicating only the beginning and ending cells, separated by a colon. If the range covers multiple rows and columns, you may refer to the range by indicating the top left cell and the bottom right cell.

For some formulas you might want to refer to many ranges of cells. For instance, you might want to total two columns with a column of text between them. In that case, you can separate each range of cells with a comma. For example, if you want to sum all of range C5 through C9 and E5 through E9, enter the formula **=SUM(C5:C9,E5:E9)**.

■ Understanding Relative and Absolute References

By default, the cells you refer to in your formulas are treated as though they refer to cells that are relative to your current cell. For this reason, you can copy the formula in cell E5 to cells E6 through E9 and still get the correct answers for each different row. This is called *relative cell referencing*, and it means that the cells you enter in your formulas are relative to the location of your formulas. Most formulas use this relative cell referencing method.

Excel also can use *absolute cell referencing*, meaning that your formulas always refer to a particular cell, no matter where you copy the formula. Understanding how relative and absolute cell referencing works is absolutely vital to mastering Excel formulas.

Using Absolute References

To enter a formula in Excel using absolute cell referencing, add a dollar sign ($) before the row and the column reference. For example, in cell E5 enter **=$D$5*A5$**. If you copy this formula to a different cell, it will still refer to cell D5 and A5.

Using Mixed References

Excel allows you to mix absolute and relative cell references. For example, you can enter the formula in cell E5 as **=$D5*$A5**—in essence, telling Excel that you want the column letters to be absolute, but that the row numbers can be relative. This formula still yields the correct answers in each cell, because only the row number actually needs to change. If you copy the formula to the right, it still works, because this formula always refers to the values found in columns A and D of the current row.

TIP. *After you enter a cell reference, you can use the F4 key to toggle between the different combinations of relative and absolute cell references. For an example of these combinations, select a blank cell and enter* **=D8**. *Before you continue, press F4 to cycle through D8, D8$, and D$8, which are the different combinations available. You also can use this method when editing a formula. Move to the formula you want to edit and press F2 to begin editing. Use the arrow keys to move the insertion point so that it is in the cell reference you want to change, then press F4 to cycle through the changes.*

■ Understanding A1 and R1C1 Cell Addressing

By default, Excel refers to cells using what is called the *A1 reference method*, which uses the alphabet to represent columns and numbers to represent rows. Columns are lettered from A through IV (A to Z, AA to AZ, BA to BZ, and so on, up to IV, which is the 256th column). Rows are numbered from 1 to 65536.

Excel also can use a different reference method, called the *R1C1 reference method*, in which the rows *and* columns are numbered.

In the R1C1 method, cells are referenced by using a combination of their row and column number. The equivalent of cell A1 is R1C1 (meaning Row #1, Column #1). Cell E5, for example, would be R5C5, and so on.

Toggling between A1 and R1C1 Addressing

To toggle Excel between the A1 and the R1C1 methods, pull down the Tools menu, select Options, then click on the General tab in the Options dialog box that appears. Select the check box marked R1C1 reference style, then click on the OK button. To toggle Excel back to the A1 method, choose the same menu command and dialog box and uncheck the R1C1 reference style option.

After you follow those steps, your formulas and cells will be referenced using this different method. Table 2.4 shows two examples of the differences you will observe.

Table 2.4

A1 versus R1C1 Formula
Changes

A1 CELL	R1C1 CELL	A1 FORMULA	R1C1 FORMULA
E5	R5C5	=D5*A5	=RC[-1]*RC[-4]
E10	R10C5	=SUM(E5:E9)	=SUM(R[-5]C:R[-1]C)

NOTE. *Using the A1 or the R1C1 method changes only the* appearance *of your worksheet. Nothing internal will change in your worksheet. If you give a copy of your worksheet to someone using a different method, they will see the formulas in the method they are using, and the worksheet will function exactly as it did using the other method.*

If you look at the first example in Table 2.4, the R1C1 formula **=RC[-1]*RC[-4]**, translated into English, reads:

```
"Take the value in the current row, one column to the left, and multiply it by
the value in the current row, four columns to the left."
```

The second example, **=SUM(R[-5]C:R[-1]C)**, translates to the following:

```
"Sum the values starting from the cell five rows up in the current column to
the cell one row up in the current column."
```

These formulas refer to cell positions that are *relative* to the current cell. The formulas in cells R5C5, R6C5, R7C5, R8C5, and R9C5 are all *exactly* the same formula. When a number is not given after the 'R' or the 'C' in the R1C1 addressing method, Excel assumes you are referring to the current row or column. Because of this assumption, it is easy to understand how formulas copied to different locations in the spreadsheet refer to cells in the same positions, relative to the cell that contains the formula. So, for example, if you copy the formula =SUM(R[-5]C:R[-1]C) to cell R19C34, it sums the values found in cells R14C34, R15C34, R16C34, R17C34, and R18C34.

If you use the R1C1 method, you also can enter formulas that are not relative to the current cell but are absolute. If, for example, you enter the formula **=R5C1*R5C4**, the formula always refers to those two cells, no matter where in the worksheet you copy the formula.

NOTE. *If you've changed to R1C1 addressing to try it out, you should switch back to A1 addressing now. The rest of the book's examples assume that you're using A1 addressing.*

■ Understanding the Importance of Names

One of the most useful, but least used, features of Excel is its ability to assign names to parts of the worksheet. In Excel, you can name ranges of cells, constant values, and formulas. Perhaps many people do not use names because they feel that normal cell references work just fine, and they don't want to take the time to learn something new. Or possibly some people think their worksheets won't grow large enough to benefit from using names—but then their worksheets do, in fact, grow! In any case, consider the following advantages and features of using names in Excel:

*   If you name cells or ranges of cells, you can then use those names in your formulas. It is far easier to remember to type =Amount*Quantity than it is to remember =D5*A5.

    TIP. *Excel 97 introduces a feature called* natural language formulas. *If your worksheet is structured with the row and column labels next to the data, you can use those labels in formulas automatically, without defining the named ranges. However, defining named ranges is still a good discipline, because natural language formulas won't necessarily guess which cells you're referring to, or you may want to use names that don't match the display label.*

*   Using names improves the ability to audit your worksheets. When you use names in your formulas, you can see easily that the formula **=Amount*Quantity** is correct, but it is not as apparent that **=D5*A5** is correct.

*   In Excel, you can assign a constant value to a name. For instance, if you work with many financial statements from many different companies, you can assign the name *Number_of_Periods* the value 12 or 13, depending on how many accounting periods the company uses. Then, use the *Number_of_Periods* name in your formulas in place of the number 12 or 13. When you need to use the same worksheet for a company with a different number of accounting periods, just change the value of the *Number_of_Periods* constant, and then all the formulas that use the name automatically are based on the new value.

*   When you need to jump around a large worksheet, it is easier to use the name to which you want to jump with the Go to command (F5), as opposed to using, for example, cell BZ157. You can press F5 for the Go to command, then just enter SALES to jump to the cells named SALES.

*   Using names can reduce the potential for errors. If you type in a formula with the column or the row even slightly wrong, Excel can give you the answer based on what is in the wrong cell, and you might think that the answer is correct. If you use a name incorrectly, however, Excel gives

you a #NAME? error, instead of using an erroneous cell and possibly giving you an incorrect answer.

- The preceding advantage is even more important when you consolidate multiple worksheets. It is far easier to validate the formula **=AUG-SUM.XLS!Units** than to validate **=AUGSUM.XLS!AR214**.

NOTE. *Technically, Excel has two types of names: book-level names and sheet-level names. Book-level names correspond to a named range that encompasses an entire workbook, while sheet-level names correspond to ranges within a single worksheet. This is an important distinction when you start referencing cells in multiple sheets.*

Creating Names

As you create and work with names, remember the following rules:

- The first character of a name must be a letter or underscore.

- **Names cannot contain spaces**. Instead, use the underscore (_) or the period (.) to separate words. For example, use West_Sales, West.Sales, or even WestSales rather than West†Sales.

- **Names cannot resemble cell addresses**.

- **Use short names**. Long names make it difficult to find the name you want when you search through a list of names in a list box. Plus, they're harder to type and to review quickly.

- **Names are not case-sensitive.** You can use any combination of upper- and lowercase letters.

You can name parts of your worksheet in two ways. The method you use will depend on the way your data is structured and the way you want to use the names. Try both of the following exercises so you can understand the differences between the two methods.

Manually

To manually name a range, follow these steps:

1. Select the range of cells A4 through A9.

2. Pull down the Insert menu, select Name, then Define. The Define Name dialog box appears as shown in Figure 2.5.

3. Click on the OK button.

Because you preselected the range you wanted to name, the dialog box already has filled in the range you want to name, as well as the name you want to use. (Excel uses the text found in the top row or far left column that

Figure 2.5

The Define Name
dialog box

you selected in order to "guess" the name, but you can enter your own if you like.) If you don't select the range before you issue the Insert Name Define command, you'll have to type the name you want in the Names in Workbook field and the range of cells in the Refers to field. Excel has also used absolute cell references in the Refers To field, which is correct.

Automatically

In Excel, you also can create names for multiple ranges at the same time, which is most useful for tables, not unlike the inventory table you have created. To use this method, follow these steps:

1. Select ranges A4:A9, D4:D9, and E4:E9. Hold down the Ctrl key when you select the second and third ranges. If you select all three ranges properly, your screen will look like Figure 2.6.

2. Pull down the Insert menu, select Name, then Create Names. The Create Names dialog box will appear (see Figure 2.7).

   In the Create Names dialog box, you can tell Excel where to look for the names you want to apply automatically to the ranges. Here, you want Excel to automatically use the titles in the top row for each range, so you need to make sure that the Top Row check box is selected.

   If you are working in a table that has labels in both the top and left rows, you can select both of those check boxes (Top Row and Left Column), which creates a name for each range.

   Important: You can have many names that all refer to the same cell. For instance, you might have vertical ranges named Q1_Sales and Q2_Sales, and horizontal ranges named West_Region and East_Region. In this example, each cell will be referenced by two different names, and you can use those two names appropriately in formulas. If you are creating a new row that adds

Figure 2.6

Multiple ranges selected

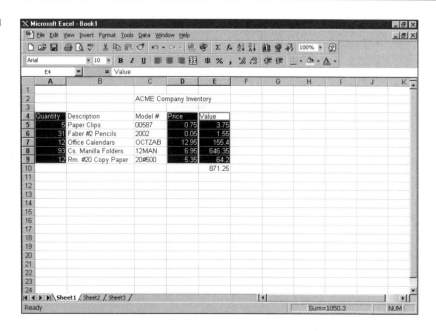

Figure 2.7

The Create Names
dialog box

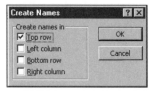

West_Region and East_Region, you can enter those names. If you are creating a column that totals Q1_Sales and Q2_Sales to the right of your table, you also can use those names.

3. With the Top Row check box selected, click on the OK button.

After you click on the OK button, Excel will open a dialog box that asks if you want to replace any existing names (in this example, Quantity was defined earlier). Click on the OK or Cancel button in that dialog box. If your worksheet has no preexisting named ranges in the area in which you are working, nothing happens when the new names are created. You can, however, test these new named ranges. To test them, follow these steps:

1. Move to cell E5.

2. Enter the formula **=Quantity*Price** and press Enter.

If you created the named ranges correctly, you'll see the same result that previously existed in cell E5, but the Formula bar will show your new formula. If the names did not exist, or if you mistyped them in the formula, you'll get a <u>#NAME?</u> error in that cell.

Creating Book-Level Names

You can create names that refer to cells in multiple sheets. Follow these steps:

1. Access the Insert, Name, Define command.

2. Type the name you want to define in the Names in workbook field.

3. Clear the Refers to field manually. Select the reference and press the Backspace key.

4. Type an equal sign (=) and then click the tab of the first sheet to be named.

5. Hold down the Shift key and click on the last sheet to be named.

6. Select the range of cells on the current sheet.

7. Click OK to close the dialog box.

This procedure results in a name that refers to the cells you selected in all of the sheets you selected. If you refer to that name in formulas, the contents of all the appropriate cells in the named sheets will be included in the result.

Applying Names

If you are working with an existing worksheet, it's hardly worth it to manually re-enter all your formulas the way you did for cell E5. Fortunately, in Excel you can take your new named ranges and automatically change all the applicable formulas to use those names. To do this with the inventory worksheet, follow these steps:

1. Select the ranges A4:A9, D4:D9, and E4:E10 (make sure to include the total at the bottom of the Value column). Press and hold down Ctrl while you use your mouse to select the second and third ranges.

2. Pull down the Insert menu, select Name, then select Apply. The Apply Names dialog box will appear, as shown in Figure 2.8.

3. Click on the OK button.

Figure 2.8

The Apply Names dialog box lets you transform your equations to use the names you assigned.

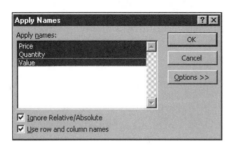

Before you use it, make sure that the names you want to apply are selected in the Apply names list box, which they are by default if you completed the range-selection process in step 1. If the names are not selected, you'll need to select them using the mouse, holding down Ctrl if you want to apply more than one name.

The Apply Names dialog box has several options, as follows:

- **Ignore Relative/Absolute**. Controls the way Excel substitutes names for relative and absolute references. If this box is not checked, Excel applies only names that match the absolute or relative reference found in the original formula. You usually want to check this box.

- **Use Row and Column Names**. Controls how liberally Excel applies names. If this box is not checked, Excel applies only names that refer to the individual cells used in the formula rather than names that might refer to an entire column or row. If this box is checked (the default), Excel uses the name for the entire row or column. Normally, you want to leave this box checked.

Check around the worksheet. All the formulas have been replaced with the simpler, name-based formulas. Even the =SUM formula reads **=SUM(Value)**, which is far easier to read, remember, and understand than **=SUM(E4:E9)**.

Creating Named Constants

One often-overlooked feature in Excel is being able to create named constants. If you use Excel's name feature, constants don't even have to take up cell space.

Use a constant when parts of your worksheet depend on a single number. One example is a sales projection worksheet that uses a single value for sales-growth assumptions. A profit and loss statement that has an assumption about your gross margin might also rely on one value. In either case, you can handle the numerical assumption in one of two ways:

- You can enter the assumption in a single cell on the worksheet, and then have your other formulas refer to that cell (using an absolute cell reference).

- You can define a named constant that contains the number.

Using the named constant keeps your worksheet a little neater, and also makes it easier to see how your formulas work.

TIP. *When you create named constants, consistently use something in the name to distinguish it as a constant rather than a named range of cells. For example, you could use only uppercase letters for the names of your constants. Or you could begin the name of each constant with C_. For example, you might create a constant named C_GROWTH. Using this kind of visual clue helps you see quickly which names in your formulas are constants and which are named cells.*

Using B_name for book-level range names and S_name for sheet-level names will also help you keep your naming conventions in check.

To create and work with named constants, use the following steps. Add a new column to your example worksheet that shows the retail value of the inventory in stock. For this exercise, create a named constant called C_MARKUP that you can use to calculate the retail value. Then follow these steps:

1. Move to cell F4 and select it, then type **Retail Value** and press Enter.

2. Reselect cell F4. Then, pull down the Insert menu, select Name, and then Define.

3. In the Define Names dialog box that appears, move to the field called Names in Workbook and type **C_MARKUP**.

4. Tab to the Refers to field and type **1.40**—a 40-percent markup after you use it in the formula to multiply against the Value.

5. Click on OK to return to the worksheet.

6. Move to cell F5 and type the formula **=Value*C_MARKUP** and press Enter. Cell F5 now shows you the retail value of the inventory in row 5.

7. Select the range F5:F9. While those cells are selected, pull down the Edit menu, select Fill, then Down (or simply press Ctrl+D).

8. While the range still is selected, pull down the Insert menu, select Name, then Define.

9. The Define Name dialog box already has its name—Retail_Value—and the range of cells entered. So just click on the OK button.

10. Move to cell F10, enter the formula **=SUM(Retail_Value)**, and press Enter.

Your worksheet now has the new column, along with the total retail value in cell F10. To change the assumption contained in the constant value C_MARKUP (your retail markup assumption), follow these steps:

1. Pull down the Insert menu, select Name, then Define.

2. In the Names in Sheet list box, select C_MARKUP. Now click in the Refers to field, and change the value from 1.40 to 1.5.

3. Click on the OK button for your changes to take effect. The results are shown in Figure 2.9.

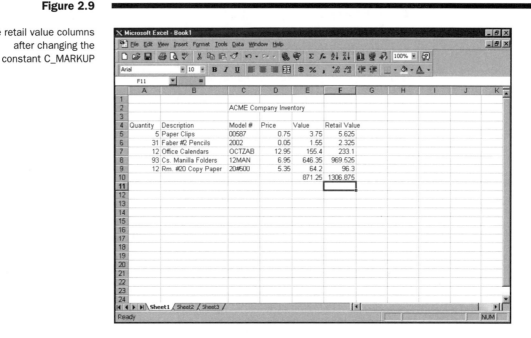

Figure 2.9

The retail value columns after changing the constant C_MARKUP

Immediately after you click on the OK button, the retail value of each item changes to reflect the new markup in the constant C_MARKUP. The total at the bottom of the column also changes to reflect the new markup assumption.

Creating Named Formulas

Even as you can define a named constant, so too can you define a named formula. While named formulas have fewer uses, they can come in handy. One situation where named formulas might be useful is when your worksheet uses a single formula in many places. If you use a named formula, you can simply change the named formula, rather than finding and changing the formula in every cell it occurs in.

To see how this works, create a named formula called Calc.Retail.Value. This named formula has the formula necessary to calculate the retail value. Follow these steps:

1. Select cell F5. Next, pull down the Insert menu, select Name, and then Define.

2. In the Define Name dialog box, move to the Names in workbook field and type **Calc.Retail.Value**.

TIP. *For the same reason you want your named constants to have a distinct naming style from named ranges, you also want named formulas to have a distinct naming style. In this example, the named formula uses periods to separate the words and also has the word Calc at the beginning of the name, which helps you see that this name refers to a named formula.*

3. Tab to the Refers to field, type **=(E5*C_MARKUP)**, press Enter to create the name and close the Define Name dialog box.

4. Move back to cell F5, type **=Calc.Retail.Value**, and press Enter.

5. Cell F5 now contains a reference to Calc.Retail.Value that contains the formula that does the calculation. To complete this change, copy the new formula down to the other cells.

6. To copy the named formula to the rest of the column, select the cells F5:F9 and press Ctrl+D (the shortcut for Edit, Fill Down).

Deleting Names

Sometimes you have to delete names from a workbook. For example, if the name in question is no longer in use, you might want to remove it from the list to reduce clutter. To remove a name, use the following procedure.

1. Pull down the Insert menu, select Name, then Define.

2. Click on the name you want to delete in the Names in Workbook list box.

3. Click on the Delete button, then the OK button.

WARNING. *If you delete a name that is being used in other formulas, Excel won't warn you. Instead, after you click on the OK button a #NAME? error message will appear in all the cells that have formulas using that name, as well as in any cells that refer to the cells using that deleted name. For example, if you delete the Price name from the example worksheet, all the cells in columns E and F will show the #NAME? error, because those cells depend on the Price name. To rectify such a mistake, you must re-create the name or edit the formulas in the affected cells.*

■ Working with Comments in Cells

Naming parts of your workbook is only the beginning of documenting it. Often, you still have to explain *why* certain calculations were made or provide other information pertinent to the workbook. Here are a couple of reasons that notes make sense:

* If you need to look at the workbook again in several months, you might not remember why you made certain choices.

* If others work with your workbooks, they might not understand why you did certain things or your reasons for choosing a particular way to do them.

In Excel, you can attach comments to individual cells—comments that you can use to explain the worksheet. In essence, you can annotate your worksheet.

Adding Comments

In the worksheet in Figure 2.10, the sales for Clyde Coyote are at zero for the month of April, but why the sales go to zero that month is totally inexplicable.

Any proper documentation must certainly explain that "zero" entry—a perfect occasion for Excel's comment feature. If you wanted to add a comment that explains the lack of sales during April, you would follow these steps:

1. Move to cell F5.

2. Pull down the Insert menu and select Comment. A cell comment window appears on the worksheet, as shown in Figure 2.11.

   TIP. *Press Shift+F2 to pull up the Cell Comment window for the active cell.*

   In the Cell Comment window, simply type the comment appropriate for the cell. In this case, you can type **Clyde on vacation in April** and click outside of the comment window to finish the comment.

Figure 2.10

The ACME Sales
Projections worksheet
with the mysterious
"zero month"

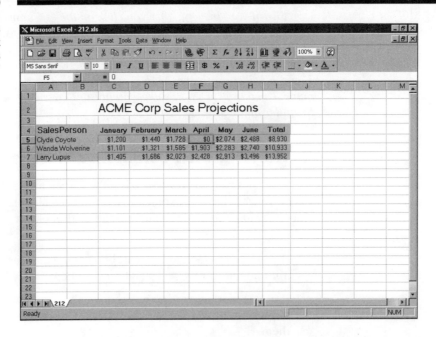

Figure 2.11

The Cell Comment window

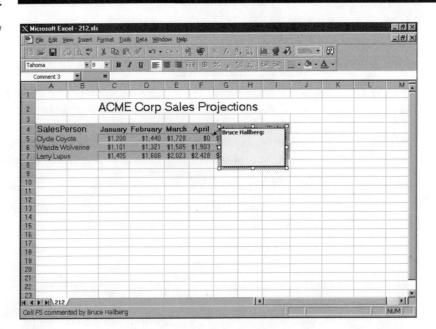

A small red triangle in the upper-right corner of a cell indicates the presence of a comment (see Figure 2.12). This red triangle will not appear on printouts of the worksheet, however.

Figure 2.12

The Comment indicator

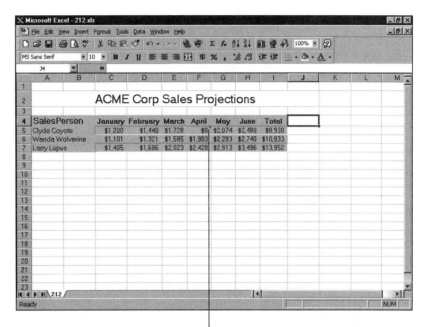

Small red triangle indicates a comment attached to cell

Showing Comments

If a comment is indicated by the presence of a small red dot, simply move your mouse pointer over the red triangle, wait a beat, and the comment will appear automatically, just like a ToolTip. You can also press Shift+F2 when the cell that contains the comment is active to display (and edit) the comment.

You can make the small red triangle disappear by following these steps:

1. Pull down the Tools menu, select Options, then click on the View tab.

2. On the View notebook page, find the check box marked None in the Comments section and select it.

3. Click on the OK button.

Finding Comments

To search the spreadsheet for a specific comment, follow these steps:

1. Pull down the Edit menu and select Find (or press Ctrl+F). The Find dialog box appears.

2. In the Find What field, type the word you want to find.

3. In the Look In drop box, select Comments.

4. Click on the Find Next button.

5. Click on the Close button.

Excel searches all the comments in the worksheet for the word you typed, and the cell that contains the comment becomes the active cell. To bring up the note, press Shift+F2 when you are on that cell.

Editing and Deleting Comments

To edit a note, perform one of these actions:

- Make the cell with the comment active and press Shift+F2. You can then edit the comment using the normal editing keys.

- Right-click on the cell containing the comment and choose Edit Comment, Delete Comment, or Show Comment from the shortcut menu.

- With the cell containing the comment active, pull down the Insert menu and choose Edit Comment. This command replaces Insert Comment when your active cell already contains a comment.

■ Rearranging Data

One of the most powerful notions behind worksheets is that they can help you work through an idea or analysis progressively. It is vital to know how to rearrange the data you enter into the worksheet as you decide to try new approaches, consider new information, and so on. Whether you want to analyze the data in a different way, rearrange the data to make it easier to graph, or accomplish some other task, manipulating data is an important skill. This section covers the following:

- Cutting data from one location and pasting it to another

- Copying data in your document

- Moving data with a single mouse movement

- Moving not only ranges, but entire rows or columns

- Filling ranges of cells automatically with numbers or text

- Using AutoFill to complete various numeric and date progressions

Cut and Paste

The basic method for moving and duplicating data in a worksheet is to Cut and Paste or Copy and Paste—similar, but not identical, activities. You can cut or copy data into the Clipboard, then paste it from the Clipboard to a new location.

For these examples, you'll use the inventory worksheet that you created at the beginning of this chapter:

1. Begin by selecting range B4:B9.

2. Pull down the Edit menu and select Cut. A marquee will surround the area you have cut, but it won't disappear right away (in many programs, your data disappears immediately after choosing Cut, but not in Excel).

3. Move your active cell to location B12.

4. Pull down the Edit menu and select Paste.

NOTE. *When you cut and paste cells that other cells depend on, Excel automatically adjusts the references so that the formulas still work properly with the data in the new location.*

Immediately, the data will vanish from its original location and reappear in the new location (see Figure 2.13). The pasted data will start in the active cell (B12) and fill the cells downward. The destination you select is always the upper-left corner of the area you want to paste to.

To reverse the process, select the data from cells B12:B17, then choose Cut from the Edit menu. Move your active cell to cell B4, then select Paste from the Edit menu.

NOTE. *Of course, if you wanted to undo the cut and paste operation, you simply choose Undo from the Edit menu.*

You'll cut, copy, and paste frequently in Excel, so you can save a great deal of time by learning to use the cut, copy, and paste shortcut keys. These keys are shown in Table 2.5.

Copying Data

Copying data works just like cutting and pasting. Instead of cutting from one location and pasting onto another, you copy the data from the selected range onto the Clipboard and then paste it onto the new location. The original data is unaffected.

Figure 2.13

The pasted data in its
new location

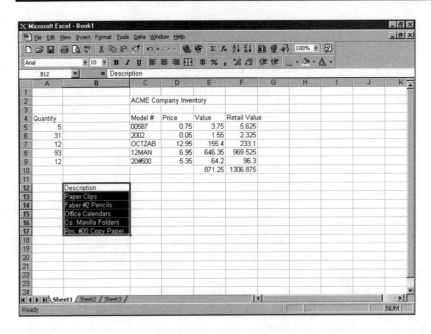

Table 2.5

Cut, Copy, and Paste
Shortcut Keys

FUNCTION	SHORTCUT KEY	MEMORY CUES
Cut	Ctrl+X	Think of 'X' as similar to a pair of scissors, or think of crossing something out on a paper document with a big X.
Copy	Ctrl+C	'C' stands for copy.
Paste	Ctrl+V	Think of the 'V' as an insertion point that you would make hand-editing a document.

For an example of how copying works, select the range B4:B9 and press
Ctrl+C (for copy). Move your active cell to B12 and press Ctrl+V (paste).
You should see a copy of the data appear in the new location.

Because the data is still in memory, you can paste the copied data into an
unlimited number of new locations until you cut or copy something else,
which will overwrite the old data in the Clipboard, or press Esc to cancel the
selection marquee. To see how this works, move to cell C12 and press Ctrl+V
again.

Deleting Data

To delete data from your worksheet, select a range (C12:C17 is used in the example), pull down the Edit menu, and choose Clear, then All.

The cascading menu is shown in Figure 2.14.

Figure 2.14

The Clear All
cascading menu

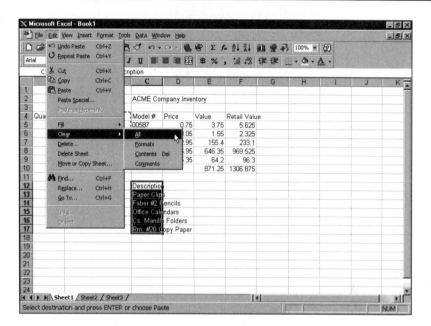

TIP. *Pressing the Del key does the same thing as selecting Clear, All from the Edit menu.*

The Clear cascading menu has four options, as follows:

- **All**. Removes the data in the selected range, as well as any formatting applied to the cell and any notes attached to the cell. When formatting is removed, the cell reverts to General—the default format.

- **Formats**. Causes the formatting for the cell to be removed. The cell reverts to the General format.

- **Contents**. Removes any cell contents, including formulas, numbers, and text labels, but does not affect the cell format or any notes attached to the cell. This is the default setting.

- **Comments**. Removes only the comment attached to the selected cells. The cell contents and formatting remain.

Rows and Columns

You can cut, copy, paste, or clear entire rows and columns. As an example, move column E to column G by using the following steps:

1. At the top of the worksheet, click once on the column marker labeled E. The entire column will be highlighted.

2. Press Ctrl+X to cut the data from column E.

3. Click on the column marker for column G.

4. Press Ctrl+V to paste the data into the new location. Depending on your computer's available memory, you might see a dialog box that warns you that the section is too large to undo. If you are sure you want to proceed, click on the OK button.

You can perform the same operation on rows by selecting the numbered row label.

You also can perform the operation on multiple rows or columns. Hold down Ctrl as you select each row or column. If you select an operation (such as Edit, Delete) that Excel cannot perform on multiple rows or columns, an error box will appear.

Drag and Drop Editing

Cutting and pasting with Ctrl+X and Ctrl+V are quick methods, but Excel includes one other shortcut that lets you move data with a simple drag of the mouse. To see how shortcuts work, move the cells D4:D9 to G4:G9, as follows:

1. Select the range D4:D9.

2. Very carefully move your pointer to the outside border of the selected cells. When your pointer is in precisely the right place, it will change into a white arrow.

3. With your pointer in the arrow shape, click and hold down the left mouse button. With the button held down, move your mouse to the right. As you move it, a thick marquee will also move.

4. Position the thick marquee so that it encloses cells G4:G9, and then release the mouse button.

This procedure works with both single cells and ranges. You even can use it with entire rows and columns!

WARNING. *When you move sections of your worksheet that contain formulas or numbers used by formulas in other cells, be careful. Moving cells can mess up the formulas they contain or formulas in other cells that use the moved* *data. Often these problems appear as #REF! or #VALUE! errors in the affected cells.*

■ Filling Ranges of Cells

Frequently you'll need to copy the contents of one cell into many cells. You can copy the data into the Clipboard, then paste it into the new cells, but there are even faster ways available to duplicate cell contents throughout many cells.

For these examples, begin a new worksheet (if you've been following along with the earlier example sheet, you can close it now). Pull down the File menu and select New. A dialog box will prompt you for the type of document that you want to create. Select Workbook and click on the OK button.

Fill Handle

Using the Fill handle is far easier than using the menu commands to fill ranges. The Fill handle also lets you do some neat tricks! For these examples, delete anything on the worksheet left over from the previous example. Select a range that includes all the worksheet contents, and press Ctrl+Delete to clear the worksheet contents.

Use Table 2.6 to set up several cells to use to explore the different ways in which the Fill handle works. After you set up the worksheet, it should look like Figure 2.15.

Table 2.6

Fill Handle Example Setup

CELL	CONTENTS
B3	1
B4	1
C4	3
B5	January
B6	Jan
C6	Apr
B7	Quarter 1
B8	1/1/97

CELL	CONTENTS
B9	1/1/97
C9	2/1/97

Figure 2.15

The example worksheet
for Fill handle examples

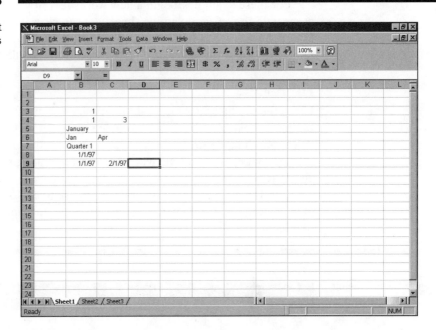

Follow these steps to start using the Fill handle:

1. Make sure that cell B3 is your active cell.

2. Locate the Fill handle. It is the small box at the lower right corner of the active cell (see Figure 2.16).

3. Carefully move your pointer until it is immediately on top of the Fill handle. When positioned correctly, the pointer changes to a small cross.

4. Hold down the left mouse button and drag the mouse to the right until the thick marquee surrounds the cells from B3 to H3.

5. When the marquee is positioned correctly, release the mouse button.

Figure 2.16

The Fill handle

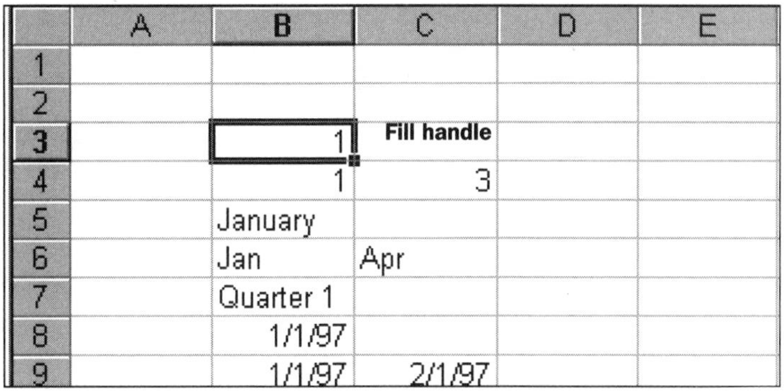

	A	B	C	D	E
1					
2					
3		1	**Fill handle**		
4		1	3		
5		January			
6		Jan	Apr		
7		Quarter 1			
8		1/1/97			
9		1/1/97	2/1/97		

The number 1 is automatically copied into each of the selected cells. You also can use the Fill handle to fill on each of the other four directions.

AutoFill

If you use the Fill handle with a single number or a text label, Excel simply copies the data. Similarly, if you use the Fill handle with a formula, Excel copies it, adjusting any relative cell references as it fills the formula.

Sometimes, however, the Fill handle activates a feature called *AutoFill*. Follow these examples to see some of the ways AutoFill works.

Linear Series

1. Select the cells B4:C4

2. Drag the Fill handle into the lower right-hand corner of cell C4 until the thick marquee extends to H3 and release the mouse button. The results are shown in Figure 2.17.

Excel determined that you had marked out two cells that contained a numeric progression. Excel assumed that you wanted to continue the numeric progression, and filled the cells accordingly.

Date Progressions

AutoFill also is very intelligent about filling dates into cells. For each of the remaining lines in the example worksheet, use the Fill handle to copy the contents to column H. In the two cases where two initial examples are provided (when column C has a value), remember to select both examples before dragging the Fill handle to the right. The results are shown in Figure 2.18.

Table 2.7 contains some comments on each of these examples.

Figure 2.17

Numeric progression with
the Fill handle

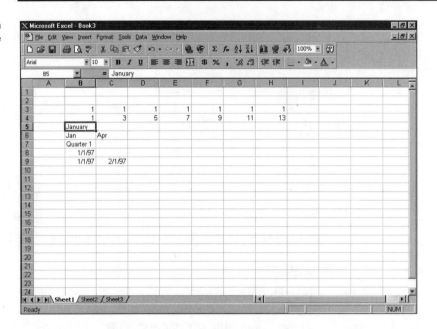

Figure 2.18

Completed examples
of AutoFill

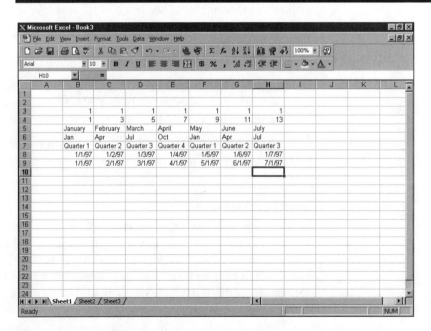

Table 2.7

ROW	STARTING DATA	COMMENTS
5	January	Excel recognizes the word "January" as a valid month name. It automatically fills the remaining months into the filled cells.
6	Jan, Apr	Excel also recognizes Jan and Apr as valid abbreviations of month names. Because you used two month names that are three months apart, Excel continues the series, even starting over again at Jan when it finishes the first year.
7	Quarter 1	Excel recognizes Quarter 1 as a common financial heading. It correctly fills the remaining three quarters, and then starts over again at Quarter 1. Excel also recognizes 'Qtr1' and 'Q1' as quarterly titles.
8	1/1/93	AutoFilling this range produces dates each one day apart. If you AutoFill many cells, you'll find that Excel knows the day on which each month ends and that it even takes leap years into account!
9	1/1/93,2/1/93	As you observed in previous progressions, Excel is fairly intelligent about making assumptions about your desires. In this case, it automatically fills each cell with the first day of each month.

As you can see, Excel's AutoFill feature is very intelligent and saves you a tremendous amount of time.

■ Inserting and Deleting Data

Aside from cut, copy, paste, and clear operations, Excel also lets you insert and delete areas on the worksheet, shifting the location of existing information in the worksheet accordingly. Using various commands on the Insert menu and the Delete commands on the Edit menu, you can accomplish the following tasks:

- Insert new rows or columns, pushing the existing rows or columns down or to the right to make room.

- Insert blocks of data, pushing the existing data to the right or down.

- Delete entire rows or columns, moving the remaining data up or to the left.

- Delete ranges of data, moving the remaining data up or to the left.

Inserting Blank Space

To insert new blank space in your worksheet, select the area in which you want the new cells to appear, pull down the Insert menu, then select Cells.

As an example, select the range C4:F7, pull down the Insert menu and then select Cells. The Insert dialog box appears, as displayed in Figure 2.19.

Figure 2.19

The Insert dialog box

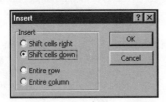

The Insert dialog box lets you choose from the following four options:

- **Shift cells right.** Makes new space by forcing the existing cells to the right of the new area.

- **Shift cells down.** Pushes the existing cells downward.

- **Entire row.** Inserts entire rows in the selected range, pushing the existing rows down.

- **Entire column.** Inserts entire columns, pushing the existing columns to the right.

For this example, select Shift Cells Down. The results are shown in Figure 2.20.

Inserting Data

You also can copy data from one location and insert it into a new location by selecting the range you want to copy, pressing Ctrl+C to copy it to the Clipboard, positioning the active cell where you want the data to be inserted, pulling down the Insert menu, and selecting Cell. The Insert dialog box will appear, permitting you to shift the existing cells to the right or down. After you make your decision in the dialog box, Excel will perform the insert operation, moving the existing cells in the direction you specify.

Figure 2.20

The inserted blank range

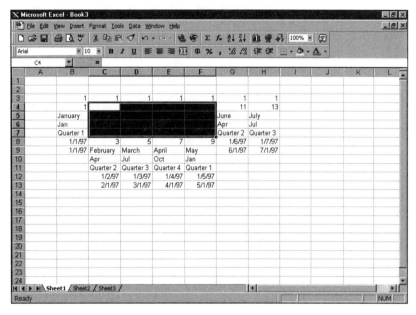

TIP. *You can perform drag-and-drop inserts, too. Select the cells that you want to move and insert, and hold down the Shift key as you drag them to a new location. Remember to drag using the border of the selected cells.*

Deleting Ranges

Deleting entire ranges is accomplished in a similar way. Select the range of cells to delete, pull down the Edit menu, and select Delete. You will be shown a Delete dialog box, which allows you to shift the cells up, to the left, or to delete entire rows and columns. Select the appropriate choice and click on the OK button.

Inserting and Deleting Entire Rows and Columns

Finally, you can insert and delete entire rows and columns by selecting the row or column. Click on the row or column label, then choose Insert, Row; Insert, Column; or Edit, Delete.

You also can select multiple rows and columns. Just hold down the mouse on the first row or column, then drag the mouse in the appropriate direction to select the desired rows or columns.

Special Paste Tricks within Excel

Excel has a few other tricks up its sleeve concerning the rearrangement of data. Under the Edit menu is a command called Paste Special. Paste Special lets you accomplish the following tasks:

- Selectively paste only cell values, formulas, formatting, validation rules, or comments.

- Automatically take the contents of the Clipboard and perform a mathematical operation with its cells using the contents of the destination cells.

- Transpose a series of cells, which has the effect of rotating the data 90 degrees. Columns of data become rows, and vice-versa.

- Create a link between the original source data and the pasted (destination) data. If the source data is modified, the destination data will reflect the change.

To understand how these features work, set up a new worksheet as follows:

1. In cell B2, enter **1.**

2. In cell C2, enter **3.**

3. Use the Fill handle to AutoFill the numeric series to column G (select B2:C2 and drag the Fill handle to cell G2).

4. In cell B3, enter **2.**

5. In cell C3, enter **4.**

6. Use the Fill handle to AutoFill the numeric series to column G.

7. In cell B4, enter the formula **=B2*B3** and press Enter.

8. Use the Fill handle to copy the formula in cell B4 to all of the cells over to cell G4.

Your worksheet should look like Figure 2.21.

Pasting Values

Excel allows you to copy a series of formulas and paste only their results. You can, for example, select a series of formulas that result in numeric values and copy those formulas into the Clipboard. Then you can move to the destination cell, use Paste Special, and select Values from the dialog box. Click on OK to complete the operation. The destination cells will contain the results, not the formulas of the originating cells.

Figure 2.21

A sample worksheet for
Paste Special examples

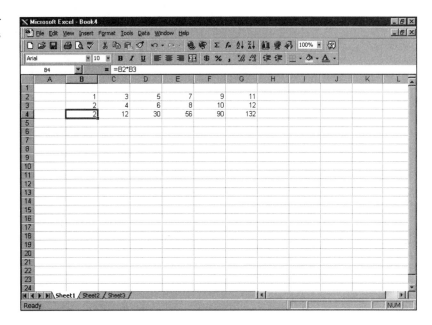

To perform this operation, do the following:

1. Select the cells B4:G4 and press Ctrl+C to copy them into the Clipboard.

2. Move to cell B6.

3. Pull down the Edit Menu and select Paste Special.

4. In the Paste Special dialog box, select Values, and click the OK button. If you look at the cell contents of the original cells (B4:G4) you can see that they contain formulas. (Select one of the original cells, then look at the Formula bar to see the contents of the cell.) The destination cells, however, contain only the resulting values. It is as if Excel took the values and simply typed the results for you in the new location (see Figure 2.22).

Performing Math Operations

Excel lets you copy one series of numbers (either derived from a formula or entered by hand) and then add, subtract, multiply, or divide those values against a different range.

To see how this operation works, follow these steps:

1. Select the series of cells B3:G3.

2. Press Ctrl+C to copy the cells into the Clipboard.

Figure 2.22

The first result
of Transpose

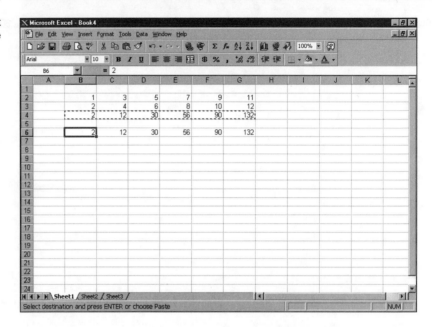

3. Move to cell B6, where the results of the previous example start.

4. Pull down the Edit menu and select Paste Special.

5. In the Paste Special dialog box, select Divide and click on the OK button.

Excel will take the numbers in the destination cells and divide them by the contents of the Clipboard. Using the same method, you also can add, subtract, or multiply two ranges of numbers against one another.

Transposing Data

You also can change the orientation of your data quickly using the Paste Special command. For example, if you have some data for which you want the rows to become columns and the columns to become rows, Paste Special allows you to "rotate" the data 90 degrees. This capability is separate from the new PivotTable feature, which is discussed in a later chapter.

WARNING. *When you transpose cells that contain formulas, you change any formulas in the transposed cells. To deal with this potential problem, select the Values option button when performing the Paste Special command. This option converts any formulas to pure numbers.*

To see how the Transpose feature in Paste Special works, follow these steps:

1. Select the range of cells B2:G4.

2. Press Ctrl+C to copy the cells to the Clipboard.

3. Move to cell B6.

4. Pull down the Edit menu and select Paste Special.

5. In the Paste Special dialog box, click on the Transpose check box, then click on the OK button.

   The results are shown in Figure 2.23.

   Excel rearranges the data 90 degrees from its original orientation in the source cells.

Figure 2.23

The second result of
Transpose

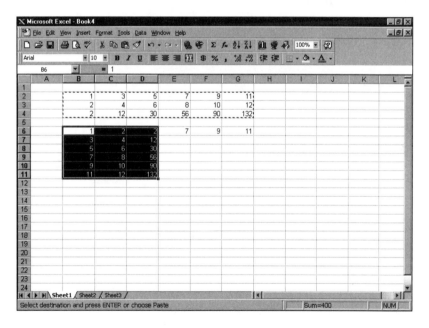

- *Activating the Formatting Toolbar*
- *Formatting Numbers*
- *Changing Row Height*
- *Changing Column Width*
- *Changing Worksheet Display Characteristics*
- *Changing Fonts*
- *Using Borders*

- *Using Colors and Patterns*
- *Aligning Text*
- *Protecting and Hiding Cells*
- *Using Styles*
- *Using AutoFormats*

3

Worksheet Formatting

Now that you understand the basics of working with data in Excel, you need to know how to make your worksheets look more professional and appealing.

In this chapter, you will learn to use Excel's formatting tools to do the following:

- Format numbers for different display styles

- Change the height of your rows and the width of your columns

- Change fonts in your worksheet

- Dress up your worksheet with border lines and shading

- Control the alignment of the data in your worksheet, including centering a title across the worksheet quickly

- Alter the protection characteristics of a cell to restrict modifications

- Use Excel's predefined styles to format your worksheets quickly, or create your own

- Format a table quickly and easily using Excel's AutoFormat feature

A nicely formatted document helps you present your information much more effectively. Setting up a worksheet, entering the data, getting all the formulas to work, and structuring the worksheet in a useful way are usually just half the battle. Before you can use Excel to share information with others, you must be able to format the worksheet in a way that communicates your information quickly and effectively.

Excel provides many tools to help you control how your worksheet looks on the screen and on paper. This chapter teaches you how to produce professional, eye-catching reports and worksheets.

■ Activating the Formatting Toolbar

This chapter explains how to use the Formatting toolbar for fast, easy formatting. To open the Formatting toolbar (if you don't see it—it appears by default when you install Excel), follow these steps:

1. Pull down the View menu and choose Toolbars. You'll see the Toolbars sub-menu, as shown in Figure 3.1.

2. Click on the Formatting command (it is selected in Figure 3.1).

Figure 3.2 shows all the buttons in the Formatting toolbar. The function of each button is described in Table 3.1.

Figure 3.1

The Toolbars sub-menu
with the Formatting
toolbar selected

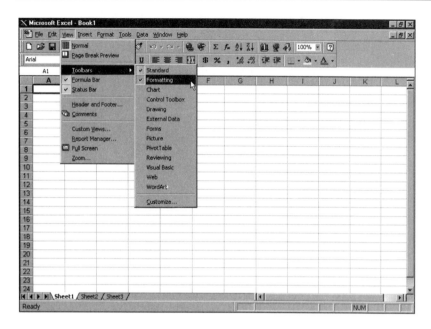

Figure 3.2

The Formatting toolbar

■ Formatting Numbers

When you format a worksheet, you begin by controlling the way numeric information appears in the individual cells. Many choices are available. Answer the following questions to choose your preferred format:

- Do you wish to use commas for the thousands separator?

- Do you want to display negative numbers in red?

- Will you use brackets for negative numbers, and if so, what characters will you use for the brackets?

- How many decimal positions do you want to show?

- What format will you use to display dates and times?

Because you can create your own numeric and date formats, the possibilities for using different numeric formats are virtually endless.

Table 3.1

Formatting Toolbar
Buttons

BUTTON IMAGE	ICON NAME	DESCRIPTION
 Arial	Font	Chooses font name for selected range
 10	Font Size	Chooses font size for selected range
 **B**	Bold	Makes selected range bold
 *I*	Italic	Makes selected range italic
 .U	Underline	Underlines selected range
 ≡	Align Left	Makes selected range left-justified
 ≡	Center	Makes selected range centered
 ≡	Align Right	Makes selected range right-justified
 ⊞	Merge and Center	Merges the selected cells and centers the text in the left-most cell across the selection
 $	Currency Style	Applies the currency style to numbers in selected range
 %	Percent Style	Applies the percentage style to numbers in selected range
 ,	Comma Style	Applies the comma style to numbers in selected range
 +.0 .00	Increase Decimal	Increases the number of digits after the decimal point for numbers in selected range

**Table 3.1
(Continued)**

Formatting Toolbar
Buttons

BUTTON IMAGE	ICON NAME	DESCRIPTION
.00 +.0	Decrease Decimal	Decreases the number of digits after the decimal point for numbers in selected range
	Decrease Indent	Decreases the indent in the selected cells
	Increase Indent	Increases the indent in the selected cells
	Borders	Chooses the border style for selected cells
	Fill Color	Chooses the color for selected cells
A	Font Color	Chooses the text color for selected cells

Using Built-In Formats

Excel lets you choose from a variety of formats, and also lets you design your own custom formats, which you'll learn about in the next section.

You can access Excel's cell display formats using the Format Cells command, which displays the Format Cells dialog box shown in Figure 3.3. Use the Number tab to determine how numbers (and some kinds of text) are displayed.

Table 3.2 shows you the different format categories in Excel, along with a couple of examples of each. If the format you need isn't shown in the table, read the following section for instructions on how to create your own custom formatting.

To apply a format to a range of cells, first select the cells and then choose Format, Cells to display the Format Cells dialog box. Choose a format from the Numbers tab and click the OK button to apply the format to the cells.

TIP. *You can quickly access the Format Cells dialog box by right-clicking on selected cells and choosing Format Cells from the shortcut menu.*

Figure 3.3

The Number tab of the
Format Cells dialog box

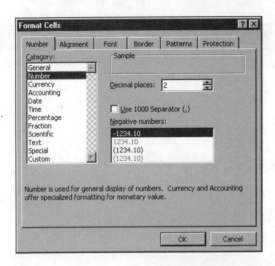

Table 3.2

Built-In Excel Formats

FORMAT CATEGORY	FORMAT SETTINGS	EXAMPLES OR COMMENTS
General	None	12345.67, -12345.67
Number	Decimal places; Thousands separator	1234.1, 1,234.567, -1234.567
Currency	Decimal places; Currency Symbol	$1,234.56, 1,234.56 kr
Accounting	Decimal places; Currency Symbol	Similar to currency, but currency symbols line up in column
Date	Date Format	1/2, 1/2/97, 01/02/97, 1-Jan, 1-Jan-97, January-97, January 1, 1997, 1/2/97 2:34 PM, 1/2/97 14:34, J, J-97
Time	Time Format	2:34, 2:34 PM, 14:34, 2:34:56
Percentage	Decimal places	Percentage automatically multiplies the cell value by 100 and displays the percent symbol. For instance, .15 would be displayed as 15% when this format is applied.

Table 3.2
(Continued)

Built-In Excel Formats

FORMAT CATEGORY	FORMAT SETTINGS	EXAMPLES OR COMMENTS
Fraction	Fraction Format	1/2, 15/21, 153/342; also can restrict display to halves, quarters, eighths, sixteenths, tenths, and hundredths.
Scientific	Decimal places	2.E+03, 1.235E+05. These are exponential representations of the numbers 2,000. and 123,500., respectively.
Text	None	Forces the cell contents to be displayed as text, even if the cell contains numbers.
Special	Zip Code, Zip Code+4, Phone Number, Social Security Number	These are special formats that make it easy to enter and display these types of data. Special characters, such as the parenthesis surrounding the area code, are supplied by the format.

Applying Built-In Formats with Keyboard Shortcuts

You can apply different numeric formats to your cells in three ways. The first way you learned, using menu commands, is the most flexible. The second way, using buttons on the Formatting toolbar, is quick but offers limited choices. The third way involves using keyboard shortcut keys, which are available for most common formatting needs.

Excel includes some key combinations that format the cells you select instantly with a number of commonly used formats. Table 3.3 shows a list of these shortcut keys.

Table 3.3

Excel Format
Shortcut Keys

KEY COMBINATION	FORMAT CODE	EXAMPLE
Ctrl+Shift+~	General	12345.67
Ctrl+Shift+!	Number	12345.67
Ctrl+Shift+@	Time	6:31 AM
Ctrl+Shift+#	Date	15-Apr-95

KEY COMBINATION	FORMAT CODE	EXAMPLE
Ctrl+Shift+$	Currency	$12,345.67
Ctrl+Shift+%	Percent	12%
Ctrl+Shift+^	Scientific	1.23E+04

Creating New Formats

To create your own custom number formats, you'll need to understand how Excel interprets its custom format codes and learn the various available codes you can specify. Excel is extremely flexible about displaying numbers, times, dates, or text, even when your needs exceed the capabilities of the built-in formats found in the Format Cells dialog box. This flexibility creates some complexity, but the following section clearly explains how these formatting codes work. You can begin writing your own formats in no time!

You can access Excel's custom format codes through the Format Cells dialog box. Use the Number tab and then select the Custom category. When you have selected the Custom category, you'll see a number of built-in custom format codes that have already been programmed into Excel. As you learn how these format codes work, you'll find that the custom format codes listed correspond to the built-in formats you've already learned about: Excel uses these codes even for the built-in formats, it just hides this complexity from you unless you need it. Figure 3.4 shows the Format Cells dialog box with the Number tab selected and the Custom category chosen.

NOTE. *When you create a new custom format using the symbols that follow, Excel automatically stores the new format in its list of custom formats. The formats you create, however, are stored only as part of the workbook in which you create them. In other workbooks, only the default Excel formats will be found in the Format Cells dialog box.*

Format Code Structure

Each format code is divided into four parts, as follows:

```
Positive_Section;(Negative_Section);Zero_Section; Text_Section
```

Codes that appear in the positive section format positive numbers; the negative section contains the format codes for negative numbers; the zero section formats zero values; and the text section formats any text entries. Each section is separated from the others with a semicolon. Only the first section, the positive section, is required. If the remaining sections are not

Figure 3.4

Use the Custom category
to gain access to Excel's
custom formatting codes.

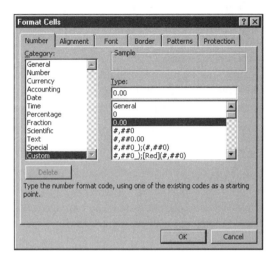

specified, Excel provides default formatting for numbers that match those
characteristics.

Consider the following custom format code:

```
#,###;[Red](#,###);0;[RED]\"@\" "is not allowed. Entry must be a number!!"
```

The preceding format specifies that positive numbers appear with a thousands separator, that negative numbers are in red with parentheses, that a
zero appears as "0," and that if text is entered into this cell, the message *x is
not allowed. Entry must be a number!!,* where *x* is whatever you typed, appears in red instead of the text you enter. The preceding format uses several
tricks. The "Format Codes" section explains how the format options work,
and teaches you how to write your own custom format codes.

Format Code Conditions

You can define the conditions Excel will use for each section of the format.
By default, the first section applies to numbers greater than zero, the second
section to numbers less than zero, and the third section to all other numbers
(usually just the number zero).

If you use a conditional operator surrounded by square brackets at the
beginning of the code section, you can specify the conditions for each of the
three format-code sections that Excel uses, rather than the default number
ranges. Consider the following format code:

```
[Blue][>100]#,##0; [Yellow][<-100]#,##0;[Green]0
```

This code specifies that numbers greater than 100 are blue and that numbers less than -100 are yellow. Numbers less than 100 or greater than -100 are green. The reason that the third position applies to the range of numbers -99 to 99 is that the third section must format everything the first two formats don't control. Usually only zero values are involved, because the first section typically formats all positive numbers, and the second section typically formats all negative numbers. When you change the numeric conditions of the first two sections, however, the third section has to take care of everything else.

Format Codes

You can use a variety of different codes in each format code. Table 3.4 lists each code symbol and explains its function.

As an exercise, use the format code explanations in Table 3.4 to examine what the standard Excel formatting codes do.

■ Changing Row Height

When designing a worksheet in Excel you might need taller rows to give your form the appearance you desire. In the past, many spreadsheet users were accustomed to inserting blank rows above their text to gain additional "white space" on the page.

NOTE. *If you change the font in a given cell, Excel will automatically increase the row height to accommodate the taller letters.*

You can alter the height of a row using the mouse or menu commands. To use the mouse, follow these steps:

1. Move your mouse pointer over to the row labels. Carefully maneuver the pointer so that it is directly on top of the line at the bottom of the row you want to adjust. When you have positioned the pointer correctly, you'll see a horizontal line with two vertical arrows, one pointing up and one pointing down.

2. Press and hold the left mouse button and drag your mouse up or down to shorten or heighten the row as you see fit. Release the mouse button.

TIP. *While you are dragging the mouse up and down, the row height appears in the upper left corner of the Excel screen in the cell indicator box to the left of the Formula bar.*

As an alternative to this method, you can select multiple rows before you adjust the height of one. When you finish sizing one row, all the other selected rows will also use the new row height.

Table 3.4

Format Symbols

SYMBOL	EXPLANATION
General	The word "General" is actually one of the format symbols. For example, you might have a specific format for positive numbers, but specify General format for negative numbers. An example follows: **$#,###;General**.
0	The symbol 0 acts as a placeholder for a number. The 0 placeholder indicates that if the number being formatted does not have as many digits as the number of 0s in the format, a zero is to appear. For example, if the number 123 is formatted with the code **0.000** the result is 123.000. If the number 23.12 is formatted with **0000.000**, the result is 0023.120. Note that zeros appear in place of the missing digits.
#	The pound sign acts much like the 0 symbol, except that it does not force a digit to appear if the digit doesn't exist in the underlying number. For example, the number 123 formatted with **#,###.##** simply appears as 123. with no decimal places, but note that the decimal point is displayed.
?	The question mark functions like the pound sign, except that it inserts a space for the missing digits. This function is useful when you need to make decimal points align with numbers for which the number of digits that follow the decimal point varies. The question mark is also used for fraction displays, as in the format **# ???/???**, which displays the fractional portion of the number with up to three-digit accuracy.
.	The period lets you define the number of digits that are to appear following the decimal point. If your format code specifies a decimal point, a decimal point will always appear, even if no digits follow it. If the format code has one or more #s before the period, Excel will display numbers less than one as starting with a decimal point. To force Excel to always display at least one zero before the decimal point, use 0 before the period, as in the format **0.0#**.
%	If you use a percent mark in your format code, Excel multiplies the number by 100 and then appends the % symbol to the resulting number that appears. For instance, when you enter .15 and the format code **0%**, the displayed result will be 15%. The underlying number will remain .15, however.
,	The comma tells Excel to include commas as a thousands separator. Also, if you put the comma after a single placeholder, Excel divides the number by 1000 before displaying it. Following a placeholder with two commas divides the number by one million before displaying it. **#,** displays the number 145000 as 145, and **#,,** displays the number 12000000 as 12. This trick is very useful for financial statements displayed in thousands or millions.
e+,e-, E+,E-	The E symbol followed by a plus or minus causes the number to appear in scientific notation, along with the letter "E" in the appropriate place on the display. **##0.0E+0** is an example of a format code using scientific notation. If this formatting instruction were applied to a cell containing the number 12345, the result would be 12.3E+3.

**Table 3.4
(Continued)**

Format Symbols

SYMBOL	EXPLANATION
-0+/()$: (space)	Including any of these characters in your format code causes them to appear. If you need to display a character other than one of these, use the backslash followed by the character you want to display. For example, the code fragment **\"** causes a double-quotation mark to appear — it's particularly useful when you want your format to display a character that is otherwise used as a formatting symbol. Accordingly, **\#** displays the pound sign in the result, which is otherwise interpreted as a formatting symbol.
\	The backslash character is a special character that is not displayed in the format. Use it to tell Excel to display the character that follows it literally. For example, **\?** displays a question mark, which Excel normally interprets as a special format-code symbol. If you need to display a backslash in your format, use two backslashes in a row.
*	The asterisk is similar to the backslash, except that it causes the following character to repeat often enough to fill up the cell. The format code **#,###;-#,###;*!** displays positive and negative numbers, but if a zero is entered, it will fill the entire cell with exclamation points.
_	The underline is used to tell Excel to insert a space in its location. For example, in a format that surrounds negative numbers with parentheses, the decimal points of positive numbers do not align, because the negative number takes more space to the right of the decimal point to display the closing parenthesis. In this case, you should use an underline at the end of the positive section of the format to tell Excel to save a space in that location for any possible parentheses.
"Text"	If you want Excel to display a text string, you should enclose it in quotation marks. The following example displays "DR" or "CR" (abbreviations for debit and credit) after positive and negative numbers, respectively: **#,###"DR";[Red]#,###"CR";0**
@	The at symbol represents any text that is entered into the cell. For instance, the code **#,###;[Red](#,###);0;[RED]\"@\" "is not allowed. Entry must be a number!!"** displays numbers in the formats shown. If text is entered, however, the last section of the format code comes into play, and you will see the text you typed plus the additional error message. If you enter None into a cell using this custom format, you'll see: *"None" is not allowed. Entry must be a number!!*.
m	Displays the month number (1 through 12).
mm	Displays the month number, but with leading zeroes for months numbered 1 through 9 (01 through 09).
mmm	Displays the month name using its three-letter abbreviation (Jan, Feb, Mar, and so on).
mmmm	Displays the full name of the month (January, February, March, and so on).
d	Displays the day of the month without leading zeroes.

Table 3.4
(Continued)

Format Symbols

SYMBOL	EXPLANATION
dd	Displays the day of the month with leading zeroes (01 through 31).
ddd	Displays the three-letter abbreviation of the day of the week (Mon, Tue, Wed, and so on).
dddd	Displays the full name of the day of the week (Monday, Tuesday, Wednesday, and so on).
yy	Displays the last two digits of the year (00 through 99).
yyyy	Displays all the digits of the year (1900 through 2078).
h	Displays the hour without leading zeroes. If the format contains an AM or PM, Excel uses the 12-hour clock; otherwise it uses the 24-hour clock.
hh	Displays the hour with leading zeroes, if necessary. If the format contains an AM or PM, Excel bases the number on a 12-hour clock; otherwise it uses the 24-hour clock.
m	Displays the minutes without leading zeroes, but must be preceded by an h or hh and a colon. Otherwise, Excel will interpret them as a request for the month.
mm	Displays the minutes with leading zeroes, if necessary. Note that the mm must be preceded by an h or hh and a colon, or Excel will treat it as a month code.
s	Displays the seconds without leading zeroes.
ss	Displays the seconds with leading zeroes, if necessary.
AM/PM	Forces Excel to use a 12-hour clock for the time display, and displays AM or PM in the location specified. You also can use **am/pm** (lowercase letters), **A/P**, or **a/p** to tell Excel to use those indicators.
[*color*]	If you place a color name in square brackets at the beginning of the appropriate section of the formatting code, Excel will display the matching number in that color. Valid colors are Black, Blue, Cyan, Green, Magenta, Red, White, and Yellow.
[*condition*]	As you saw in an earlier section, you can tell Excel which condition to use for each different section of the format code. Valid operators include <, <=, >, >=, =, and <> (not equal).

TIP. *If a row doesn't display the full height of any text in the row, you can command Excel to set the row height automatically to display all text. To make that command, move your mouse so that it is on top of the line at the bottom of the row label you want to change, and double-click your mouse. Excel uses a "best fit" method to determine the row height. This method also works if you* *select multiple rows before double-clicking on one of the rows' adjustment lines.*

To change the height of a row using menu commands, follow these steps:

1. Select the row you want to format, then pull down the Format menu and select Row. You will see the cascading menu shown in Figure 3.5. The Row menu offers the following choices:

    - **Height.** Brings up a dialog box in which you can enter the desired row height for the selected rows or the current row manually.

    - **AutoFit.** Sets the row height to accommodate the tallest characters in the entire row.

    - **Hide.** Hides the selected rows.

    - **Unhide.** Reveals the hidden rows.

Figure 3.5

The Row menu selected from the Format menu

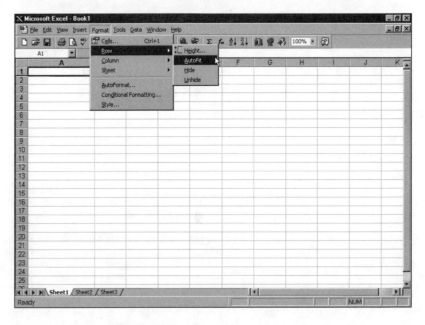

2. Select Height from the Row menu. The Row Height dialog box appears, as shown in Figure 3.6.

3. Enter the height you want for your row in the Row Height field. Enter the value as a decimal figure in typographical points.

4. Click on the OK button.

Figure 3.6

The Row Height dialog box

TIP. *In typographical terms, 72 points is approximately equal to one inch, so 36 points would be one-half of an inch, 18 points would be one-fourth of an inch, and so forth.*

Hiding a Row

You can hide a row the same way you change its height. Drag the height-adjustment line for the row until the row height is zero, or use the Hide command. To use the Hide command, select the row or rows you want to hide, pull down the Format menu, select Row, and then select Hide.

TIP. *When you have a row or rows selected, you can press Ctrl+9 to hide them.*

Unhiding a Row

You can unhide a row the same way you hide a row, except you must select the rows that surround the hidden row. Select the rows that include the hidden rows. If row 10 is hidden, for example, select rows 9 and 11. Then pull down the Format menu, select Row, and then select Unhide.

TIP. *When you have selected the rows, including the hidden rows, press Ctrl+Shift+(to unhide the row.*

■ Changing Column Width

Changing column widths is similar to adjusting row heights. The main difference is that you drag the line to the right of the column label to adjust a given column. You also can double-click on that column-heading border to have Excel examine all the entries in that column, and adjust the column width so that all entries fit within the column's borders.

TIP. *When the pointer has changed to a vertical bar with two horizontal arrows, you can simply double-click to automatically give the column the appropriate width.*

To see the Column Width menu, pull down the Format menu and select Column (see Figure 3.7).

As you can see, the Column Width menu is much the same as the Row menu, and it functions in the same way. The only difference is the addition of the Standard Width option. Selecting Standard Width opens a dialog box that allows you to change the default width for all columns in the worksheet (see Figure 3.8).

Figure 3.7

The Column Width menu

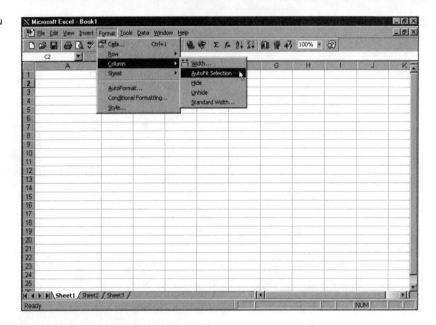

Figure 3.8

The Standard Width
dialog box

■ Changing Worksheet Display Characteristics

Excel has many default settings for displaying workbooks, but you can easily change these defaults to suit your tastes or needs. To do so, pull down the Tools menu and select Options. The Options notebook will appear. Click on the View tab to see the View settings shown in Figure 3.9.

The View page has many settings, each of which is discussed in Table 3.5.

TIP. *Press Ctrl+`, the left single quote that's located beneath the tilde (~) on most keyboards, to switch quickly between the normal worksheet and*

Figure 3.9

The View notebook page lets you choose default view options for workbooks.

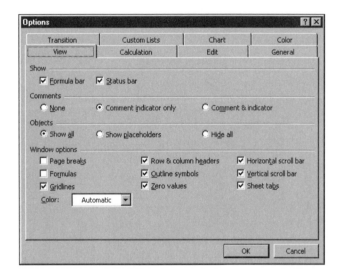

formulas. See Chapter 6, "Advanced Worksheet Features," to learn more about Excel's outlining features.

■ Changing Fonts

Choosing the typeface used in your worksheets is an important step in communicating with your readers or audience. Different typefaces encourage different impressions of the data being presented. Also, good use of different sizes of type and of type emphasis, such as bold, italic, and underline, can call the reader's attention to key points of the data. Excel has many tools for formatting the fonts—typefaces, sizes, and styles—that your worksheet uses.

Understanding Different Font Types

A wide variety of fonts and tools for working with them is available for use with Excel. You can add additional fonts and font-formatting tools to your system if you wish. Each type of font looks different on your screen, and each will print differently on your printer. The most popular types of fonts include the following:

- **Bitmapped Screen Fonts.** Windows includes several screen fonts that approximate the fonts your printer uses. For these fonts to print correctly, similar fonts must be built into your printer. Examples of screen fonts on a standard Windows system are Roman, Helvetica, Modern, Script, and Symbol. These fonts are available only in the sizes installed

Table 3.5

View Tab Settings

SECTION	SETTING	EXPLANATION
Show	Formula Bar	Controls the presence of the Formula bar. If this box is not selected, the Formula bar is not shown.
	Status Bar	The status bar is the area at the bottom of the screen that shows you the status of various options in Excel. Deselect this check box to hide the status bar.
Comments	None	Attached comments are not indicated on the worksheet.
	Comment Indicator only	Displays a red triangle in the upper-right corner of cells that have attached comments.
	Comment & Indicator	Displays both the comment and the indicator for cells that have attached comments.
Objects	Show All	If this option button is selected, all graphic objects in the workbook (buttons, graphics, etc.) are displayed.
	Show Placeholders	If this option button is selected, a gray rectangle appears on your screen in place of any graphic objects. This option can help you scroll through the worksheet more quickly.
	Hide All	This option button causes all embedded graphic objects to be hidden. They also are not printed.
Window	Page breaks	This check box causes Excel's automatically determined page breaks to appear.
	Formulas	Choose this check box to show the formulas in the cells instead of the results. At the same time, it doubles the width of the cells so that they are likely to be capable of displaying the formulas, and it left-justifies all the formulas displayed. This option is useful for checking the validity of the formulas in your worksheet and for documenting your work.
	Gridlines	Deselect this option to turn off the gridline display in the worksheet.

**Table 3.5
(Continued)**

View Tab Settings

SECTION	SETTING	EXPLANATION
Window	Color	This drop-down list lets you choose the color of the gridlines in the worksheet.
	Row and column headers	Deselect this choice to turn off the labels for rows and columns. If you are developing worksheet-based forms, this option can be useful when you distribute the worksheet, because the people who are completing the form should have little need for the row and column headers.
	Outline symbols	This check box controls whether Excel displays the symbols used by its outline feature.
	Zero values	If this option is unchecked, cells that have a zero value and are formatted using the General format are displayed as blank. Cells formatted with a specific format calling for zeroes still display the zeroes.
	Horizontal scroll bar	This check box hides or unhides the horizontal scroll bar.
	Vertical scroll bar	This check box hides or unhides the vertical scroll bar.
	Sheet Tabs	This check box controls the display of the workbook sheet tabs at the bottom of the screen.

in your system: if you choose a size that your system doesn't have, Windows will try to approximate it on-screen, but the results will usually be poor.

- **TrueType Fonts.** TrueType fonts were introduced in Windows 3.1. They include both *display fonts,* which you can see on your worksheet, and equivalent *printer fonts*, which Windows can generate for your printer when you print. Even if your printer does not contain that font, Windows (and therefore Excel) can make your printer use them. TrueType fonts can be scaled to different sizes, and the underlying Windows TrueType software generates the appropriate display and printer fonts automatically so that what you see on the screen is as close as possible to what you see when you print. TrueType fonts have a 'TT' symbol before their names in the Excel font dialog box.

- **PostScript Fonts.** PostScript fonts are the most professional available. Although the untrained eye often cannot distinguish between TrueType fonts and PostScript fonts, most graphic artists prefer PostScript fonts because of their precise design quality and adaptability. PostScript fonts can be printed in any size desired, from one point up to 999 points. If you have a PostScript printer, Excel can print these fonts, and will display your documents using screen fonts that are roughly the same as what you'll see on paper.

- **ATM (PostScript) Fonts.** Many Windows-based applications include a program called *Adobe Type Manager* (ATM). ATM gives users the ability to use and print with PostScript fonts without having to own a PostScript-capable printer. You also can purchase ATM separately.

  NOTE. *You should know that when you use ATM, PostScript, or TrueType fonts with a printer that does not support TrueType or PostScript fonts, printing will take longer because Windows has to draw the letters for your printer. In other words, rather than instructing the printer to print the letter 't' in a certain location and at a certain size, Windows must download the letter to the printer as a graphic image, or as an outline instruction that describes the letter to your printer.*

How to Change Fonts

Excel includes several tools to quickly change the current font. You can make the current font bold, italic, or underlined. You can change fonts, and you can change the size of the selected font.

Many of these functions can be accomplished using the Formatting toolbar. Figure 3.10 shows the toolbar buttons for these font styles.

To use these buttons, select the cells you want to format and click on the appropriate button.

You also can change fonts and font styles by using the Font dialog box and following these steps:

1. Pull down the Format menu, select Cell, then click on the Font tab in the Format Cells dialog box. You will see the Font notebook page, shown in Figure 3.11.

   TIP. *To access the Format Cells dialog box quickly, select the cells you want to format and then click your right mouse button in the selected region. This procedure causes a shortcut menu to appear. From the shortcut menu, select Format Cells from menu.*

2. In the Font box, select or enter the typeface you want to use. When you select the font, Excel shows an example of the font in the Preview window.

Figure 3.10

The toolbar buttons for
font styles and sizes

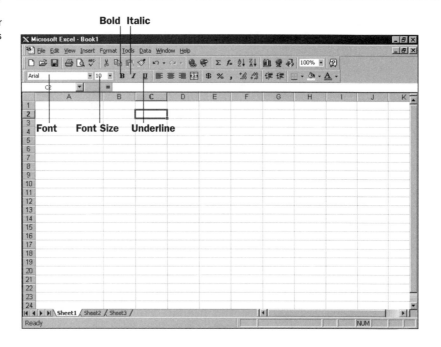

Figure 3.11

The Font page of the
Format Cells dialog box

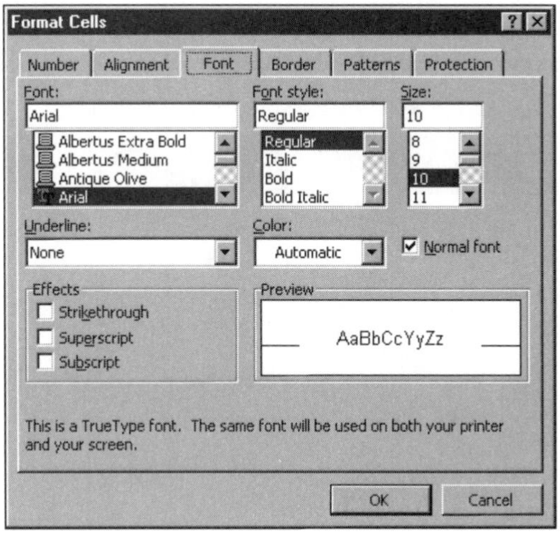

3. In the Font Style list box, select the display style of the font (Bold, Bold Italic, Italic, and so on).

4. You also can use the Underline list box to select from a variety of underline styles.

5. Use the Strikethrough, Superscript, and Subscript list boxes for those effects.

6. Finally, select the size you want from the Size list box.

7. After you finish making the font choices you want, click on the OK button.

Font vs. Typeface

Here is a bit of typography trivia: The term *font* is often used incorrectly. A set of letters in a particular style (like Courier, Times Roman, or Helvetica) is actually a *typeface*. When you take a typeface and define the size and attributes (bold, italic, and so on), you end up with a *font*. Many incorrectly call a typeface a font. The Excel dialog box makes this mistake, for example. Many programs do!

Excel also has shortcut keys for changing many font attributes. Table 3.6 shows these shortcut keys.

Table 3.6

Font Style Shortcut Keys

FUNCTION	SHORTCUT KEY
Bold	Ctrl+B
Italic	Ctrl+I
Underline	Ctrl+U
Strikethrough	Ctrl+5

■ Using Borders

You can spice up your worksheets with borders. By drawing lines around certain portions of your worksheets, you can make them more attractive, and you can separate them visually into distinct sections. Borders make your work more presentable and easier for others to understand.

TIP. *You can make a border around a cell or group of cells quickly by using the toolbar. An example featuring the Border button can be seen in Figure 3.2 near the beginning of this chapter.*

To use the Border button to quickly create a border, follow these steps:

1. Select the cell or group of cells that you want the border to surround.

2. Click on the down arrow next to the Border button, which causes a palette of borders to appear, as you can see in Figure 3.12.

Figure 3.12

The Border drop-box lets
you choose a border style.

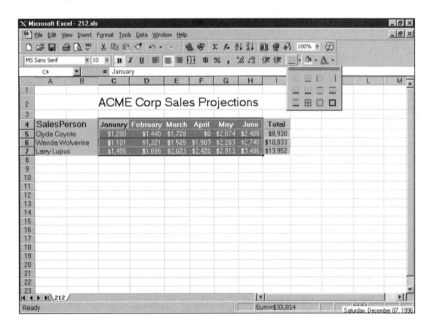

3. Examine the Border drop-box to find the border style you want. After you find the right style, click on that particular box to apply it to the selected cells.

After you have chosen a particular border, the Border button will change to show the most recently used border. You simply can click on that button again to choose it immediately.

TIP. *If you do a lot of work with borders, the Border palette accessed from the toolbar can be "torn off" and left on top of your worksheet. To "tear off" the Border list, pull down the list by clicking on the down arrow to the right of the* *border button. Then, click and hold the mouse button on the line at the top of the border box, and drag your mouse down out of the border drop-box. Now you'll be able to access the Border palette quickly.*

You can achieve even more control over the borders you create by using the Border page in the Format Cells notebook. To use this page, pull down the Format menu and select Cell. When you see the Cell notebook, click on the tab marked Border. The Border page is shown in Figure 3.13.

Figure 3.13

The Border page gives you a dizzying array of border choices.

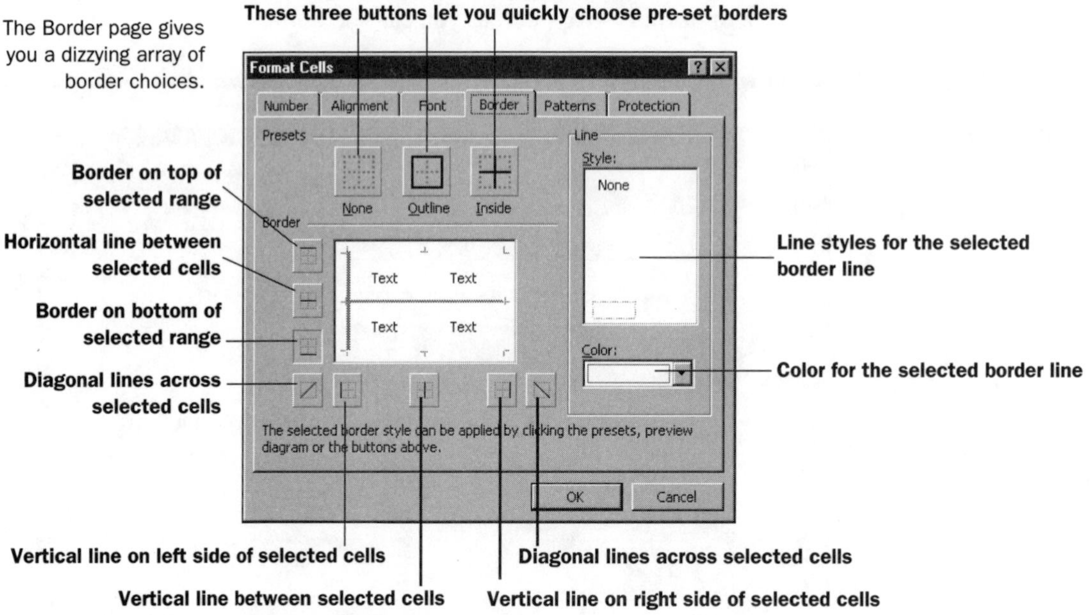

These three buttons let you quickly choose pre-set borders

Border on top of selected range

Horizontal line between selected cells

Border on bottom of selected range

Diagonal lines across selected cells

Line styles for the selected border line

Color for the selected border line

Vertical line on left side of selected cells

Vertical line between selected cells

Diagonal lines across selected cells

Vertical line on right side of selected cells

■ Using Colors and Patterns

You also have many choices about changing the color and shading of cells in your worksheet, just as you do with the Border command. You can color cells and text with the Fill Color and Font Color buttons on the Formatting toolbar. These buttons are shown near the beginning of the chapter in Figure 3.2.

To change the color of specific cells, follow these steps:

1. Select the cells you want to color.

2. Click on the down arrow to the right of the Fill Color button to show the colors available. This Color palette is shown in Figure 3.14.

3. Click on the color you want for the selected cells.

Figure 3.14

The Fill Color box

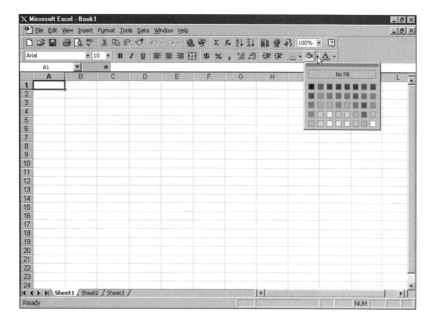

The color and background pattern can be controlled in selected cells with the Format Cell notebook by following these steps:

1. Select the cells you want to format.

2. Pull down the Format menu and select Cells. Then click on the Patterns tab in the formatting notebook (see Figure 3.15).

3. Choose the color you want from the selection of colors available.

4. Open the drop-down box labeled Pattern to see a variety of patterns that you can use. Click on the pattern you want.

After you choose a color and pattern, you can see an example of the way they look in the Sample box on the Pattern page.

The final coloring option comes from the Font Color button on the Formatting toolbar. You can change the color of the text in cells. Select the cells you want to affect, and then click on the down arrow to the right of the Font Color button. You see a list of colors that you can use. Choose one to change the text color for the cells you selected.

Figure 3.15

The Pattern page

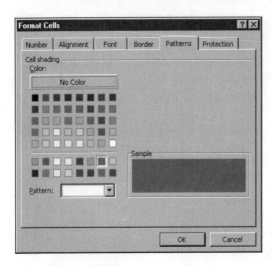

■ Aligning Text

By default, Excel aligns text to the left edges of cells and numbers to the right. You can override these default alignments.

The Formatting toolbar contains three buttons to control text alignment within cells. Figure 3.2, at the beginning of this chapter, shows these buttons.

To use the Toolbar alignment buttons, select the cells whose contents you want to realign and click on the desired alignment button.

Excel has some other text-alignment tricks up its sleeve. You can align text at any angle, and you can arrange text so that the words appear vertically. To access these options, do the following:

1. Select the cells you want to change.

2. Pull down the Format menu and select Cells to cause the Format Cell dialog box to appear.

3. Click on the Alignment tab. You'll see the page shown in Figure 3.16.

The page is grouped into three sections: Text Alignment, Orientation, and Text Control. Table 3.7 describes some of these choices.

Centering Text across a Range

Often, you want centered titles at the tops of your worksheets. Achieving a perfectly centered title can be difficult, however, given the number of columns in your worksheet, the width of each column, and the width of your title.

Figure 3.16

The Alignment tab of the
Format Cells dialog box

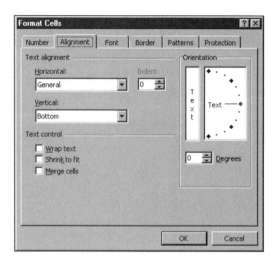

Centering Text

In the early days of spreadsheets with VisiCalc, Lotus 1-2-3, Multiplan, and the like, the only way to center text across the page was to manually insert spaces in the title cells. With the advent of proportional typefaces, even that trick became impossible, because each letter takes up a different amount of space.

Excel can center text across a range automatically using two different methods. The first method lets you merge multiple cells into a single cell and then centers the text within the merged cell. To do this, follow these steps:

1. Type a title in the far-left column of the range in which you want the text to appear centered. For example, if you want the text centered between columns A and I, put the text in column A.

2. Select the range of cells starting from the cell that contains your title, and extending to the last cell within which you want to center the text.

3. Click on the Merge and Center button on the Formatting Toolbar. Alternately, pull down the Format menu, choose Cell, click on the Alignment tab, and then choose the Merge cells check box and the Center option in the Horizontal drop-down list box, and click on OK.

Table 3.7

Alignment Dialog Choices

SECTION	OPTION	FUNCTION
Text Alignment	Horizontal	Lets you choose to horizontally align text using General (default alignment), Left, Center, Right, Fill, Justify, and Center Across Selection. Choosing Left lets you also choose an Indent for the text in the cells.
	Vertical	Lets you align text vertically in a cell along the Top or Bottom. You can also choose Center and Justify. Center aligns text midway between the top and bottom of the cell, while Justify aligns words along both the top and bottom of a cell.
	Orientation	Selecting the left-most button displays text from top to bottom in a cell, such that letters in words display as shown. You can also choose varying degrees of text rotation in the "half-clock" control shown, or you can choose the exact number of degrees of rotation with the Degrees spin box.
Text Control	Wrap Text	When cells contain many words they extend into adjacent cells, or they are cut off if the next cell over has something in it. Choosing Wrap Text causes text to wrap to multiple lines within a single cell.
	Shrink to Fit	Sometimes you care more about the size of a cell than the size of the text that must display within it. In cases like these, choose Shrink to Fit to cause the font size of a cell's contents to be automatically adjusted so that it fits within the current cell size.
	Merge cells	When you choose multiple cells before entering the Format Cells dialog box, and then select this check box, all of the selected cells are merged into one larger cell. If you've selected a number of ranges of cells, each range is consolidated into a single cell when you select this check box.

To "unmerge" a merged set of cells, choose the merged cell, access the Format Cells dialog box and, on the Alignment tab, clear the Merge cells check box.

You can also center text across a range of cells without merging the cells into one. To do this, enter your text into the left-most cell of the range into which you want the text centered. Select the complete range of cells, starting with the one containing the text and extending to the right-most cell that defines the centering area. Access the Format Cells dialog box and, on the Alignment tab, choose Center Across Selection in the Horizontal drop-down list box and then click the OK button. Your text is automatically centered, but the individual cells remain and can still accept data (the cells are still present, but their grid lines are turned off to show you the range you are centering it across). Keep in mind, however, that entering data into the cells involved in a Center Across Selection will readjust the centering, as Center Across Selection only centers the left-most cell across empty cells.

Filling a Range with Text

Excel also can take a piece of text—a single letter, word, or sentence—and fill that text across a range. You usually do this for formatting reasons, like when you want to splash the asterisk character across a bunch of cells just for the effect. To do so, follow these steps:

1. Type the text to be repeated in the far-left cell of the range you want to fill.

2. Select the range of cells, starting with the cell that contains the text to be repeated and extending as far to the right as you want to repeat it.

3. Pull down the Format menu, select Cell, then click on the Alignment tab.

4. Choose the Fill option from the Horizontal drop-down list box, and click on the OK button.

■ Protecting and Hiding Cells

When you develop worksheets for others to use, it is sometimes wise to restrict their ability to change certain characteristics of the worksheet. For instance, certain cells should be unmodifiable, while others should hide their formulas. This makes your worksheet easier for others to use, and protects your worksheet from being modified in such a way that it stops working properly or gives erroneous results.

By default, cells you create are marked as already being *locked*. After the entire document is protected, locked cells cannot be modified. You can designate certain other cells as *hidden*, which doesn't mean that the cell itself is hidden, only that the underlying formulas are hidden.

To change the protection characteristics of a cell or group of cells, follow these steps:

1. Select the cell or group of cells you want to protect.

2. Pull down the Format menu and choose Cells. Click on the Protection tab to display the protection page. You'll see the page shown in Figure 3.17.

Figure 3.17

The cell protection page

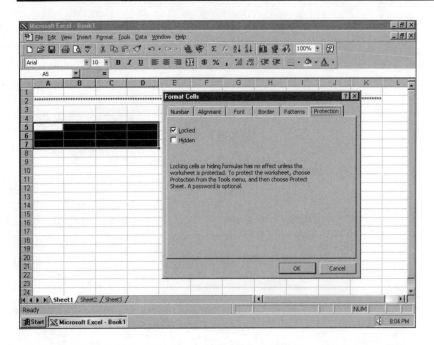

3. In the dialog box, click on the Locked or Hidden check boxes. Then, click on the OK button.

After you've finished your worksheet, you'll need to protect the document so that these settings take effect. Follow these steps:

1. Pull down the Tools menu and select Protection to display a cascading menu, from which you can select Protect Sheet, Protect Workbook, or Protect and Share Workbook. Selecting Protect Sheet displays the dialog box shown in Figure 3.18.

Figure 3.18

The Protect Sheet
dialog box

2. If necessary, enter a password in the Password field (passwords are optional).

   WARNING. *Passwords in Excel are case-sensitive. In other words, they depend on exact capitalization. Also, when you use a password in a document, be sure to use one that you can remember. If the document you work on is important to your company, make sure someone else knows your password. Your computer department may have stringent policies regarding the use of application-specific passwords. Follow them!*

3. Choose from the remaining three check boxes:

   - **Contents.** Causes the cells you mark as hidden to hide their formulas, or the cells you mark as locked to be unchangeable.

   - **Objects.** Causes objects embedded in your worksheet, such as graphics, to be made unmodifiable.

   - **Scenarios.** Makes the scenarios in a workbook unmovable and unsizable.

4. With the appropriate options selected, click on the OK button to protect the document.

The Protect Workbook dialog box also lets you enter a password required to unprotect the workbook, and lets you choose to protect the workbook's Structure and its Windows. Protecting its structure means that individual worksheets cannot be deleted, inserted, moved, renamed, or unhidden. Protecting its windows means that the arrangement of worksheet windows for the workbook cannot be changed; they cannot be moved, resized, hidden, or otherwise changed unless the workbook is first unprotected.

The third command found in the Protection sub-menu of the Tools menu, Protect and Share workbook, displays the dialog box shown in Figure 3.19. In this dialog box, you can choose to enable sharing of the workbook with Track Changes, so that any changes anybody makes to the shared workbook are tracked and you can see them (and accept or reject them accordingly). If you enter a password in this dialog box, others cannot turn off the Track Changes feature without using the password.

To unprotect a worksheet or workbook, pull down the Tools menu, select Protection, and then select either Unprotect Sheet or Unprotect Workbook. If a password was used to protect the sheet or workbook, you'll need to enter it before they become unprotected. If no password was used, the sheet or workbook is unprotected instantly.

Figure 3.19

You can ensure that others don't make untracked changes with the Protect Shared Workbook dialog box.

■ Using Styles

Styles allow you to predefine collections of formatting settings and apply those settings to selected cells. Rather than choosing a range and then tediously selecting the typeface, font style, size, alignment, shading, and so on, you can define entire styles that you commonly use and then apply them to a cell or collection of cells quickly and easily.

Styles let you define the following properties:

- Typeface (Font)
- Number format
- Cell alignment
- Borders
- Cell patterns
- Cell protection

Applying a Style

Apply styles that already exist by following these steps:

1. Select the cells you want to format.

2. Pull down the Format menu and select Style. You'll see the dialog box shown in Figure 3.20.

3. Pull down the Style Name drop-down list and choose the style you want.

4. Click on the OK button to close the Style dialog box.

Figure 3.20

The Style dialog box

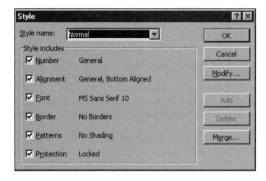

Creating a Style

To create a new style, use the Style dialog box that you saw in Figure 3.20.

Probably the first thing you'll notice on the dialog box is a series of check boxes: Number, Alignment, Font, Border, Patterns, and Protection. These check boxes define which formatting aspects the style contains. If you want a style that controls only the font, for example, deselect all of the check boxes except for Font.

To begin creating your new style, click on the Style name box and type in the name for your style. Then, using the check boxes, choose the formatting elements that you want your new style to affect and click on the Modify button. This procedure brings up the Format Cell notebook. Any changes you make to the notebook now, however, impact only the style you are creating. Use the notebook to change all the aspects of the style until they are satisfactory. After you are finished, click on the OK button to return to the Style dialog box.

You'll also see a button marked Merge on the Style dialog box. Click on this button to import styles that you have created in other workbooks. The other workbooks must be open in a different Excel window to make their styles available.

NOTE. *Styles that you create appear only in the workbook in which you create them. To move them to other workbooks, use the preceding Merge procedure.*

After you are finished with changing the style attributes, click on the Add button to create the new style. The new style can then be applied just like any other style in the list. Similarly, if you want to delete an existing style, select it in the Style Name list box and click on the Del button.

To finish working with the Style dialog box, click on the OK button.

■ Using AutoFormats

Examine the worksheet in Figure 3.21. You could spend a lot of time reformatting the table to give it a polished, professional appearance. Fortunately, instead of spending much time on reformatting, you can use the Excel Auto-Format feature to format a table quickly in one of many predefined, professionally designed formats.

Figure 3.21

The sample sales table, prior to formatting

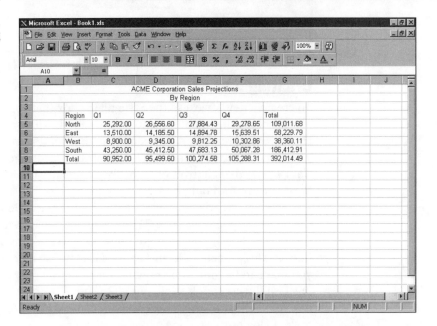

Before you use AutoFormat, make sure that your active cell is within the table to be formatted, and that the table elements are contiguous. If blank columns or rows are in the table, then select the entire range of cells that contains the table: otherwise Excel will not know where your table begins and ends. After you have selected the table, follow these steps:

1. Pull down the Format menu and choose AutoFormat. The AutoFormat dialog box will appear, as shown in Figure 3.22.

2. Scroll through the list of formats. If you click on a format, you can preview the results of a particular AutoFormat in the Sample window.

3. After you find a format you like, click on the OK button to apply it.

Figure 3.22

The AutoFormat dialog box

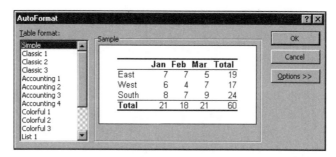

When using the AutoFormat dialog box, you also can control which parts of the format to apply by clicking on the Options button, which expands the dialog box, as shown in Figure 3.23.

Figure 3.23

The expanded
AutoFormat dialog box

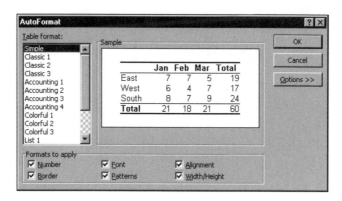

The expanded AutoFormat dialog box lets you select the aspects of the format you want to apply with the various check boxes.

Figure 3.24 shows the example table with the List 1 table format applied.

Figure 3.24

The formatted table. Producing a professional-looking table like this by hand takes a long time, but AutoFormat takes care of all of the details for you!

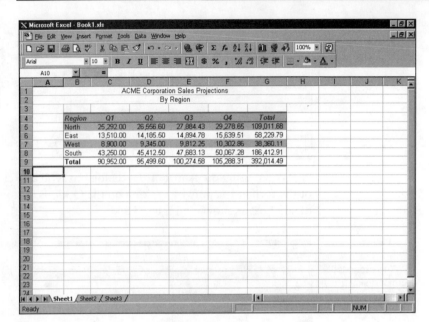

- *Understanding Your Printer's Capabilities*
- *Printing Worksheets*

Printing Documents

PUTTING YOUR WORK ON PAPER IS ONE GOAL WHEN YOU ARE using Excel. Whether you are printing to proofread your work, to get a better look at the overall picture your work represents, or to distribute your worksheets and charts to others, you'll need to master Excel's printing tools.

In this chapter, you will learn the following:

- Using different types of printers, graphics, and fonts

- Printing with Excel

- Adjusting Excel's printing with print-to-fit and the new page break feature

- Creating and editing headers and footers

- Setting up titles to repeat

- Previewing your printout, and adjusting the columns and margins

The tasks and tips you learn in this chapter will help you produce high-quality, professional-looking worksheets every time.

Printing is usually easy: you select the area to print, click on a given print button, and that's it—you're done. In Excel, however, you can do a variety of printing tricks when your needs extend beyond the basics. This chapter covers using Excel's printing features to get the results you want when it's time to commit your workbook to paper.

■ Understanding Your Printer's Capabilities

Before you can understand your printer, you'll need to know what type of printer it is and which fonts are built into it. This section discusses different types of printers, built-in fonts, and print quality.

Dot-Matrix Printers

Dot-matrix printers fire little pins into an inked printer ribbon. The resulting pattern of dots forms the letters and images that appear on the paper. Dot-matrix printers are relatively slow, and the output quality varies considerably from model to model.

Some dot-matrix printers use nine pins to form characters; these offer poor print quality. Some use 24 pins and perform better than their nine-pin counterparts, but still not as well as laser printers.

Dot-matrix printers typically have a limited number of preinstalled fonts, often with fixed sizes. If your printer supports graphics printing, as many do, Excel can use TrueType fonts to create different typefaces, sizes, and styles on the printer.

Impact Printers

Few impact printers are in use today. Impact printers form characters just like a typewriter: they hammer individually formed metal or plastic letters into an inked printer ribbon, which then hits the page. These printers are really slow and noisy in comparison to other types of printers. Although text quality is very high (just like a typewriter), you are limited to the one font installed in the printer at a time, and generally have no graphics capabilities.

Inkjet Printers

Inkjet printers shoot small amounts of ink directly onto the paper. These printers are very quiet, form near-laser-quality text and graphics, and are relatively inexpensive. The main drawbacks to inkjet printers are that they are fairly slow compared to laser printers, and they don't offer the same sharpness of printing as laser printers do. Plus, the per-page cost of printing on an inkjet printer is usually higher than the cost of using a laser printer, even though the initial investment for the printer is lower.

Most inkjet printers have a limited number of typefaces and sizes pre-installed. Due to the fairly high resolution (generally about 360 dots per inch or more) of these printers, however, you often can get good print quality by using TrueType fonts. Windows incorporates these fonts, which print letters to the inkjet printer as a graphic image. Printing this way is slower than using the printer's built-in fonts, but offers flexibility you don't otherwise have—an inkjet printer's built-in fonts rarely handle multiple type sizes beyond those built into the printer.

One advantage of inkjet printers over laser printers is that many good color inkjet printers are available. With a color inkjet printer, you can produce color charts and overhead transparencies. Equivalent color capabilities on laser printers still cost $5,000 or more, but color inkjet printers can be purchased for as little as $300.

Laser Printers

Laser printers set the standard for high-quality output in today's business world. They are fast, quiet, and have become fairly inexpensive in recent years, with some personal models selling for less than $500.

Laser printers shoot a laser beam onto a drum. The drum picks up an electrical charge in the areas that the laser hits. Then the drum rolls through powdered ink, known as *toner*, which sticks to the charged places on the drum. When the drum rolls onto the paper, it deposits these toner particles. Finally, the paper is passed through a very hot roller called a *fuser*, which fuses the toner particles onto the paper.

In the world of laser printers, two major standards exist that control how text and graphics are laid out on the pages: *PostScript* and *Printer Control Language* (PCL). PostScript laser printers are the most expensive, but give you the greatest capabilities for accurate graphics and text. PCL printers have somewhat less capability, but more recent versions of PCL (Version 4 and up) can scale the printer's built-in typefaces to different sizes and perform other tricks. Hewlett-Packard sets the standard in the PCL world, although almost all laser printers are PCL-compatible and can emulate HP LaserJet printers. PostScript printers also are available from a number of different printer manufacturers.

Graphics

By default, Excel prints graphics at the highest resolution allowed by your printer. You can also select a different resolution using the Printer Setup dialog box.

Fonts

Font support is one of the more complex areas of effective printing—so many fonts are available, and each one has its own limitations and abilities. Windows (and, therefore, Excel) offers four major font types: see the following list.

- Screen Fonts
- TrueType Fonts
- PostScript Fonts
- ATM (PostScript) Fonts

NOTE. *TrueType fonts work with any printer that can print graphics. The TrueType software in Windows prints these fonts at the highest resolution your printer allows. You also can adjust the resolution with which Windows prints TrueType fonts by accessing the Page Setup command in the File menu, then choosing the Options button. TrueType fonts are an economical alternative to PostScript fonts, often costing only 1 percent of the price. TrueType fonts are usually a better value because when they are compared to PostScript fonts, the quality is nearly the same as printed with most laser printers.*

As a general rule, use PostScript fonts if you are doing work that a professional printing company will print for you. To use PostScript fonts, you must have a PostScript-based printer or Adobe Type Manager, a special software program that emulates a PostScript printer and prints the graphic images to a non-PostScript printer, rather than the actual fonts.

If your printer can print graphic images, then ATM can print the PostScript fonts at the highest resolution your printer supports.

Knowing which types of fonts are best for different tasks and which fonts work best with your printer can make your job of turning out attractive output much easier. For more information on each of the printable fonts, see the "Fonts" section in Chapter 3.

■ Printing Worksheets

Excel prints your entire worksheet automatically when you select the Print command. To print your entire worksheet, click on the Print button in the Standard toolbar.

When you need to exert more control over your printouts, use the following procedure:

1. Pull down the File menu and select Print. The Print dialog box will appear, as shown in Figure 4.1.

Figure 4.1

The Print dialog box

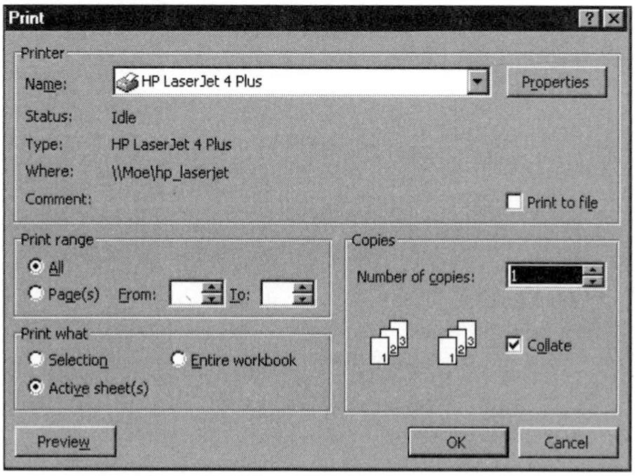

Table 4.1 shows the options available in the Print dialog box.

Table 4.1

Print Dialog Box Options

OPTION	DESCRIPTION
Page Range	Here you choose whether to either print all pages of the worksheet or to print a range of pages. You can do the latter by selecting Pages, then entering the number of a starting page (From) and an ending page (To).
Selection	If you select a range of cells prior to selecting the Print menu, then click on the Selection option button: only the preselected range of cells will be printed.
Active Sheets	Excel allows you to print multiple worksheets from your workbook simultaneously. You must click on the first sheet you want to print, then click on the remaining sheets while holding the Ctrl key. When you print, use the Active Sheet(s) option button to print only those sheets.

**Table 4.1
(Continued)**

Print Dialog Box Options

OPTION	DESCRIPTION
Entire Workbook	Choose this option button to print all sheets in your workbook.
Copies	The number you enter in this field is the number of copies of the worksheet Excel prints. In most offices, it is easier, cheaper, and faster to use the photocopier than printing multiple copies of your documents on the laser printer.
Collate	When printing multiple copies, selecting Collate causes a complete copy of all pages to be printed before succeeding copies are printed. Unchecking this option means that Excel will print the number of copies selected of page one, then the number of copies selected of page two, and so forth.
Preview	If you click on this button, Excel will display a rough representation of how the printed output should appear. You can use this option to resolve problems with different fonts, graphic positioning, and other design issues, without having to print each time. Because you might need to print many times to resolve printing problems with your worksheet, using the Print Preview option can greatly speed up this process.
Print to File	Choosing this check box causes the printed output to be redirected to a file instead of to the printer. A dialog box called Print to File will appear when you print the document with this option selected. It lets you choose the filename, which will contain the redirected output.
Name	Click on this drop-down list-box button to choose which printer to use, if you have more than one printer installed. You can also choose a valid faxmodem, if you have one installed, that can emulate a printer—for instance, Microsoft Fax, which is included with Windows 95.

After you have selected the options you want to use, click on the OK button to print your document.

Selecting Areas to Print

Often, you don't want to print the entire worksheet. Sometimes you do not need parts of the worksheet, or parts of the worksheet contain only support information used to generate the actual worksheet. For example, you might have detailed sales records in your worksheet, but you only use them to generate the totals you are using in a sales report, and don't want to print the raw data.

In such cases, follow these steps:

1. Select the range of cells you want to print.

2. Pull down the File menu and select Print.

3. When the Print dialog box appears, click on the Selection option button to print only the selected area.

Excel uses dashed lines to show you where your worksheet will break into multiple pages. If the location and number of these page breaks is not acceptable, you have several choices, as follows:

- You can reformat your worksheet to fit in the number of pages you want, usually by choosing smaller fonts and reducing the width of columns and the height of rows. You might also rearrange your data to print the way you want, inserting or deleting rows and columns in order to fit everything on the pages.

- You can insert page breaks to force Excel to break the pages earlier. You can also change how pages break in order to lay out the printed pages the way you want them.

- You can use Excel's print-to-fit feature, which automatically shrinks the entire selected print area to fit on a single page. You also can choose varying levels of reduction or enlargement.

Working with Page Breaks

In Excel, you can print certain parts of your worksheet on specific pages by inserting page breaks into the document. To insert page breaks, use the following procedure:

1. Decide where you want to begin a new page.

2. Move your active cell to immediately below and to the right of where you want the page break to occur. The page break will be created at the upper-left corner of the active cell.

3. Pull down the Insert menu and select Page Break.

The page-break indicator lines will show you the new page layout. Excel will automatically adjust the other page breaks in the document according to your changes. To remove an inserted page break, use the following procedure:

1. Move your active cell to immediately below and to the right of the page break.

2. Pull down the Insert menu and select Remove Page Break.

The Remove Page Break menu option is in the same place on the menu as the Set Page Break command, but appears in place of Set Page Break when your active cell is next to an inserted page break. If you see the Set Page Break command instead of the Remove Page Break command, then your active cell is in the wrong location, or you are trying to remove a page break that Excel has inserted because no room is available on the page. You cannot remove Excel's automatic page breaks. You can, however, insert new page breaks before the Excel-inserted page breaks and let Excel reformat the rest of the document accordingly.

Using Page Break Preview and Draggable Page Breaks

New to Excel 97 is the ability to preview and visually choose how your worksheet pages will break when you print. Sometimes working with page breaks can be frustrating, particularly with multipage, complex worksheets. The new Page Break Preview mode helps you control page layouts easier than ever before in Excel.

You can access the Page Break Preview command from Excel's View menu. When you do so, you'll see a reduced-size version of your worksheet with the page breaks clearly indicated, as shown in Figure 4.2. To change the page breaks, simply drag the page borders or the dashed page breaks with your mouse to reposition them as you wish.

Figure 4.2

Use Excel 97's new Page Break Preview mode to easily control how your worksheets are printed out.

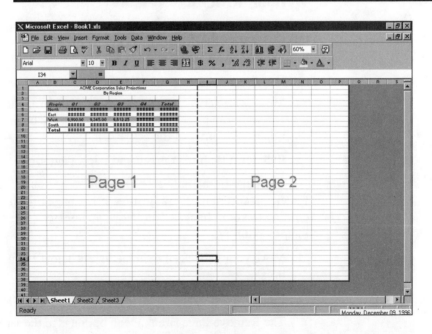

Once you've arranged the page breaks to your liking, choose the Normal command in the View menu to return to normal worksheet views.

Printing to Fit

You can instruct Excel to automatically reduce a print area so that the entire area fits on one page, or even on a given number of pages. Of course, it might be reduced so much that you can't read it, so this option won't prove useful if you ingeniously try to cram a twenty-page document onto a single page. The reduction in size is accomplished by Excel choosing exactly the right font shrinkage to fit all of your work onto the selected number of pages. To use the print-to-fit feature (actually called "Fit to"), follow this procedure:

1. Select the range of cells that you want to print.

2. Pull down the File menu and choose Page Setup; the Page Setup notebook will now appear. Click on the Page tab. The Page notebook page will appear, as shown in Figure 4.3.

Figure 4.3

The Page Setup page

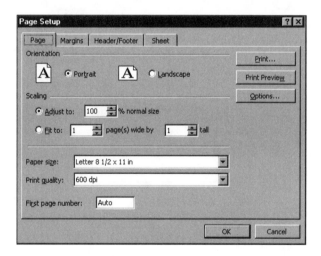

3. Click on the Fit to option button.

4. If you need to modify the number of pages into which Excel fits your selected area, change each field appropriately.

If you follow the preceding instructions, Excel will automatically calculate the necessary percentage of the reduction.

You also can manually adjust the percentage of any reduction or enlargement by selecting the Adjust to button, and then entering a percentage amount.

NOTE. *If your printer doesn't support scaleable typefaces, or if you use fixed-size typefaces in your document, you might be unable to reduce or enlarge the* *page exactly as you want. To avoid this problem, try to use scaleable typefaces (such as PostScript or TrueType fonts) as often as possible.*

Using Headers and Footers

By default, Excel does not print headers and footers on your printouts. You can, however, choose from a number of predefined headers and footers, and you can easily create your own. Some uses for headers and footers include confidentiality notices, specially formatted page numbers, dates and times, or attaching the author's name to the pages of a worksheet.

Headers and footers are managed with the Page Setup dialog box shown in Figure 4.3. Clicking on the Header/Footer brings up the Header/Footer page, as shown in Figure 4.4.

Figure 4.4

The Header/Footer page

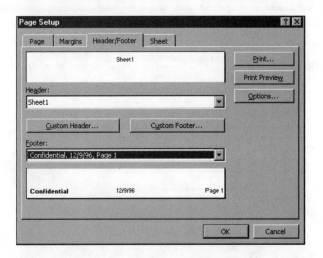

NOTE. *Headers and footers are printed in a half-inch border at the top and bottom of the page. If you use headers or footers that exceed this amount of space, your worksheet contents will probably print on top of the header or footer. To avoid this problem, change the top or bottom margins with the Page Setup command in the File menu.*

Note also that if you use a laser or inkjet printer, you may have as much as a one-third-inch unprintable area on the borders of your pages due to your printer's limitations.

One of the more thoughtful touches included in Excel is predefined headers and footers. To use these, pull down the Header or Footer drop-down list and select one of the many styles available from the list. Figure 4.5 shows the predefined header list.

Figure 4.5

The predefined
headers list

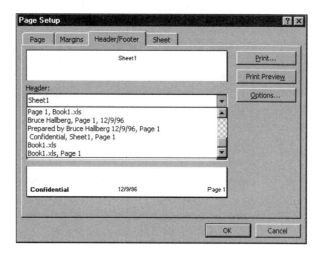

In the Header/Footer page, you can see two windows. The top window shows you what the header will look like, while the bottom window shows the footer. You cannot edit these two windows directly, because they are preview windows. To change the header or footer, you must choose from Excel's predefined headers and footers, or create your own.

Creating headers and footers works the same way. The following example shows you the screens for creating a footer, but the steps shown work identically for creating headers. Click on the Custom Footer button. The Footer dialog box will appear (see Figure 4.6).

Figure 4.6

The Footer dialog box

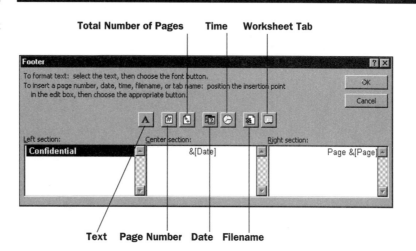

The Footer dialog box has three panes—the Left section, Center section, and Right section—that are used to enter information that should be left-aligned, centered, or right-aligned, respectively. In each pane, you can enter text information or special codes. Use the special codes to insert things like the system date and time, the name of the worksheet, or formatting commands that select a particular font and type style. Clicking the buttons shown in Figure 4.6 will insert many of the allowed codes for you, or you can type the codes directly into one of the windows.

To enter text in any window, simply click in that window and type the text you want. To insert a code, either click one of the buttons representing the most commonly used codes, or enter one of the codes shown in Table 4.2.

Table 4.2

Header and Footer Codes

CODE	RESULT
&"*fontname*"	Text that follows this code uses the font specified in *fontname*. The name used in *fontname* must be exactly as spelled in the Font dialog box, and the surrounding quote marks are required.
&xx	Replace xx with the point size of the font desired. Be sure to use two-digit point sizes: 06, 08, 12, and so on. Also, be sure to leave a space after the numbers for the font size.
&B	Makes the following text bold. The next &B turns bold printing off, then the next occurrence of &B turns it back on, and so forth.
&I	Makes the following text italic. The second &I turns italic printing off, and so on.
&S	Causes the following text to be printed with strikethrough emphasis. The second &S turns strikethrough printing off.
&U	Underlines the following text. The second &U turns underline off, and so forth.
&D or &[Date]	Prints the system date.
&F or &[File]	Prints the name of the workbook.
&[Tab]	Prints the name of the worksheet tab.
&T or &[Time]	Prints the system time.
&P or &[Page]	Prints the current page number.
&N or &[Pages]	Prints the total number of pages. Useful for footers that read Page 1 of 12, which would be accomplished with this entry: Page &P of &N.

**Table 4.2
(Continued)**

Header and Footer Codes

CODE	RESULT
&P+x	These two header or footer code forms instruct Excel to print the page number plus or minus the number specified by x and are useful when your worksheet is part of a larger report. Use this code to have Excel print the correct page numbers for your report instead if its own page numbers. For example, if you have several sheets that need to be numbered from page 10 to page 15, you can use this code to start the page numbers at 10 instead of 1.
&&	Prints an ampersand. Because Excel normally interprets an ampersand as part of a header or footer code, the double-ampersand code is provided in case you need to print an ampersand in the header or footer itself rather than have Excel try to interpret it as a code.

Figure 4.7 shows an example of a custom footer created using some of these codes.

Figure 4.7

A sample custom footer

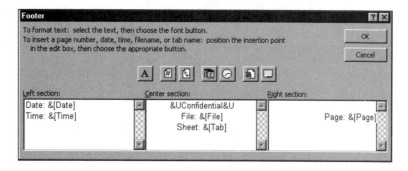

Setting Up Repeating Titles

When tables span many pages, finding specific data can be difficult, because the labels that define the data often end up on a different page. You can avoid this problem by using an Excel feature called Print Titles to automatically print the labels for your data on each page.

Consider the worksheet shown in Figure 4.8.

When you print your worksheet using a normal font, the results appear as shown in Figures 4.9 and 4.10.

This example illustrates the problems that exist in a strictly horizontal format. In reality, you must work in both dimensions, sometimes crossing many pages. The cure is Print Titles, which causes part of your worksheet to repeat automatically on each page. You can select the rows or columns that contain the titles you want repeated so that they print on each page.

Figure 4.8

The large worksheet

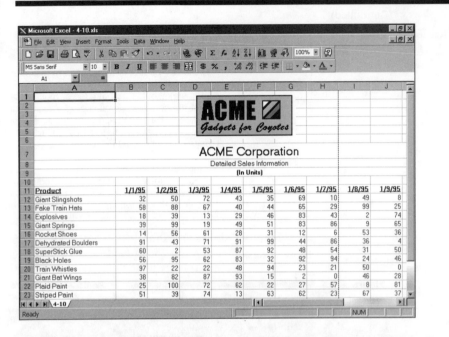

Figure 4.9

The first page looks fine.

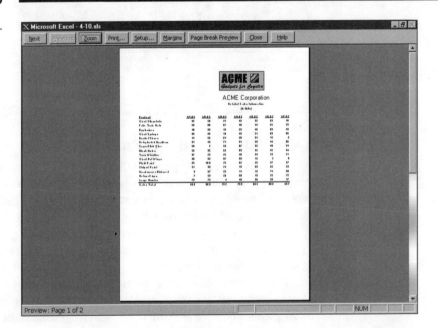

Figure 4.10

The second page is
difficult to interpret.

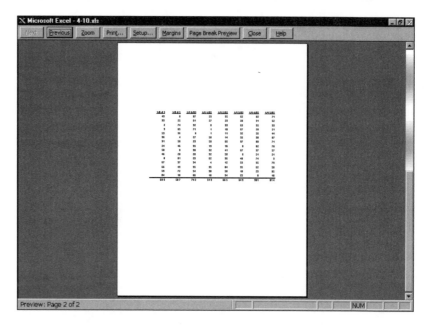

In this example, you want to make the row titles (the product names)
into print titles. To make print titles, use the following procedure:

1. Pull down the File menu and select Print Setup. The Page Setup notebook will appear.

2. Click on the Sheet tab to display the Sheet page, as shown in Figure 4.11.

3. On the Sheet page, click once on Rows to Repeat at Top or Columns to
   Repeat at Left field. Then use your mouse to select the rows or columns
   you want to repeat. The rows or columns you select must be contiguous.

4. On the Sheet page, click once on Rows to repeat at top or Columns to repeat at left field.

5. Click the Collapse Dialog Box button on the right side of the field to
   temporarily move the dialog box out of the way.

6. Use your mouse to select the rows or columns you want to repeat. The
   rows or columns you select must be contiguous. Notice that the column
   range is entered into the field automatically.

7. Click the Collapse Dialog Box button again to restore the dialog box to
   its previous size.

Figure 4.11

The Sheet page of the
Page Setup notebook

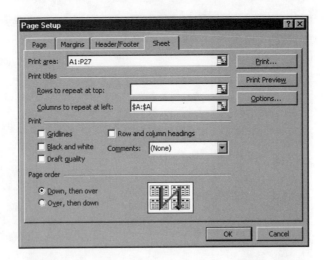

NOTE. *Either field will accept a named range of columns or rows rather than column letters or row numbers.*

8. Click on OK to close the Page Setup dialog box.

Figure 4.12 shows the new page 2 of the example printout, complete with titles.

Previewing Your Printout

With Excel, you can preview your printouts before printing out hard copy. Excel shows you, as closely as possible, exactly what you will see when you print out to paper. You also can adjust certain print characteristics when you are in the Print Preview mode, until you are happy with the results. When you are satisfied, you can print the final document quickly and easily.

To preview a document, pull down the File menu and select Print Preview. Alternately, click on the Print Preview button on the Standard toolbar. The preview will now appear, as shown in Figure 4.13.

Along the top of the screen you'll see a number of buttons. These are listed and defined in Table 4.3.

In this example, the document might benefit from a number of changes. Clicking on the Setup button allows you to make the following changes:

• Switch from Portrait to Landscape orientation on the Page page.

• Remove the gridlines. Use the Sheet page and deselect the Gridlines check box.

Figure 4.12

Page 2 looks better—
and is easier to
interpret—with titles.

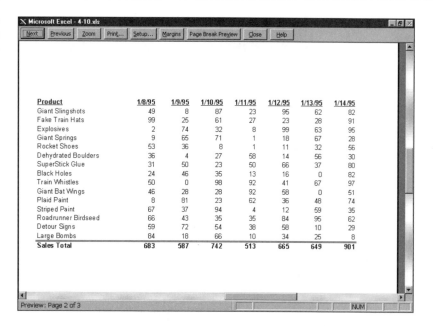

Figure 4.13

The Print Preview screen

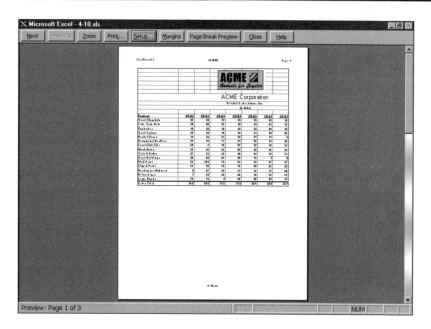

Table 4.3

Print Preview Buttons

BUTTON NAME	FUNCTION
Next	In a multipage document, click on this button to move to the next page. If no more pages remain, this button will be grayed out.
Previous	In a multipage document, click on this button to move to the previous page. If you are on the first page, this button will be grayed out.
Zoom	This button acts as a toggle switch. Click on it once to zoom in for a closer view of your document. Click on it again to view the entire page. You can also simply point to a particular region of the screen with the magnifying-glass pointer. A "zoomed" view of that particular area then appears. Click again with the magnifying-glass pointer to return to viewing the full page.
Print	Clicking on this button closes the Preview window and returns you to the document, automatically bringing up the Print dialog box.
Setup	Click on this button to bring up the Page Setup dialog box. You can make almost any changes you want. However, you cannot establish a print area or print titles when you access the Page Setup dialog box through Print Preview. When you click on the OK button, the preview window will reflect your changes.
Margins	Clicking on this button brings up the margin handles that let you set the margins and column widths visually, as explained in the next section.
Page Break Preview	Use this button to change to Page Break Preview mode, in which you can choose where your worksheet's pages will break.
Close	This button closes the Print Preview window and returns you to your worksheet.

- Remove the header and footer. Use the Header/Footer page. Pull down the Header and Footer list box and choose (none). The (none) entry can be found at the top of the list box.

- Automatically center the document vertically and horizontally. Use the Margin page and select the Horizontally and Vertically check boxes in the Center on Page section of the page.

After these changes are made in the Page Setup dialog and the OK button has been selected, the results will appear (see Figure 4.14).

Adjusting Margins and Column Widths in Print Preview

When you are in the preview window, you can adjust the margin and column widths visually by clicking on the Margins button. Control handles will appear, as shown in Figure 4.15.

Figure 4.14

The Preview example
after changes

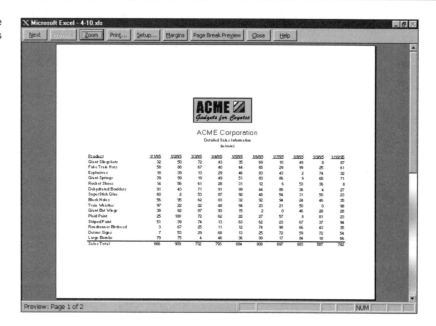

Figure 4.15

The margin and column
control handles

**Column margin
handles**

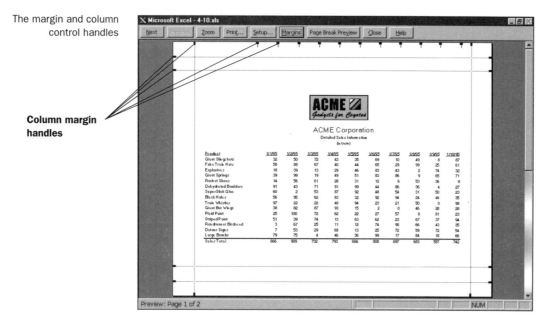

To adjust the margins or column widths, position your pointer on top of the relevant control handle and drag it to the new position. The results will appear instantly. It's often easier to see the result of your margin changes if you turn off the margin handle display.

- *Splitting the Worksheet*
- *Using Multiple Views of a Single Workbook*
- *Controlling Workbook Sheets*
- *Linking Data between Sheets*
- *Linking to Other Applications*
- *Setting Up Templates*

5

Working with Multiple Windows

O NE OF THE REAL STRENGTHS OF EXCEL IS ITS ABILITY TO HELP
users manage complex data. You can view and work with large
amounts of information fairly effortlessly by using the program's
built-in tools. You can view one or more documents in multiple
windows or views, and easily consolidate information from different worksheets—even when they are in different workbooks. You
also can set up titles and create multiple scrollable areas within a
single worksheet to make your tasks even easier.

In this chapter, you'll learn about these tools, including the following:

- Viewing and working with multiple windows in the Excel work area

- Managing sheets within the workbook: inserting new sheets, deleting sheets, and renaming sheets

- Managing and switching between multiple worksheets

- Using three-dimensional references in your workbooks

- Linking data between multiple worksheets or workbooks

- Linking Excel with other Windows applications through OLE

- Setting up and using Excel templates

Once you've learned to manipulate multiple windows and views, you'll be able to work more efficiently. The features discussed in this chapter can help you put more of Excel's power to work for you.

One of Excel's most valuable aspects is its ability to help you consolidate and analyze data that would otherwise be very cumbersome. With the improved workbook feature in Excel 97 for Windows, such tasks become even easier. The workbook-organizing metaphor makes it simple to keep similar types of data together, with different sheets for different parts of your data or for charts.

■ Splitting the Worksheet

In many cases, you might want to view different parts of a single sheet at the same time. You might want to keep the labels of a table visible, for example, or to view multiple parts of the worksheet to better understand the way a complex formula works as you scroll across it.

Creating Multiple Viewing Areas

To split the worksheet into multiple *panes* (different scrollable portions of the same sheet) with the mouse, either drag the horizontal split bar down, or drag the vertical split bar to the left. Figure 5.1 shows you the location of the two split bars. When you put your mouse pointer on top of the split bar, the pointer will change into two vertical or horizontal bars with arrows, which indicate that you can move the bar. When your pointer is in the right place, click and drag the bar to the position you want.

Figure 5.2 shows the effect of dragging the vertical split bar to the left side of the worksheet.

Figure 5.1

Split bar locations

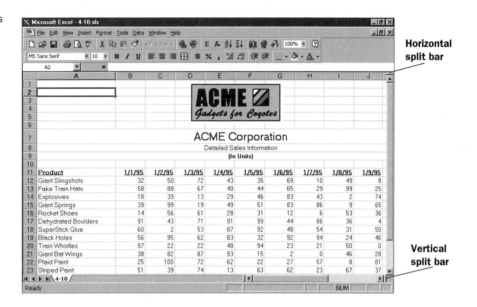

Horizontal
split bar

Vertical
split bar

Figure 5.2

The vertical split bar

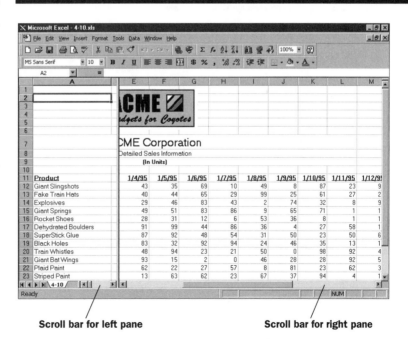

Scroll bar for left pane   **Scroll bar for right pane**

You also can split the worksheet into four parts instantly with the menu command provided. Use the following procedure:

1. Position your active cell to the right of the column and below the row where you want the split to occur. In other words, if you wanted to create a split between columns A and B and rows 11 and 12, you would make cell B12 the active cell.

2. Pull down the Window menu.

3. Choose Split from the menu.

You can move between panes simply by clicking your mouse in the pane with which you want to work. Each pane area can scroll independently of the other panes. As you see in Figure 5.2, each pane has its own scroll bars for this purpose.

Freezing Panes

You can also "freeze" the window panes in a single position. Freezing is useful when you are working with large tables. Look at the sales worksheet shown in Figure 5.3 for an example.

Figure 5.3

The table example

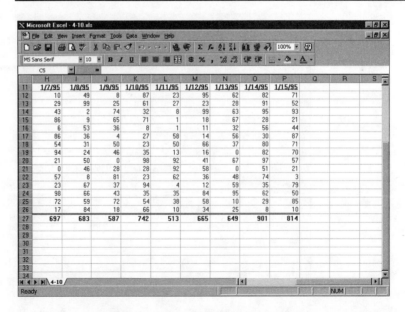

When you look at the data to the right of the table, you really can't tell what each line represents, because the labels in column A are not visible (they are far to the left of the visible portion of the worksheet). This example shows the problem in only one dimension. If the table extended down further, you would have similar problems with the dates at the top of the table—they would not be visible while looking at the lower parts of the table. To help you deal with this problem, Excel allows you to freeze portions of the worksheet so that the row and column labels always remain visible. The Freeze Panes command differs from splitting in that you cannot scroll the frozen panes.

As with splitting panes, you begin by placing the active cell to the left of the column and below the row that are to become the boundaries of the frozen area. Using Figure 5.2 as an example, it's clear that column A should remain visible when you scroll the worksheet to the right, and row 11 should always be visible when you scroll down through the worksheet. Thus, the active cell should be cell B12, because it defines the boundaries of the area to be frozen. To see how the command works, follow these steps:

1. Move to cell A1.

   TIP. *Ctrl+Home quickly takes you to cell A1.*

2. Pull down the Window menu and choose Split.

3. Position your mouse pointer directly over the intersection of the two panes. Drag the panes so that the two lines intersect at cell A11, as shown in Figure 5.4.

Figure 5.4

Correctly positioned split panes

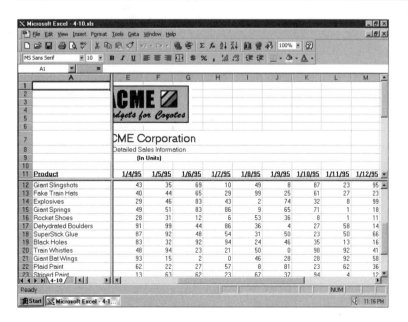

> **TIP.** *Excel normally creates the split above or to the left of the active cell. For the preceding example, you could position the active cell to B12 before using the Split command to automatically create the split in the correct position.*

4. Pull down the Window menu again and choose Freeze Panes. The result is shown in Figure 5.5.

Figure 5.5

Frozen panes

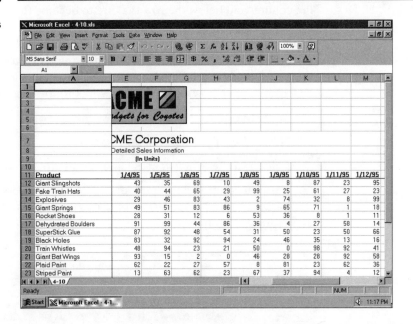

After you have completed the previous step, you'll notice that several things have happened. First, the pane indicators are now made up of fine lines rather than the thicker lines shown in Figure 5.4. Second, the worksheet only has a single set of scroll bars, because you can no longer scroll the frozen portions independently as you could before you chose the Freeze Panes command. Now, when you scroll the worksheet, you scroll everything *except* the frozen panes (in this case, rows 1 through 11 and column A). If, for example, the worksheet is scrolled down and to the right, the frozen pane areas still are visible, as in Figure 5.6. When navigating large tables, using frozen panes makes it easy to always keep the table labels visible as you look through the data.

Figure 5.6

Scrolled worksheet
with frozen panes

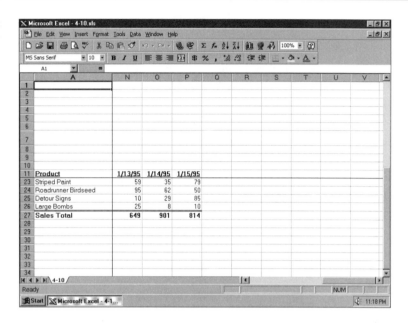

Removing Frozen Panes

To unfreeze the existing panes, pull down the Window menu and choose Unfreeze Panes. You also can remove the panes without unfreezing them first by pulling down the Window menu and choosing Remove Split.

■ Using Multiple Views of a Single Workbook

Another useful trick is working with multiple windows that contain a single workbook. This makes it easy to compare disparate areas of a worksheet, and also makes it possible to quickly switch between different areas of the worksheet. For instance, imagine that you're working with two areas of a worksheet. One area is near the top of the sheet, and the other area is quite far from the first. You need to rapidly switch between these two areas as you work with the data. Instead of constantly scrolling back and forth between the areas, you can open two windows containing the same workbook: one focusing on the first area, and the other focusing on the second area. Simply switch between the windows to move back and forth between the two areas. Using a related feature (see the "Arranging Windows" section following this one), you also can show multiple workbooks or copies of a single workbook on the screen at one time.

To open a second window of a single workbook, do the following:

1. Pull down the Window menu.

2. Choose New Window.

This procedure creates a second *instance* of the workbook, so you can switch using the Window menu, as shown in Figure 5.7.

Figure 5.7

The Window menu

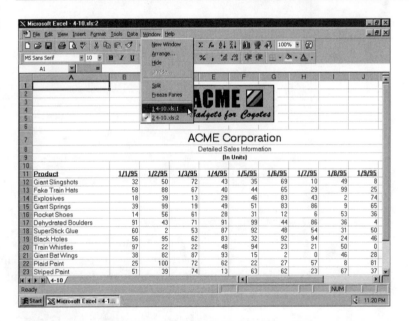

Choosing either window at the bottom of the Window menu takes you to that instance of the workbook. Notice that each workbook has a colon following its name, with a number after the colon, indicating that these are different windows of the same workbook. Changes to one window are shown instantly in the other.

Arranging Windows

You also can arrange the windows on your screen so that you can view them all simultaneously. To make this arrangement using the mouse, first click on the worksheet's Restore button, found below Excel's Restore button. This button reduces the current view to a window that can be moved and resized on the Excel work area. Figure 5.8 shows what this view looks like after you have clicked on the document's Restore button.

Figure 5.8

The windowed view
of a workbook

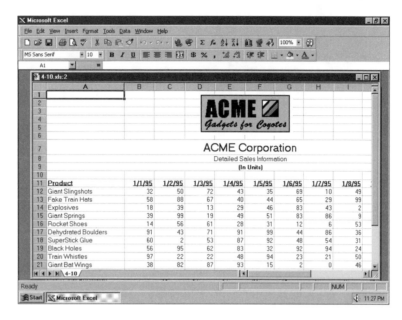

Some Excel commands rearrange multiple windows automatically. You can follow these steps:

1. Pull down the Window menu.

2. Choose Arrange. The Arrange Windows dialog box will appear, as shown in Figure 5.9.

The Arrange Windows dialog box offers several options, as follows:

- **Tiled.** Arranges windows so that they each use an equal portion of the screen, as in Figure 5.10.

- **Horizontal.** Arranges windows so that they span the entire screen and are arrayed vertically, as in Figure 5.11.

- **Vertical.** Arranges windows so that they stretch from the top of the screen to the bottom, and are arranged next to each other, as in Figure 5.12.

- **Cascade.** Arranges the windows vertically, as you can see in Figure 5.13. The Cascade option gives each window the most space possible, while still allowing you to click on any exposed area of a window at any time to bring it to the front.

Figure 5.9

The Arrange
Windows dialog box

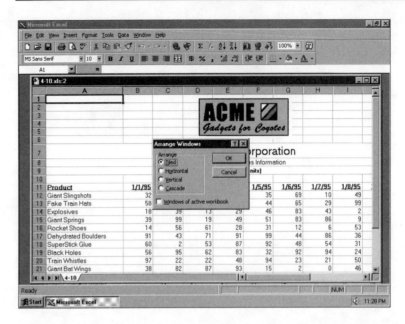

Figure 5.10

The Tiled option

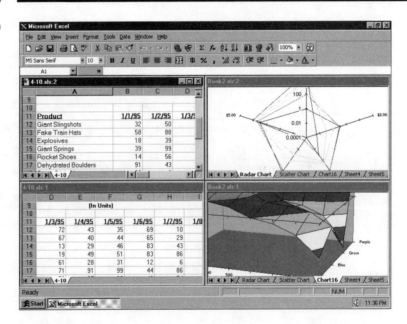

Figure 5.11

The Horizontal option

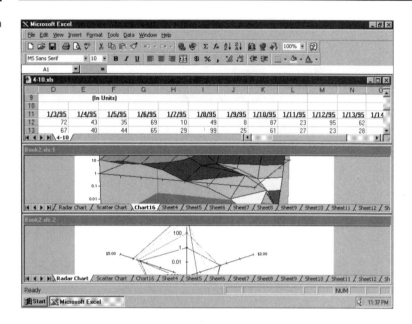

Figure 5.12

The Vertical option

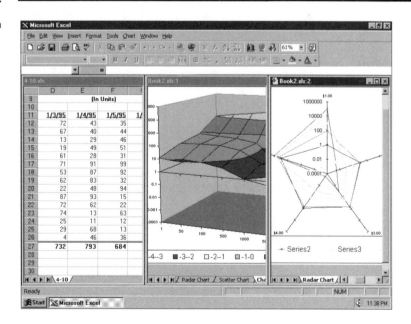

Figure 5.13

The Cascade option

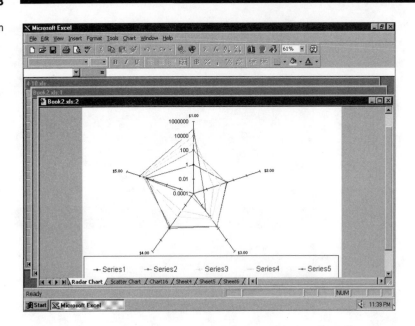

The Arrange Windows dialog box also has a check box called Windows of Active Workbook. If this option is selected before you click on the OK button in the dialog box, Excel will only include those views of the workbook that are currently selected in the Arrange operation.

NOTE. *When you choose File, Close with one of the multiple windows of a single workbook active, all of the windows of the workbook will be closed. Opening the workbook later will open it with the same multiple windows.*

You can close any of the views by clicking on that window's Close button. The remaining views are renumbered accordingly.

TIP. *Normally, you switch between windows by using the Window menu. You also can switch between all open windows by pressing Ctrl+Tab.*

Hiding and Showing Windows

You can easily hide any of the open windows by using the Window menu's Hide command. Make sure the window you want to hide is active, then select Hide. The window vanishes, and so does not appear in the Window menu as it normally would. This option is valuable for worksheets that you distribute to others. You can hide the underlying details of the worksheet, if necessary.

To reveal a hidden window, pull down the Window menu and choose Unhide. The Unhide dialog box, shown in Figure 5.14, lists all currently hidden windows. Select the window you want to unhide from the list, and click on OK.

Figure 5.14

The Unhide dialog box

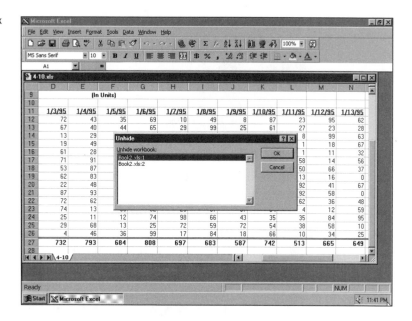

Locking Down Windows

When you are developing workbooks for others to use, you might want to take away the user's ability to rearrange the windows. For example, if your workbooks might be used by novice Excel users, they could become confused and disoriented if they mistakenly close a needed window in the workbook. Prevent this possibility by locking the windows of the workbook into positions assigned by you.

To lock windows, follow these steps:

1. Arrange the windows in exactly the way you wish them to remain.

2. Pull down the Tools menu, choose Protection, and then choose Protect Workbook. You will see the Protect Workbook dialog box, shown in Figure 5.15.

3. Before protecting the workbook, make sure that the Windows check box is selected. This step ensures that the border around each window that normally enables you to resize it is disabled. Also, attempts to use the Arrange option on the Window menu will now be ignored.

4. If you do not want to prevent the user from otherwise modifying the workbook, clear the Structure check box.

5. Click OK.

Figure 5.15

The Protect
Workbook dialog box

To restore Excel's capability to arrange the windows, simply unprotect the workbook. Pull down the Tools menu, choose Protection, and then choose Unprotect Workbook.

WARNING. *Be very careful in assigning passwords to protected workbooks. Without the correct password, you will not be able to access the protected portions of the workbook again.*

■ Controlling Workbook Sheets

You can move easily between different worksheets in your workbook by clicking on the tabs found at the bottom of the workbook.

You also can switch between your active sheets using a keyboard combination. Ctrl+PgDn moves you to the next sheet in the workbook; Ctrl+PgUp moves you to the previous sheet.

Rearranging Sheets

To rearrange the order of sheets in your workbook, click on the sheet tab you want to move, hold down the left mouse button, and drag to the right or left. A small arrow indicates where the sheet will be "dropped" when you release the mouse button.

You also can use the shortcut menu to move or copy sheets in your workbook via the following method:

1. Click the right mouse button on the tab of the sheet you want to copy or move.

2. From the menu, choose Move or Copy. You will see the dialog box shown in Figure 5.16. This dialog box offers many options, as follows:

   • **To Book.** Allows you to choose any other open workbook to which to move the sheet.

Figure 5.16

The Move or Copy
dialog box

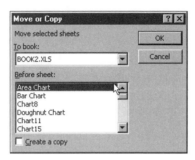

- **Before Sheet.** Permits you to choose a position for the moved sheet in the target workbook. Choose the sheet before which you want the moved or copied sheet to be inserted.

- **Create a Copy.** Tells Excel to make a copy of the sheet rather than moving it.

3. After you have selected the options you want, click on the OK button.

TIP. *To see fewer or more tabs displayed on the tab line, grab the tab split box just to the left of the horizontal scroll bar's left-pointing arrow, and drag it to the left or right for better visibility.*

To see the next tab label quickly, click once on the tab split box to slide one tab to the right.

Creating Sheets

The easiest way to create new sheets in an existing workbook is to use the shortcut menu. Right-click on one of the sheet tabs, then choose Insert from the shortcut menu. You will see the dialog box shown in Figure 5.17.

As you can see from the dialog box, Excel supports many types of sheets:

- **Worksheet.** A worksheet is an Excel spreadsheet.

- **Chart.** Excel supports charts embedded in worksheets, as well as charts that exist as separate sheets in the workbook. If you want to create a chart on a separate sheet in the workbook, choose this option.

- **MS Excel 4.0 Macro.** The old macro language used in Excel 4 was replaced with Visual Basic for Application tools. Excel 97 for Windows still supports Excel 4 macros, however. To use a macro from Excel 4, include it in an MS Excel 4.0 Macro sheet in your workbook.

- **MS Excel 5.0 Dialog.** For use with Excel 5 Modules, Dialog sheets contain dialog boxes that accept input and choices from the user of the VBA application.

Figure 5.17

The Insert dialog box

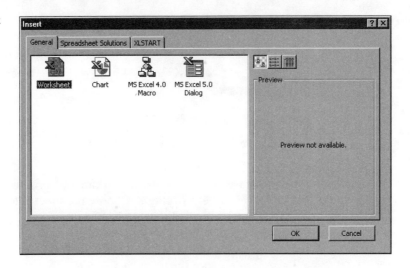

After you have chosen the type of sheet you want to insert, click on the OK button to create a sheet of that type.

You can also insert new sheets by using the Insert menu. You can create a new worksheet with the Insert, Worksheet command. To create a new chart, access the Insert, Chart command and then use the Chart Wizard dialog boxes to create the new chart sheet.

Deleting Sheets

To delete a sheet or sheets in Excel, follow these steps:

1. Select the sheet you want to delete. If you want to delete more than one sheet, Ctrl+click on the worksheet tabs to select additional sheets.

2. Pull down the Edit menu and choose Delete Sheet. Alternately, you can access the shortcut menu from here by clicking your right mouse button on one of the selected sheet tabs. From the shortcut menu, choose Delete.

3. Click OK.

Renaming Sheet Tabs

You will probably find it difficult to manage your sheets if you continue to use the default names of Sheet1, Sheet2, Sheet3, and so on. Fortunately, Excel lets you rename the sheet tabs so that each sheet has a more meaningful name. To rename tabs using the menus, follow these steps:

1. Select the sheet you want to rename.

2. Pull down the Format menu and choose Sheet. Choose Rename from the cascading menu.

3. Type the new sheet name on the worksheet tab.

As with almost all Excel commands, you also can rename tabs using the shortcut menus. Right-click on the sheet tab and choose Rename from the shortcut menu.

Adding an Existing Worksheet to a Workbook

Excel 4 didn't support tabbed workbooks. To take an existing Excel 4 worksheet and add it to a tabbed workbook, follow these steps:

1. Open the workbook of which you want the existing worksheet to be a part.

2. Open the existing Excel 4 worksheet. It will open into a single-sheet workbook, with the file name located where you normally see the tab name.

3. With the Excel 4 worksheet active, pull down the Edit menu and then choose Move or Copy Sheet from the menu.

4. In the Move or Copy dialog box, select the name of the destination workbook in the To Book drop box.

   NOTE. *Sheets are inserted to the left of the active sheet by default.*

5. In the list labeled Before sheet, select the sheet in the workbook before which you want the existing worksheet to appear.

6. If you want to insert a copy of the Excel 4 worksheet rather than move it, enable the Create a copy check box at the bottom of the dialog box.

7. Click on the OK button.

■ Linking Data between Sheets

The workbook is one of Excel's most powerful features. It allows you to organize your worksheets more logically, with major sections of your project contained in their own worksheets. You'll spend less time worrying about organizing your data and more time actually getting answers and analyzing your data as a result. Also, workbooks make developing more complicated worksheets, such as multi-company spreadsheets, much easier.

NOTE. *The following sections discuss various ways to link data between different sheets, whether they are in the same workbook or different workbooks. Table 5.1 defines many terms you'll need to know in order to understand these sections.*

Table 5.1

Linked Data Terms

TERM	DEFINITION
3D Reference	A reference to another sheet in the current workbook. These references are updated automatically when Excel recalculates the workbook.
Source Document	When linking different files (workbooks), this document contains the source data.
Dependent Document	When linking different files, the dependent document is the one that relies on data in other documents.
External Reference	A cell reference that refers to cells in a different workbook.
Remote Reference	A remote reference refers to data in a file that was created by an application other than Excel. This data might be graphic data from a drawing program or text data from a word processing application. The program containing the source data must support DDE (Dynamic Data Exchange).

To access the full power of the workbook, you must learn to link data between the different sheets of the workbook. From these examples, you can learn to create a simple income statement, with individual sheets for each major division in the company and a sheet that combines all divisions into a consolidated total. The consolidated sheet is made up of formulas that automatically total each of the other sheets in the workbook. After the consolidated sheet is completed, changes in any of the divisional sheets are reflected there automatically. Consider Figure 5.18, which shows all four sheets in the same workbook.

Creating 3D References

The easiest way to link cells from different sheets into a formula is to use the mouse. This section shows you how to perform mouse references, and tells you what to type when you want to enter 3D references manually.

To see how a 3D reference works, follow these steps:

1. Move to the cell in which you want the total placed from another sheet.

2. Type the equal sign to begin the formula.

3. Click on the tab of the sheet that contains the data you want.

4. Click on the cell you want to reference.

5. Press Enter to complete the formula.

After you press Enter, Excel returns to the sheet that contained the formula, and the data from the other sheet now appears in the cell. This data is said

Figure 5.18

The ACME consolidated
3D workbook

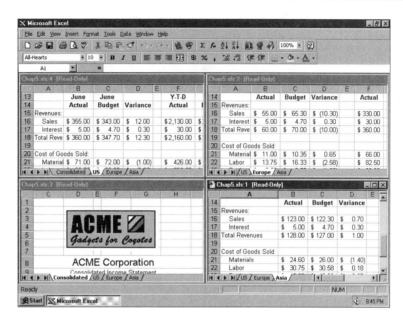

to be *dynamic*. In other words, if you change the source cell, the destination cell (which contains the formula) instantly changes to reflect the new number.

Also, as you can see, Excel entered the formula in the format:

```
=SheetName!CellName
```

NOTE. *Sheet names in a 3D reference are always absolute. Individual cells or ranges in the 3D reference can be absolute or relative.*

This method is the general way in which references to other sheets are entered. The only exception occurs when you have spaces in the sheet name, in which case Excel will surround the sheet name with single quote marks, as in the following example:

```
='Sheet with a Space'!CellName
```

NOTE. *When you enter references to other sheets using the mouse, Excel automatically uses single quote marks, if needed.*

The next step in entering multisheet references with the mouse is performing some arithmetic. In Figure 5.19, the formula bar shows one way to add cells from three sheets into a total in the consolidating sheet. You can type, as in this example, **=US!B16+Europe!B16+Asia!B16** to add cells from multiple sheets together.

Figure 5.19

3D arithmetic

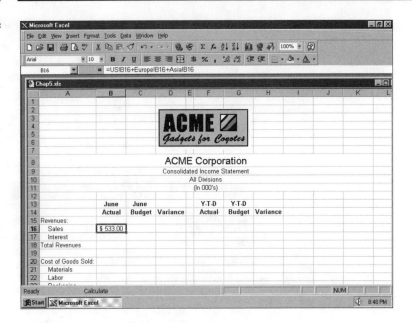

Working with Sheet Ranges

Excel also permits you to use references that refer to many sheets all in one reference. The example in Figure 5.19 is not very practical if you are consolidating tens or hundreds of worksheets—and Excel *can* handle hundreds of worksheets! In such cases, you'll want to use the SUM function and enter the sheet names as a range. This operation can be done entirely with mouse commands, as follows:

1. Move to the cell that will contain the formula.

   NOTE. *When using sheet ranges in formulas, it's important to ensure that all the worksheets being referenced have the same structure. In other words, if you're summing all of the values in cell B12 across multiple sheets, cell B12 should contain the same kind of information in all of the sheets, and you should double-check to make sure of this.*

2. Start the formula by entering **=SUM(**.

3. Click on the first sheet tab in the range and then click on the cell you want to total, or drag to select the range you want to use.

4. Shift-click on the last sheet tab in the range that you want included in the formula.

5. Press Enter to complete the formula (pressing Enter automatically enters the closing parenthesis for you).

Figure 5.20 shows the range of sheets with the completed formula.

Figure 5.20

A range of sheets referenced by the formula in the formula bar

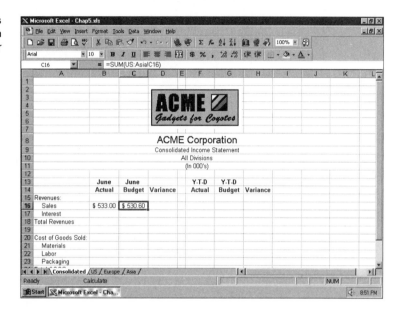

As you can see, multisheet references are given in the following form:

```
FirstSheet:LastSheet!Cell_Or_Range
```

You can perform this action with a range of cells in each sheet. For example, **=SUM(US:Asia!B21:B23)** would total cells B21, B22, and B23 in all three sheets.

WARNING. *If you rearrange the order of the sheets in your workbook, you might change the way sheet ranges are calculated. In the range Sheet4:Sheet8, for instance, if you move Sheet6 somewhere outside of the range in the formula, its cells will no longer be part of the solution. Similarly, if you insert a new sheet in a range of sheets, the new sheet's data will become part of the answer.*

If you move the first or last sheet to an area outside of the original range, the formula will adjust to exclude that sheet. In the preceding example, if Sheet4 is moved to follow Sheet8, then the formula changes to Sheet5:Sheet8.

The result in either case will probably be confusion on your part, as your formulas will no longer work correctly. For this reason, be careful when you rearrange sheets in a workbook that contains 3D references.

Using References to Other Workbooks

Linking between different workbooks (and not just different worksheets within a workbook) has many possible uses, including the following:

- **Looking at different analyses of your data.** You can create new workbooks from your source workbooks to present key data in different ways without changing the structure of the original data. This procedure helps you look at your data differently.

- **Simplifying complex workbooks.** In very large workbooks, you can often simplify the organization of your data by breaking it down into different workbooks.

- **Conserving memory.** You can conserve your computer's memory by breaking large workbooks into smaller pieces. In fact, if you are working with a workbook that includes many sheets and you start getting *Out of Memory* error messages, break the large workbook into smaller workbooks.

- **Creating a hierarchy of different workbooks for very large projects.** You can create multiple levels of linked workbooks, if necessary. In other words, workbook No. 1 can refer to workbook No. 2, which references workbooks Nos. 3 and 4 (or any other hierarchical organization that makes sense for your project).

- **Coordinating large projects.** You can use Excel to do your company's budgeting, for example, or to prepare and distribute workbooks for budgeting managers. When the managers complete and return the workbooks, you can consolidate them into a single, company-wide budget workbook.

You can use all the tools you just learned about to link workbooks. You can use the mouse, as you saw earlier, to create the links between the different workbooks. The only exception is that you should open the workbooks you want to link, and use the Window menu to switch between the workbooks instead of just clicking on the workbook tabs.

References to other workbooks that are open in Excel take the following form:

```
=[Workbook_Filename]Sheet_Name!Cell_Or_Range
```

When the workbook you want to reference is not open in Excel, the full path name of the workbook is shown at the beginning of the reference, as in the following example:

```
='C:\EXCEL\DATA\[WORKBOOK.XLS]Sheet_Name'!Cell_Or_Range
```

NOTE. *Make sure that the entire sequence of path name, workbook file name, and sheet name is enclosed with single quote marks before the exclamation point.*

Also, if the workbook to which you are linking is located in the same directory as the dependent workbook, you do not need to type the path name.

When opening a workbook that contains links to other Excel workbooks stored on your computer's disk, you will see the message shown in Figure 5.21. (You will see this message either in the dialog box shown in Figure 5.21, or in a message from the Office Assistant if it's running, but the message will be the same.)

Figure 5.21

The Update Reference message box

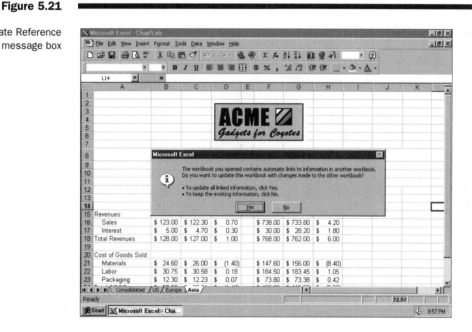

If you click on Yes, Excel will automatically go into the referenced workbooks to find the most recent data, and it will update all formulas that access that data.

If you select No, Excel will simply show you the answer that was stored the last time you saved the dependent workbook. The links to the other workbook will still be present, but will not necessarily be accurate if the other workbooks have been updated. You might want to choose the No button if you are working with a very large workbook that contains many links to many different workbooks. If you do not need the most current data, you can save time by telling Excel to skip the update process.

Managing Workbook Links

You can manage the links between your workbooks to do the following tasks:

- Update the dependent workbook at any time

- Redirect a workbook link from one workbook to another

- Open the source workbooks

NOTE. *A dependent document is one that contains a formula that uses data from another document. The document that contains the original data is the* source document.

To manage your document links, pull down the Edit menu and choose Links. You'll see the dialog box shown in Figure 5.22.

Figure 5.22

The Links dialog box

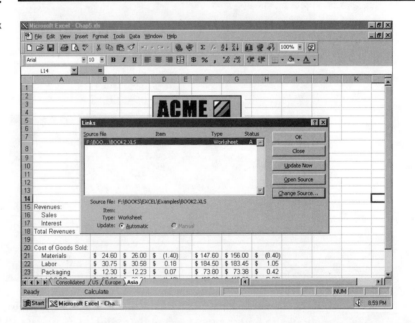

The Links dialog box shows you all active links in the current document. You can select the link with which you want to work by clicking on it. After you have selected a link, you can perform the following functions:

- Click on the Update Now button to update the link immediately with any new information in the source document.

- Click on the Open Source button to open the source document.

- Click on the Change Source button to tell Excel to link to a different workbook. You will be shown the Change Links dialog box, which looks much like the File Open dialog box. Use the Change Links dialog box to find and open the new document to which you want to link. The links automatically use the same ranges in the new source document that you select.

NOTE. *The Links dialog box shows all the links available for you to control. Links are not limited to other Excel workbooks. Excel allows linked graphics, word-processing files, and so on. The Links dialog box shows all these links for your current workbook.*

Save the source workbook first when you are saving linked workbooks. This precaution ensures that the data is calculated properly before the dependent workbook is closed.

Be careful when renaming or moving workbooks when you have links established. If you rename a source workbook, do the following two things to make sure that all the dependent references are properly updated:

1. Check to see that the source and dependent workbooks are open simultaneously so that Excel can automatically correct any dependent references to the renamed workbook.

2. Use the Excel Save As command to rename the source workbook.

If a source workbook is renamed or moved with Windows Explorer or by using the folders in My Computer or Network Neighborhood, you must update the links in the dependent workbook manually, because Excel will not know what you did with the source workbook. When you open the dependent workbook, it will automatically note that the source workbook is no longer present. It will then bring up the File Not Found dialog box, allowing you to locate the correct file for the links. Use this dialog box to relocate the file that contains the source data.

Using Paste Special

You will often want to share data in different sheets, but when you use the normal copy-and-paste operation between worksheets, you do not create a link between those sheets. Instead, you have to use Paste Special to copy data to a new sheet that is still linked back to the original sheet. To use Paste Special, follow these steps:

1. Select the source range of cells.

2. Pull down the Edit menu and choose Copy.

3. Move to the destination workbook, and click on the cell into which you want the data to be copied.

4. Pull down the Edit menu and choose Paste Special. You will see the dialog box shown in Figure 5.23.

5. Click on the Paste Link button.

6. Press Esc to deactivate the copy marquee.

Figure 5.23

The Paste Special dialog box

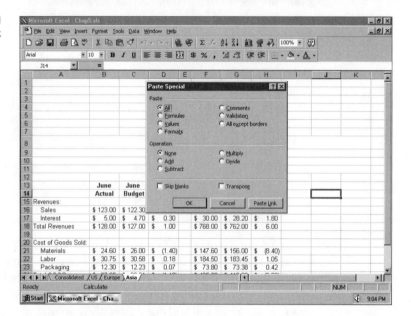

The data will be placed in your chosen destination cells, with an automatic link back to the source document. If the source information changes, the cells containing the linked information will automatically be updated.

Removing Links

To remove a link but retain the results, follow these steps:

1. Select the range you want to retain.

2. Pull down the Edit menu and choose Copy.

3. Pull down the Edit menu again and choose Paste Special. In the Paste Special dialog box, click on the Values option button and then click on the OK button, then press Esc to deactivate the copy marquee.

When you follow the preceding steps, the links will be removed but the results that were present will be converted to regular data, as if you had simply retyped them.

■ Linking to Other Applications

Many business and scientific documents are really *compound documents*. They are composed of information from a variety of sources: spreadsheets, charting programs, drawing programs, word processors, and so on. Instead of cutting and pasting information from all of these sources, you can use a Windows technology called *Object Linking and Embedding* (OLE, pronounced like a bullfighter saying "Olé!") to make the creation of compound documents much easier.

OLE gives you the following capabilities:

- **In-place editing of embedded (linked) objects.** If you double-click on an Excel chart embedded in a word processor that supports OLE, you are able to edit the chart without leaving your word-processing document. The word processor's menus become Excel menus, and you have full access to Excel's power—it's almost as if Excel is now built into the word processor!

- **Dragging and dropping objects.** This capability lets you grab data in one application and simply "drag-and-drop" it into another application.

Using OLE

You can take information from one Windows application and link it to another application in two ways. You can take the source data and drag it to the destination, or you can use the Copy command in the Edit menu of the source program, and then use some form of Paste Special in the destination program.

NOTE. *Although Microsoft programs generally use a command called Paste Special for linked pastes, other programs might call this command something else. Some, for instance, call it Paste Link. When in doubt, consult the documentation for the program you are linking to Excel.*

Using Drag and Drop

Drag and drop might also function differently with various applications. Some programs might interpret a drag-and-drop operation as a command to move data from the source application to the destination application. Others might assume that you are attempting to create a link. It all depends on the application you are using, and also on the specific data you are trying to drag and drop.

NOTE. *For drag and drop to work with Excel, you must enable a check box in the Options dialog box. Pull down the Tools menu and choose Options. Then click on the Edit tab in the Options notebook. Make sure that the check box labeled Allow cell drag and drop is checked. This option is already activated by default when you install Excel.*

Figure 5.24 shows a chart that was dragged from Excel to Microsoft Word.

Figure 5.24

A demonstration of
drag and drop

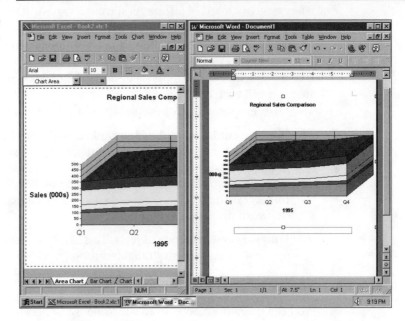

To perform the drag-and-drop function, follow these steps:

1. Arrange the applications on the screen so that you can see them both at
   the same time. (To do this quickly, right-click the task bar and choose
   Tile Vertically from the shortcut menu.)

2. Select the graphic object (such as a chart) or range of cells that you want
   to drag and drop.

3. If you are selecting a graphic object, click on the object and hold down
   the left mouse button. Then drag the mouse to the destination application. If you are copying a range of cells, point to the border of the selected range, making sure the mouse pointer looks like a white arrow,
   before dragging.

4. Position the cursor in the destination application, and release the left
   mouse button.

TIP. *Dragging an object from one application window to another generally
moves the object to the destination program. However, if you need to force the
drag-and-drop function to move the data, hold down the Shift key while you
perform the operation. To copy the data from Excel and place it in the
destination application, hold down Ctrl during the drag-and-drop operation.*

After the object has been dragged to the destination application, you can edit the data simply by double-clicking on it. This operation brings up Excel with the data ready for editing—unless Excel was not running when you double-clicked on the data, in which case Word will use Excel's capabilities to help you edit the data. Excel will start in the background and "insert" itself into Word so that it still appears that you are working with Word, even though you have full access to all of the power of Excel. Excel menu commands will appear in place of the Word menu commands, and so forth. When you finish editing the Excel object, click outside of the object. The native application's menus and toolbars will be restored. This capability is called *in-place editing*.

Some applications do not support in-place editing of Excel objects. In those cases, when you double-click on the Excel data in the destination application Excel will be launched with the data loaded in it. Edit the data in Excel and exit Excel to update the data in the destination application.

Controlling Link Requests

While Excel is running, it services any requests for link updates from other applications. You can control whether Excel responds to these requests by following these steps:

1. Pull down the Tools menu and choose Options.

2. Click on the Calculation tab.

3. Select or deselect the check box labeled Update Remote References.

Using Snapshots of Excel Data

You can prepare a "snapshot" of part of an Excel document that can be placed easily in another program (or in another sheet in Excel, for that matter). If, for example, you use the Copy and Paste commands to move part of a worksheet into a Word document, you actually paste only the data: you do not place the data so that it appears with all of its Excel-based formatting intact. Instead, use a snapshot to prepare a part of your worksheet (which includes all formatting), then place the resulting image into the other application. Follow these steps:

1. Select the part of your worksheet you want to present in a different application (in this example, Microsoft Word).

2. Hold down the shift key, access the Edit menu, and use the Copy Picture command. You will see the Copy Picture dialog box, which offers the following choices:

   - **As shown on screen.** Choosing this option creates the snapshot exactly as it appears on the screen at the time you take it.

- **As shown when printed.** Creates the snapshot as if it were taken from a printed version of the range.

- **Picture.** Creates the snapshot as a Windows Metafile, which can be resized in the destination application.

- **Bitmap.** Creates the snapshot using the exact screen or printer pixels you see: the resulting image cannot be resized in the destination application. Furthermore, the resolution of the destination application (or computer) must match your system in order for the image to appear correctly.

3. Choose the Paste command in another part of the worksheet or workbook, or in the destination application. Figure 5.25 shows some cells pasted into an area below the data, as well as into Microsoft Word.

Figure 5.25

The worksheet image
pasted as a snapshot

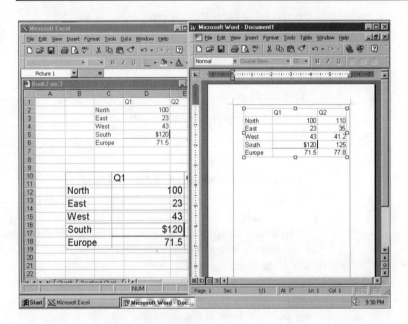

■ Setting Up Templates

One useful Excel application is setting up template workbooks that can be completed by other people you work with. Typically, such templates are created to apply all the desired formatting and formulas, and the template's user has only to fill in the necessary cells to complete the document based on the template. (This is a perfect application for Expense Reports, for example.) Another advantage of creating templates is that users do not directly work on the templates themselves, so users cannot inadvertently change the formulas or formatting in the template.

To set up template workbooks, follow these steps:

1. Prepare the workbook you want to make into a template.

2. Pull down the File menu and choose Save As.

3. In the Save As dialog box, click on the button to the right of the Save File as Type field to see a list of the different types of files you can save from Excel.

4. Choose Template from the list, enter a file name, then click on the OK button to save the document, which will be given an XLT extension.

After you have created the template and it is subsequently opened with the File New command by you or by someone else, a copy of the document will be loaded and given a temporary name to preserve the original template file from changes. This prevents anyone from accidentally changing your template.

However, you will sometimes need to update templates to reflect changes, or to incorporate improvements you have made. To edit a template file, follow these steps:

1. Pull down the File menu and choose Open.

2. Open the Template folder and select the template file.

3. Click on the Open button.

This procedure opens the template file for editing. Make any necessary changes, and resave the template.

- *Mastering Excel's Outlining Feature*
- *Using the Scenario Manager*
- *Using PivotTables*
- *Importing Text Files*
- *Auditing Workbooks*
- *Validating Data*

Advanced Worksheet Features

Excel has some advanced features that the typical user won't need on a day-to-day basis. However, these features can be real time-savers. In this chapter, you will learn about the following procedures:

- Using the Excel outlining feature
- Creating different scenarios with the Scenario Manager
- Using the PivotTable Wizard, which allows you to look at information in a table by rotating data categories to show new relationships
- Importing text files using the Text Import Wizard
- Auditing workbooks
- Validating worksheet data

By taking advantage of Excel's powerful worksheet tools, you can go far beyond the basics and become an Excel "power user."

Excel includes many advanced features that are available to you when needed. This chapter discusses a number of these features, many of which have been improved over previous versions in Excel 97 for Windows. The features included in this chapter are not needed by everyone who wants to benefit from using Excel; for those who do need them, however, they can be incredible allies.

■ Mastering Excel's Outlining Feature

Excel's outlining feature permits you to hide or show detail in your worksheets. You can designate ranges of rows or columns, and group them so that you can quickly hide or show their detail. You also can create *nested outline groups* (groups within groups), allowing you to provide exactly the level of detail that you want.

Examine the worksheet shown in Figure 6.1 and Figure 6.2. This worksheet shows a detailed income statement, organized by quarter, that has been outlined.

Figure 6.1

An expanded income statement

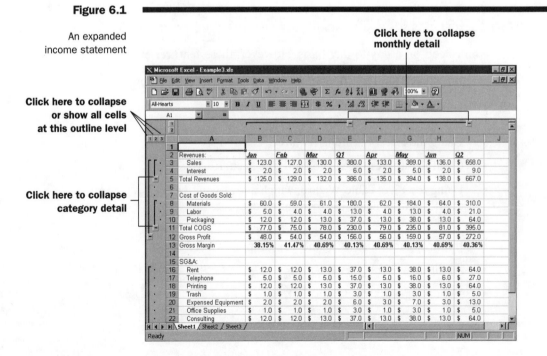

Figure 6.2

A collapsed
income statement

Click here to expand to
this outline level

Click here to show
category detail

Click here to show
monthly detail

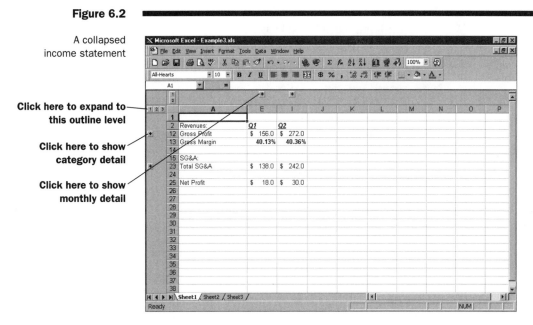

By using the outlining tools on the worksheet shown in Figures 6.1 and 6.2, you can switch quickly to any level of detail. In a large and complex worksheet, you can navigate faster with collapsed groups. When you get to the area of the worksheet where you want to work in greater detail, just click on the appropriate outline button to reveal the detailed information.

Creating an Outline Range Manually

To create an outline range manually, follow these steps:

1. Select a range of rows or columns by dragging across the row- or column-heading buttons. Be sure to select the rows or columns themselves, rather than cells within the worksheet.

2. Pull down the Data menu, choose Group and Outline, and then choose Group from the cascading menu that appears.

TIP. *After you have selected a range of rows or columns, you can quickly group or ungroup them for the outline by pressing Alt+Shift+right arrow to group or Alt+Shift+left arrow to ungroup.*

You don't always have to select whole rows or columns, as you did in the previous example. You also can select a range of cells on the worksheet before you select the Group command. When you select a range of cells and then Group them, the Group dialog box will appear, asking whether you want to group the rows or columns for the selected range of cells (see Figure 6.3).

Select Rows to group the rows that contain the selected cells, or Columns to group the columns in the selected cell range.

Figure 6.3

The Group dialog box

Creating an Outline Automatically

With most worksheets, Excel can examine the structure of the worksheet and generate all the appropriate outlining levels automatically. Excel bases its decisions on factors like the location of formulas compared to actual data, or the location of SUM formulas. Excel then creates an outline level for each consistent structure in the worksheet.

If you want to control how Excel looks for this consistency before you create the automatic outline, pull down the Data menu and select Group and Outline. When you choose Settings from the cascading menu, the Outline dialog box will appear (see Figure 6.4).

Figure 6.4

The Outline dialog box

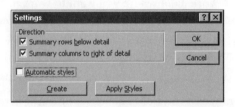

In the Outline dialog box, select the Summary rows below detail check box if your data is summarized downward (in other words, if the totals are at the bottom of each range of data in the worksheet). If your summary formulas are above the details they represent, deselect this check box. Also, if your column summaries are to the right of the details they represent, select the Summary columns to right of detail check box.

If you select the Automatic Styles check box, Excel will format your document with boldface in the summary-cell locations. This is intended to help you distinguish summary information from detailed information.

If you want to create the outline from the Outline dialog box, click on the Create button. Otherwise, pull down the Data menu, select Group and Outline, and then select Auto Outline. Excel will then apply the rules you set in the Outline dialog box, and it will automatically create all the appropriate outline levels for your worksheet.

TIP. *To restrict the area that Excel outlines with the Auto Outline feature, select the cells you want to outline before executing the command. Otherwise, Excel will outline the entire worksheet.*

If you restructure your data, you can select the Auto Outline command again to rebuild the outline levels based on the new data structure.

Deleting Outlines

Excel offers two ways to delete outlines. You can either delete individual outline levels or you can delete all outlines in the worksheet with a single action.

To delete individual outline levels, select the rows or columns in the outline level you want to remove. Then pull down the Data menu, select Group and Outline, and then select Ungroup. You also can press Alt+Shift+left arrow instead of using the menu command.

To delete all outline levels on your worksheet, begin with no rows or columns selected. Then pull down the Data menu, select Group and Outline, and then select Clear Outline.

■ Using the Scenario Manager

Excel has a tool called the *Scenario Manager* that can help you track multiple scenarios created with your data within a single workbook. The Scenario Manager permits you to define *changing cells* for a single worksheet. You can then define different scenarios based on those changing cells. Using this feature, you can store multiple scenarios created with your data in a single worksheet, without having to maintain multiple copies of the data itself. This is a fundamentally better method for building multiple scenarios—if you change the formulas that make up your worksheet and are not using the Scenario Manager, you might forget to update all copies of your worksheet. When you use the Scenario Manager to model many scenarios, you'll need to make structural changes to your worksheet in only one place instead of many.

When you create different scenarios, you can use the Scenario Manager to switch quickly between the different sets of data. This lets you quickly examine and compare the different scenarios. As an example, you might want to examine three budget "cases" on your worksheet that use the same basic data: Projected (or expected), Best Case, and Worst Case. Or, you might define scenarios such as "Best case if the Johnson deal goes through" or "Projected profits if we freeze salaries."

NOTE. *For even more complex and powerful analysis, use the Scenario Manager together with PivotTables. PivotTables are discussed in the next section of this chapter.*

Examine the worksheet shown in Figure 6.5. This worksheet shows a sales budget for four different regions in the company. Each region has a projected sales-growth target, which is defined below in the Sales Growth cells. The Q1 column contains actual assumed starting values, while the Q2 through Q4 columns use the growth rates in cells B15:B18 to calculate each quarter's sales.

Figure 6.5

The Scenario Manager sample worksheet

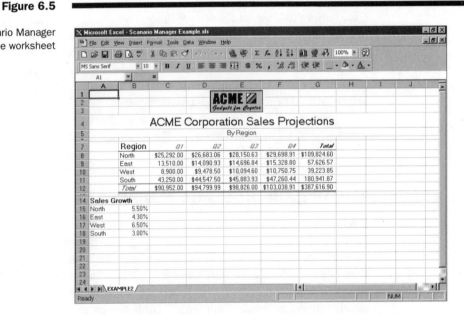

You could use the Scenario Manager to look at what the total company sales will be if regions experience different sales-growth rates. This example defines simple Projected, Best Case, and Worst Case scenarios, but you could also define scenarios that examine different events in each of the individual regions (such as Projected: West Loses Sales Manager, or Best Case: New Product Introduction in East).

Creating a Scenario

To create a scenario, pull down the Tools menu and select Scenarios. The Scenario Manager dialog box appears, as shown in Figure 6.6.

Begin to define the new scenario by clicking on the Add button in the Scenario Manager dialog box, which brings up the Add Scenario dialog box shown in Figure 6.7.

Figure 6.6 ██

The Scenario
Manager dialog box

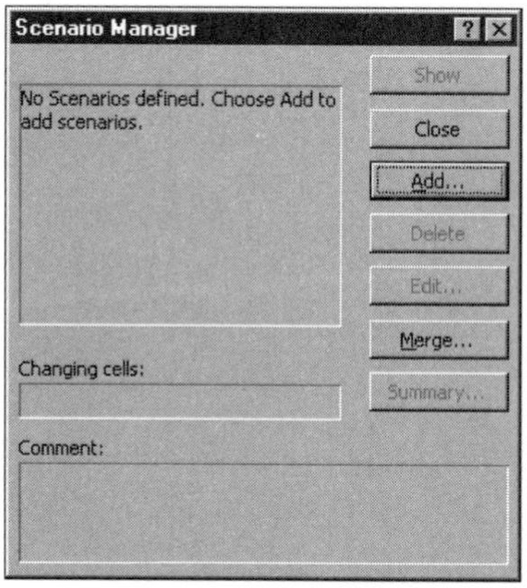

Figure 6.7 ██

The Add Scenario
dialog box

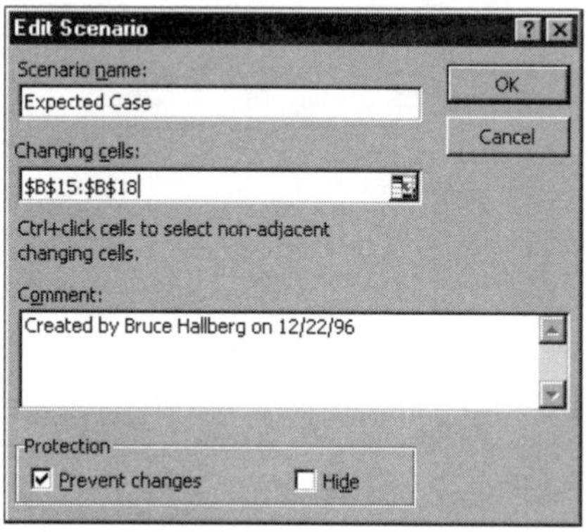

Type the name of your scenario in the Scenario Name field. Define the
changing cells by clicking in the Changing Cells field, and then select the
cells in the worksheet. For this example, you want to define each scenario
based on different assumptions for the sales growth percentages shown in
cells B15:B18, so those cells are selected for the Changing Cells field. (Remember, you can click the Collapse Dialog button to temporarily put the dialog box aside while you select the changing cells in your worksheet. Click the
button again when you are ready to expand the dialog box.) Excel will automatically put your name and the date you created the scenario in the Comment field, although you can easily edit this information. The Add Scenario
dialog box also has two check boxes: Prevent Changes and Hide. Select the
Prevent Changes check box to prevent other users from modifying your

scenario. Select the Hide check box to prevent the new scenario from appearing in the Scenario Manager dialog box.

NOTE. *The Changing Cells are those that you will change for the different scenarios you create: in this case, the different scenarios will be based on different projected sales-growth rates for the different regions.*

After you select the changing cells (in this case, cells B15:B18), click on OK. The Scenario Values dialog box will appear (see Figure 6.8).

Figure 6.8

The Scenario
Values dialog box

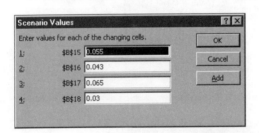

Use the Scenario Values dialog box to define the values in the changing cells for the new scenario. You are limited to 32 changing cells per scenario. For each cell in the dialog box, there is a corresponding field in which you input the value for the cell. After you have entered the values for the new scenario, click on OK and then close the Scenario Manager dialog box.

TIP. *If you need to define a scenario that uses more than 32 changing cells, create multiple scenarios, each of which changes a different range of cells. For example, you can define scenario No. 1 to change cells A1:A32, scenario No. 2 to change cells B1:B32, and so forth.*

Switching between Scenarios

You can quickly switch between scenarios with the Scenario Manager dialog box.

To display different scenarios using the Scenario Manager dialog box, follow these steps:

1. Access the Scenario Manager dialog box via the Scenarios command in the Tools menu.

2. Click on the desired scenario in the Scenarios list.

3. Click on the Show button.

After you click on the Show button, the scenario you selected will appear. When you finish viewing scenarios, or have found the scenario you want to work with, click on the Close button to return to the worksheet.

Creating a Scenario Summary Report

You can create a summary report of your different scenarios. This report will show the different assumptions you worked with, and the results you got based on each scenario. To create a scenario summary report, follow these steps:

1. Access the Scenario Manager dialog box by pulling down the Tools menu and selecting Scenarios.

2. Click on the Summary button in the Scenario Manager dialog box. The Scenario Summary dialog box will appear, as shown in Figure 6.9.

Figure 6.9

The Scenario
Summary dialog box

3. Confirm that the Scenario summary option is selected in the Report Type box.

4. Select the contents of the Result Cells field, if necessary, and then select the cells in your worksheet that have the results you want to see in your scenario summary report. In this example, select the range G8:G12. Remember, you can hold down the Ctrl key to select multiple ranges.

5. Click on the OK button to create the scenario summary report.

The preceding steps will create the scenario summary report in a new sheet in your workbook (see Figure 6.10).
Note the following features of the scenario summary report:

• Excel automatically creates the formatting you see in Figure 6.10.

• Excel automatically outlines the report for you.

• You can view the comments (creation date and creator) for each scenario by clicking on the Outline button to the left of row 3 (the row that includes the scenario names).

• The scenario summary report is somewhat difficult to understand if it only includes cell references for the categories in the report. You can correct this problem by using named ranges in your worksheet. Figure 6.11 shows a scenario summary report with named ranges.

Figure 6.10

A scenario
summary report

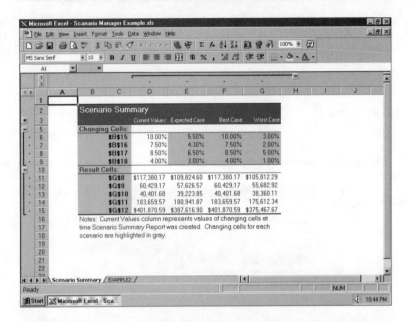

Figure 6.11

A scenario summary
report with named ranges

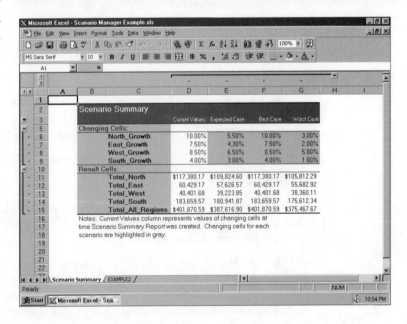

Creating a Scenario PivotTable

You can create a scenario PivotTable to view your scenarios by following these steps:

1. Access the Scenario Manager dialog box by pulling down the Tools menu and choosing Scenarios.

2. Click on the Summary button in the Scenario Manager dialog box. The Scenario Summary dialog box shown in Figure 6.9 will appear.

3. Select Scenario PivotTable from the Report Type box.

4. Select the contents of the Result Cells text box, then select the cells in your worksheet that contain the results you want to view in the summary report. In this example, select the range G8:G11.

5. Click on the OK button to create the scenario PivotTable shown in Figure 6.12.

NOTE. *Scenario PivotTables, like scenario summary reports, can make use of named ranges to make the results more easily understood. The example in Figure 6.12 uses named ranges, so the names are automatically displayed for the row and column headings.*

Figure 6.12

A scenario PivotTable

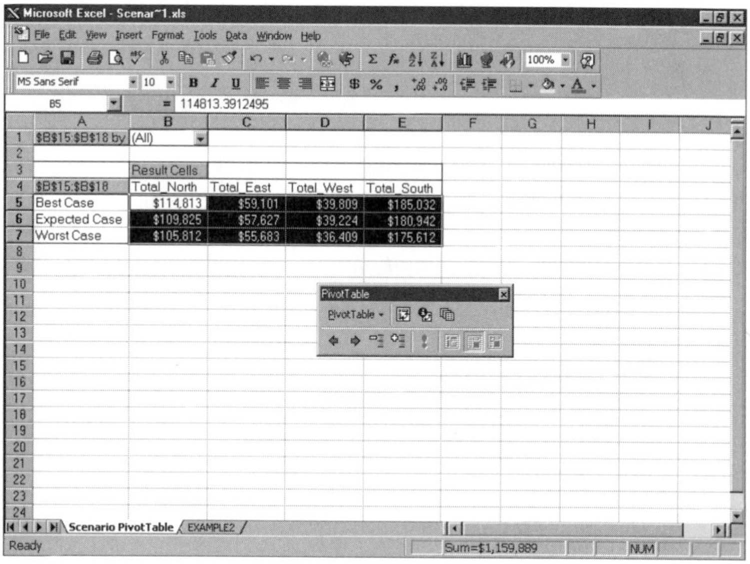

■ Using PivotTables

One of the most powerful tools in Excel 97 for Windows is the PivotTable feature. PivotTables allow you to summarize detailed information for easier analysis. You can use PivotTables to analyze many types of data, including the following:

- Detailed sales records

- Shipping cost statistics

- Purchase order details

- Engineering safety records

PivotTables have many other potential applications as well. You can summarize a detailed list or database records (such as those in the preceding list) into PivotTables, which show summary information only. You can then *rotate* the data with your mouse to analyze it in different ways. These rotations aren't actual rotations of what you see on the screen, but rather are movements of the table headers. Drag a column heading to a row, for instance, and the summary data will change instantly to reflect the new layout.

This section teaches you about Excel's PivotTable feature by using sample call records from a call-accounting system. Figure 6.13 shows the top of the worksheet that contains the detailed records.

NOTE. *Approximately 500 call records have been imported into Excel for this example, although you can work with thousands of records without any trouble. You only see a few of these records in Figure 6.13, but the example PivotTables in this section use all of the records for their source data.*

NOTE. *A* call-accounting system *is software that runs on a computer connected to your telephone system. A call-accounting system captures telephone statistics so you can manage your telephone costs. Most such systems can output their data into text files that Excel can read.*

Table 6.1 shows the fields in the sample worksheet.

If you were the telecommunications manager at your company, you might want to ask certain types of questions about the telephone data, such as the following:

- **What were the total dollars spent by each telephone extension?** Because you know who is assigned to each extension, you can figure out the amount each person spends from the data. You might even provide the data to accounting so that each person's department can be charged for their calls.

Figure 6.13

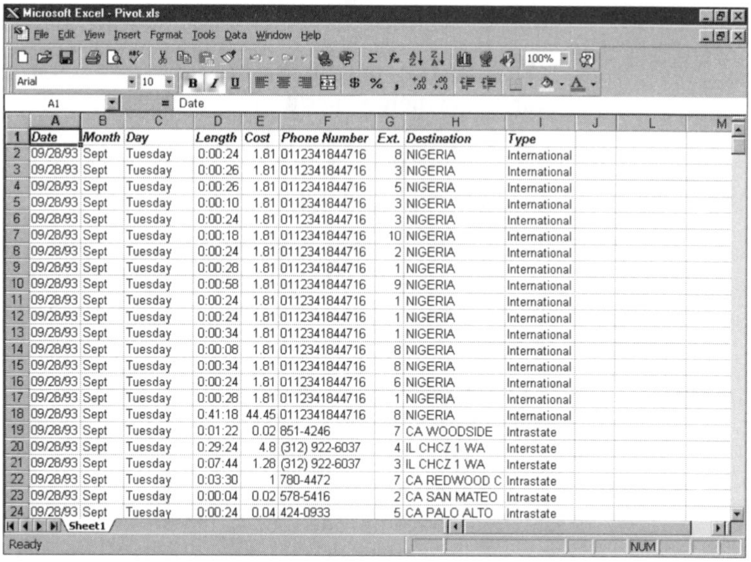

Call records

Table 6.1

Worksheet Fields

FIELD NAME	DESCRIPTION
Date	The date the call was placed
Month	The month in which the call was placed
Day	The day of the week when the call was placed
Length	The length of the call in minutes
Cost	The estimated cost of the call (generated by the call-accounting system)
Phone Number	The phone number dialed
Extension	The extension number from which the call was placed
Destination	The name of the geographic destination
Type	The type of call: international, interstate, or intrastate

- **How much is spent on different call types?** In other words, how much is spent on international, interstate, and intrastate calls? This information might help you justify a different telephone carrier that has cheaper rates for the most common types of calls.

- **What are the most expensive destinations called?** If you can identify a couple of frequently called and expensive destinations, you can use that data to negotiate targeted discounts with your telephone carrier.

- **What are the traffic patterns by day of week or by time of day?** This data can help you look at different carriers' rates for different time periods. Also, if you make the assumption that outgoing call volume has a rough relationship to incoming calls, this information can help you schedule your telephone operators more effectively.

- **What is the average time spent on each call for each extension?** These statistics can indicate, for example, that you need to work with a couple of people to try to make their expensive international calls briefer.

The preceding questions are only a few of the valid questions you can ask with the data shown in the sample worksheet. You also can use Excel's capability to manipulate the records to ask even more questions. You might use the MID() function, for example, to strip out the area code called in the telephone number field and then get cost summaries by area code. Use Excel's extensive list of functions to massage your data into different categories, so that you can ask detailed questions about the data. You can't easily answer such questions by manually looking through hundreds or thousands of data records. PivotTables work well with this type of project.

Figure 6.14 shows an example of a PivotTable created from the sample data. This PivotTable shows the total dollar amount of calls made by type of call (international, intrastate, or interstate) for each extension, and also has a Page field that lets you look at all calls or at just the total calls made in a given month.

Using the PivotTable Wizard

You use the PivotTable Wizard to generate the sample PivotTable shown in Figure 6.14. To begin creating a PivotTable, pull down the Data menu and select PivotTable Report. The first page in the PivotTable Wizard will appear (see Figure 6.15).

In Step 1 of the PivotTable Wizard, select from the four choices explained in Table 6.2.

For this example, select Microsoft Excel List or Database, and then click on the Next button (or press Enter) to proceed to Step 2 of the PivotTable Wizard (see Figure 6.16).

In Step 2 of the PivotTable Wizard, you select the range of data you want to report on. If the range Excel guesses for you is incorrect (Excel assumes you want to create the PivotTable using all cells with data that are contiguous with your active cell), use your mouse to select the range that

Figure 6.14

A sample PivotTable

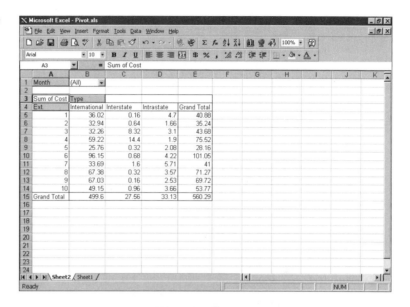

Figure 6.15

The PivotTable
Wizard: Step 1

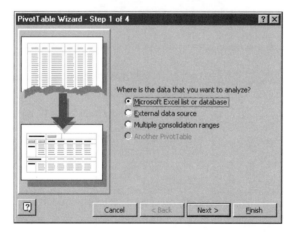

contains the desired data. You also can click on the Browse button to select a
file on the disk that has the data, if the data is in a different worksheet. After
you have selected the range of data for the PivotTable, click on the Next button to go to Step 3 of the PivotTable Wizard (see Figure 6.17).

Step 3 of the PivotTable Wizard is the most important step. To the right
of the screen, a number of buttons are arrayed, one for each category of
data. In the center of the page is the layout area, divided into four different
sections as described in Table 6.3.

Table 6.2

PivotTable Wizard:
Step 1 Options

OPTION	DESCRIPTION
Microsoft Excel List or Database	Choose this option to use data in a single worksheet in your workbook.
External Data Source	Choose this option to automatically start Microsoft Query, a tool that comes with Excel and is used to query other database files or sources.
Multiple Consolidation Ranges	Choose this option to build the PivotTable from multiple worksheets in your workbook.
Another PivotTable	If your workbook contains other PivotTables, choose this option to incorporate one of them in the new PivotTable.

Figure 6.16

The PivotTable
Wizard: Step 2

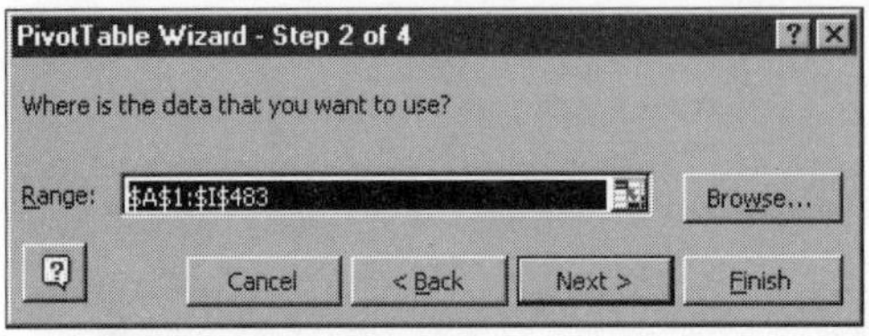

Figure 6.17

PivotTable Wizard: Step 3

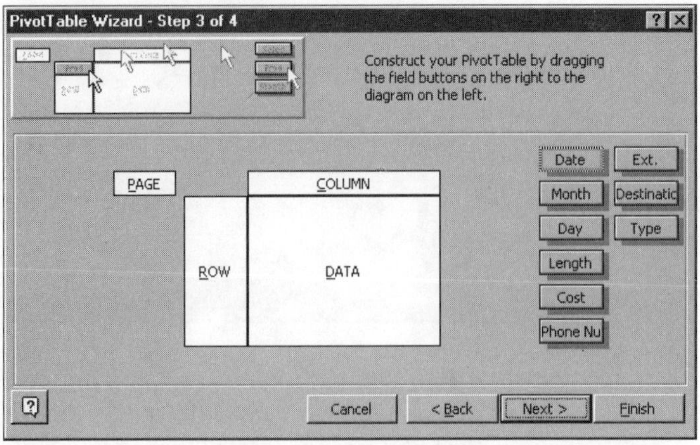

Table 6.3

PivotTable Wizard
Layout Sections

SECTION	DESCRIPTION
Page	Defines a section of the PivotTable in which you can select the records shown in the table. For example, you could drag the Type field to the Page section to allow you to show only international calls in the resulting PivotTable. The variable you choose for Page is used to restrict the data that fills the rest of the PivotTable.
Row	Permits you to choose the categories to be shown in the PivotTable rows.
Column	Controls which categories appear along the horizontal axis of the table.
Data	Can be summarized in different ways. You can show totals, counts, or averages of the category in the Data section.

After you have dragged the categories you want to report on into the layout area, click on the Next button to display the fourth and final step of the PivotTable Wizard (see Figure 6.18).

Figure 6.18

The PivotTable
Wizard: Step 4

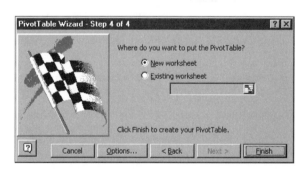

In the fourth step of the PivotTable Wizard, you decide whether your PivotTable will be created as a new worksheet in the existing workbook, or placed into an existing worksheet. You can also click on the Options button to set a number of important options for the PivotTable. The PivotTable Options dialog box that appears when you click the Options button is shown in Figure 6.19.

Table 6.4 shows the settings available in the PivotTable Options dialog box.

Click OK to close the Options dialog box, and then click on the Finish button to complete the creation of the PivotTable. Figure 6.20 shows the completed PivotTable.

Figure 6.19

The PivotTable
Options dialog box

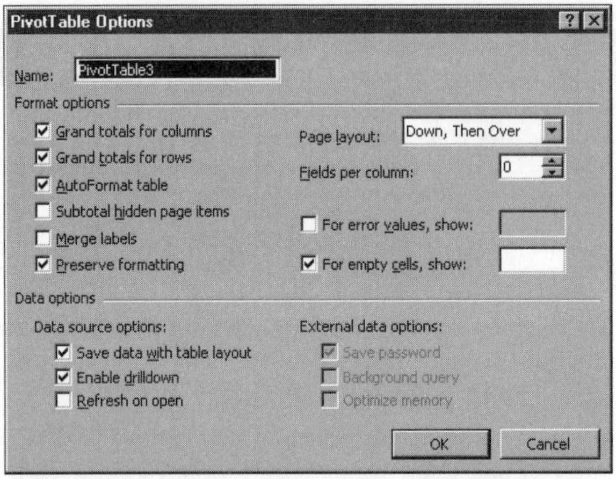

Table 6.4

PivotTable Wizard:
PivotTable Options
Dialog Box Settings

SETTING	DESCRIPTION
Name	Enter the name of the sheet that will be created for the new PivotTable.
Grand totals for columns	If this check box is selected, the PivotTable Wizard automatically creates grand totals for all the columns in your PivotTable.
Grand totals for rows	If this check box is selected, the PivotTable automatically creates grand totals for all the rows in your PivotTable.
AutoFormat table	Select this check box to automatically format the PivotTable with the default table AutoFormat. You can also use the Format AutoFormat command after the PivotTable is created to apply a different format.
Subtotal hidden page items	If the PivotTable includes hidden page field items, selecting this includes such items in a subtotal.
Merge labels	Merges cells for outer row and column labels.
Preserve formatting	When changing an existing PivotTable using the PivotTable Wizard, this setting preserves your PivotTable formatting.
Page layout	Choose the default (Down, Then Over) or the alternate choice (Over, Then Down) to control how the PivotTable orients its results by the data you selected for the Page field.
Fields per column	If you are displaying multiple "pages" of data based on the Page field, use this spin button to control the number of Page fields that are included before a new row or column is started.

SETTING	DESCRIPTION
For error values, show	When selected, lets you enter a result that will display in place of any errors in the PivotTable.
For empty cells, show	When this is selected, you can choose what is displayed in place of empty cells in the PivotTable. If the default is selected, a blank cell will be displayed.
Save data with table layout	Normally, the PivotTable contains a copy of the source data in a hidden area, and uses that copy for its results. Doing so makes the PivotTable calculate more quickly. However, if you are having memory-constraint problems, you can clear this check box to avoid creating the duplicate data. The PivotTable will calculate more slowly in some circumstances, but you will potentially free up enough of the computer's memory to render a complex PivotTable. If you later wish to modify the PivotTable, you will have to refresh the data manually.
Enable drilldown	New to Excel 97, this feature lets you double-click on a PivotTable cell to see the detailed data the cell represents. If you want to hide the source data, you can clear this check box.
Refresh on open	When selected, this feature lets the PivotTable refresh its source data when you open the workbook that contains the PivotTable. When PivotTables use data that takes a long time to query, as would be the case with an external database accessed through a slow network connection, or when you know the source data has not changed, clear this check box to prevent automatic updates.
Save password	When working with an external data source for a PivotTable, you may need a password to access the external data source. Checking this option stores your password as part of the PivotTable query so you don't have to re-enter the password every time you update the source data for the PivotTable.
Background query	When selected, this feature lets Excel query an external data source in the background while you continue to use Excel. This slows the query process, but lets you remain productive while the query runs.
Optimize memory	Selecting this option slows the PivotTable query somewhat, but conserves memory on your computer.

Changing the PivotTable

Not only can you use the PivotTable Wizard to create PivotTables, you also can use it to determine which categories to include in the PivotTable. To change categories, place your active cell anywhere in the PivotTable, then access the PivotTable Report command in the Data menu. The layout page of the PivotTable Wizard will immediately appear. You can then drag categories and drop them in different locations. Just as you can drag new categories

Figure 6.20

The completed PivotTable

	A	B	C	D	E
1	Month	(All)			
2					
3	Sum of Cost	Type			
4	Ext.	International	Interstate	Intrastate	Grand Total
5	1	79.07	4.16	2.22	85.45
6	2	19.83	10.72	2.81	33.36
7	3	59.69	1.28	1.78	62.75
8	4	26.31	1.44	3.14	30.89
9	5	94.88	7.36	5.95	108.19
10	6	27.42	1.12	1.96	30.5
11	7	23.01	0.16	4.31	27.48
12	8	70.72	0.32	4.69	75.73
13	9	35	0.32	4.31	39.63
14	10	63.67	0.68	1.96	66.31
15	Grand Total	499.6	27.56	33.13	560.29

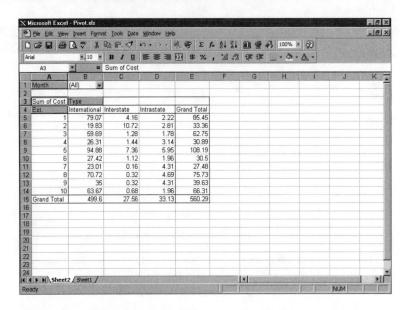

from the right into the layout area, you can delete categories by dragging them from one of the layout sections to a blank part of the screen.

Manipulating the PivotTable

Figure 6.21 shows a new PivotTable created from the sample data. This PivotTable shows the call totals by looking at the mix of calls placed on different days of the week. This PivotTable also has two Page fields: Month and Extension.

Figure 6.21

A sample PivotTable

	A	B	C	D	E	F	G	H	I
1	Month	(All)							
2	Ext.	(All)							
3									
4	Sum of Cost	Day							
5	Type	Sunday	Monday	Tuesday	Wednesday	Thursday	Friday	Saturday	Grand Total
6	International	101.8	0	233.4	0	0	0	164.4	499.6
7	Interstate	2.24	0.16	10.24	0	0	0.52	14.4	27.56
8	Intrastate	1.61	2.97	9.51	3.86	2.47	9.26	3.45	33.13
9	Grand Total	105.65	3.13	253.15	3.86	2.47	9.78	182.25	560.29

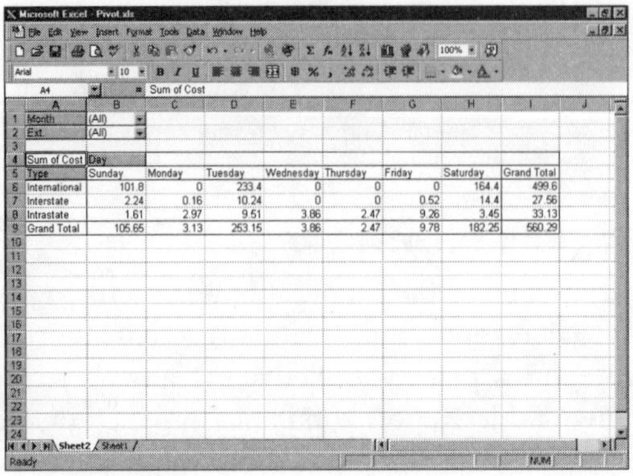

You use the Page fields to restrict the data being displayed. To use the Page fields, click on the drop-down arrow to display the valid choices. When you make a selection, your PivotTable shows only that category of data. On the sample PivotTable shown in Figure 6.21, it is easy to show the information for only one telephone extension by using the Ext. Page field. You can also look at one telephone extension in a given month or all extensions for a given month by using the appropriate combination of choices in the Page fields.

You can drag and drop the categories used in the PivotTable: this can be easier than accessing the PivotTable Wizard again to change how the data is displayed. Figure 6.22 shows the result of dragging the Extension field to the vertical axis of the table. You can see that the breakdown is according to call type sorted by telephone extension. You can see that whoever uses Ext. 1, for example, does most of his or her calls on Saturday, and that these calls are mostly international (at least in terms of the cost of the calls).

Figure 6.22

Comparing the mix of type per extension

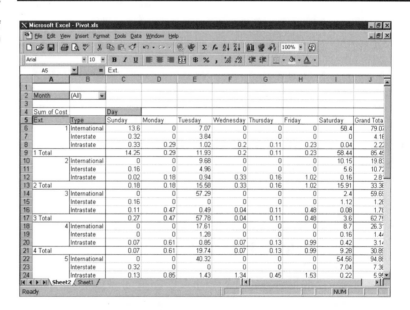

The new format is not useful if you want to compare the mix of calls made by each extension. For example, you now know that Ext. 1 makes many international calls, but does Ext. 1 make the most international calls? To change the PivotTable to show that information, drag the Ext. field to the right of the Type field so that the Ext. field becomes a subcategory of Type, as shown in Figure 6.23.

On the new PivotTable, you can easily see that Ext. 5 makes more international calls than Ext. 1.

Figure 6.23

Comparing the type of
call for extensions

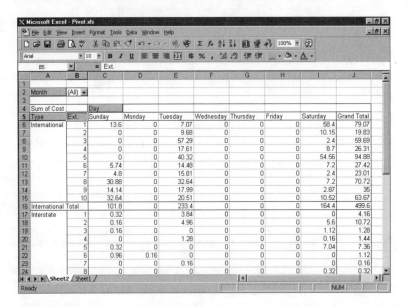

Figure 6.24 shows a new configuration of the fields in the PivotTable. The new arrangement shows only international calls, and also shows that most international calls are made on Tuesday. This example was created by dragging the Type field to the page area (below the Month field), and then selecting International from its drop-down list.

NOTE. *In Figure 6.24, only three days are listed (Sunday, Tuesday, and Saturday). The PivotTable lists only these three days, because no international calls were made by any extension in the database on the other days of the week. PivotTables automatically filter out completely blank categories.*

Controlling Fields

You can control the treatment of different categories by using the PivotTable Field dialog box. Right-click two times on the name of the field you want to work with, and choose Field from the pop-up menu. If you select an axis field, such as Ext., and then choose the command, the PivotTable Field dialog box will appear, as shown in Figure 6.25.

You can change the name of the category by typing a new name in the Name field. If you want to reposition the category without dragging and dropping, select the Row, Column, or Page option button. If the category you format is divided into subcategories, select the different summarization options in the Subtotals box. Choose from the various methods listed, such as Sum, Average, Count, and so on. You can select as many subtotals as you want by

Figure 6.24

International call totals

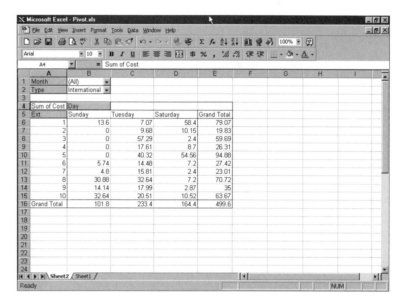

Figure 6.25

The PivotTable
Field dialog box

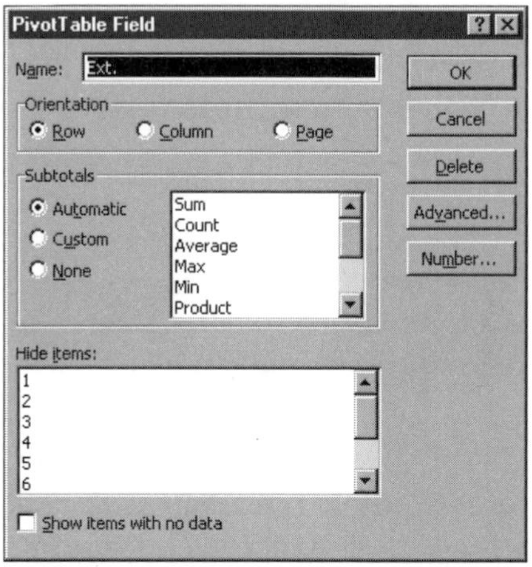

clicking on each one individually. Finally, you can choose to hide parts of the
data by selecting from the list in the Hide Items list box. When you finish
changing the settings in the PivotTable Field dialog box, click OK to close it.

You also can reformat the data portion of the PivotTable. For example, if
you want to show the number of calls rather than total dollars spent, reformat the data area accordingly. Right-click on a cell in the data area, and

choose Field from the pop-up menu. A somewhat different version of the PivotTable Field dialog box will appear, as shown in Figure 6.26.

Figure 6.26

The PivotTable Field dialog box with the data area selected

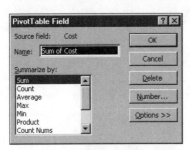

Use the Name field to change the name of the subtotal. Select the type of subtotal from the Summarize by list box in the PivotTable Field dialog box. Click on the Number button to choose what number format to use to format the subtotals, or use the Options button to see additional result-formatting options.

Refreshing Data

PivotTables do not automatically update themselves when the data on which they are based changes. You have to use the Refresh Data command to get the most recent data. Select the Refresh Data command from the Data menu or, if the Query and Pivot toolbar is displayed, click on the Refresh Data button.

Removing Categories

You can remove categories by dragging them out of the PivotTable area. When you do this, your pointer changes to a category button that has a large X in it. If the X is displayed and you drop the category by releasing the mouse button, you will remove the category from the table.

TIP. *Instead of removing categories from the PivotTable that you might want to use again later, you can drag the category to the Page area of the PivotTable and set it to display all records. You get the same result as far as the data shown in the table is concerned, and you can drag the category back into the PivotTable later without having to call up the PivotTable Wizard again.*

Grouping Data in a PivotTable

Sometimes groups that you might want to view in a PivotTable do not exist within the data you are using. In these cases, you can group together similar types of records. For example, what if you wanted to look at the costs of international calls compared to non-international calls in this example? There's no field in the data that breaks down the calls in this way—instead, you would have to tell the PivotTable to combine Interstate and Intrastate calls into a single group, and then compare this new group to the International totals.

To group data like this, select the records you want to group in the PivotTable, then either click on the Group button in the PivotTable toolbar, or select the Data menu, choose Group and Outline, and then choose Group. Figures 6.27, 6.28, and 6.29 show a before-and-after look at this grouping operation.

Figure 6.27

Starting our analysis with this summary, which breaks down call costs by call type, use Ctrl+Click to select Interstate and Intrastate. Next, use the Group command in the Group and Outline submenu in the Data menu.

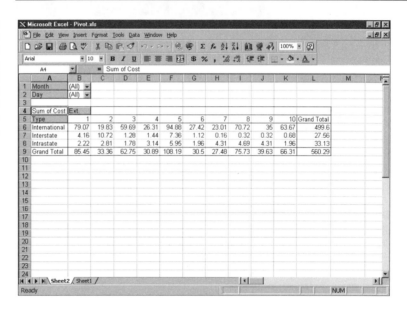

Charting PivotTables

You can generate charts from your PivotTables using all the charting tools covered in Part 3 of this book. When you change your PivotTable, the charts you have made will be updated with the changes automatically.

■ Importing Text Files

Although Excel can read and write many different file formats, sometimes you have to import text files into Excel. Some examples of cases where you would want to import text files into Excel include the following:

- Downloading stock data from an online service such as CompuServe, and then importing the stock data into Excel.

Figure 6.28

Now your group is created, but you still can't compare totals the way you want to. With Interstate and Intrastate still selected, right-click on either one of them and choose Hide Detail in the Group and Outline sub-menu of the shortcut menu.

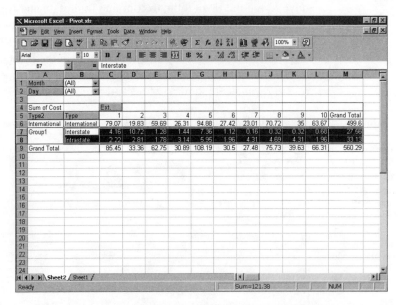

Figure 6.29

Now you can directly compare the international and non-international (Group1) calls.

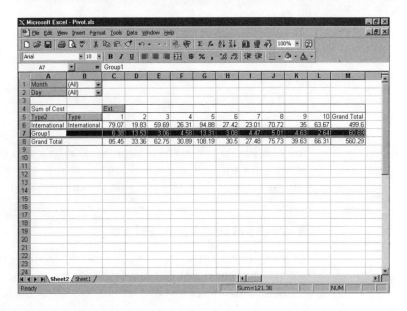

- Taking the output of another program and importing it into Excel: for instance, you might want to import detailed measurements from a piece of test equipment. Most automated test devices have interface software that can export the test data into text files, which can then be used in Excel.

- Importing accounting data from your accounting system into Excel. Very few accounting systems can create Excel files for analysis, but almost all accounting systems can create a text file that can be used in Excel. After you load the detailed accounting data (General Ledger transactions, for example), you can use the PivotTable feature to analyze the data.

Any time you open a text file in Excel, the Text Import Wizard starts automatically. The *Text Import Wizard* is a tool that enables you to import almost any format of text data into Excel.

Using the Text Import Wizard

To use the Text Import Wizard, simply open a text file by accessing the Open command in the File menu. If the file you open has an extension other than the normal Excel file extension (which it probably does), make sure that List Files of Type is set to All Files (*.*). Select your file in the File Open dialog box, then click on the Open button.

Excel should recognize the file as a text file and start the Text Import Wizard, as shown in Figure 6.30. In some cases, Excel recognizes that it doesn't need any help importing a text file. When this is the case, Excel simply converts the file and shows you the resulting worksheet rather than the Text Import Wizard.

Figure 6.30

The Text Import
Wizard: Step 1

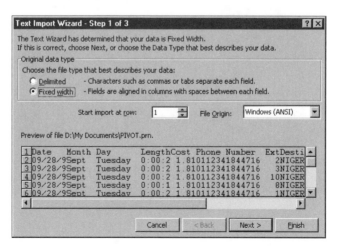

The Text Import Wizard examines the data in the text file and guesses whether its fields are delimited in some way or if the file is composed of fixed-width fields. *Delimited data* generally separates each field with a comma, but some use spaces, tabs, or other characters. Contrast this with *fixed-width data*, in which records are set up in such a way that each field is at exactly the same horizontal position within each line. If Excel guesses incorrectly about your data, select the appropriate option button (Delimited or Fixed width) before proceeding.

The Step 1 page also has two other fields. The first field, Start import at row, lets you choose a row in the data to begin reading at. Often the first row or rows have header information for the file that you might not want or need. In such cases, set Start Import at Row to the appropriate value. You can use the Preview window to help determine which row the import should start at. The second field is labeled File Origin. You can choose from three file origins: DOS or OS/2 (PC-8), Windows (ANSI), and Macintosh. The File Origin field determines the way certain control characters in the file should be interpreted. Usually, DOS or OS/2 (PC-8) is the best choice, although Windows (ANSI) works with almost all files as well. If the data you see in the Preview window is garbled, try selecting another type of file origin. If the data appears garbled using any of the file-origin choices, then the file is not a text file; you need to go back to the originating application and re-export the data into an ASCII or ANSI text-based format.

Importing a Delimited File

Assuming that your file is delimited, select the Delimited option button before you click on the Next button to move to Step 2, as shown in Figure 6.31.

Figure 6.31

The Text Import Wizard:
Delimited Step 2

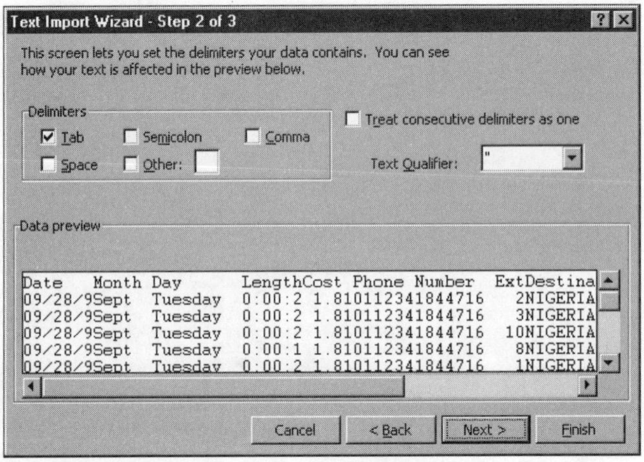

NOTE. *If your file is fixed width, see the following section. Fixed-width files go through different steps in the Text Import Wizard.*

The second step for importing delimited files involves telling Excel what character was used to delimit the fields in each record. Examine the Preview window of this screen to see what the delimiting character is. In most cases, Excel correctly guesses what the delimiter is, but you may need to change the check boxes shown if Excel guesses wrong. A horizontal line will be shown after each delimiter to help you see if you've correctly identified it or not.

In addition to the Delimiters section of this dialog box, you can set two other choices: Treat consecutive delimiters as one, and Text Qualifier. Selecting Treat consecutive delimiters as one has the effect of making the import records vary in the number of fields for each record, so this option is not normally set (such files are very rare).

You can use the Text Qualifier field to indicate which character has been used in the text file to indicate textual data as opposed to numeric or date information. Most delimited text files surround purely textual data with quotation marks ("). Because you want to import text data as text, and because you probably don't want the text-qualifier character to be imported along with the text, this field is important to set if a text qualifier is being used in the text file.

To finish the Text Import Wizard import of a delimited file, skip the following section.

Importing a Fixed-Width File

If you select Fixed Width in Step 1 of the Text Import Wizard, you see a different Step 2 screen than if you choose Delimited (see Figure 6.32).

Figure 6.32

The Text Import Wizard: Fixed Width Step 2

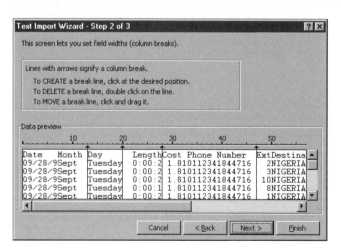

In Step 2 of a fixed-width file import, you will see a preview of the data with a ruler above it, as shown in Figure 6.32. For fixed-width files, Excel does not have the ability to recognize where each field is separated from the adjacent fields: you will need to indicate where each field starts and ends by clicking at the ruler position for each field. Each time you click in the Preview window, a new vertical line will be created that shows where Excel will break the field. You can move these lines by clicking and dragging them to a new position, and you can delete these lines by double-clicking on them. After you have placed all the field markers, click on the Next button to proceed to Step 3.

Finishing a Text Import Wizard Operation

In the final step of using the Text Import Wizard, you tell Excel what type of data each field should contain (see Figure 6.33).

Figure 6.33

The Text Import
Wizard: Step 3

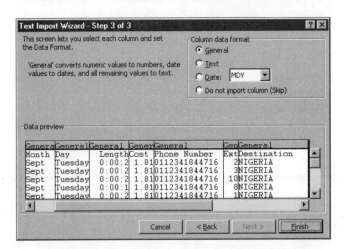

Each field has a button above it with the type of data in the field listed inside the button. By default, all fields are marked as having General data, which causes them to be created in Excel with the General cell format. To change the field format, click on the button for the field you want to change and then select the appropriate option button from the Column Data Format box. The Column data format box permits you to choose from the options listed in Table 6.5.

After you have designated the fields in Step 3, click on the Finish button to complete the operation and import the data into Excel.

Table 6.5

Field Format Options

OPTION	DESCRIPTION
General	This option uses the Excel General cell format when the data is imported.
Text	This option forces the field to be treated as text, even if it contains only numbers. It can be important to force some numeric fields to be treated as text, particularly if you want to retain any leading zeros. For example, the Phone Number field in the illustration should be formatted as text. Otherwise, the international phone numbers will be displayed in Scientific notation when Excel imports the data.
Date	Select this option if the field contains dates. Furthermore, choose the format the dates are in by using the drop-down list to the right of the Date option button.
Do not import column	Select this option to avoid loading the selected field.

■ Auditing Workbooks

Complex workbooks can quickly become difficult to validate or troubleshoot. So many interdependencies develop that making changes that don't cause many problems elsewhere in the workbook is particularly tough. You can help to alleviate the situation by using named cells and cell comments, but even that doesn't always help to sort out a complex workbook.

Excel 97 for Windows includes auditing tools that let you visualize how a worksheet or workbook is put together, and that help you to validate the results in the workbook. You can access these features with the Auditing toolbar shown in Figure 6.34.

Figure 6.34

The Auditing toolbar

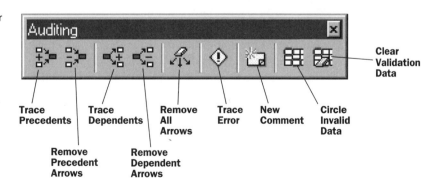

NOTE. *The Auditing Toolbar is not selected like other toolbars, and is not shown in the Toolbars submenu of the View menu. Instead, pull down the Tools menu, choose the Auditing sub-menu, and then choose Show Auditing Toolbar.*

To audit the sources for a particular cell in a workbook, first make that cell your active cell. Then click on the Trace Precedents button, which reveals the immediate source of the data (see Figure 6.35).

Figure 6.35

Clicking on Trace
Precedents shows the
source of a cell's
data or results.

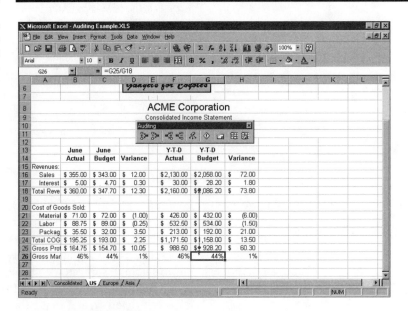

To follow the formulas further back, continue clicking on Trace Precedents to find your way back to the original data upon which the cell is based. For example, Figure 6.36 shows the appearance of the screen after you have traced precedents three more times.

If you are working in a multidimensional workbook, you may also see precedents that point to other sheets in the workbook. Figure 6.37 shows such references, indicated with small worksheet icons. You can jump to the source worksheet by double-clicking on the line that connects the icon to the cell it points to. This brings up the Go To dialog box, shown in Figure 6.37.

The example in Figure 6.37 shows three source sheets and cells, because the formula in this particular case sums up the values across the U.S., Europe, and Asia worksheets. Select the appropriate reference in the Go To dialog box and then click on the OK button to jump to that reference. Your active cell in the destination sheet will be the one referenced by the tracing action.

Figure 6.36

Continue tracing precedents to see more and more underlying detail.

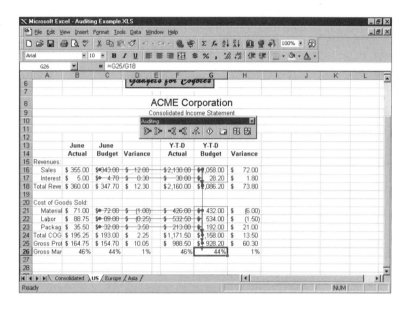

Figure 6.37

The Go To dialog box

Tracing dependents works exactly the same as tracing precedents, except that you will see cells that are based on your active cell, rather than sources for your active cell.

When you're finished with tracing cells, click on the Erase All Arrows button to remove them from the workbook.

■ Validating Data

You can define what constitutes valid data for cells in your worksheet. For instance, you may know that a particular value will always be between, say, 2 and 5. Any other value is known by you to be invalid and therefore a data-entry mistake. You can define such validity checks for Excel using the Data Validation dialog box, a new feature in Excel 97. You can assign validity checks to individual cells or to multiple cells: just select the cells for which you want to define validity checks before accessing the Data Validation dialog box.

Data Validation Settings

Bring up the Data Validation dialog box with the Validation command in the Data menu. You will see the dialog box shown in Figure 6.38.

Figure 6.38

The Data Validation
dialog box

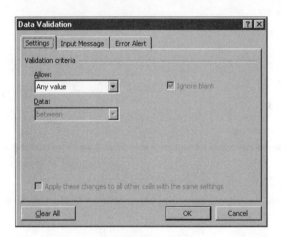

There are three tabs in the Data Validation dialog box: Settings, in which you define the valid data; Input Message, in which you enter a message that displays when the validated cell is selected for editing; and Error Alert, in which you can control how data-entry errors are handled.

The Allow drop-down list box on the Settings tab lets you control what types of data are allowed for the selected cells. Your choices include Any value, Whole number, Decimal, List, Date, Time, Text length, and Custom. Most of these options cause additional fields to be displayed on the Settings dialog-box tab. For instance, when you choose Decimal, you can then choose the valid range of values that can be entered. Choosing List lets you define a valid list of choices that can be entered without error. Custom lets you enter a validation formula for the cell. Figure 6.39 shows an example where only values between 0 and 50 are allowed.

TIP. *In the example shown in Figure 6.39, you can enter values in the Minimum and Maximum fields, but you can also refer to cells by selecting the field and then clicking on the cell you want to use.*

Figure 6.39

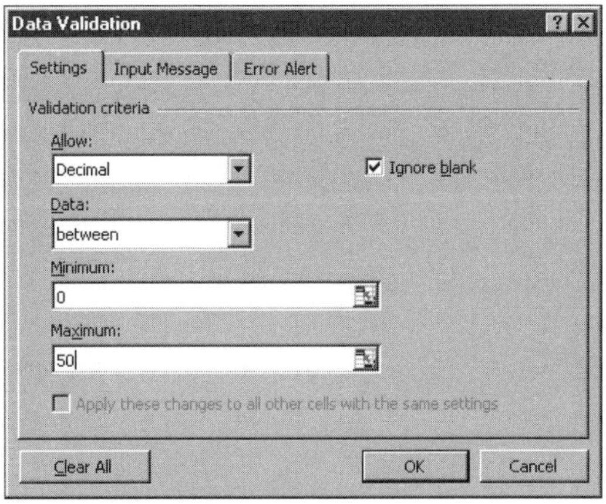

An example of Data Validation where only decimal values between 0 and 50 are allowed

The Input Message tab lets you enter an input message that will be shown when data is entered into a validated cell. Figure 6.40 shows such a message being entered, while Figure 6.41 illustrates how the message appears when it is activated.

Figure 6.40

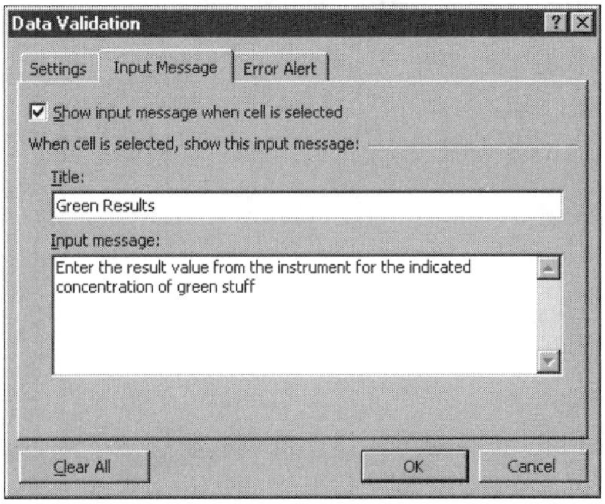

Defining a validated cell's input message

Use the Error Alert tab to control what Excel displays when someone tries to enter data that is invalid. Figure 6.42 shows an example of a message defined in the Error Alert tab, while Figure 6.43 shows how this message looks to the person entering the erroneous data.

Figure 6.41

How input messages
are displayed to the
person entering data

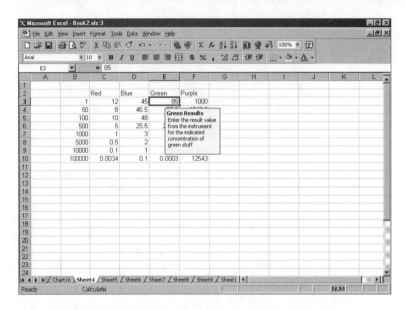

Figure 6.42

Defining an error
message in the Error
Alert dialog box

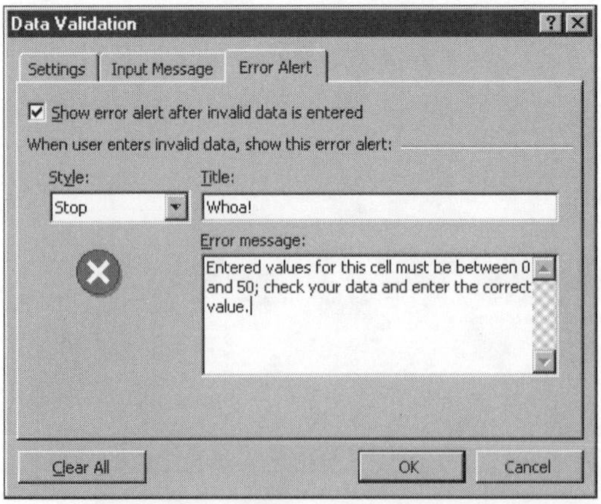

Figure 6.43

An Error Alert dialog
box being displayed

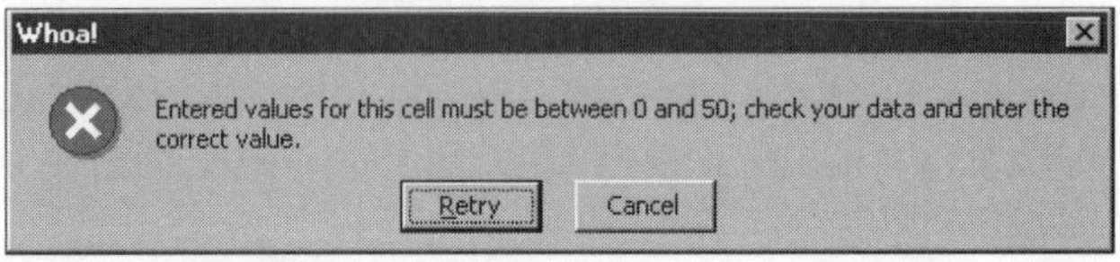

Circling Invalid Data

When you define validation rules and need to quickly find invalid data, you can use the Circle Invalid Data button on the Auditing Toolbar. Pull down the Tools menu, choose Auditing, and then choose Show Auditing Toolbar. On the Auditing Toolbar, click on the Circle Invalid Data button to show entries that don't conform to the data-validation rules you've defined, as shown in Figure 6.44.

Figure 6.44

Circling invalid data provides a visual cue that helps you quickly focus on erroneous data.

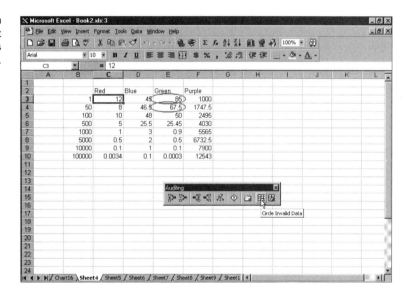

When you're done viewing and correcting the invalid data, you can click on the Clear Validation Circles button on the Auditing toolbar to remove the circles.

- *Understanding Functions*
- *Entering Functions*
- *Troubleshooting Function and Syntax Messages*

7

Mastering Functions

THIS CHAPTER COVERS THE FUNCTIONS INCLUDED IN EXCEL. Knowing how to use these functions can help you create worksheets that solve what-if questions, assist with special analysis tasks, and much more. Functions are the backbone of Excel's power.

Chapter 7 helps you to utilize this power by including the following:

- Understanding what a function is
- Understanding the parts of a function
- Understanding how to create a function
- Using the Paste Function command and the Formula Palette
- Using functions to answer refinancing questions
- Troubleshooting functions

In this chapter, you will see how easy it is to use and master functions in Excel. Even if you feel that functions are sometimes intimidating, you can learn about tools like Function Palette and Help, which make using functions simple. Using Excel to its full potential will make your computing life much more pleasant.

■ Understanding Functions

How often have you repeated a certain task or calculation, all the while wishing that you could just snap your fingers and be done with it automatically? With the aid of the functions featured in Excel 97, you can come quite close to doing just that. You can make your life significantly simpler—just automate repetitive procedures by using some of the methods covered in this chapter.

A *function* is a formula that can automatically calculate results, perform worksheet actions, or assist with decision-making based on information you provide. You can use the functions that Microsoft has built into Excel for Windows, or you can write your own. This chapter discusses the functions provided with Excel, which are called *worksheet functions*.

NOTE. User-defined functions, *those that you write for yourself, can be used in your worksheet just like normal worksheet functions. User functions can be programmed using Excel's Visual Basic for Applications.*

Functions are most commonly used to generate calculated results. You might, for example, want to find out what your monthly payment would be if you refinanced your house, or you might need to track revenues and expenses to calculate your profit margin. Maybe you are developing a marketing survey and want to analyze the statistics you gather. To meet these kinds of needs, Microsoft has included a wide variety of functions with Excel.

Function Groups

Excel has hundreds of built-in functions available to you. They have been categorized into the following groups:

- **Database.** Helps with database information, like selecting the minimum or maximum value from database entries.

- **Date & Time.** Calculates the number of days between two dates based on a 360-day year, translates dates to serial numbers, and so on.

- **DDE and External**. While not shown in the Paste Function dialog box, these functions can still be used to perform Dynamic Data Exchange (DDE) and communicate with external programs. You can find more information on these functions in Chapter 8, "A Complete Guide to Functions."

- **Engineering.** Useful for converting feet to meters, a binary number to hexadecimal, or complex numbers.

- **Financial.** Calculates interest, depreciation, return on investment, and other types of financial information.

- **Information.** Returns general information about your worksheet, such as formatting or the contents of a cell.

- **Logical.** Produces results based on certain conditions in your worksheet.

- **Lookup & Reference.** Provides information about your worksheet, such as returning the column number of a reference or the number of areas in a reference.

- **Math & Trigonometry.** Useful for setting up and solving basic engineering and math problems, such as calculating the cosine or tangent of a number.

- **Statistical.** Helps with statistical problems, like calculating the binomial distribution probability.

- **Text.** Helps you manipulate text data.

- **User Defined**. Excel lets you use Visual Basic for Applications to program your own functions.

The organization of functions into these categories helps you find the right function quickly.

Components of a Function

No matter what type of function you use, you will always express the function in the same way. You can see an example of a function in Figure 7.1. This worksheet is a template for projecting sales at the fictitious ACME Corporation. In this worksheet, starting values are entered into the first-quarter column, and then sales growth rates are calculated for the remaining quarters using the growth-rate assumptions in cells B15 through B18. As data is entered for different quarters, row 12 will reflect totals and column G will automatically reflect the YTD totals, because formulas have been entered into these cells that can perform these summations.

When you select a cell that contains a formula, the formula will appear in the formula bar. The formula bar shows an equal sign followed by the function name, then a set of parenthesis enclosing the information that is used to calculate the result (the instructions enclosed in the parentheses are called *arguments*).

Figure 7.1

The form of a function

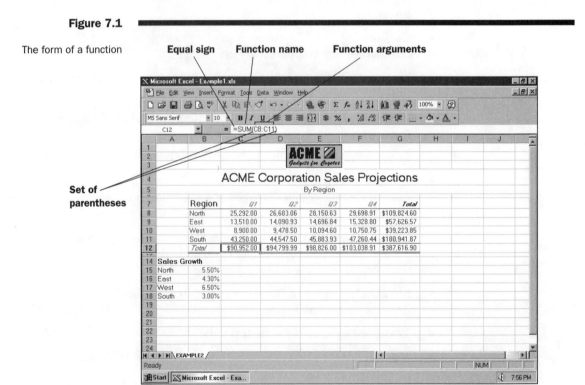

Each component provides meaning to the function so that Excel can determine how to process the information, as follows:

- **Equal sign.** This tells Excel to display the *results* of the function. Without the equal sign, there is no calculation made, and the cell shows the remaining function syntax as text.

- **Function name.** The referenced function can be any function provided by Excel or a user-defined function.

- **Parentheses.** Every function requires at least one argument, and all of its associated arguments must be enclosed in a set of parentheses.

- **Arguments.** Different functions have their own requirements for the type of information that can be used for each of their arguments. There are numerous ways you can provide the data for an argument, however. Arguments can be literal (constants), formulas or expressions, references to cells, or other functions. Each argument is separated with a comma when multiple arguments are required. Cell references and ranges are most commonly used as arguments in functions. When using functions within functions, called *nesting functions*, you are limited to seven nested levels. You do not use the equal sign in front of a nested function (you provide the equal sign for the first function, but each nested function thereafter does not require its own equal sign).

Together, the components provide a structure or format to the function. This format is known as the *syntax*, the rules or "model" you must follow to describe the information you want to use in the function. The syntax for each function is different. Thus, you must pay attention to the way Excel looks for information, or you might get some very strange results.

Using Arguments

The information you provide to a function is called an *argument*. A function can include more than one argument, because different kinds of information might be needed to calculate the desired answer. Each function includes a predetermined set of arguments, always separated by commas.

TIP. *Particular function syntax and arguments are documented in the Excel documentation. You also can use the Paste Function dialog box or the online help, both discussed later in the chapter, to help you with your functions and argument lists.*

In the example illustrated in Figure 7.1, you need to calculate the total of first-quarter sales for each territory in the United States. The function name, SUM, is followed by the information you want to sum enclosed in parentheses. The regions for the first quarter are located in cells C8 through C11. The argument to the SUM function is a reference to those cells.

You can describe function arguments in several ways. The preceding example uses *cell ranges*. You told the Excel function SUM which cells to reference to find the information to calculate the sum. Another way to describe what we want to sum, however, is to use *cell references*, or a list of cells. In the next example, shown in Figure 7.2, you use *cell references* to calculate the second-quarter sales.

Figure 7.2

The SUM function using cell references as its arguments

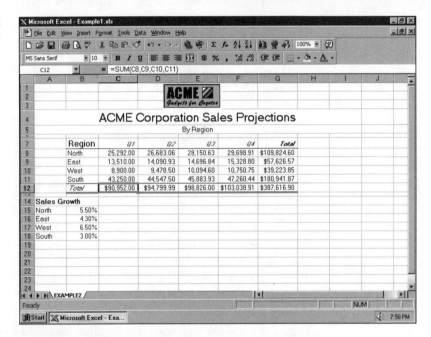

This example contains four arguments: the individual cells that will be summed. The example shown in Figure 7.1 using cell ranges is generally easier, but using cell references adds some capabilities—for example, what if you didn't want to include all of the regions in the total? With cell references, you can refer to just the cells you want.

You need to understand how Excel deals with cell references when you add and remove rows or columns from your sheets. For instance, look at the Total line, now located at C13 (see Figure 7.3). Notice that after you insert a row to add a new Central region, Excel changes the last two arguments in that SUM function to reflect the new location of the West and South regions, which are now in cells C11 and C12. It does not change the first two arguments, C8 and C9, because the location of first-quarter sales for the North and East regions did not change. If we were to add a number to show Central first-quarter sales in C10, it would not be included in the total at C13.

Now look at the total in C13, as shown in Figure 7.4. If the Central row is added when a cell range was used, the SUM function will adjust to properly reflect the new range (C8:C11 becomes C8:C12), and values added to the Central row will be automatically included in the total in C13.

Figure 7.3

Individual cell references
not adjusted to include
added row

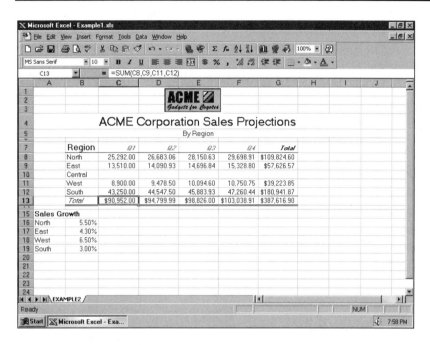

Figure 7.4

Cell range automatically
adjusts to include
added row.

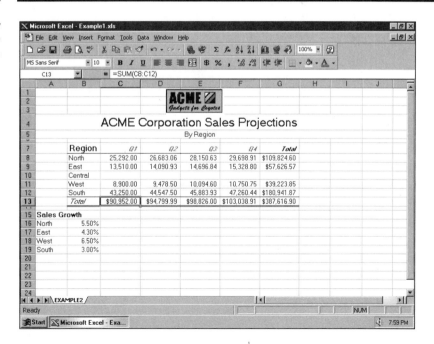

TIP. *If all you want to do is get a quick look at the sum of a group of numbers, take advantage of the AutoCalculate feature. Look at the status bar at the bottom of Figure 7.5—the AutoCalculate box is showing the sum of the selected cells; the answer is automatically displayed on the status bar. You no longer need to use a calculator or use a temporary formula in a worksheet when you want to quickly check a total. You can also average the numbers or count the entries by clicking on the Auto Calculate area in the status bar with the right mouse button.*

Figure 7.5

The AutoCalculate box

AutoCalculate area

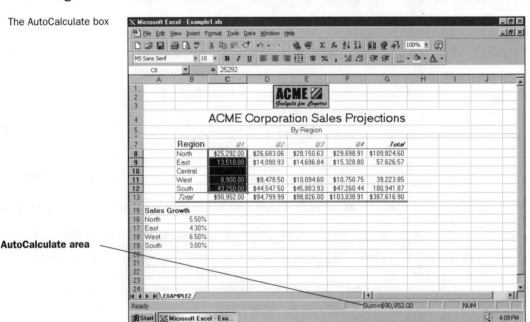

Paste Function and Function Palette

Mastering function construction is one of the most difficult steps to becoming a proficient Excel user. Fortunately, Microsoft has made it easier. To assist you in choosing functions and determining the information Excel needs to calculate them, Excel provides the *Paste Function* dialog box and the *Formula Palette*, step-by-step tools that helps you choose and build functions in your worksheet.

Activate the Paste Function dialog box by choosing Insert, Function, or by clicking on the Paste Function tool on the Standard toolbar (see Figure 7.6).

Figure 7.6

The Paste Function Tool

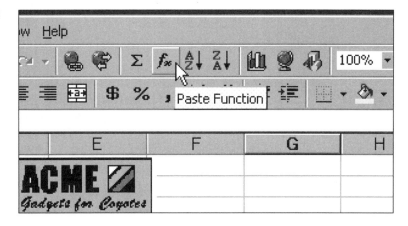

To help you understand how the Paste Function dialog box works, the next demonstration adds a logical function to the worksheet. In the following exercise, you need to know which salespeople met their sales quotas, because those salespeople are going to win a trip. You'll see how this is done with the sheet shown in Figure 7.7.

Figure 7.7

The Sales by Salesperson Example spreadsheet

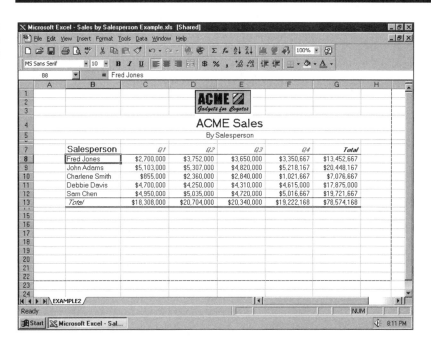

Total year-to-date sales for each person is shown in cells G8 through G12. Annual quota by region is in cells J6 through J10 (these cells are not visible in the screen in Figure 7.7). You'll use these numbers to determine which salespeople win the trip. If sales were greater than or equal to quota, you want Excel to put an asterisk (*) in column H. To begin, select H6, then click on the Paste Function button. A dialog box will appear, as shown in Figure 7.8.

Figure 7.8

The Paste Function
dialog box

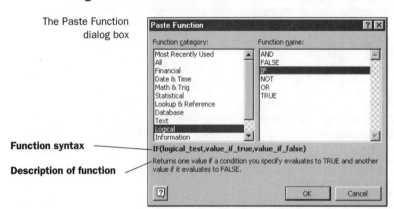

Function syntax

Description of function

The Paste Function dialog box shows the function categories on the left, and specific function names on the right. As you select different categories, the function-name list will change. Below the list boxes, Excel provides a description of the currently highlighted function and its syntax.

For this example, click on the category Logical, then select the IF function by clicking on the function name or by pressing the Tab key and then the arrow keys. Paste Function tells you that the first argument for this function is *logical_test*, the second argument is *value_if_true*, and the last argument is *value_if_false*.

TIP. *This information might be enough to allow you to complete your function. If you need more guidance, click on the Office Assistant button at the bottom-left corner of the dialog box, or press F1. Then click on the Help with this feature option button and then on the Help on selected function option button in the Office Assistant bubble. A Help window containing information about the selected function will be displayed. To exit Help, click the Close button at the top-right corner of the Help window (see Figure 7.9).*

After selecting the function you want, click on the OK button in the Paste Function dialog box. You now see Formula Palette, which will help you build the function (see Figure 7.10).

Figure 7.9

Help for the IF function

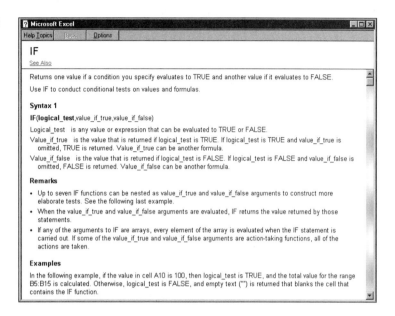

Figure 7.10

The Formula Palette

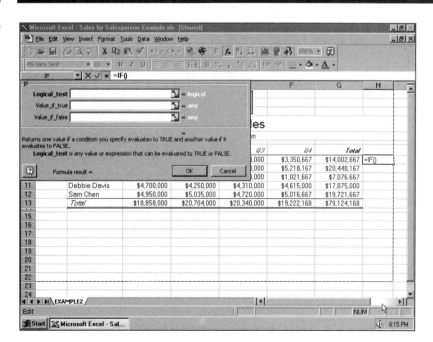

The Formula Palette gives you three edit boxes in which you can provide the three arguments for the IF function. Notice that the first argument, *logical_test*, is bold, which means it is required. You must enter a value or expression that can be evaluated to TRUE or FALSE. In this example, you want to know if Total YTD Sales for the first salesperson in G8 is greater than or equal to his or her quota in cell J8.

Enter the expression **G8>=J8** into the *logical_test* box. Because this expression can be evaluated to true or false, it is a legitimate logical test. In this case, the expression evaluates to TRUE. Notice that the expression also appears in the formula bar, because the Formula Palette builds the function as you proceed.

TIP. *When an argument is in bold type, it is required. If it is in regular type, it is optional. If you omit the optional arguments, Excel applies an assumed value. This assumption is documented in the Help file and also in the Excel documentation.*

To enter the second argument, *value_if_true*, click on the second box or press Tab. You want H8 to show an asterisk if sales met the quota, so enter * in the second edit box (see Figure 7.11). Because *value_if_true* is optional, you could omit this argument, and Excel would display the value TRUE, as you learned from reading the Help screen in Figure 7.9.

Figure 7.11

Entering the second argument

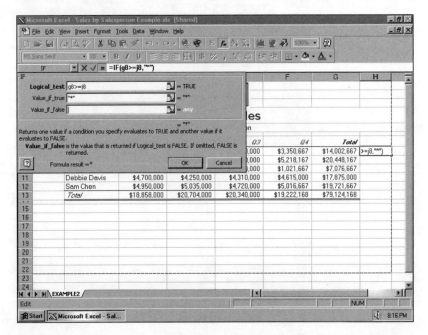

To enter the third argument, *value_if_false*, click on the third edit box or press Tab. If sales did not meet quota, you want H6 to be blank, so you enter two quote marks with nothing between them (see Figure 7.12). This argument also is optional. If you omit it, Excel will display the value FALSE.

Figure 7.12

Enter the third argument.

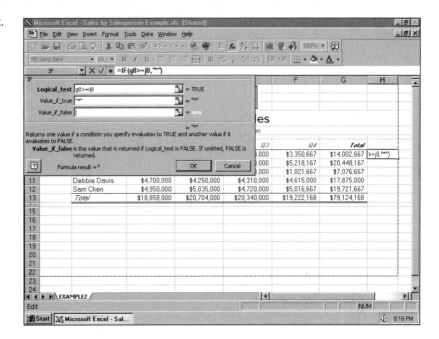

You now are finished with building your function. Click on the OK button. Figure 7.13 shows the completed IF function in the formula bar and the * at H6 to demonstrate that the salesperson met their quota. The Formula Palette put quotation marks around the asterisk in *argument2* and the space in *argument3*. The Formula Palette understands that you want these entries to be treated as text values (all text values must be enclosed in quotation marks).

Select H8 through H12 and choose Down under the Fill option from the Edit menu. Now cells H9 through H12 contain similar IF functions, which will show what other territories will win the trip. In the end, your analysis shows that Fred Jones, John Adams, and Charlene Smith will be winning the incentive trip.

Figure 7.13

The completed IF function

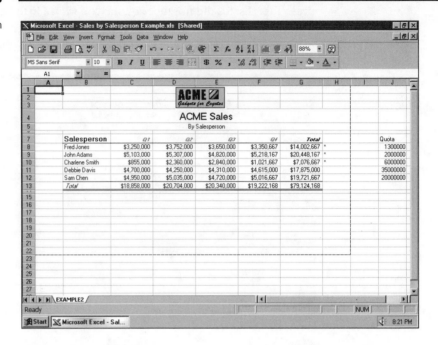

Nesting Functions

Excel allows you to include functions inside other functions. This process is called *nesting* functions. You can use functions and nested functions as arguments. Suppose, for example, that the vice president of sales gets to accompany her sales team on the incentive trip if Total YTD sales is greater than or equal to the sum of all quotas. One way to construct the IF function might be as follows:

```
=IF(SUM(G8:G12)>=SUM(J8:J12),"*****"," ")
```

The SUM function is nested within the IF function.

■ Entering Functions

You'll now see how to build a worksheet that calculates mortgage payments based on mortgage amount, points, interest and term. To build the worksheet, start with a blank worksheet and enter the values and labels shown in Table 7.1.

Table 7.1

Mortgage Payment
Worksheet Values

CELL	CONTENTS
C4	"Refinance Analysis"
B6	"Mortgage Amount"
C6	$80,000
B7	"Refinancing Fees"
C7	$1,300
B8	"Refinancing Points"
C8	$1,600
B10	"Total Amount Financed"
B12	"Points"
C12	2
B13	"Fixed Interest Rate"
C13	8.25%
B14	"Term in Years"
C14	30
B15	"Payment"

When you're done, your worksheet should look like the one shown in Figure 7.14.

For this analysis, you'll want to finance the fees and points along with the mortgage. To calculate the total amount financed, you will again use the SUM function. Select cell C10 and enter =**SUM(C6:C8)** so your worksheet looks like the one in Figure 7.15.

Note that the function appears in C10, as well as in the formula bar. When you press Enter, Excel calculates the equation, and $82,900 then appears in cell C10. Also, note that SUM appears in capital letters in the formula bar after you've entered it, telling you that Excel recognizes the function and can calculate the formula based on the argument you specified: the range C6:C8, as shown in Figure 7.16.

Figure 7.14

The Mortgage Payment Worksheet

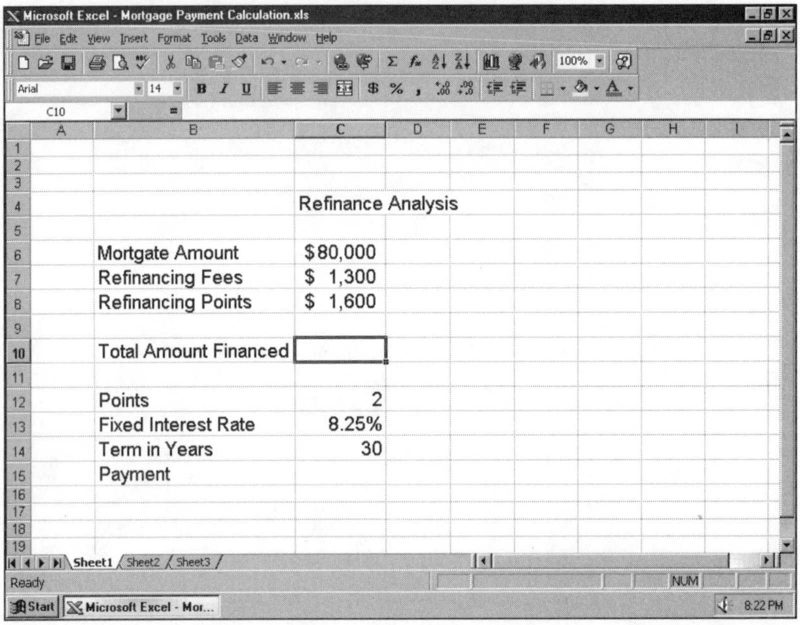

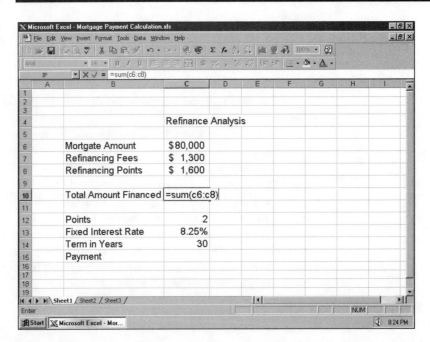

Figure 7.15

The SUM function keyed from the keyboard

Figure 7.16

The SUM function
calculated

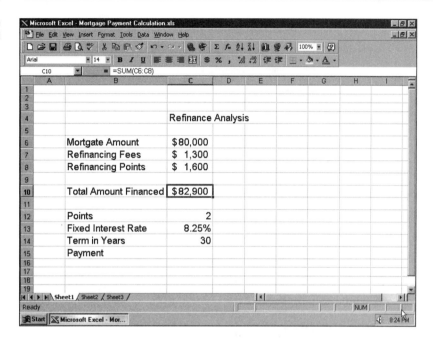

The next step is to construct the payment function. You can enter it from the keyboard as you did in C10, use the Paste Function process as you did in your sales recap worksheet, or use a combination of methods. For this function, you'll use the Paste Function dialog to get the syntax of the PMT function, and the Formula Palette to complete the function.

1. Select cell C15.

2. Activate the Paste Function dialog box (click on its button on the toolbar).

3. Select the Financial Category and then the function name PMT. Your screen should look like Figure 7.17.

Click on OK to paste the function and bring up the Formula Palette. You now need to fill in the fields of the Formula Palette, which is shown in Figure 7.18.

You'll notice that Rate, the first argument, is in bold. That means it is required. To enter the rate's cell, make the Rate field in the palette active and then click on cell C13. (You may need to click the Collapse Dialog button in order to see the cell. After you click on the cell, click the Collapse Dialog button again to restore the Formula Palette.) The cell reference will automatically be entered. Because the rate you enter is annual, but you want to calculate monthly payments, you will need to divide the rate by 12 months to make the

Figure 7.17

The PMT function
activated by Paste
Function

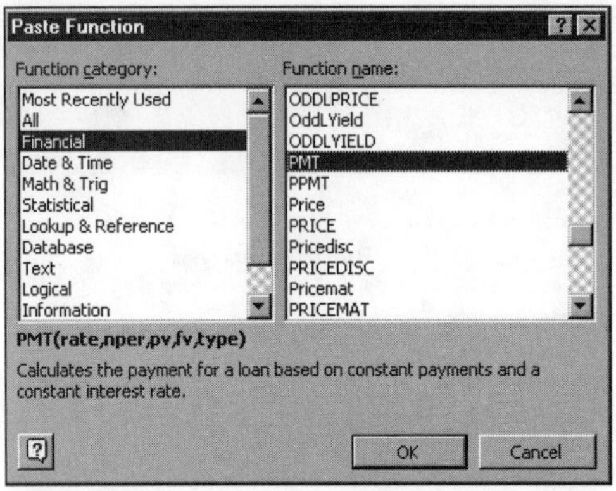

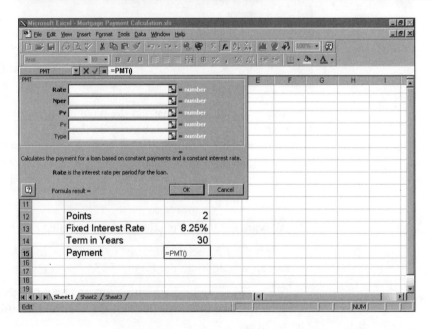

Figure 7.18

The Formula Palette for
the PMT function

function work properly. Type **/12** immediately after the cell reference in the Rate field to do so. Figure 7.19 shows the completed Rate argument.

The next step is to complete the rest of the arguments: *nper*, *pv*, *fv*, and *type*. If you want help with this part of the function construction, activate the Help screen.

Notice that *rate*, *nper* and *pv* are in bold, because they are also required arguments. The *fv* and *type* variables are optional arguments. As discussed in

Figure 7.19

The completed Rate
argument in the
Formula Palette

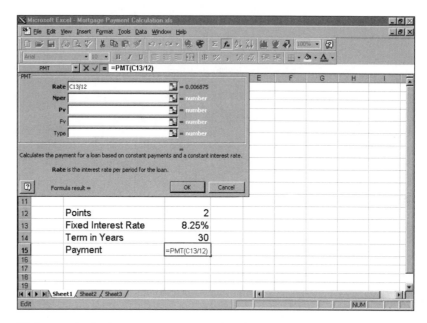

Help, *rate* is the interest rate per period (in this case, per month); *nper* is the total number of payment periods; *pv* represents the total payments' present value; *fv* is the future value, or cash balance after the last payment is made; and *type* indicates when payments are due. (Leases are calculated assuming payments are made at the beginning of each period—in *advance*, while loans are calculated assuming payments are made at the end of each period—in *arrears*.)

NOTE. *You must be consistent about the units you use for specifying* rate *and* nper. *If you use monthly payments on a four-year loan at 12 percent annual interest, use 12%/12 for* rate *and 4*12 for* nper.

To put this in simpler terms, you are making monthly payments, so your units must be in monthly terms. To complete the *Nper* field, make it active, click on cell C30, and then type ***12** after the cell reference to yield the total number of payments.

To enter the *Pv* argument, you may first note that you can't see the cell that contains the amount financed. It might be obscured by the Formula Palette, depending on how you're viewing your worksheet and the resolution of your screen. You have a couple of choices here. You can simply type in the cell reference if you know it (it's cell C10) or you can use the Collapse Dialog button on the far right side of the field. Clicking on this shrinks the Formula

Palette to its minimum size and lets you select cells that are otherwise obscured. Figure 7.20 shows the Formula Palette reduced in this fashion.

Figure 7.20

Using the Collapse Dialog button shrinks the Formula Palette so you can select cells behind it

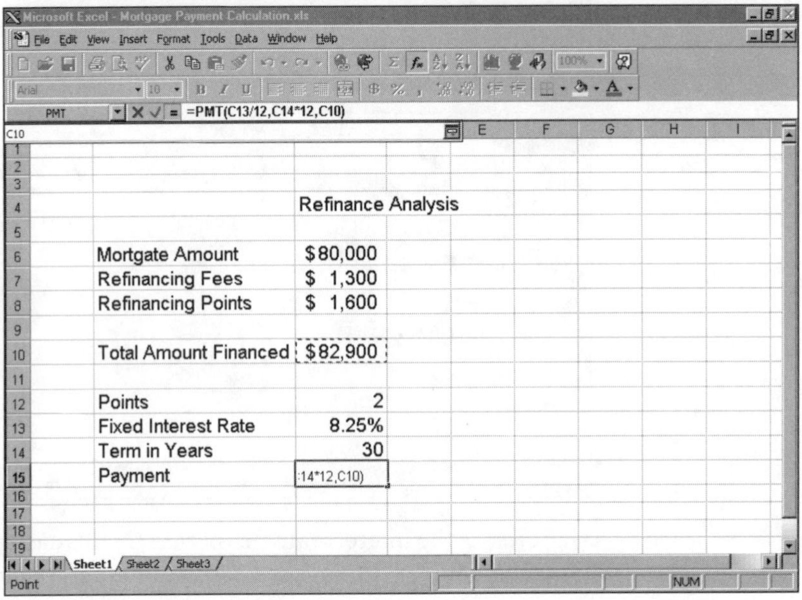

After selecting cell C10, click on the Collapse Dialog button again to restore the Formula Palette to its original size.

You do not need to complete the Fv and Type fields, because the future value for this loan will be zero, and the default for the Type field is already correct for this type of payment calculation. Click on the OK button to complete the formula and view the result, shown in Figure 7.21.

Note that the payment appears as ($622.80). The parentheses mean it is a negative number—money paid out.

You can use the Formula Palette in the following ways:

- When you enter a function from the keyboard, enter the equal sign and function name and press Ctrl+A to display the Formula Palette, then use it to assist you when you enter arguments.

- When you select a cell that contains a function and then activate the Paste Function button, the Formula Palette becomes active immediately so that you can make changes to arguments. You can also click the Edit Formula button on the Formula bar (the button displaying an equal symbol) to display the Formula Palette.

Figure 7.21

The PMT function
complete

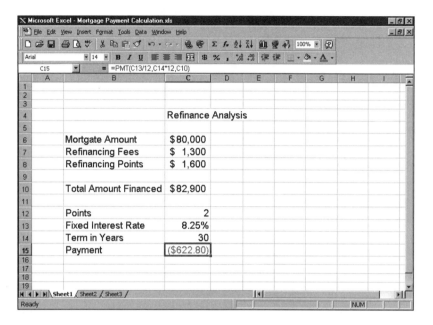

- When you enter a formula, after you type the equal symbol you can select a function from the Function Box located on the left side of the Formula bar.

- Use the same order of precedence for Excel functions as you do for other Excel formulas. Excel performs operations in the following order:

()	Parentheses
:	Range
Space	Intersection
,	Union
-	Negation (single operand)
%	Percent
^	Exponentiation
* and /	Multiplication and Division
+ and -	Addition and Subtraction
&	Text joining
=	Equals

<	Less than
>	Greater than
<=	Less than or equal
>=	Greater than or equal
<>	Not equal

■ Troubleshooting Function and Syntax Messages

If a function name remains in lowercase after you complete the formula and press Enter, check for spelling errors in the function name.

TIP. *Get into the habit of using lowercase so that Excel can help you spot spelling errors. When you enter a function name in lowercase letters and then press Enter, the function name will be converted to all uppercase letters by Excel. If Excel doesn't recognize the function name (and it won't if it's misspelled), the function name will remain in lowercase.*

When Excel displays an error message rather than a calculated result from the worksheet function, check the following:

- Check for typing errors.

- Make sure all your parentheses match and are in the right places.

- Make sure all the required arguments are defined, and in the order that Excel expects to see them.

- Make sure all data types are valid for each argument: you can't use numbers with arguments that expect text, and vice-versa.

- Make sure cell references contain valid data. Use the auditing tool to help trace any dependencies your referenced cells have on other cells.

- Make sure you leave out commas in numbers you enter into a formula, or Excel will think you are separating arguments. (1,000 should be entered as **1000**, for example.)

- When you omit an optional argument and you want to define another argument later in the list, make sure you place a comma (,) as a placeholder for the omitted argument.

Excel also displays formula errors instead of function results when you make an error in a formula that serves as an argument. These errors include:

- #DIV/0, means you entered a formula with a division-by-zero error

- #N/A, means that some data referred to by the formula isn't available

- #NAME?, means that text entered in a formula wasn't recognized by Excel

- #NULL!, means that an intersection you specified doesn't actually intersect

- #NUM!, means that you entered an incorrect value as an argument

- #REF!, means that a cell reference isn't valid

- #VALUE!, means that an argument you provided doesn't use the type of value that Excel expects for that argument

When you see these error messages, carefully inspect the arguments you provided to the function, using the guide above as a starting point to identifying the incorrect argument.

- *Database Functions*
- *Date and Time Functions*
- *DLL and External Functions*
- *Engineering Functions*
- *Financial Functions*
- *Information Functions*
- *Logical Functions*

- *Look-Up and Reference Functions*
- *Math and Trigonometric Functions*
- *Statistical Functions*
- *Text Functions*
- *User-Defined Functions*

Complete Guide to Excel Functions

THIS CHAPTER PICKS UP WHERE THE LAST ONE LEFT OFF, SHOWING in more detail the functions available in Excel 97 for Windows. This reference explores the following information about each function:

- The function's group or category, as defined by the Function Wizard
- The purpose of the function
- The correct syntax of the function
- The function's available arguments or variables

NOTE. *Keep this function reference in mind as you use Excel functions in your daily work.*

The last chapter discussed ways to use functions in your Excel spreadsheets. This chapter provides you with a complete guide to the functions available in Excel.

NOTE. *All of the functions discussed here are included with Excel. However, not all of them are available from a typical installation. To add these, run Excel's Setup program (or run Office Setup and then choose Microsoft Excel) and select Add/Remove Components. Make sure the Add-Ins box is checked, and click the Configure button. Check the box for the Analysis ToolPak and choose OK twice (three times if you're using Office Setup). Now you can add the remainder of the functions from the Tools menu. Select Add-Ins... and click the Analysis ToolPak check box. This adds almost 100 functions to the Function Wizard's listings. See Chapter 9, "Mastering Excel Analytical Tools," for more information about installing the Analysis ToolPak.*

The functions are divided into the groups you see in the Function Wizard for easy reference, as shown in the following list:

- Financial
- Date and Time
- Math and Trigonometric
- Statistical
- Look-Up and Reference
- Database
- Text
- Logical
- Information
- Engineering

We've include two additional groups of functions in this chapter to complete the set of functions available in Excel. These two additional groups are shown below:

- DDE and External
- User Defined

Within each category, functions are listed alphabetically. An explanation of what each function does is provided, as well as its correct syntax and options available with the function.

NOTE. *The category DDE and External Functions is not included for use by the Function Wizard, but is included with Excel and documented in the Help Function Reference.*

TIP. *To see examples of each function in use, consult the built-in help that accompanies Excel. From the Help Contents tab, double-click on Creating Formulas and Auditing Workbooks, and then double-click on Worksheet Function Reference. Double-click the function category to access examples of the functions alphabetically by function name.*

In addition, you can open the worksheet SAMPLES.XLS, which you can find in the EXAMPLES folder within the EXCEL folder (or within the Office folder, if you installed Excel as part of the Office 97 suite). This worksheet contains examples of almost all the Excel worksheet functions correctly formatted and operating. Several of the other spreadsheet examples in this directory also illustrate worksheet functions.

■ Database Functions

The database and list-management functions included in Excel allow you to extract information from a database or list, and let you perform operations on the information you have extracted. With these functions, you can access databases you have defined within Excel and databases you maintain with database software that is external to Excel. If you are working with an external database, you can bring your data in with SQLREQUEST and then manipulate the data using functions that work on databases internal to Excel. All database function examples refer to Figure 8.1, which shows a sample database defined by the range A1:E10.

NOTE. *When you enter a function into a worksheet cell, remember to include an equal sign (=) before the function's name.*

DAVERAGE

Purpose: Arithmetically averages the database entries you have selected.
Syntax: DAVERAGE(database,field,criteria)
Arguments: Database is the range of cells that define the database. Field is the named field or range of cells representing the column to average. Criteria is the named field or range of cells containing any criteria that define which values of field to include in the average.

Figure 8.1

A sample Excel worksheet using database functions

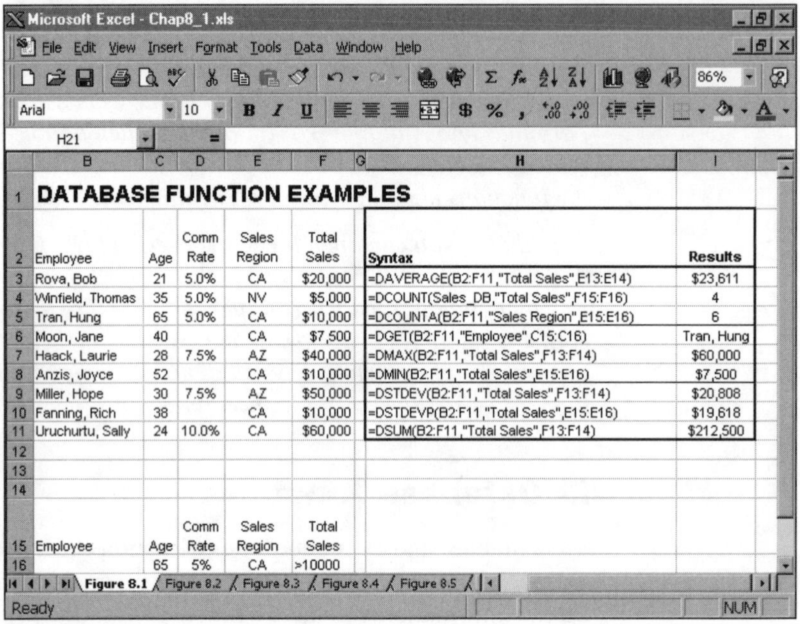

	B	C	D	E	F	H	I
1	DATABASE FUNCTION EXAMPLES						
2	Employee	Age	Comm Rate	Sales Region	Total Sales	Syntax	Results
3	Rova, Bob	21	5.0%	CA	$20,000	=DAVERAGE(B2:F11,"Total Sales",E13:E14)	$23,611
4	Winfield, Thomas	35	5.0%	NV	$5,000	=DCOUNT(Sales_DB,"Total Sales",F15:F16)	4
5	Tran, Hung	65	5.0%	CA	$10,000	=DCOUNTA(B2:F11,"Sales Region",E15:E16)	6
6	Moon, Jane	40		CA	$7,500	=DGET(B2:F11,"Employee",C15:C16)	Tran, Hung
7	Haack, Laurie	28	7.5%	AZ	$40,000	=DMAX(B2:F11,"Total Sales",F13:F14)	$60,000
8	Anzis, Joyce	52		CA	$10,000	=DMIN(B2:F11,"Total Sales",E15:E16)	$7,500
9	Miller, Hope	30	7.5%	AZ	$50,000	=DSTDEV(B2:F11,"Total Sales",F13:F14)	$20,808
10	Fanning, Rich	38		CA	$10,000	=DSTDEVP(B2:F11,"Total Sales",E15:E16)	$19,618
11	Uruchurtu, Sally	24	10.0%	CA	$60,000	=DSUM(B2:F11,"Total Sales",F13:F14)	$212,500
12							
13							
14							
15	Employee	Age	Comm Rate	Sales Region	Total Sales		
16		65	5%	CA	>10000		

DCOUNT

Purpose: Counts the number of cells containing numbers that match the criteria defined in the last argument.

Syntax: DCOUNT(database,field,criteria)

Arguments: Database is the range of cells that define the database. Field is the named field or range of cells representing the column in which to count. (The field argument is optional. If it is absent, the count applies to the entire database). Criteria is the named field or range of cells containing the conditions that define which fields to include in the count.

DCOUNTA

Purpose: Counts the number of nonblank cells matching the criteria defined in the last argument.

Syntax: DCOUNTA(database,field,criteria)

Arguments: Database is the range of cells that define the database. Field is the named field or range of cells representing the column in which to count. Criteria is the named field or range of cells containing any conditions that define which fields to include in the count.

DGET

Purpose: Gets a single value from a field that matches the criteria identified in the third argument.

Syntax: DGET(database,field,criteria)

Arguments: Database is the range of cells that define the database. Field is the named field or range of cells representing the column from which to extract the value. Criteria is the named field or range of cells containing any conditions that define which value to extract. This function returns the #VALUE! error value if no match is found. It returns the #NUM! error value if more than one match is found.

DMAX

Purpose: Gets the largest number in a column of data records.

Syntax: DMAX(database,field,criteria)

Arguments: Database is the range of cells that define the database. Field is the named field or range of cells representing the column in which to find the maximum value. The field argument can be represented either by the field name enclosed in quotation marks or as a number representing the position of the column in the list. Criteria is the named field or range of cells containing any conditions that define any constraints on the search for a maximum value (such as within all the employees whose name begins with "J" represented in the "Years with Company" column).

DMIN

Purpose: Gets the smallest number in a field that matches the criteria you specify.

Syntax: DMIN(database,field,criteria)

Arguments: Database is the range of cells that define the database. Field is the named field or range of cells representing the column in which to find the minimum value. The field argument can be represented either by the field name enclosed in quotation marks or as a number representing the position of the column in the list. Criteria is the named field or range of cells containing any criteria that define any constraints on the search for a minimum value (such as within all the employees whose name begins with "J" represented in the "Years with Company" column).

DPRODUCT

Purpose: Multiplies (takes the product of) the numbers in the column identified by the field parameters that match the stated criteria.

Syntax: DPRODUCT(database,field,criteria)

Arguments: Database is the range of cells that define the database. Field is the named field or range of cells representing the column in which to multiply. The field argument can be represented either by the field name enclosed in quotation marks or as a number representing the position of the column in the list. Criteria is the named field or range of cells containing any criteria that define which fields to include in the product.

DSTDEV

Purpose: Calculates the standard deviation for a sample of cells in the column named in the field parameter. The criteria parameter defines the way in which the sample is selected.

Syntax: DSTDEV(database,field,criteria)

Arguments: Database is the range of cells that define the database. Field is the named field or range of cells representing the column for which to calculate the standard deviation. Criteria is the named field or range of cells containing any criteria that define which fields to include in the calculation.

DSTDEVP

Purpose: Calculates the standard deviation for a sample of cells in the column named in the field parameter as if the cells defined were the entire population. The criteria parameter defines the way in which the sample is selected.

Syntax: DSTDEVP(database,field,criteria)

Arguments: Database is the range of cells that define the database. Field is the named field or range of cells representing the column for which to calculate the standard deviation. The field argument can be represented either by the field name enclosed in quotation marks or as a number representing the position of the column in the list. Criteria is the named field or range of cells containing any criteria that define which fields to include in the calculation.

DSUM

Purpose: Sums the numbers in the column named by the field parameter that meet the specified criteria.

Syntax: DSUM(database,field,criteria)

Arguments: Database is the range of cells that define the database. Field is the named field or range of cells representing the column of numbers to sum. The field argument can be represented by either the field name enclosed in quotation marks or as a number representing the position of the column in the list. Criteria is the named field or range of cells containing any conditions that define which fields to include in the calculation.

DVAR

Purpose: Estimates the variance for a sample of cells in the column named in the field parameter. The criteria parameter defines the way in which the sample is selected.

Syntax: DVAR(database,field,criteria)

Arguments: Database is the range of cells that define the database. Field is the named field or range of cells representing the column containing the values to calculate. The field argument can be represented either by the field name enclosed in quotation marks or as a number representing the position of the column in the list. Criteria is the named field or range of cells containing any conditions that define which fields to include in the calculation.

DVARP

Purpose: Calculates the variance of a population based on the entire population, not just a sample. The field parameter defines the column to be used in the function. The criteria parameter refers to the cells that contain the conditions you set.

Syntax: DVARP(database,field,criteria)

Arguments: Database is the range of cells that define the database. Field is the named field or range of cells representing the column for which to calculate the variance. The field argument can be represented either by the field name enclosed in quotation marks or as a number representing the position of the column in the list. Criteria is the named field or range of cells containing any criteria that define which fields to include in the calculation.

GETPIVOTDATA (New in Excel 97!)

Purpose: Retrieves data from in a PivotTable. GETPIVOTDATA can also be used to retrieve summary data from a PivotTable, assuming that the summary data is visible in the PivotTable.

Syntax: GETPIVOTDATA(pivot_table,name)

Arguments: Pivot_Table is a reference to a cell or range of cells in the PivotTable that contains the data you want to retrieve. Name is a text string enclosed in double quotation marks that describes the cell in the PivotTable containing the value you want to retrieve. For example, if your PivotTable contains one row field in cell A1 that represents employees, and you wanted to retrieve the Sum of February sales for an employee named "Wright," then your function statement would look like: GETPIVOTDATA(A1,"Wright Sum of February").

SQL.REQUEST

Purpose: Runs a external data-source query from within an Excel worksheet. SQL.REQUEST statements do not need to be invoked from an Excel macro. Results of an SQL.REQUEST statement are returned in an array. External data sources must support ODBC conventions to be used with this statement.

Syntax: SQL.REQUEST(connection_string,output_ref, driver_prompt,query_text,col_names_logical)

Arguments: Connection_string supplies information including data-source name, user ID, and passwords, which are required by the data-source driver. The connection_string must adhere to the driver's format. If the connection_string exceeds 250 characters, you must enter it as an array. For information on creating arrays, consult Excel's Help feature. Table 8.1 shows examples of connection strings for three drivers.

Table 8.1

Sample Connection String for Three Databases

DRIVER	CONNECTION_STRING
dBASE	DSN=STind;PWD=woof
SQL Server	DSN=Server;UID=fhoulet; PWD=123;Database=Pubs
ORACLE	DSN=My Oracle Data Source;DBQ=MYSER VER; UID=ForrH;PWD=Quack

NOTE. *You may be wondering about the abbreviations used in the connection_strings above. If so, here's the definitions: DSN = Data Source Name, UID = User Identification, PWD = Password, and DBQ = Database Query.*

Output_ref is the cell in your Excel spreadsheet into which you want the completed connection string placed. Driver_prompt is a number that defines the way in that the dialog box for the external database driver is displayed. Its values are shown in Table 8.2.

Query_text is the text of the actual query statement you are sending to the external database. If Query_text exceeds 255 characters, you must enter the query's text in a vertical range of cells, and then use that range of cells in place of Query_text.

Column_names_logical takes a value of TRUE if you want column names returned as the first row of results, and a value of FALSE if you do not. If column_names are not entered, then no column names are returned.

Table 8.2

Driver_prompt Values

DRIVER_PROMPT	DESCRIPTION
1	Dialog box is always displayed.
2	Dialog box is displayed only if there is not enough information in the function parameters to complete the connection to the external database. All options in the dialog box are available.
3	Dialog box is displayed only if there is not enough information in the function parameters to complete the connection to the external database. Dialog-box options are only available for required options.
4	Dialog box is not displayed. If no connection is made, the function returns an error.

SQL.REQUEST returns an array of data if it is successful, and the #N/A error if it is not.

■ Date and Time Functions

Date and time functions allow you to look up dates and times, and to perform mathematical calculations on dates and times with ease. Excel 97 for Windows uses a serial number system to work with dates. Although this system might seem strange at first, it calculates dates and times efficiently.

In Excel's system, each date between January 1, 1900, and December 31, 2078, is assigned a serial number between 0 and 63,918. Times are assigned serial numbers as well, so you can represent a date and time in the same string, separated by a decimal point. The number to the left of the decimal is the date serial number, while the number to the right is the time serial number. The number 367.5, for instance, represents 12:00 noon on January 1, 1901.

Many of the date and time functions work with serial numbers. Their use is demonstrated in the worksheet shown in Figure 8.2.

DATE

Purpose: Returns a date's serial number.
Syntax: DATE(year,month,day)
Arguments: Each argument is a number representing the year, month, and day for which a serial number is desired. If the day value is larger than the number of days in the month indicated, the month value will be incremented and the extra days will be added to the day value for the incremented month. DATE(91,1,35) gives the same serial number as DATE(91,2,4), for example.

Figure 8.2

A worksheet showing the use of date and time functions

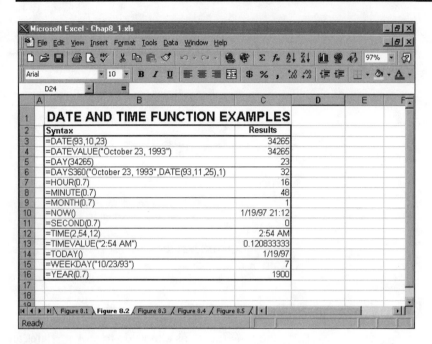

DATEVALUE

Purpose: Returns a serial number for a date written as text, as long as the date falls between January 1, 1900, and December 31, 2078.

Syntax: DATEVALUE(date_text)

Arguments: The only argument is a date written as text and enclosed in quotation marks. If the year is not present, Excel will assume that the date refers to the year set on the system clock. If the year is included, separate it with a comma. The format is better expressed as DATEVALUE(month day, year) where month is at least the first three characters of the month, day is simply the day of the month, and year is either a two-digit or four-digit number representing the year. Notice that with our alternate syntax, there is no comma between month and day.

DAY

Purpose: Converts a serial number to a day of the month.

Syntax: DAY(serial_number)

Arguments: Serial_number is a number you want to convert to a date. It can be expressed either as a serial number or text enclosed in quotation marks, such as "8-2-75".

DAYS360

Purpose: Calculates the number of days between two dates based on a 360-day year (twelve thirty-day months). This function is used when an accounting system is based on twelve thirty-day months.

Syntax: DAYS360(start_date,end_date,method)

Arguments: Start_date and end_date can be text strings (for example, "03/02/96" or "03-02-1996") or serial numbers. Method takes a value of 1 if you are using the US (NASD) method. Method is 2 if you are using the European method of calculating a 360-day year. If you omit method, Excel assumes the US convention.

EDATE

Purpose: Gives the serial number for a date and the indicated number of months afterward or before.

Syntax: EDATE(start_date,number_of_months)

Arguments: Start_date is serial number for the date in question. Number_of_months is the number of months after start_date. You can use a negative number to calculate the number of months before a date.

NOTE. *If EDATE is not listed in with the other Excel functions, you'll need to install the Analysis ToolPak. Step-by-step instructions on how to install the Analysis ToolPak are in Excel's on-line Help. From Excel's Help menu, click on Contents and Index, select Index, and type Analysis ToolPak. Click the Display button twice to see instructions for installing.*

EOMONTH

Purpose: Gives the serial number for a date at the end of the month, and for the indicated number of months afterward or before.

Syntax: EOMONTH(start_date,number_of_months)

Arguments: Start_date is serial number for the date in question. Number_of_months is the number of months after start_date. You can use a negative number to calculate the number of months before a date.

NOTE. *If EOMONTH is not listed in with the other Excel functions, you'll need to install the Analysis ToolPak. Step-by-step instructions on how to install the Analysis ToolPak are in Excel's on-line Help. From Excel's Help menu, click on Contents and Index, select Index, and type Analysis ToolPak. Click the Display button twice to see instructions for installing.*

HOUR

Purpose: Converts a serial number for a time into an hour, represented as an integer (0 through 23).

Syntax: HOUR(serial_number)

Arguments: Serial_number is a serial number that represents a date-time code. You also can include the time string as text, surrounded by quotation marks.

MINUTE

Purpose: Converts a serial number for a time into a minute expressed as an integer (0 through 59).

Syntax: MINUTE(serial_number)

Arguments: Serial_number is a serial number that represents a date-time code. You also can include the time string as text, surrounded by quotation marks.

MONTH

Purpose: Converts a serial number for a date into a month returned as an integer (1 through 12).

Syntax: MONTH(serial_number)

Arguments: Serial_number is a serial number that represents a date-time code. You also can include the time string as text, surrounded by quotation marks.

NETWORKDAYS

Purpose: Calculates the number of working days, excluding weekends and identified holidays, between two dates.

Syntax: NETWORKDAYS(start_date,end_date,holidays)

Arguments: Start_date and end_date are serial numbers representing the dates in question. Holidays is an optional list of serial numbers to exclude from the count of working days.

NOTE. *If NETWORKDAYS is not listed in with the other Excel functions, you'll need to install the Analysis ToolPak. Step-by-step instructions on how to install the Analysis ToolPak are in Excel's on-line Help. From Excel's Help menu, click on Contents and Index, select Index and type Analysis ToolPak. Click the Display button twice to see instructions for installing.*

NOW

Purpose: Gives the serial number for the current date and time.

Syntax: NOW()

Arguments: None. The current data and time is determined from the computer's internal clock.

SECOND

Purpose: Converts a serial number for a time into a second returned as an integer (0 through 60).

Syntax: SECOND(serial_number)

Arguments: Serial_number is a serial number that represents a date-time code. You also can include the time string as text, surrounded by quotation marks.

TIME

Purpose: Gives the serial number for the time indicated. A time serial number is reported as a decimal fraction (for example, .99999, 11:59:59pm).

Syntax: TIME(hour, minute, second)

Arguments: Hour is a number (0 through 23) indicating the hour, minute a number (0 through 59) indicating the minute, and second a number (0 through 59) indicating the second.

TIMEVALUE

Purpose: Gives the serial number (0 through 0.99999) for a time represented as text.

Syntax: TIMEVALUE(time_text)

Arguments: Time_text is a text string that represents the time in question.

TODAY

Purpose: Gives the serial number for the current date.

Syntax: TODAY()

Arguments: None. The date is determined from the computer's internal clock.

WEEKDAY

Purpose: Converts a serial number to a day of the week.

Syntax: WEEKDAY(serial_number,return_type)

Arguments: Serial_number is the date-time code to be converted or a text representing the date. Return_type takes values from Table 8.3.

WORKDAY (New in Excel 97!)

Purpose: Returns the serial date number of a workday that falls before or after a given start date. Weekends and user specified holidays are excluded as workdays.

Table 8.3

Return Types for
WEEKDAY

RETURN_TYPE	RANGE FOR NUMBER RETURNED
1 (or omitted)	1 (Sunday) to 7 (Saturday)
2	1 (Monday) to 7 (Sunday)
3	0 (Monday) to 6 (Sunday)

NOTE. *If WORKDAY is not listed with the other Excel functions, you'll need to install the Analysis ToolPak. Step-by-step instructions on how to install the Analysis ToolPak are in Excel's on-line Help. From Excel's Help menu, click on Contents and Index, select Index, and type Analysis ToolPak. Click the Display button twice to see instructions for installing.*

Syntax: WORKDAY(start_date,days,holidays)

Arguments: Start_date is the user specified start date. Days is the number of nonweekend and nonholiday days before or after start_date. A positive value for days returns a date after the start date; a negative value returns a date before the start date. Holidays can be a range of cells or an array of numbers that represent the dates to exclude.

YEAR

Purpose: Gives the year (1900 through 2078) associated with a serial number.

Syntax: YEAR(serial_number)

Arguments: Serial_number is the serial number to be converted. You also can use a text string to represent this date.

YEARFRAC

Purpose: Gives the fraction of the year represented by the number of whole days between two dates.

Syntax: YEARFRAC(start_date,end_date,basis)

Arguments: Start_date and end_date are the serial numbers representing the two dates. Basis is method Excel should use to count days. Valid Basis arguments are shown in Table 8.4.

NOTE. *If YEARFRAC is not listed in with the other Excel functions, you'll need to install the Analysis ToolPak. Step-by-step instructions on how to install the Analysis ToolPak are in Excel's on-line Help. From Excel's Help menu, click on Contents and Index, select Index and type Analysis ToolPak. Click the Display button twice to see instructions for installing.*

Table 8.4

Values of Basis for
YEARFRAC

BASIS	DESCRIPTION
0 (or omitted)	30/360 (US/NASD)
1	Actual/Actual
2	Actual/360
3	Actual/365
4	30/360 (European)

■ DLL and External Functions

Excel's external functions permit you to call routines in Dynamic Link Libraries (DLLs, which are files of executable functions external to Excel. Using this feature, you can execute code that belongs to other applications or that you have programmed yourself and stored in a DLL. External routines are the ultimate in customization. You can make Excel do anything you want it to, as long as you can program the function that will execute the activity. The catch is that you need a fairly sophisticated knowledge of Windows programming to create a DLL.

CALL

Purpose: Calls a function in a Dynamic Link Library or other type of code resource.

Syntax: CALL(register_id,argument1,...) or CALL(module_text,procedure,type_text,argument1,...)

Arguments: Use the first form of the function to call a DLL or code resource previously registered using the REGISTER.ID function. Use the second form to simultaneously register and call a DLL or code resource.

In the first form, register_id is a value returned from a call of the REGISTER.ID function. Argument1 and subsequent arguments are the arguments to be passed to the function called.

In the second form, module_text is a text string enclosed in quotes identifying the name of the DLL or other code resource. Procedure is a text string specifying the name of the function you are calling. Type_text is a text string specifying the name of the Windows data type returned by the function — see the Excel Development Kit documentation and the Windows Software Development Kit documentation for more information about Windows data types). Argument1 and subsequent arguments are the arguments passed to the function.

REGISTER.ID

Purpose: Collects the register ID of a Dynamic Link Library or code resource. The register ID is a unique number that identifies the DLL or code resource to Excel. If the DLL or code resource has not previously been registered, the function will register it and then return the ID.

Syntax: REGISTER.ID(module_text,procedure,type_text)

Arguments: Module_text is a text string that gives the name of the DLL or other code resource containing the function. Procedure is a text string that specifies the name of the function. Type_text is a text string specifying the name of the Windows data type returned by the function — see the Excel Development Kit documentation and the Windows Software Development Kit documentation for more information about Windows data types). If the function has already been registered somewhere else on a worksheet, you can omit type_text.

■ Engineering Functions

Excel's engineering functions allow engineers to include specialized calculations and conversions in their worksheets. To use these functions, however, you must install the Analysis ToolPak Add-in.

BESSELI, BESSELJ, BESSELK, BESSELY

Purpose: These four functions return the values of different forms of the Bessel function. BESSELI returns the modified Bessel function $In(x)$, BESSELJ the Bessel function $Jn(x)$, BESSELK the modified Bessel function $Kn(x)$, and BESSELY the Bessel function $Yn(x)$.

Syntax: BESSELI(x,n), BESSELJ(x,n), BESSELK(x,n), or BESSELY(x,n)

Arguments: X represents the value at which the function evaluates. N is the function's order.

BIN2DEC, BIN2HEX, BIN2OCT

Purpose: These three functions convert binary numbers to other bases. BIN2DEC converts from binary to decimal, BIN2HEX from binary to hexadecimal, and BIN2OCT from binary to octal.

Syntax: BIN2DEC(number), BIN2HEX(number,places), or BIN2OCT(number,places)

Arguments: Number is the binary number to be converted. Places is the number of characters to use in the conversion. If the number of places is omitted, Excel uses the minimum number of characters necessary. If you specify extra characters, Excel pads with leading zeros.

COMPLEX

Purpose: Combines real and imaginary coefficients, and converts them to a complex number.

Syntax: COMPLEX(real_num,i_num,suffix)

Arguments: Real_num is the real coefficient, i_num is the imaginary coefficient, and suffix is the suffix to be used to identify the imaginary component of the converted complex number. (If suffix is omitted as an argument, the suffix "i" is used. Note that the suffix must be expressed with a lowercase letter).

CONVERT

Purpose: Converts numbers among several units of measurement.

Syntax: CONVERT(number,from_unit,to_unit)

Arguments: Number is the number to be converted from one unit to another. It is a value expressed in from_units. From_unit is a text string denoting the measurement system to convert from. To_unit is a text string denoting the measurement system to which you want to convert. Table 8.5 shows the text strings you can use to represent various units of measure as arguments to the CONVERT function.

Table 8.5

Text Strings for Use as From_unit or To_unit

UNIT	TEXT STRING
Angstrom	"ang"
Atmosphere	"atm"
BTU	"BTU"
Cup	"cup"
Day	"day"
Degree Celsius	"C"
Degree Fahrenheit	"F"
Degree Kelvin	"K"

**Table 8.5
(Continued)**

Text Strings for Use as
From_unit or To_unit

UNIT	TEXT STRING
Dyne	"dyn"
Electron volt	"eV"
Erg	"e"
Fluid ounce	"oz"
Foot	"ft"
Foot-pound	"flb"
Gallon	"gal"
Gauss	"ga"
Gram	"g"
Horsepower	"HP"
Horsepower-hour	"HPh"
Hour	"hr"
Inch	"in"
IT calorie	"cal"
Joule	"J"
Liter	"l"
Meter	"m"
Minute	"mn"
mm of Mercury	"mmHg"
Nautical mile	"Nmi"
Newton	"N"
Ounce mass (avoir-dupois)	"ozm"
Pascal	"Pa"
Pica (1/72 in.)	"Pica"

UNIT	TEXT STRING
Pint	"pt"
Pound force	"lbf"
Pound mass (avoir-dupois)	"lbm"
Quart	"qt"
Second	"sec"
Slug	"sg"
Statute mile	"mi"
Tablespoon	"tbs"
Teaspoon	"tsp"
Tesla	"T"
Thermodynamic cal-orie	"c"
U (atomic mass unit)	"u"
Watt	"W"
Watt-hour	"Wh"
Yard	"yd"
Year	"yr"

Table 8.6 shows the set of prefixes that can be added to the text strings for metric measurements.

COMMON METRIC PREFIX	MULTIPLIER FOR MEASUREMENT UNIT	TEXT STRING PREFIX TO ADD IN CONVERT
atto	1E-18	"a"
centi	1E-02	"c"

COMMON METRIC PREFIX	MULTIPLIER FOR MEASUREMENT UNIT	TEXT STRING PREFIX TO ADD IN CONVERT
deci	1E-01	"d"
dekao	1E+01	"e"
exa	1E+18	"E"
femto	1E-15	"f"
giga	1E+09	"G"
hecto	1E+02	"h"
kilo	1E+03	"k"
mega	1E+06	"M"
micro	1E-06	"u"
milli	1E-03	"m"
nano	1E-09	"n"
peta	1E+15	"P"
pico	1E-12	"p"
tera	1E+12	"T"

If a conversion is not possible for some reason, the function will returns the #N/A error value.

DEC2BIN, DEC2HEX, DEC2OCT

Purpose: These three functions convert decimal numbers to other bases. DEC2BIN converts from decimal to binary, DEC2HEX from decimal to hexadecimal, and DEC2OCT from decimal to octal.

Syntax: DEC2BIN(number,places),DEC2HEX(number, places), or DEC2OCT(number,places)

Arguments: Number is the decimal number to be converted. Places is the number of characters to use in the conversion. If the number of places is omitted, Excel uses the minimum number of characters necessary. If you specify extra characters, Excel pads with leading zeros.

DELTA

Purpose: Verifies that two numbers are equal, returning a value of 1 if so and 0 if not.

Syntax: DELTA(number1,number2)

Arguments: Number1 and number2 are the two numbers whose equality are to be verified. If number2 is omitted, Excel assumes the value is zero.

ERF

Purpose: Integrates the error function between the specified lower and upper limits.

Syntax: ERF(lower_limit,upper_limit)

Arguments: The two arguments are the lower and upper limits for integration. If upper_limit is omitted, the function integrates between lower_limit and 0.

ERFC

Purpose: Evaluates the complementary ERF function between the value specified and 0.

Syntax: ERFC(x)

Arguments: X is the lower bound for the ERF function involved in the calculation.

GESTEP

Purpose: Determines whether a number is greater than the specified threshold value. This function returns the value 1 if number>=step, and 0 otherwise.

Syntax: GESTEP(number,step)

Arguments: Number is the number to be tested. Step is the threshold value. If step is omitted, the threshold of 0 is used.

HEX2BIN, HEX2DEC, HEX2OCT

Purpose: These three functions convert hexadecimal numbers to other bases. HEX2BIN converts from hexadecimal to binary, HEX2DEC from hexadecimal to decimal, and HEX2OCT from hexadecimal to octal.

Syntax: HEX2BIN(number, places), HEX2DEC(number), or HEX2OCT(number, places)

Arguments: Number is the hexadecimal number to be converted. Places is the number of characters to use in the conversion. If the number of places is omitted, Excel uses the minimum number of characters necessary. If you specify extra characters, Excel pads with leading zeros.

IMABS

Purpose: Gives the absolute value in modulus form of a complex number.
Syntax: IMABS(inumber)
Arguments: Inumber is that complex number in x+yi or x+yj format for which you want the absolute value.

IMAGINARY

Purpose: Gives the imaginary coefficient of a complex number.
Syntax: IMAGINARY(inumber)
Arguments: Inumber is a complex number in x+yi or x+ji form for which you want the imaginary coefficient.

IMARGUMENT

Purpose: Calculates the argument of a complex number, and returns it as an angle measured in radians.
Syntax: IMARGUMENT(inumber)
Arguments: Inumber is the complex number whose argument you want.

IMCONJUGATE

Purpose: Calculates and returns the complex conjugate of a complex number.
Syntax: IMCONJUGATE(inumber)
Arguments: Inumber is the complex number in x+yi or x+yj form for which you want the conjugate.

IMCOS

Purpose: Calculates and returns the cosine of a complex number.
Syntax: IMCOS(inumber)
Arguments: Inumber is the complex number in x+yi or x+yj form for which you want the cosine. Inumber is in text format.

IMDIV

Purpose: Divides two complex numbers in x+yi or x+yj text format and returns the quotient.
Syntax: IMDIV(number1,number2)
Arguments: Number1 and number2 are complex numbers in x+yi or x+yj form. Number1 is the numerator or dividend. Number2 is the denominator or divisor.

IMEXP

Purpose: Calculates and returns the exponential for a complex number.
Syntax: IMEXP(inumber)
Arguments: Inumber is the complex number in x+yi or x+yj form for which you want the exponential.

IMLN

Purpose: Calculates and returns the natural logarithm for a complex number.
Syntax: IMLN(inumber)
Arguments: Inumber is the complex number in x+yi or x+yj form for which you want the natural logarithm.

IMLOG10

Purpose: Calculates and returns the common logarithm (base 10) for a complex number.
Syntax: IMLOG10(inumber)
Arguments: Inumber is the complex number in x+yi or x+yj form for which you want the common logarithm.

IMLOG2

Purpose: Calculates and returns the base-2 logarithm for a complex number.
Syntax: IMLOG2(inumber)
Arguments: Inumber is the complex number in x+yi or x+yj form for which you want the base-2 logarithm.

IMPOWER

Purpose: Calculates a complex number raised to an integer power.
Syntax: IMPOWER(inumber,power)
Arguments: Inumber is the complex number in x+yi or x+yj form that you want to raise to an integer power. Power is the integer.

IMPRODUCT

Purpose: Calculates the product of between two and 29 complex numbers.
Syntax: IMPRODUCT(inumber1,inumber2, ...)
Arguments: Inumber1 and so on are the complex numbers in x+yi or x+yj form that you want to multiply together.

IMREAL

Purpose: Returns the real coefficient for the complex number specified.

Syntax: IMREAL(inumber)

Arguments: Inumber is the complex number in x+yi or x+yj form for which you want the real coefficient.

IMSIN

Purpose: Calculates the sine of a complex number.

Syntax: IMSIN(inumber)

Arguments: Inumber is the complex number in x+yi or x+yj form for which you want the sine.

IMSQRT

Purpose: Calculates the square root of a complex number.

Syntax: IMSQRT(inumber)

Arguments: Inumber is the complex number in x+yi or x+yj form for which you want the square root.

IMSUB

Purpose: Calculates the difference of two complex numbers.

Syntax: IMSUB(inumber1,inumber2)

Arguments: Inumber1 and inumber2 are the complex numbers in x+yi or x+yj form that you want to subtract. Inumber2 is subtracted from inumber1.

IMSUM

Purpose: Calculates the sum of between two and 29 complex numbers.

Syntax: IMSUM(inumber1,inumber2…)

Arguments: Inumber1 and so on are the complex numbers in x+yi or x+yj form that you want to add together.

OCT2BIN, OCT2DEC, OCT2HEX

Purpose: These three functions convert octal numbers to other bases. OCT2BIN converts from octal to binary, OCT2DEC from octal to decimal, and OCT2HEX from octal to hexa-decimal.

Syntax: OCT2BIN(number,places), OCT2DEC(number), or OCT2HEX(number,places)

Arguments: Number is the octal number to be converted. Places is the number of characters to use in the conversion. If the number of places is omitted, Excel uses the minimum number of characters necessary. If you specify extra characters, Excel pads with leading zeros.

■ Financial Functions

The financial functions provided by Excel let you make financial calculations a part of your worksheets. You can calculate principal and interest for loans and make several related calculations. You also can calculate depreciation and yields for a variety of assets. Examples that show how many of the financial functions can be used are provided in the spreadsheet shown in Figure 8.3.

Figure 8.3

A sample spreadsheet showing the use of financial functions

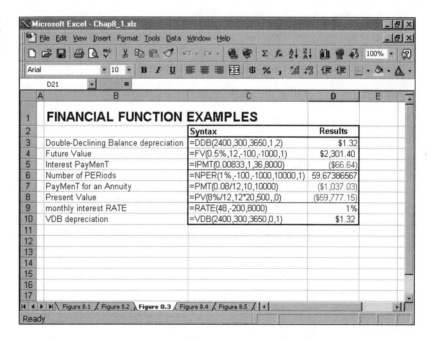

Many financial functions require the use of a code indicating the day count basis to be used. Table 8.7 gives the codes used by the financial functions for this purpose.

Financial functions also use codes for different year bases. Table 8.8 shows the codes used for year basis.

In addition, certain financial functions need codes that represent the timing of payments. Table 8.9 shows the codes used for this purpose.

Table 8.7

Codes for Day Count Basis

CODE	BASIS
0 or omitted	US (NASD) 30/360
1	Actual/actual
2	Actual/360
3	Actual/365
4	European 30/360

Table 8.8

Year Basis Codes for Financial Functions

CODE	YEAR BASIS
0	360 days (NASD method)
1	Actual
3	365 days in a year
4	360 days in a year (European method)

Table 8.9

Payment Timing Codes for Financial Functions

CODE	TIMING OF PAYMENTS
0	Payment at the end of the period
1	Payment at the beginning of the period

NOTE. *In many of the functions in Excel, date values must be expressed as serial numbers. For instance, if you wanted to represent a date value for January 1, 1997, the serial number entered in the formula would be 35431. (The number is based internally on the number of days since 01/01/1900). Instead of figuring the serial number yourself, being mindful of leap years, use a nested DATE(year, month, day) function.*

ACCRINT

Purpose: Calculates accrued interest for a security paying periodic interest.

Syntax: ACCRINT(issue,first_interest,settlement,rate,par,frequency,basis)

Arguments: Issue is the security's issue date. First_interest is the first date the security paid interest. Settlement is the settlement date for the security. Rate is the annual coupon rate. Par is the par value for the security. If you omit par, Excel assumes a par value of $1,000. Frequency is an integer representing the number of coupon payments in one year. Basis is day count basis code from Table 8.7 in the introduction to the financial functions. Date arguments need to be expressed as serial date numbers.

NOTE. *If ACCRINT is not listed in with the other Excel functions, you'll need to install the Analysis ToolPak. Step-by-step instructions on how to install the Analysis ToolPak are in Excel's on-line Help. From Excel's Help menu, click on Contents and Index, select Index and type Analysis ToolPak. Click the Display button twice to see instructions for installing.*

ACCRINTM

Purpose: Calculates the accrued interest for a security that pays interest at maturity.

Syntax: ACCRINTM(issue,maturity,rate,par,basis)

Arguments: Issue is the issue date of the security (entered as a serial date number). Maturity is the maturity date (entered as a serial date number). Rate is the coupon rate. Par is the par value. If you omit par, Excel assumes a value of $1,000. Basis is the day count basis from Table 8.7.

AMORDEGRC

Purpose: Calculates the depreciation for each accounting period. (This function is provided for those using the French accounting system).

Syntax: AMORDEGRC(cost,date_purchased,first_period,salvage,period,rate,basis)

Arguments: Cost is the amount that the asset cost. Date_purchased is the purchase date for the asset. First_period is that date that ends the first period. Salvage is the value of the asset at the end of its life. Period is the period. Rate is the depreciation rate. Basis is the year basis to be used from Table 8.8.

AMORLINC

Purpose: Calculates the depreciation for each accounting period. (This function is provided for those using the French accounting system).

Syntax: AMORLINC(cost,date_purchased,first_period,salvage, period,rate,basis)

Arguments: Cost is that amount the asset cost. Date_purchased is the purchase date for the asset. First_period is the date that ends the first period.

Salvage is the value of the asset at the end of its life. Period is the period. Rate is the depreciation rate. Basis is the year basis to be chosen from Table 8.8.

COUPDAYBS

Purpose: Calculates the number of days from the beginning of the coupon period to the settlement date.

Syntax: COUPDAYBS(settlement,maturity,frequency,basis)

Arguments: Settlement is a the settlement date. Maturity is for the maturity date. Frequency is the number of coupon payments annually. Basis is the day count basis from Table 8.7 in the introduction to the financial functions.

COUPDAYS

Purpose: Calculates the number of days in the coupon period containing the settlement date.

Syntax: COUPDAYS(settlement,maturity,frequency,basis)

Arguments: Settlement is the settlement date. Maturity is the maturity date. Frequency is the number of coupon payments annually. Basis is the day count basis from Table 8.7 in the introduction to the financial functions.

COUPDAYSNC

Purpose: Calculates the number of days from the settlement date to the next coupon date.

Syntax: COUPDAYSNC(settlement,maturity,frequency,basis)

Arguments: Settlement is the settlement date. Maturity is the maturity date. Frequency is the number of coupon payments annually. Basis is the day count basis from Table 8.7 in the introduction to the financial functions.

COUPNCD

Purpose: Calculates the next coupon date after the settlement date.

Syntax: COUPNCD(settlement,maturity,frequency,basis)

Arguments: Settlement is the settlement date. Maturity is the maturity date. Frequency is the number of coupon payments annually. Basis is the day count basis from Table 8.7 in the introduction to the financial functions.

COUPNUM

Purpose: Calculates the number of coupons payable between settlement and maturity dates.

Syntax: COUPNUM(settlement,maturity,frequency,basis)

Arguments: Settlement is the settlement date. Maturity is the maturity date. Frequency is the number of coupon payments annually. Basis is the day count basis from Table 8.7 in the introduction to the financial functions.

COUPPCD

Purpose: Calculates the coupon date before the settlement date.
Syntax: COUPPCD(settlement,maturity,frequency,basis)
Arguments: Settlement is the settlement date. Maturity is the maturity date. Frequency is the number of coupon payments annually. Basis is the day count basis from Table 8.7 in the introduction to the financial functions.

CUMIPMT

Purpose: Calculates the cumulative interest paid between two periods of a loan.
Syntax: CUMIPMT(rate,nper,pv,start_period,end_period,type)
Arguments: Rate is the interest rate, nper the number of payment periods, and pv the present value. Start_period is the first period for the purposes of the calculation, and end_period the last period for the calculation. Type is the payment timing, as shown in Table 8.9 in the introduction to the financial functions.

CUMPRINC

Purpose: Calculates the cumulative principal paid between the starting period and ending period of a loan.
Syntax: CUMPRINC(rate,nper,pv,start_period,end_period,type)
Arguments: Rate is the interest rate, nper the number of payment periods, and pv the present value. Start_period is the first period for the purposes of the calculation, and end_period the last period for the calculation. Type is the payment timing, as shown in Table 8.9 in the introduction to the financial functions.

DB

Purpose: Calculates depreciation for an asset, using the fixed-declining balance method, for a specified period.
Syntax: DB(cost,salvage,life,period,month)
Arguments: Cost is what you paid for the asset, salvage its value after depreciation, life is the number of periods in the useful life of the asset, period is the period for which depreciation is to be calculated, and month is the number of months in the first year. (If month is omitted, Excel assumes a value of 12.)

DDB

Purpose: Calculates depreciation for an asset for a specified period using the double-declining balance method, or another method you specify.

Syntax: DDB(cost,salvage,life,period,factor)

Arguments: Cost is what you paid for the asset, salvage is its value after depreciation, life is the number of periods in the useful life of the asset, period is the period for which depreciation is to be calculated, and factor is the rate at which the balance declines. If factor is omitted, Excel will assume a value of 2. All arguments must be positive numbers.

DISC

Purpose: Calculates a security's discount rate.

Syntax: DISC(settlement,maturity,pr,redemption,basis)

Arguments: Settlement is the settlement date. Maturity is the maturity date. Pr is the price per $100 of face value of the security. Redemption is the redemption value per $100 of face value. Basis is the day count basis, given in Table 8.7 in the introduction to the financial functions.

DOLLARDE

Purpose: Converts a dollar price written as a fraction to a dollar price written as a decimal.

Syntax: DOLLARDE(fractional_dollar,fraction)

Arguments: Fractional_dollar is the dollar amount expressed as a fraction. Fraction is the integer used as the denominator of the fraction.

DOLLARFR

Purpose: Converts a dollar price written as a decimal number to a dollar price written as a fraction.

Syntax: DOLLARFR(decimal_dollar,fraction)

Arguments: Decimal_dollar is the dollar amount expressed as a decimal number. Fraction is the denominator for the fraction you wish to use in the conversion.

DURATION

Purpose: Calculates the duration of a security having an assumed par value of $100.

Syntax: DURATION(settlement,maturity,coupon yld,frequency,basis)

Arguments: Settlement is the date representing the security's settlement date. Maturity is the security's maturity date. Coupon is the annual coupon rate, yld the annual yield, and frequency the number of payments in a given year. Basis is the day count basis given in Table 8.7 of the introduction to the financial functions.

EFFECT

Purpose: Calculates the effective annual interest rate.
Syntax: EFFECT(nominal_rate,npery)
Arguments: Nominal_rate is the nominal interest rate involved. Npery is the number of periods for compounding the interest in a given year.

FV

Purpose: Calculates the future value of an investment that has constant periodic payments and a constant interest rate.
Syntax: FV(rate,nper,pmt,pv,type)
Arguments: Rate is the interest rate expressed as a per period value. Nper is the total number of payment periods. Pmt is the payment made each period. Pv is the present value. Type is the payment timing code shown in Table 8.9 in the introduction to the financial functions.

FVSCHEDULE

Purpose: Calculates the future value of an investment with variable or adjustable compound interest rates.
Syntax: FVSCHEDULE(principal,schedule)
Arguments: Principal is the present value of the investment. Schedule is an array of interest rates that apply.

INTRATE

Purpose: Calculates the interest rate for a security that is fully invested.
Syntax: INTRATE(settlement,maturity,investment,redemption,basis)
Arguments: Settlement is the settlement date, and maturity is the maturity date. Investment is the amount invested, redemption the amount received at maturity, and basis the day count basis given in Table 8.7 in the introduction to the financial functions.

IPMT

Purpose: Calculates the interest payment over a given period of time for an investment based on constant, periodic payments and a fixed interest rate.
Syntax: IPMT(rate,per,nper,pv,fv,type)
Arguments: Rate is the constant interest rate per the period over which you want to calculate the interest rate, and nper the total number of periods in the investment. Pv is the present value. Fv is the future value you want to

attain — if fv is omitted, Excel will assume the future value of 0. Type is the payment timing code shown in Table 8.9 in the introduction to the financial functions.

IRR

Purpose: Calculates the internal rate of return based on a series of cash flows.

Syntax: IRR(values, guess)

Arguments: Values is an array or reference containing the numbers representing a series of cash flows. Guess is a number representing your estimate of the result of the calculation. The guess parameter is optional — the default for guess is 10 percent (0.1). Excel uses the guess parameter as a starting point for calculating the result. After 20 attempts at resolving the calculation without success, Excel will return the #NUM! error value. If you get the #NUM! error message, try a different value for guess.

NOTE. *For the purposes of this function, your initial investment should be entered as a negative number, such as -$70,000.*

MDURATION

Purpose: Calculates the modified Macauley duration for a security. The function assumes a par value of $100.00.

Syntax: MDURATION(settlement,maturity,coupon,yld,frequency,basis)

Arguments: Settlement is the settlement date. Maturity is the maturity date. Coupon is the annual coupon rate. Yld is the annual yield. Frequency is the number of coupon payments annually. Basis is the day count basis from Table 8.7 in the introduction to the financial functions.

MIRR

Purpose: Calculates the modified internal rate of return for a series of periodic cash flows. The function includes the cost of investment and interest on reinvestment of cash.

Syntax: MIRR(values,finance_rate,reinvest_rate)

Arguments: Values is an array or reference to cells containing the values that represent the series of cash flows. Finance_rate is the interest rate paid on the money used for the cash flows. Reinvest_rate is the interest the reinvested cash flows generate.

NOMINAL

Purpose: Calculates the nominal annual interest rate.

Syntax: NOMINAL(effect_rate,npery)

Arguments: Effect_rate is the effective interest rate, and npery the number of compounding periods in one year.

NPER

Purpose: Calculates the number of periods necessary for an investment. NPER assumes constant payments and a fixed interest rate.

Syntax: NPER(rate,pmt,pv,fv,type)

Arguments: Rate is one period's rate of interest, pmt the payment made during each period, pv the present value, and fv the future value. Type is the payment timing code given in Table 8.9 in the introduction to the financial functions.

NPV

Purpose: Calculates the net present value for an investment, assuming a discount rate and a series of periodic cash flows representing future payments and income.

Syntax: NPV(rate,value1,value2,...)

Arguments: Rate is one period's discount rate. The values are up to 29 values that represent the future payments (negative values) and income (positive values). The order of values must be entered in the order of cash flows.

ODDFPRICE

Purpose: Calculates the price per $100.00 face value for a security with an odd first period.

Syntax: ODDFPRICE(settlement,maturity,issue,first_coupon,rate,yld,redemption,frequency,basis)

Arguments: Settlement is the settlement date. Maturity is the maturity date. Issue is the issue date. First_coupon is the first coupon date. Rate is the interest rate, yld is the annual yield, redemption the redemption value per $100 of face value, frequency the number of coupon payments per year, and basis the day count basis given in Table 8.7 in the introduction to the financial functions.

ODDFYIELD

Purpose: Calculates the yield of a security with an odd first period.

Syntax: ODDFYIELD(settlement,maturity,issue,first_coupon,rate,pr,redemption,frequency,basis)

Arguments: Settlement is the settlement date. Maturity is the maturity date. Issue is the issue date. First_coupon is the first coupon date. Rate is the interest rate, pr the security's price, redemption the redemption value per

$100 of face value, frequency the number of coupon payments per year, and basis the day count basis given in Table 8.7 in the introduction to the financial functions.

ODDLPRICE

Purpose: Calculates the price per $100.00 of face value for a security with an odd last period.

Syntax: ODDLPRICE(settlement,maturity,last_interest,rate,yld,redemption,frequency,basis)

Arguments: Settlement is the settlement date. Maturity is the maturity date. Last_interest is the last coupon date. Rate is the interest rate, yld is the annual yield, redemption the redemption value per $100 of face value, frequency the number of coupon payments per year, and basis the day count basis given in Table 8.7 in the introduction to the financial functions.

ODDLYIELD

Purpose: Calculates the yield for a security with an odd last period.

Syntax: ODDLYIELD(settlement,maturity,last_interest,rate,pr,redemption,frequency,basis)

Arguments: Settlement is the settlement date. Maturity is the maturity date. Last_interest is the last coupon date. Rate is the interest rate, pr the security's price, redemption the redemption value per $100 of face value, frequency the number of coupon payments per year, and basis the day count basis given in Table 8.7 in the introduction to the financial functions.

PMT

Purpose: Calculates the payment for an annuity or loan built on fixed payments and a fixed interest rate.

Syntax: PMT(rate,nper,pv,fv,type)

Arguments: Rate is the interest rate per period, nper the number of periods for the annuity or loan, pv the present value, fv the future value, and type the payment timing code given in Table 8.9 in the introduction to the financial functions.

PPMT

Purpose: Calculates the payment on the principal in a given period for an investment built on fixed payments and fixed interest.

Syntax: PPMT(rate,per,nper,pv,fv,type)

Arguments: Rate is the interest rate per period, per identifies the period, nper is the number of payment periods, pv the present value, fv the future value, and type the payment timing code given in Table 8.9 in the introduction to the financial functions.

PRICE

Purpose: Calculates the price per $100.00 of face value for a security paying periodic interest.

Syntax: PRICE(settlement,maturity,rate,yld,redemption,frequency,basis)

Arguments: Settlement is the settlement date. Maturity is the maturity date. Rate is the annual coupon rate, yld the annual yield, redemption the redemption value per $100 of face value, frequency the number of payments annually, and basis the day count basis given in Table 8.7 in the introduction to the financial functions.

PRICEDISC

Purpose: Calculates the price per $100.00 of face value for a discounted security.

Syntax: PRICEDISC(settlement,maturity,discount,redemption,basis)

Arguments: Settlement is the settlement date. Maturity is the maturity date. Discount is the discount rate, redemption the redemption value per $100 of face value, and basis the day count basis given in Table 8.7 in the introduction to the financial functions.

PRICEMAT

Purpose: Calculates the price per $100.00 of face value for a security that pays its interest at maturity.

Syntax: PRICEMAT(settlement,maturity,issue,rate,yld,basis)

Arguments: Settlement is the settlement date. Maturity is the maturity date. Issue is the issue date. Rate is the interest rate at date of issue, yld the annual yield, and basis the day count basis given in Table 8.7 in the introduction to the financial functions.

PV

Purpose: Calculates the present value for an investment.

Syntax: PV(rate,nper,pmt,fv,type)

Arguments: Rate is the interest rate per period, nper the number of payment periods in an annuity, pmt the payment for each period, fv the future value, and type the payment timing code given in Table 8.9 in the introduction to the financial functions.

RATE

Purpose: Calculates the interest rate per period for an annuity.

Syntax: RATE(nper,pmt,pv,fv,type,guess)

Arguments: Nper is the number of payment periods in an annuity, pmt the payment for each period, pv the present value, fv the future value, type the payment timing code given in Table 8.9 in the introduction to the financial functions, and guess is your estimate of what the rate will be. If you do not make a guess, Excel will assume a guess value of 10 percent. If Excel returns a $NUM! error, try a different guess.

RECEIVED

Purpose: Calculates the amount received at maturity for a security that is fully invested.

Syntax: RECEIVED(settlement,maturity,investment,discount,basis)

Arguments: Settlement is the settlement date. Maturity is the maturity date. Investment is the amount invested, discount the discount rate, and basis the day count basis given in Table 8.7 in the introduction to the financial functions.

SLN

Purpose: Calculates straight-line depreciation for an asset over one period.

Syntax: SLN(cost,salvage,life)

Arguments: Cost is the initial cost of the asset, salvage the value of the asset after the depreciation period (salvage value), and life the number of periods over which you depreciate the asset (the useful life of the asset).

SYD

Purpose: Calculates the sum-of-years' digits depreciation for an asset over one period.

Syntax: SYD(cost,salvage,life,per)

Arguments: Cost is the initial cost of the asset, salvage the value of the asset after the depreciation period (salvage value), and life the number of periods over which you depreciate the asset (useful life of the asset). Per is the period in question.

TBILLEQ

Purpose: Calculates a Treasury bill's bond-equivalent yield.

Syntax: TBILLEQ(settlement,maturity,discount)

Arguments: Settlement is the settlement date. Maturity is the maturity date, and discount is the discount rate.

TBILLPRICE

Purpose: Calculates a Treasury bill's price per $100.00 of face value.
Syntax: TBILLPRICE(settlement,maturity,discount)
Arguments: Settlement is the settlement date. Maturity is the maturity date, and discount is the discount rate.

TBILLYIELD

Purpose: Calculates a Treasury bill's yield.
Syntax: TBILLYIELD(settlement,maturity,pr)
Arguments: Settlement is the settlement date. Maturity is the maturity date, and pr is the price per $100 of face value.

VDB

Purpose: Calculates the variable declining baland (depreciation) of an asset over a specified period using the depreciation method you specify.
Syntax: VDB(cost,salvage,life,start_period,end_period,factor,no_switch)
Arguments: Cost is the initial cost of the asset, salvage the value of the asset after the depreciation period (salvage value), and life the number of periods over which you depreciate the asset (the useful life of the asset). Start_period is the starting period for the depreciation calculation. End_period is the ending period for the calculation. Factor is the rate of decline for the balance (the rate is assumed to be 2 if factor is omitted). No_switch is a logical value that causes the calculation to switch to straight-line depreciation if depreciation is greater using this method. (TRUE enables the switch, and FALSE disables it. Excel will assume FALSE if you omit this argument).

XIRR

Purpose: Calculates the internal rate of return for a nonperiodic schedule of cash flows.
Syntax: XIRR(values,dates,guess)
Arguments: Values is an array of cash flows. Dates is an array of payment dates corresponding to these cash flows. Guess is your estimate of the result of the function.

XNPV

Purpose: Calculates net present value for a nonperiodic schedule of cash flows.
Syntax: XNPV(rate,values,dates)
Arguments: Rate is the discount rate. Values is an array of cash flows. Dates is an array of payment dates corresponding to the cash flows.

YIELD

Purpose: Calculates yield for a security that pays periodic interest.

Syntax: YIELD(settlement,maturity,rate,pr,redemption,frequency,basis)

Arguments: Settlement is the settlement date. Maturity is the maturity date. Rate is the annual coupon rate. Pr is the price per $100 of face value, redemption the redemption value per $100 face value, frequency the number of coupon payments per year, and basis the day count basis given by Table 8.7 in the introduction to the financial functions.

YIELDDISC

Purpose: Calculates the annual yield of a discounted security.

Syntax: YIELDDISC(settlement,maturity,pr,redemption,basis)

Arguments: Settlement is the settlement date. Maturity is the maturity date. Pr is the price per $100 of face value, redemption the redemption value per $100 of face value, and basis the day count basis given by Table 8.7 in the introduction to the financial functions.

YIELDMAT

Purpose: Calculates the annual yield for a security paying interest at maturity.

Syntax: YIELDMAT(settlement,maturity,issue,rate,pr,basis)

Arguments: Settlement is the settlement date. Maturity is the maturity date. Issue is the issue date. Rate is the interest rate at date of issue. Pr is the price per $100 of face value, and basis the day count basis given by Table 8.7 in the introduction to the financial functions.

■ Information Functions

Excel's information functions allow you to collect information about the cells on your worksheets. You can determine the nature of information stored in any cell. You also can collect information about error types. Relevant examples of how these functions may be used are shown in the sample spreadsheet in Figure 8.4.

CELL

Purpose: Gets information regarding formatting, location, or contents for the upper-left cell in a reference.

Syntax: CELL(info_type,reference)

Arguments: Info_type is a text string that identifies the type of information requested. Appropriate text strings are shown in Table 8.10.

Figure 8.4

A sample spreadsheet
showing the use of
information functions

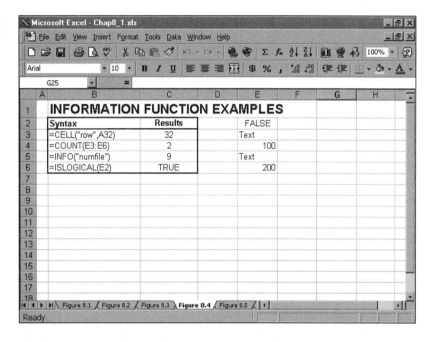

Table 8.10

Text Strings for Info_type

INFO_TYPE	RETURNS
"address"	First cell's reference.
"col"	First cell's column number.
"color"	1 if the cell is formatted in color; 0 if not.
"contents"	Upper-left cell's contents.
"filename"	File name containing the reference ("" if the worksheet has not been saved).
"format"	Text expressing the number format of the cell. "-" appended if cell is in color for negative values. "()" appended if parentheses for positive values or all values.
"parentheses"	1 if the cell uses parentheses for either positive or all values; 0 if not.

Table 8.10 (Continued)

Text Strings for Info_type

INFO_TYPE	RETURNS
"prefix"	Text expressing the label prefix of the cell. "'" if text is left-aligned. """ if the text is right-aligned. "^" if text is centered. "\ " if text is fill-aligned. "" if the cell contains anything else.
"protect"	0 if cell is unlocked, and 1 if cell is locked.
"row"	Row number for the first cell.
"type"	Text expressing the type of data in the cell. "b" if the cell is blank. "l" if the cell contains a label (text). "v" if the cell contains any other value.
"width"	Cell's column width rounded to the nearest integer. Units of column width equal one character in the default font.

When info_type is "format," this function will return one of the codes shown in Table 8.11.

Table 8.11

Return Codes for Info_type "Format"

FORMAT	CODE RETURNED
General	"G"
0	"F0"
#,##0	",0"
0.00	"F2"
#,##0.00	",2"
$#,##0_);($#,##0)	"C0'
$#,##0_);[Red]($#,##0)	"C0-"
$#,##0.00_);($#,##0.00)	"C2"
$#,##0.00_);[Red]($#,##0.00)	"C2-"
0%	"P0"
0.00%	"P2"
0.00E+00	"S2"
# ?/? or # ??/??	"G"

FORMAT	CODE RETURNED
m/d/yy or m/d/yy h:mm or mm/dd/yy.	"D4"
d—mmm—yy or dd—mmm—yy	"D1"
d—mmm or dd—mmm	"D2"
mmm—yy	"D3"
mm/dd	"D5"
h:mm AM/PM	"D7"
h:mm:ss AM/PM	"D6"
h:mm	"D9"
h:mm:ss	"D8"

Reference is the reference for any cell in the worksheet.

COUNTBLANK

Purpose: Gets the number of blank cells in a range.

Syntax: COUNTBLANK(range)

Arguments: Range is the range of cells in which you want to count the blank cells.

ERROR.TYPE

Purpose: Gets a number that corresponds to an Excel error value.

Syntax: ERROR.TYPE(error_val)

Arguments: Error_val is the error value whose number you want to have. Numbers associated with error values are shown in Table 8.12.

ERROR VALUE	ERROR NUMBER RETURNED
#NULL!	1
#DIV/0!	2
#VALUE!	3

ERROR VALUE	ERROR NUMBER RETURNED
#REF!	4
#NAME?	5
#NUM!	6
#N/A	7
Other values	#N/A

INFO

Purpose: Gets information about the current operating environment.

Syntax: INFO(type_text)

Arguments: Type_text is a text string that determines what information is collected. Valid values for type_text appear in Table 8.13.

TYPE_TEXT	VALUE RETURNED
"directory"	Current directory or folder path
"memavail"	Memory available, expressed in bytes
"memused"	Memory used to store data
"numfile"	Number of worksheets loaded
"origin"	Absolute A1-style reference, as text, prepended with "$A:" for Lotus 1-2-3 release 3.x compatibility. Returns the cell reference of the top-left cell visible in the window, based on the current scrolling position.
"osversion"	Operating system version
"recalc"	Recalculation mode that is current, either "Automatic" or "Manual"
"release"	Text expressing Excel version
"system"	Operating environment, either "mac" for Macintosh or "pcdos" for Windows
"totmem"	Memory available for use, including memory currently in use, expressed in bytes

ISBLANK, ISERR, ISERROR, ISEVEN, ISLOGICAL, ISNA, ISNONTEXT, ISNUMBER, ISODD, ISREF, ISTEXT

Purpose: These nine functions test the type of a value or reference. They return TRUE if the value is of the type being tested for, and FALSE if not.

Syntax:

ISBLANK(value)

ISERR(value)

ISERROR(value)

ISLOGICAL(value)

ISNA(value)

ISNONTEXT(value)

ISNUMBER(value)

ISREF(value)

ISTEXT(value)

Arguments: Value is the value to be tested. These functions perform the tests indicated in Table 8.14.

Table 8.14

Tests Performed by the
Nine IS Functions

FUNCTION	TRUE IF:
ISBLANK	The cell is empty
ISERR	Refers to an error code, except #N/A
ISERROR	Refers to any error value, including #N/A
ISLOGICAL	Is a logical value
ISNA	Is the #N/A error code
ISNONTEXT	Is any value, including a blank cell, that is not text
ISNUMBER	Is a number
ISREF	Is a reference
ISTEXT	Is text

N

Purpose: Converts a value to a number.

Syntax: N(value)

Arguments: Value is the value to convert. A number is, of course, converted to that number. Dates are converted to serial numbers. TRUE is converted to 1. All other values are converted to 0.

NA

Purpose: Returns the "no value is available" (#N/A) error value.

Syntax: NA()

Arguments: None. Note that the empty parentheses must be included, even though there is no argument.

TYPE

Purpose: Gets the type of a value.

Syntax: TYPE(value)

Arguments: Value is the value whose type you want to know. TYPE returns the values shown in Table 8.15.

Table 8.15

Return Types for the TYPE Function

TYPE	RETURN CODE
Number	1
Text	2
Logical value	4
Formula	8
Error value	16
Array	64

■ Logical Functions

Excel's logical functions let you make decisions about information in various cells on your worksheets. You can check to see whether certain conditions are true. If they are, you can take appropriate action with another function. The logical functions allow you to take complex actions using Excel's simple functions.

In many uses of logical functions, you will need to build logical expressions — several types of logical expressions can be evaluated. Comparisons are a common form, and can be numeric, text, and date expressions using <, >, =, <=, >=. Numbers other than zero are evaluated to TRUE, zero returns FALSE. The text values of "true" or "false" are converted to their corresponding values of TRUE or FALSE — any other text value will result in the #VALUE! error. Examples of their use appear in the sample worksheet shown in Figure 8.5.

Figure 8.5

A sample spreadsheet showing the use of logical functions.

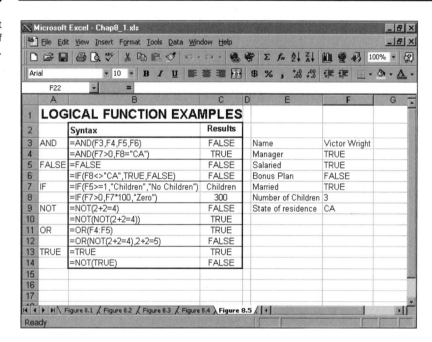

AND

Purpose: Evaluates to TRUE if all the arguments are TRUE, FALSE if one or more arguments are FALSE.

Syntax: AND(logical1, logical2,...)

Arguments: Each logical argument represents a condition that can evaluate to TRUE or FALSE. You can include up to 30 conditions.

FALSE

Purpose: Returns the value FALSE.

Syntax: FALSE()

Arguments: None. You may even omit the parentheses with this function, and Excel will still interpret it as the FALSE condition.

IF

Purpose: Returns a specified value if the logical test evaluates as TRUE, and another specified value if the test evaluates as FALSE.

Syntax: IF(logical_test,value_if_true,value_if_false)

Arguments: Logical_test is an expression or value that can evaluate to TRUE or FALSE. Value_if_true is the value returned if logical_test evaluates to TRUE. Value_if_false is the value returned if logical_test evaluates to FALSE. You can include up to seven nested IF functions for the value_if_true and value_if_false arguments. Listed below is an example showing nested IF statements for assigning letter grades to students, based on a typical academic grading standard:

IF(ClassPoints>=90,"A",IF(ClassPoints>=80,"B",
IF(ClassPoints>=70,"C",IF(ClassPoints>=60,"D","F"))))

NOT

Purpose: Converts the value of the argument to its reverse.

Syntax: NOT(logical)

Arguments: Logical is any value or expression that can evaluate to TRUE or FALSE.

OR

Purpose: Returns a value of TRUE if any argument evaluates to TRUE, and a value of FALSE if all arguments evaluate to FALSE.

Syntax: OR(logical1,logical2,...)

Arguments: Each logical argument is a condition that can evaluate to TRUE or FALSE. You can include up to 30 logical arguments.

TRUE

Purpose: Returns the value TRUE.

Syntax: TRUE()

Arguments: None. Similar to the FALSE function. You may omit the parentheses and Excel will still interpret it as the TRUE condition.

■ Look-Up and Reference Functions

Look-up and Reference functions, as their names imply, are useful when you need to look up a value in an Excel database or need a reference to a cell.

For example, suppose you have created a database in Excel to hold a typical tax table. Excel's Look-up functions can be used to look up tax values, given an income amount and marital status. Reference functions, on the other hand, can provide useful information about cell references. For example, say you need to know the column number of the cell reference AA100. Entering the function reference statement "=Column(AA100)" would return 27, the number of the column in which cell AA100 resides. Examples of some of these useful functions appear in the sample worksheet shown in Figure 8.6.

Figure 8.6

A sample spreadsheet showing the use of Look-up and Reference functions

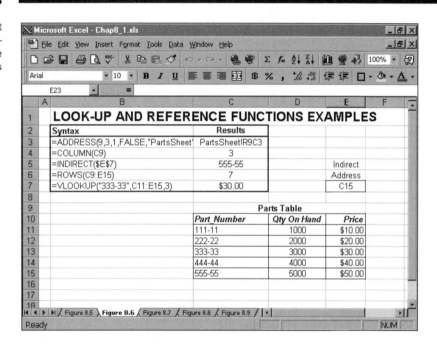

ADDRESS

Purpose: Creates a cell address to text, given specified row and column positions.

Syntax: ADDRESS(row_num,column_num,abs_num,a1,sheet_text)

Arguments: Row_num is the row number. Column_num is the column number. Abs_num is 1 (or omitted) for an absolute reference, 2 for an absolute row but relative column reference, 3 for a relative row but absolute column reference, or 4 for a relative reference. A1 is TRUE (or omitted) for an A1 style reference, or FALSE for an R1C1 style reference. Sheet_text is a text string that names the worksheet or macro sheet to be used as external reference. (If omitted, no such name is used.)

AREAS

Purpose: Gets the number of areas, ranges of contiguous cells, or single cells in a given reference.

Syntax: AREAS(reference)

Arguments: Reference is a cell or a range of cells. You can refer to multiple areas.

CHOOSE

Purpose: Returns one of up to 29 values from the list provided, using an index number.

Syntax: CHOOSE(index_num,value1,value2,...)

Arguments: Index_num indicates the position in the list to choose. The value arguments represent the values in the list. You can include up to 29 values.

COLUMN

Purpose: Gets the column number for the specified reference.

Syntax: COLUMN(reference)

Arguments: Reference is a cell or a range of cells for which you need a column number. If the argument is omitted, Excel will assume that you are referring to the column in which the function is located.

COLUMNS

Purpose: Gets the number of columns in an array or a reference.

Syntax: COLUMNS(array)

Arguments: Array is an array, array formula, or range of cells for which you want to count the number of columns used.

HLOOKUP

Purpose: Searches the top row of an array for a specified value, and returns the value in the same column from a specified row.

Syntax: HLO-OKUP(lookup_value,table_array,row_index_num,range_lookup)

Arguments: Lookup_value is the value you are searching for in the first row of the array. Table_array is the reference to the table of information. Row_index_num is the row number in the table from which you want the data returned — it serves as the offset from the first row for selecting the cell from which to return information). Range_lookup is TRUE (or omitted) if you want an approximate match, or FALSE if you want an exact match.

HYPERLINK (New in Excel 97!)

Purpose: Creates an Internet, Intranet, or network-server shortcut ("jump") to open a file. Clicking on a cell that contains a HYPERLINK function opens the file stored at link_location.

Syntax: HYPERLINK(link_location,friendly_name)

Arguments: Link_location includes the path and file name of the document to be opened. Link_location can refer to a specific cell or named range in a Microsoft Excel file or to a Microsoft Word bookmark. The path can reference a file stored on a hard drive, a Universal Naming Convention (UNC) path on a server, or a Uniform Resource Locator (URL) path on the Internet or an Intranet. Friendly_name is the shortcut text or numeric value that is displayed in the cell. If friendly_name is omitted, the cell will display the link_location as the shortcut text.

INDEX

Purpose: Gets the reference to a cell or set of cells, or value of a cell in an array, or an array of values from an array.

Syntax: This function has two forms:

INDEX(reference,row_num,column_num,area_num)

INDEX(array,row_num,column_num)

The first form returns a reference to a cell or cells. The second form returns the value of a cell or an array of cells.

Arguments: Reference is a reference to cells in the worksheet. References to noncontiguous ranges must be enclosed in parentheses. Array identifies an array. Row_num is the row number, column_num is the column number, and area_num selects a range in reference from which to return the intersection or row_num and column_num. The first area selected is numbered 1, the second is 2, and so on. If area_num is not entered, the INDEX function will use 1

INDIRECT

Purpose: Gets the reference stored in a cell.

Returns the value of a cell referred to by an intermediary cell. In other words, if cell A5 contains a reference to cell C6, which in turn contains the number 15, the result of the formula =INDIRECT(A5) will be 15.

Syntax: INDIRECT(ref_text,A1)

Arguments: Ref_text is the cell containing a reference. The reference stored in the cell may be expressed in A1 style, R1C1 style, or as a name. A1 is TRUE (or omitted) if the style of ref_text is A1, or FALSE if the style is R1C1.

LOOKUP

Purpose: Looks up and returns values in a vector or array.

Syntax: The function has two forms: the first for vectors, the second for arrays.

LOOKUP(lookup_value,lookup_vector,result_vector)

LOOKUP(lookup_value,array)

Arguments: Lookup_value is the value you search for. Lookup_vector is a reference to one row or column, and its values must be in ascending order. Result_vector is a reference to a single row or column and must be the same size as lookup_vector. Array is a range of cells containing values, which can be text, numbers, or logical values, and which must be in ascending order. If the function cannot match the specified value, it will return the highest value that is less than or equal to the lookup_value argument..

MATCH

Purpose: Gets the relative position of an array element that matches a specified value in a specified order.

Syntax: MATCH(lookup_value,lookup_array,match_type)

Arguments: Lookup_value is the value to find. Lookup_array is a reference to the array to search. Match_type is 1 if you want to match the largest value less than or equal to lookup_value, 0 if you want an exactly equal match, or -1 if you want to match the smallest value greater than or equal to lookup_value. If match_type is 1, the array must be in ascending order. If match_type is -1, the array must be in descending order. If match_type is 0, the array can be in any order. If you omit match_type, Excel will assume a value of 1.

OFFSET

Purpose: Gets a reference to a range located a specific number of rows and columns away from a specified range.

Syntax: OFFSET(reference,rows,cols,height,width)

Arguments: Reference is a reference to the region serving as the basis for the offset. Rows is the number of rows up (negative) or down (positive) specifying the upper left cell of the new region. Cols is the number of columns right (positive) or left (negative) specifying the upper left cell of the new region. Height is the number of rows high the new region will be. Width is the number of columns wide the new region will be. If you omit either height or width, the height or width for the reference argument will be used.

ROW

Purpose: Gets the row number of a reference.
Syntax: ROW(reference)
Arguments: Reference is a reference to the cell or cells for which you want the row number. If no row is specified, Excel will assume the row in which the ROW function is located.

ROWS

Purpose: Gets the number of rows in a reference or array.
Syntax: ROWS(array)
Arguments: Array is an array, an array formula, or a reference to cells that defines the array.

TRANSPOSE

Purpose: Shifts the vertical and horizontal orientation of an array, returning the array's transpose.
Syntax: TRANSPOSE(array)
Arguments: Array is a reference to the array that you want to transpose.

VLOOKUP

Purpose: Looks up a value in the far left column of an array, and returns the value of the cell indicated.
Syntax:
VLOOKUP(lookup_value,table_array,col_index_num,range_lookup)
Arguments: Lookup_value is the value to find in the first column. Table_array is a reference to the table to be searched. Col_index_number is the column number from which the value should be returned. Range_lookup is TRUE (or omitted) if you want an approximate match, or FALSE if you want an exact match.

■ Math and Trigonometric Functions

Excel's mathematical and trigonometric functions perform a variety of calculations. They form the core of Excel's mathematical capabilities. Examples of their use appear in the spreadsheet shown in Figure 8.7.

ABS

Purpose: Gets the absolute value of a number.
Syntax: ABS(number)

Figure 8.7

A spreadsheet showing
the use of Excel's math
and trig functions

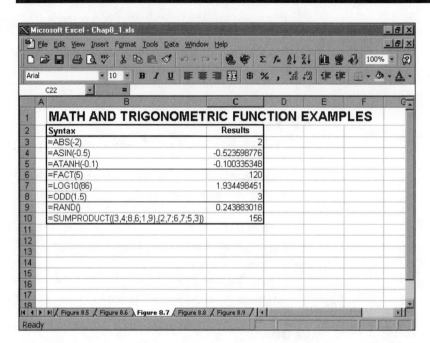

Arguments: Number is a real number for which you want the absolute value, regardless of whether it is positive or negative.

ACOS

Purpose: Calculates a number's arccosine. The angle is returned in radians ranging from 0 to pi.

Syntax: ACOS(number)

Arguments: Number is the cosine of the angle in question. It must range between 1 and -1.

ACOSH

Purpose: Calculates a number's inverse hyperbolic cosine.

Syntax: ACOSH(number)

Arguments: Number is a real number greater than or equal to 1.

ASIN

Purpose: Calculates a number's arcsine.

Syntax: ASIN(number)

Arguments: Number is the sine of the angle in question. It must range between 1 and -1. The arcsine can be expressed in degrees by multiplying the result by 180/PI().

ASINH

Purpose: Calculates a number's inverse hyperbolic sine.
Syntax: ASINH(number)
Arguments: Number is a real number.

ATAN

Purpose: Calculates a number's arctangent.
Syntax: ATAN(number)
Arguments: Number is the tangent of the angle in question.

ATAN2

Purpose: Calculates the arctangent from x/y coordinates.
Syntax: ATAN2(x_num,y_num)
Arguments: X_num is the x-coordinate and y_num is the y-coordinate of the point in question.

ATANH

Purpose: Calculates a number's inverse hyperbolic tangent.
Syntax: ATANH(number)
Arguments: Number is a real number ranging from 1 to -1.

CEILING

Purpose: Rounds numbers up to the nearest multiple of significance.
Syntax: CEILING(number, significance)
Arguments: Number is the value to round, significance the multiple to which you want to round: CEILING(423, 5) equals 425, for example.

COMBIN

Purpose: Calculates the number of possible combinations for a group of objects.
Syntax: COMBIN(number,number_chosen)
Arguments: Number is the number of objects in the set from which to choose. Number_chosen is the number of objects in each combination.

COS

Purpose: Calculates a number's cosine.
Syntax: COS(number)
Arguments: Number is the angle in question, measured in radians.

COSH

Purpose: Calculates a number's hyperbolic cosine.
Syntax: COSH(number)
Arguments: Number is the number for which you want the hyperbolic cosine.

COUNTIF

Purpose: Counts the number of non-blank cells meeting the given criteria.
Syntax: COUNTIF(range,criteria)
Arguments: Range is the set of cells within which you want to count. Criteria is a number, expression, or text that defines whether a cell is counted. For text cells, enclose the text to be compared in quotes. For example, use "expense" to count all cells in the range that contain the word expense. For numeric cells, use >, <, =, and so forth as comparisons. The entry >50 would include all cells with a value greater than 50 in the count.

DEGREES

Purpose: Converts from radians to degrees.
Syntax: DEGREES(angle)
Arguments: Angle is an angle measured in radians.

EVEN

Purpose: Rounds a number up to the nearest even integer.
Syntax: EVEN(number)
Arguments: Number is the number to round.

EXP

Purpose: Calculates e, the base of the natural logarithm (2.7182812845904) raised to a given power.
Syntax: EXP(number)
Arguments: Number is the value to be used as the exponent.

FACT

Purpose: Calculates the factorial of a number.

Syntax: FACT(number)

Arguments: Number is a positive number or 0 for which you want the factorial.

FACTDOUBLE

Purpose: Calculates the double factorial of a given number.

Syntax: FACTDOUBLE(number)

Arguments: Number is the number for which you want a double factorial.

FLOOR

Purpose: Rounds a number down to the nearest multiple of significance.

Syntax: FLOOR(number,significance)

Arguments: Number is the number to round, significance is the multiple to round to: FLOOR(728, 5) equals 725, for example.

GCD

Purpose: Calculates the greatest common divisor of two or more integers.

Syntax: GCD(number1,number2,...)

Arguments: Number is up to 29 values to be included in the calculation.

INT

Purpose: Rounds a number down to the nearest integer.

Syntax: INT(number)

Arguments: Number is a real number.

LCM

Purpose: Calculates the least common multiple for a set of integers.

Syntax: LCM(number1,number2,...)

Arguments: Number is up to 29 values to be included in the calculation.

LN

Purpose: Calculates the natural logarithm for a number.

Syntax: LN(number)

Arguments: Number is a positive real number.

LOG

Purpose: Calculates the logarithm of a number in a specified base.

Syntax: LOG(number,base)

Arguments: Number is a positive real number. Base is the value to be used as the base of the logarithm. If base is not present, Excel will assume that the base is 10.

LOG10

Purpose: Calculates the logarithm of a number in base 10.
Syntax: LOG10(number)
Arguments: Number is a positive real number.

MDETERM

Purpose: Calculates the matrix determinant of an array.
Syntax: MDETERM(array)
Arguments: Array is an array of numbers with the same number of rows as columns.

MINVERSE

Purpose: Calculates the inverse matrix of a matrix stored in an array.
Syntax: MINVERSE(array)
Arguments: Array is an array of numbers with the same number of rows as columns.

MMULT

Purpose: Calculates the matrix product of two arrays.
Syntax: MMULT(array1,array2)
Arguments: Array1 and array2 are the two arrays.

MOD

Purpose: Gets the remainder in a division problem.
Syntax: MOD(number,divisor)
Arguments: Number is the number for the numerator. Divisor is the number by which you want to divide.

MROUND

Purpose: Rounds a number to the specified multiple.
Syntax: MROUND(number,multiple)
Arguments: Number is the number to round. Multiple is the multiple to which you want to round.

MULTINOMIAL

Purpose: Calculates the ratio of the factorial of a sum of values to the product of the factorials.

Syntax: MULTINOMIAL(number1,number2,...)

Arguments: Number is up to 29 values to be included in the calculation.

ODD

Purpose: Rounds a number up to the nearest odd integer.

Syntax: ODD(number)

Arguments: Number is the number to round.

PI

Purpose: Returns the value of Pi calculated to 15 digits.

Syntax: PI()

Arguments: None.

POWER

Purpose: Raises the given number to the specified power.

Syntax: POWER(number,power)

Arguments: Number is the base. Power is the exponent.

PRODUCT

Purpose: Multiples the specified numbers.

Syntax: PRODUCT(number1,number2,...)

Arguments: Number is up to 30 values to multiply. You can use cell references.

QUOTIENT

Purpose: Calculates the integer portion of a division problem.

Syntax: QUOTIENT(numerator,denominator)

Arguments: Numerator is the number for the numerator, denominator the number for the denominator.

RADIANS

Purpose: Converts from degrees to radians.

Syntax: RADIANS(angle)

Arguments: Angle is an angle measured in degrees.

RAND

Purpose: Gets an evenly distributed random number between 0 and 1. This function gets a new number each time the worksheet is recalculated.

Syntax: RAND()

Arguments: None.

RANDBETWEEN

Purpose: Gets a random number between the specified numbers. This function gets a new random number each time the worksheet is recalculated.

Syntax: RANDBETWEEN(bottom,top)

Arguments: Bottom is the smallest integer to return, and top is the largest.

ROMAN

Purpose: Converts an Arabic numeral to text representing a Roman numeral.

Syntax: ROMAN(number,form)

Arguments: Number is an Arabic numeral. Form is 0 (or omitted) for a Classic Roman numeral. The values 1, 2, 3, and 4 specify increasingly concise (shorter) numerals. If form is TRUE, the number is classical; if FALSE, it is a simplified form.

ROUND

Purpose: Rounds a number to the number of digits indicated.

Syntax: ROUND(number,num_digits)

Arguments: Number is the real number to round. Num_digits gives the number of digits to which you want to round.

ROUNDDOWN

Purpose: Rounds a number down to the specified number of digits.

Syntax: ROUNDDOWN(number,num_digits)

Arguments: Number is the real number to round. Num_digits gives the number of digits to which you want to round.

ROUNDUP

Purpose: Rounds a number up to the specified number of digits.

Syntax: ROUNDUP(number,num_digits)

Arguments: Number is the real number to round. Num_digits gives the number of digits to which you want to round.

SERIESSUM

Purpose: Calculates the sum of a power series.

Syntax: SERIESSUM(x,n,m,coefficients)

Arguments: X is the input value. N is the initial power which you want to raise x. M is the step by which to increase n. Coefficients is a set of coefficients for multiplying each successive power of x.

SIGN

Purpose: Gets the sign of a number, returning 1 if the number is positive, 0 if the number is 0, and -1 if the number is negative.

Syntax: SIGN(number)

Arguments: Number is a real number.

SIN

Purpose: Calculates an angle's sine.

Syntax: SIN(number)

Arguments: Number is an angle measured in radians.

SINH

Purpose: Calculates a number's hyperbolic sine.

Syntax: SINH(number)

Arguments: Number is a real number.

SQRT

Purpose: Calculates the positive square root of a number.

Syntax: SQRT(number)

Arguments: Number is any number greater than 0.

SQRTPI

Purpose: Calculates the square root of a number multiplied by Pi.

Syntax: SQRTPI(number)

Arguments: Number is any number greater than 0.

SUBTOTAL (New in Excel 97!)

Purpose: Returns a subtotal in a database or list.

Syntax: SUBTOTAL(function_num,ref1,ref2,…)

Arguments: Function_num is a number between 1 and 11 that maps to a specific function used to calculate the subtotals. Ref1, ref2,... refers to the ranges or references you want to subtotal. The maximum number of ranges and/or references is 29. Table 8.16 maps the Function_num argument to its corresponding Function.

Table 8.16

Function_Num to
Function Map

FUNCTION_NUM	FUNCTION
1	AVERAGE
2	COUNT
3	COUNTA
4	MAX
5	MIN
6	PRODUCT
7	STDEV
8	STDEVP
9	SUM
10	VAR
11	VARP

SUM

Purpose: Adds the numbers listed as its arguments.
Syntax: SUM(number1,number2,...)
Arguments: Number is up to 30 numbers that you want to add together.

SUMIF

Purpose: Adds the cells that match the criteria specified.
Syntax: SUMIF(range,criteria,sum_range)
Arguments: Range is a reference to a set of cells that contain the values tested by criteria. Criteria is a number, expression, or text string that determines which cells to sum. Sum_range is a reference to cells paired with range that are the cells containing the values to be summed. If sum_range is omitted, the cells referenced by the range argument are summed.

SUMPRODUCT

Purpose: Multiplies the corresponding cells in two or more arrays and adds the products calculated.

Syntax: SUMPRODUCT(array1,array2,array3,...)
Arguments: Array is two to 30 arrays to include in the operation.

SUMSQ

Purpose: Squares its arguments, then adds the squares.
Syntax: SUMSQ(number1,number2,...)
Arguments: Number is up to 30 numbers to include in the operation.

SUMX2MY2

Purpose: Squares the corresponding values in two arrays, determines the difference between the corresponding squared values, and adds the resulting differences.
Syntax: SUMX2MY2(array_x,array_y)
Arguments: Array_x and array_y are two arrays containing the x and y values for the calculation.

SUMX2PY2

Purpose: Squares the corresponding values in two arrays and then sums the sum of the squared values.
Syntax: SUMX2PY2(array_x,array_y)
Arguments: Array_x and array_y are two arrays containing the x and y values for the calculation.

SUMXMY2

Purpose: Determines the difference between corresponding values in two arrays, squares the differences, then sums the squared differences.
Syntax: SUMXMY2(array_x,array_y)
Arguments: Array_x and array_y are two arrays containing the x and y values for the calculation.

TAN

Purpose: Calculates the tangent of an angle.
Syntax: TAN(number)
Arguments: Number is the measure of an angle in radians.

TANH

Purpose: Calculates a number's hyperbolic tangent.
Syntax: TANH(number)
Arguments: Number is a real number.

TRUNC

Purpose: Truncates a number to an integer according to the precision you specify.

Syntax: TRUNC(number,num_digits)

Arguments: Number is the number to truncate. Num_digits is the precision of truncation. (If num_digits is omitted, Excel assumes a value of 0.)

■ Statistical Functions

Excel's statistical functions permit you to analyze the data stored in your spreadsheets. They form Excel's core analytical engine. You can use them to determine trends and make statistical decisions. Examples of their use appear in the spreadsheet shown in Figure 8.8.

Figure 8.8

A spreadsheet showing the use of statistical functions

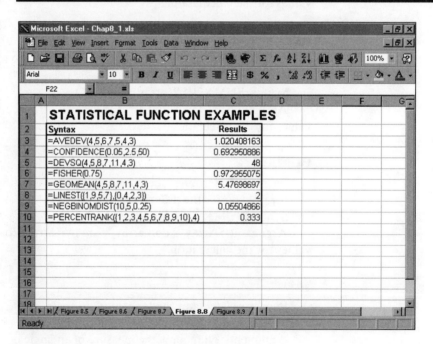

AVEDEV

Purpose: Averages the absolute deviation of data points from the mean.

Syntax: AVEDEV(number1,number2,...)

Arguments: Number is up to 30 numbers to include in the operation.

AVERAGE

Purpose: Calculates the arithmetic mean of its arguments.
Syntax: AVERAGE(number1,number2,...)
Arguments: Number is up to 30 numbers to include in the operation.

AVERAGEA (New in Excel 97!)

Purpose: Calculates the average for a the list of arguments. The list of arguments can include numbers, text and logical values such as TRUE and FALSE.
Syntax: AVERAGEA(value1,value2,...)
Arguments: Value1, value2,... list of up to 30 arguments. The arguments in the list can include ranges of cells or values on which the average is calculated.

BETADIST

Purpose: Calculates the cumulative beta probability density function. This function is used to study variation in a percentage across samples, as in the percentage of the day Americans spend driving automobiles.
Syntax: BETADIST(x,alpha,beta,A,B)
Arguments: X is the value at which to evaluate the function, and is a value between A and B. Alpha and beta are parameters for the distribution. A and B are optional, and represent the lower and upper bounds for the interval of x.

BETAINV

Purpose: Calculates the inverse of the cumulative beta probability density function. This distribution often is used to model the probable completion time of a project when you know the expected completion time and variability.
Syntax: BETAINV(probability,alpha,beta,A,B)
Arguments: Probability is the probability value for the beta distribution. Alpha and beta are the parameters for the distribution. A and B are the optional lower and upper bounds for the interval of x, the value that is the result of applying this function.

BINOMDIST

Purpose: Calculates the individual term binomial distribution probability. The binomial distribution is used to study problems consisting of a fixed number of trials with only two possible outcomes. A common example is predicting the outcome of a coin toss.
Syntax: BINOMDIST(number_s,trials,probability_s,cumulative)

Arguments: Number_s is the number of successes. Trials is the number of trials. Probability_s is the probability of success in a trial. Cumulative is TRUE for calculating the cumulative distribution function, the probability that there are at most number_s successes, and FALSE for calculating the probability mass function, the probability that there are number_s successes.

CHIDIST

Purpose: Calculates the one-tailed probability of the chi-squared distribution. This distribution is used when comparing observed and expected values in relation to contingency tables.

Syntax: CHIDIST(x,degrees_freedom)

Arguments: X is the value at which to evaluate the function. Degrees_freedom is the degrees of freedom associated with x.

CHIINV

Purpose: Calculates the inverse of the one-tailed probability of the chi-squared distribution. This function is used to compare observed results with expected results.

Syntax: CHIINV(probability,degrees_freedom)

Arguments: Probability is the probability associated with the distribution. Degrees_freedom is the degrees of freedom associated with the distribution.

CHITEST

Purpose: Calculates the chi-squared test for independence.

Syntax: CHITEST(actual_range,expected_range)

Arguments: Actual_range is a reference to the cells containing the observations to test against expected values. Expected_range is a reference to the cells containing the expected values.

CONFIDENCE

Purpose: Calculates a confidence interval for a population mean.

Syntax: CONFIDENCE(alpha,standard_dev,size)

Arguments: Alpha is the significance level. Standard_dev is the population standard deviation for the data. Size is the sample size.

CORREL

Purpose: Calculates the correlation coefficient for the values stored in two arrays. You use this value to study the relationship between two properties.

Syntax: CORREL(array1,array2)

Arguments: Array1 and array2 represent the two arrays to be correlated.

COUNT

Purpose: Determines how many numbers are in a list of arguments.
Syntax: COUNT(value1,value2,...)
Arguments: Value is a reference to up to 30 spreadsheet regions that can contain any kind of data. Only numbers are counted, however.

COUNTA

Purpose: Determines how many nonblank values are in a list of arguments.
Syntax: COUNTA(value1,value2,...)
Arguments: Value is up to 30 references to spreadsheet regions containing information of any type. Only nonblank cells, including cells containing "", are counted.

COVAR

Purpose: Calculates the covariance for data points stored in two arrays. Covariance can be used to study the relationship between two data sets.
Syntax: COVAR(array1,array2)
Arguments: Array1 and array2 are references to the arrays containing the two data sets.

CRITBINOM

Purpose: Determines the smallest value for which the cumulative binomial distribution is less than or equal to the criterion you set. This value is often used to determine the maximum number of defective products allowed to come off an assembly line before rejecting the entire lot.
Syntax: CRITBINOM(trials,probability_s,alpha)
Arguments: Trials is the number of Bernoulli trials. Probability_s is the probability of success of a trial. Alpha is the criterion.

DEVSQ

Purpose: Calculates the sum of squares of deviation of data points from the mean.
Syntax: DEVSQ(number1,number2,...)
Arguments: Number is up to 30 values to include in the calculation.

EXPONDIST

Purpose: Calculates the exponential distribution. EXPONDIST is used to study problems in which the time between events is of interest.
Syntax: EXPONDIST(x,lambda,cumulative)

Arguments: X is the value at which to evaluate the function. λ is the parameter value for the distribution. Cumulative is TRUE to calculate the cumulative distribution function, and FALSE to calculate the probability density function.

FDIST

Purpose: Calculates the F probability distribution. FDIST is used to study whether different data sets possess different degrees of diversity.
Syntax: FDIST(x,degrees_freedom1,degrees_freedom2)
Arguments: X is the value at which the function will evaluate. Degrees_freedom1 is the degrees of freedom for the numerator. Degrees_freedom2 is the degrees of freedom for the denominator.

FINV

Purpose: Calculates the inverse of the F probability distribution. You can use this function to compare the variation in two data sets.
Syntax: FINV(probability,degrees_freedom1,degrees_freedom2)
Arguments: Probability is the probability associated with the cumulative distribution. Degrees_freedom1 is the degrees of freedom for the numerator. Degrees_freedom2 is the degrees of freedom for the denominator.

FISHER

Purpose: Calculates the Fisher transformation at a given value. This function is used to test hypotheses regarding the correlation coefficient.
Syntax: FISHER(x)
Arguments: X is the value for which to calculate the transformation.

FISHERINV

Purpose: Calculates the inverse of the Fisher transformation. This function can be used to analyze the correlations between data sets.
Syntax: FISHERINV(y)
Arguments: Y is the value for which to calculate the inverse transformation.

FORECAST

Purpose: Calculates predicted values for the x and y terms of a linear regression model. This function is used to predict unknown values, such as future sales, in a correlation study.
Syntax: FORECAST(x,known_y's,known_x's)
Arguments: X is the value for which to predict a y value. Known_x's and known_y's are references to cells containing known x and y values.

FREQUENCY

Purpose: Calculates a frequency distribution as a vertical array of cells. This function sorts the data values into a set of intervals, so that you can know how many values occur within each interval.

Syntax: FREQUENCY(data_array,bins_array)

Arguments: Data_array is an array or a reference to an array of values within which you wish to count the frequencies. Bins_array is an array or a reference to an array that contains values defining the intervals over which to count the frequencies. The numbers in bins_array represent the endpoints of the frequency intervals. The array {10,20,30} defines intervals of 0 to 10, 11 to 20, and 30 to the endpoint of the data.

FTEST

Purpose: Calculates the one-tailed F test, the one-tailed probability that the variances of two arrays of values are not significantly different. You can use this test to compare the test scores of students entering public and private universities, for example.

Syntax: FTEST(array1,array2)

Arguments: Array1 and array2 are references to the two sets of data to be compared.

GAMMADIST

Purpose: Calculates the gamma distribution, used to study variables whose distribution might be skewed, as in queuing analysis.

Syntax: GAMMADIST(x,alpha,beta,cumulative)

Arguments: X is the value at which to evaluate the distribution. Alpha and beta are the parameters of the distribution. Cumulative is TRUE to calculate the cumulative distribution function, and FALSE to calculate the probability mass function.

GAMMAINV

Purpose: Calculates the inverse of the gamma cumulative distribution, used in studying variables whose distribution might be skewed.

Syntax: GAMMAINV(probability,alpha,beta)

Arguments: Probability is the probability associated with the distribution. Alpha and beta are parameters for the distribution.

GAMMALN

Purpose: Calculates the gamma function's natural logarithm.

Syntax: GAMMALN(x)

Arguments: X is the value for which you want the natural logarithm of the gamma function.

GEOMEAN

Purpose: Calculates the geometric mean of positive data points. This function often is used in calculating issues that involve compound interest with variable rates, such as growth rates.

Syntax: GEOMEAN(number1,number2,...)

Arguments: Number is up to 30 numbers to include in the calculation. You can substitute a single array or a reference to an array instead of listing the numbers as arguments.

GROWTH

Purpose: Calculates an exponential curve to fit known data points, and calculates predicted y values for x values that you supply.

Syntax: GROWTH(known_y's,known_x's,new_x's,const)

Arguments: Known_y's and known_x's are arrays of known values (known_x's are optional). New_x's are x values for which you want corresponding y values. Const is TRUE (or omitted) to calculate the constant b normally, FALSE to force b equal to 1.

HARMEAN

Purpose: Calculates a data set's harmonic mean, the reciprocal of the arithmetic mean of reciprocals.

Syntax: HARMEAN(number1,number2,...)

Arguments: Number is up to 30 values to include in the calculation. You can use a reference to an array.

HYPGEOMDIST

Purpose: Calculates the hypergeometric distribution, used to study problems within a finite population in which observations are either successes or failures, and from which each subset is chosen with equal likelihood.

Syntax: HYPGEOM-DIST(sample_s,number_sample,population_s,number_population)

Arguments: Sample_s is the number of successes appearing in the sample. Number_sample is the sample size. Population_s is the number of successes appearing in the population. Number_population is the size of the population.

INTERCEPT

Purpose: Calculates the y intercept for a regression line.

Syntax: INTERCEPT(known_y's,known_x's)

Arguments: Known_y's and known_x's are sets of data that represent the x and y values defining the regression line.

KURT

Purpose: Calculates the kurtosis, the relative peakedness or flatness of the curve describing the data distribution, for a data set.

Syntax: KURT(number1,number2,...)

Arguments: Number is up to 30 values to include in the calculation. You can use a reference to an array.

LARGE

Purpose: Gets the k-th largest value in the data set.

Syntax: LARGE(array,k)

Arguments: Array is the array of data from which to select the value. K is the position from the largest value to return.

LINEST

Purpose: Calculates a straight line to best fit a data set, using the least squares method.

Syntax: LINEST(known_y's,known_x's,const,stats)

Arguments: Known_y's and known_x's are the sets of known data points that will define the line (known_x's is optional). Const is TRUE if the constant b is to be calculated normally, FALSE if b is to be forced to 0. Stats is TRUE to return regression statistics, FALSE (or omitted) to return only the m coefficients and the constant b.

LOGEST

Purpose: Fits an exponential curve that best describes a data set.

Syntax: LOGEST(known_y's,known_x's,const,stats)

Arguments: Known_y's and known_x's are the set of known data points that will define the curve (known_x's is optional). Const is TRUE if the constant b is to be calculated normally, FALSE is b is to be forced to 1. Stats is TRUE to return regression statistics, FALSE (or omitted) to return only the m coefficients and the constant b.

LOGINV

Purpose: Calculates the inverse of the lognormal cumulative distribution, used for analyzing logarithmically transformed data.

Syntax: LOGINV(probability,mean,standard_dev)

Arguments: Probability is the probability associated with the distribution. Mean is the mean and standard_dev the standard deviation of ln(x).

LOGNORMDIST

Purpose: Calculates the cumulative lognormal distribution for a given value. This function is used to analyze logarithmically transformed data.

Syntax: LOGNORMDIST(x,mean,standard_dev)

Arguments: X is the value at which the function is to be evaluated. Mean is the mean, and standard_dev is the standard deviation of ln(x).

MAX

Purpose: Gets the maximum value from its argument list.

Syntax: MAX(number1,number2,...)

Arguments: Number is up to 30 numbers from which you want to select the maximum value.

MAXA (New in Excel 97!)

Purpose: Returns the largest value in a list of arguments. Arguments can include numbers, text, and logical values, such as TRUE and FALSE.

Syntax: MAXA(value1,value2,...)

Arguments: Value1, Value2,... a maximum of 30 values for which you want to find the largest value.

MEDIAN

Purpose: Calculates the median for a set of numbers.

Syntax: MEDIAN(number1,number2,...)

Arguments: Number is up to 30 numbers to include in the calculation.

MIN

Purpose: Gets the smallest number from the list of arguments.

Syntax: MIN(number1,number2,...)

Arguments: Number is up to 30 numbers from which you want to select the minimum value.

MINA (New in Excel 97!)

Purpose: Returns the smallest value in the list of arguments. Arguments can include numbers, text, and logical values, such as TRUE and FALSE.

Syntax: MINA(value1,value2,...)

Arguments: Value1, value2,... are a maximum of 30 values for which you want to find the smallest value.

MODE

Purpose: Gets the most frequent value in a data set.

Syntax: MODE(number1,number2,...)

Arguments: Number is up to 30 numbers for which you want the mode.

NEGBINOMDIST

Purpose: Calculates the negative binomial distribution, the probability that there will be a given number of failures before a given success.

Syntax: NEGBINOMDIST(number_f,number_s,probability_s)

Arguments: Number_f is the number of failures, number_s the threshold number of successes, and probability_s the probability of a success.

NORMDIST

Purpose: Calculates the normal cumulative distribution with a given mean and standard deviation.

Syntax: NORMDIST(x,mean,standard_dev,cumulative)

Arguments: X is the number for which the distribution is to be calculated, mean is the arithmetic mean for the distribution, standard_dev is the standard deviation for the distribution. Cumulative is TRUE to calculate the cumulative distribution function, FALSE to calculate the probability mass function.

NORMINV

Purpose: Calculates the inverse of the normal cumulative distribution with a given mean and standard deviation.

Syntax: NORMINV(probability,mean,standard_dev)

Arguments: Probability is the probability associated with the distribution, mean the mean for the distribution, and standard_dev the standard deviation for the distribution.

NORMSDIST

Purpose: Calculates the standard normal cumulative distribution function, which has a mean of 0 and a standard deviation of 1.

Syntax: NORMSDIST(z)
Arguments: Z is the value for which you want to calculate the distribution.

NORMSINV

Purpose: Calculates the inverse of the standard normal cumulative distribution.
Syntax: NORMSINV(probability)
Arguments: Probability is the probability associated with the distribution.

PEARSON

Purpose: Calculates the Pearson product moment correlation coefficient (r) for two data sets.
Syntax: PEARSON(array1,array2)
Arguments: Array1 is the set of independent values, and array2 the set of dependent values, for the calculation.

PERCENTILE

Purpose: Calculates the k-th percentile for a range of values. This function is often used to calculate thresholds, as when deciding to examine only job candidates who score above the 90th percentile on an evaluation criterion.
Syntax: PERCENTILE(array,k)
Arguments: Array is the range of data defining relative standing, and k is the percentile value desired.

PERCENTRANK

Purpose: Calculates the percentile rank for a given value in a set of data.
Syntax: PERCENTRANK(array,x,significance)
Arguments: Array is a reference to an array of numeric values defining relative standing. X is the value to be ranked. Significance is an optional value expressing the number of significant digits to include in the percentage value returned (three significant digits are included by default).

PERMUT

Purpose: Calculates the number of permutations for a set of objects to be selected from a larger set of objects.
Syntax: PERMUT(number,number_chosen)
Arguments: Number is an integer expressing the number of objects, and number_chosen is an integer expressing the number of objects in each permutation.

POISSON

Purpose: Calculates the Poisson distribution, used for predicting the number of events in a fixed period of time.

Syntax: POISSON(x,mean,cumulative)

Arguments: X is the number of events, mean the expected numeric value. Cumulative is TRUE to calculate the cumulative probability function, and FALSE to calculate the probability mass function.

PROB

Purpose: Calculates the probability that a set of values are between two limits.

Syntax: PROB(x_range,prob_range,lower_limit,upper_limit)

Arguments: X_range is the range of values for x with associated probabilities. Prob_range is the probabilities associated with x_range. Lower_limit and upper_limit represent the lower and upper bounds of the value for which you calculate the probability.

QUARTILE

Purpose: Calculates the quartiles for a data set.

Syntax: QUARTILE(array,quart)

Arguments: Array is a reference to the values to be split into quartiles. Quart is which quartile to return.

RANK

Purpose: Determines the rank of a number in a given list of numbers.

Syntax: RANK(number,ref,order)

Arguments: Number is the number to be ranked, ref is an array or list of numbers, and order is 0 (or omitted) if reference is to be sorted in descending order of a non-zero value or if reference is to be sorted in ascending order.

RSQ

Purpose: Calculates the square of the Pearson product moment correlation coefficient, a value that gives the percentage of the variance in one factor y attributable to the variance in another factor x.

Syntax: RSQ(known_y's,known_x's)

Arguments: Known_y's and known_x's are the sets of data points for which you want the squared correlation coefficient.

SKEW

Purpose: Calculates the skewedness, the degree of asymmetry in a distribution's curve, for a set of data.

Syntax: SKEW(number1,number2,...)

Arguments: Number is up to 30 numbers to include in the calculation. You can use a reference to cells.

SLOPE

Purpose: Calculates the slope of a linear regression line.

Syntax: SLOPE(known_y's,known_x's)

Arguments: Known_y's is an array of dependent data points, and known_x's an array of independent data points.

SMALL

Purpose: Gets the k-th smallest value in a set of data.

Syntax: SMALL(array,k)

Arguments: Array is an array of data from which to select the value. K is the position from the smallest value to make the selection.

STANDARDIZE

Purpose: Normalizes a value from a distribution with a given mean and standard deviation, transforming it to a value on a scale with a mean of 0 and a standard deviation of 1.

Syntax: STANDARDIZE(x,mean,standard_dev)

Arguments: X is the value to normalize, mean the mean of the distribution, and standard_dev is the distribution's standard deviation.

STDEV

Purpose: Estimates the standard deviation based on a sample.

Syntax: STDEV(number1,number2,...)

Arguments: Number is up to 30 values to be included in the calculation. You can use a reference to a range of cells.

STDEVA (New in Excel 97!)

Purpose: Estimates standard deviation based on a sample. Arguments can include text and logical values such as TRUE and FALSE.

Syntax: STDEVA(value1,value2,...)

Arguments: Value1,value2,... are a maximum of 30 values corresponding to a sample population. A single array or a reference to an array can be used instead of arguments separated by commas.

STDEVP

Purpose: Calculates a standard deviation based on an entire population.
Syntax: STDEVP(number1,number2,...)
Arguments: Number is up to 30 values to include in the calculation. You can use a reference to cells.

STDEVPA (New in Excel 97!)

Purpose: Calculates standard deviation based on an entire population specified in the argument list. Arguments can include text and logical values such as TRUE and FALSE.
Syntax: STDEVPA(value1,value2,...)
Arguments: Value1,value2,... are a maximum of 30 values corresponding to an entire population. A single array or a reference to an array can be specified instead of arguments separated by commas.

STEYX

Purpose: Calculates the standard error of predicted y values for the x values in a regression problem.
Syntax: STEYX(known_y's,known_x's)
Arguments: Known_y's and known_x's are arrays of dependent and independent data points, respectively.

TDIST

Purpose: Calculates the T distribution, used for hypothesis testing in small data sets.
Syntax: TDIST(x,degrees_freedom,tails)
Arguments: X is the value for which to evaluate the function, degrees_freedom is the number of degrees of freedom, and tails is the number of tails (two or one).

TINV

Purpose: Calculates the inverse of the T distribution with given degrees of freedom.
Syntax: TINV(probability,degrees_freedom)
Arguments: Probability is the probability associated with a two-tailed text, and degrees_freedom is the number of degrees of freedom.

TREND

Purpose: Calculates values along a linear trend.
Syntax: TREND(known_y's,known_x's,new_x's,const)

Arguments: Known_y's and known_x's are arrays of known values (known_x's are optional). New_x's are x values for which you want corresponding y values. Const is TRUE (or omitted) to calculate the constant b normally, and FALSE to force b equal to 0.

TRIMMEAN

Purpose: Calculates the mean of an interior data set. You can use this function to exclude spurious outliers from your data analysis.

Syntax: TRIMMEAN(array,percent)

Arguments: Array is the range of values to use, and percent is the fractional number of data points to trim from the data set.

TTEST

Purpose: Calculates the probability value associated with the t-test, which determines whether two samples come from the same or different underlying populations.

Syntax: TTEST(array1,array2,tails,type)

Arguments: Array1 and array2 are the two data sets. Tails is the number of tails in the test (one or two). Type is the kind of t-test to perform (1=paired, 2=two-sample equal variance, 3=two-sample unequal variance).

VAR

Purpose: Calculates the variance of a sample.

Syntax: VAR(number1,number2,...)

Arguments: Number is up to 30 values to be included in the calculation. You can use a reference to cells.

VARA (New in Excel 97!)

Purpose: Estimates variance based on a sample population specified in the argument list. Arguments can include numbers, text and logical values such as TRUE and FALSE.

Syntax: VARA(value1,value2,...)

Arguments: Value1,value2,... are a maximum of 30 values corresponding to a sample of a population.

VARP

Purpose: Calculates the variance for an entire population.

Syntax: VARP(number1,number2,...)

Arguments: Number is up to 30 values to be included in the calculation. You can use a reference to cells.

VARPA

Purpose: Calculates variance based on the entire population. VARPA accepts text and logical values such as TRUE and FALSE as arguments.

Syntax: VARPA(value1,value2,...)

Arguments: Up 30 values corresponding to a population.

WEIBULL

Purpose: Calculates the Weibull distribution, used in reliability analysis.

Syntax: WEIBULL(x,alpha,beta,cumulative)

Arguments: X is the value at which the function will evaluate, alpha and beta are parameters for the distribution, and cumulative determines the form of the function (TRUE for the cumulative distribution, FALSE for the probability mass function).

ZTEST

Purpose: Calculates the two-tailed probability value associated with the z-test, used to determine whether data was drawn from the same or different populations.

Syntax: ZTEST(array,x,sigma)

Arguments: Array is the data set to test. X is the value to test for the likelihood it was drawn from the population. Sigma is the population standard deviation. (If omitted, the sample standard deviation substitutes).

■ Text Functions

Excel's text functions allow you to manipulate text in your worksheets. You can format text, search for text, substitute text, join text, and perform other such operations outlined for each function. Examples for functions described in this section appear in the spreadsheet in Figure 8.9.

CHAR

Purpose: Gets the character associated with a code number.

Syntax: CHAR(number)

Arguments: Number is the number that represents the character set code for the character you want. Number must be between 1 and 255.

CLEAN

Purpose: Strips nonprintable characters from text.

Syntax: CLEAN(text)

Figure 8.9

An example spreadsheet
showing the use of text
functions

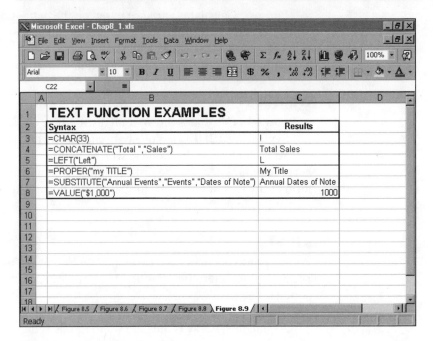

Arguments: Text is the worksheet information you want to clear of non-printing characters.

CODE

Purpose: Gets the numeric code associated with the first character in a text string.

Syntax: CODE(text)

Arguments: Text is the text string for which the function returns the code of the first character.

CONCATENATE

Purpose: Links several text strings into a single text string.

Syntax: CONCATENATE(text1,text2,...)

Arguments: Text is up to 30 text strings that you want to concatenate into a single text string. You can use references to cells containing text as arguments.

DOLLAR

Purpose: Converts a number to text in an appropriate currency format.

Syntax: DOLLAR(number,decimals)

Arguments: Number is a numeric value, a formula that evaluates as a numeric value, or a reference to a cell holding a numeric value. Decimals is the number of decimal places to include. (If decimals is omitted, Excel assumes a value of 2.)

EXACT

Purpose: Returns TRUE if the text strings in the argument list are exactly the same.

Syntax: EXACT(text1,text2)

Arguments: Text1 and text2 are the two text strings to compare.

FIND

Purpose: Searches for a string of text within another string of text. The return value is the position of the first character in the found string. This function is case-sensitive, and will not accept wildcard characters.

Syntax: FIND(find_text,within_text,start_num)

Arguments: Find_text is the text to find. Within_text is the text to search in. Start_num is the position in the string at which to start the search.

FIXED

Purpose: Rounds a number to the given number of decimal places, and converts the number to text with the appropriate use of periods and commas.

Syntax: FIXED(number,decimals,no_commas)

Arguments: Number is the number to round and convert. Decimals is the number of decimal places. No_commas is a logical value. If TRUE, no commas appear in the text returned. If FALSE or omitted, the text returned includes commas.

LEFT

Purpose: Returns the far left number of characters specified from a text string.

Syntax: LEFT(text,num_chars)

Arguments: Text is the text string from which to get characters. Num_chars is the number of characters to get. (If omitted, Excel assumes a value of 1 for num_chars.)

LEN

Purpose: Gets the number of characters that make up a text string. This function counts spaces as characters.

Syntax: LEN(text)
Arguments: Text is the text whose length is determined.

LOWER

Purpose: Converts a text string to all lower case.
Syntax: LOWER(text)
Arguments: Text is the text to convert.

MID

Purpose: Gets the specified number of characters from a text string, starting at the position you indicate.
Syntax: MID(text,start_num,num_chars)
Arguments: Text is the string from which to get characters. Start_num is the position at which to begin selection. Num_chars is the number of characters to get.

PROPER

Purpose: Capitalizes the first letter of each word in a text string, as well as any letters that come after characters that are not letters, like spaces and punctuation marks. All other characters are converted to lowercase. This function can be used to capitalize all words in a title.
Syntax: PROPER(text)
Arguments: Text is the text to convert.

REPLACE

Purpose: Replaces a given number of characters starting at a given position with a new set of characters.
Syntax: REPLACE(old_text,start_num,num_chars,new_text)
Arguments: Old_text is the text in which characters are replaced. Start_num is the position of the character to be replaced. Num_chars is the number of characters to replace. New_text is the text that replaces characters in old_text.

REPT

Purpose: Repeats a text string a specified number of times. This function can fill a cell with a fixed number of instances of the same text string.
Syntax: REPT(text,number_times)
Arguments: Text is the text to repeat. Number_times is the number of times to repeat.

RIGHT

Purpose: Gets the far right number of characters specified in a text string.

Syntax: RIGHT(text,num_chars)

Arguments: Text is the text string or reference to a cell containing text from which to get characters. Num_chars is the number of characters to get. If this value is omitted, Excel will assume a value of 1 for num_chars.

SEARCH

Purpose: Gets the number of the character at which the specified text is found, going from left to right, in a text string. This function accepts wildcard characters.

Syntax: SEARCH(find_text,within_text,start_num)

Arguments: Find_text is the text to find. Within_text is the text to search within. Start_num is the position within within_text at which to start the search.

SUBSTITUTE

Purpose: In a text string, substitutes the new text you specify for the old text you specify.

Syntax: SUBSTITUTE(text,old_text,new_text,instance_num)

Arguments: Text is the text string or reference to a cell holding text in which to substitute characters. Old_text is the text to replace. New_text is the text to substitute in place of the old_text. Use instance_num if you want to specify the occurrence of old_text you want to replace with new_text. Otherwise, every occurrence of old_text in your text will be changed to new_text.

T

Purpose: Gets the text referred to by a value. Generally, you do not need to use this function, because Excel automatically performs this action for you.

Syntax: T(value)

Arguments: Value is the value to test. Value can be a reference to a cell, a text string, or any other value. If value refers to text, the text is returned. Otherwise, "" is returned.

TEXT

Purpose: Converts a numeric value to text in the numeric format you specify.

Syntax: TEXT(value,format_text)

Arguments: Value is a number, a formula that evaluates a number, or a reference to a cell containing a number. Format_text is the number format in text form that you want to use.

TRIM

Purpose: Removes all leading and trailing spaces. Single spaces between words are not affected.

Syntax: TRIM(text)

Arguments: Text is the text string or reference to a cell holding text from which you want the spaces removed.

UPPER

Purpose: Converts a text string to uppercase.

Syntax: UPPER(text)

Arguments: Text is the string or reference to a cell holding text that you want to convert.

VALUE

Purpose: Converts the text to number.

Syntax: VALUE(text)

Arguments: Text is the text string or reference to a cell holding text that you want to convert.

■ User-Defined Functions

Excel allows users to define custom functions that meet their unique needs. User-defined functions are created on a Visual Basic module sheet. The module must begin with the word FUNCTION, and end with words END FUNCTION. What falls between FUNCTION and END FUNCTION are the user-defined function name, the function arguments, and the function code.

To create a user-defined function, you'll need a new module sheet. To create a new module sheet, open the Tools menu, point to Macro, and click on Visual Basic Editor (see Figure 8.10). From the Visual Basic Window click on the Insert Menu and select Module, as in Figure 8.11.

Remember to begin the module with the word FUNCTION, and your user-defined function name. Next, type the function arguments. The argument list is enclosed in parentheses and separated by commas.

When you press the ENTER key to move to a new line, The Visual Basic Editor checks the syntax of the line you just entered. As you enter the function code, use the Tab key to indent your code and make it easier to read.

Figure 8.10

Starting the Visual Basic Editor

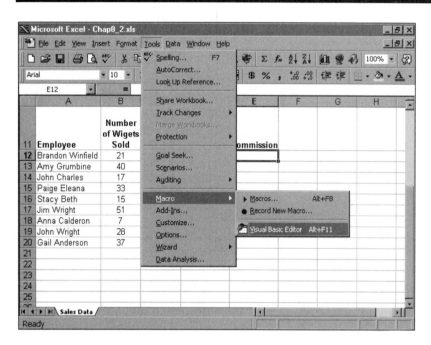

Figure 8.11

Creating a new module sheet

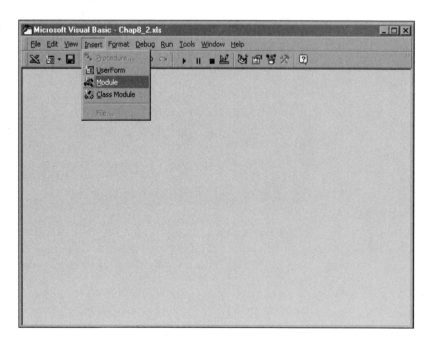

Figure 8.12 shows a user-defined function that computes a conditional sales commission.

If you enter invalid code and it causes a syntax error, The Visual Basic Editor will display an error-message dialog box. The error message will point to the first part of the code that is invalid. A Help button in the error-message dialog box is also available, and can provide additional information to help you correct the error.

Syntax rules for individual keywords are available in Visual Basic's Help feature. To get Help on a keyword from within a module, select the keyword and press the F1 Key.

TIP. *You can add comments to a function to explain its purpose. In Visual Basic, a comment starts with REM or an apostrophe ('), followed by one or more spaces.*

Figure 8.12

A user-defined function

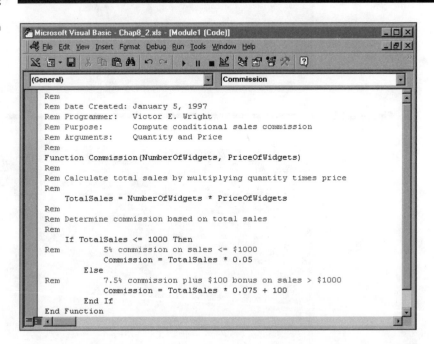

```
Microsoft Visual Basic - Chap8_2.xls - [Module1 (Code)]
File  Edit  View  Insert  Format  Debug  Run  Tools  Window  Help

(General)                                          Commission

Rem
Rem Date Created: January 5, 1997
Rem Programmer:   Victor E. Wright
Rem Purpose:      Compute conditional sales commission
Rem Arguments:    Quantity and Price
Rem
Function Commission(NumberOfWidgets, PriceOfWidgets)
Rem
Rem Calculate total sales by multiplying quantity times price
Rem
    TotalSales = NumberOfWidgets * PriceOfWidgets
Rem
Rem Determine commission based on total sales
Rem
    If TotalSales <= 1000 Then
Rem        5% commission on sales <= $1000
           Commission = TotalSales * 0.05
        Else
Rem        7.5% commission plus $100 bonus on sales > $1000
           Commission = TotalSales * 0.075 + 100
        End If
End Function
```

A user-defined function can return any valid Excel value (for example, number, date, text) and is used in the same manner as other Excel functions. In Figure 8.13, you can see how the user-defined commission function is called.

Figure 8.13

Calling a user-defined
function

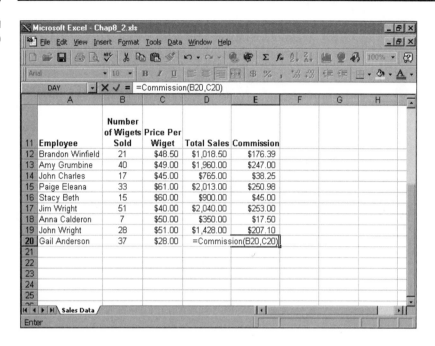

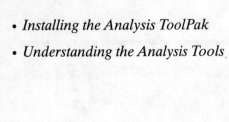

- *Installing the Analysis ToolPak*
- *Understanding the Analysis Tools*

9

Mastering Excel Analytical Tools

In THIS CHAPTER, YOU WILL LEARN ABOUT USING THE ANALYSIS ToolPak provided with Excel. This bonus package of software applications and Excel functions lets you apply statistical analysis in an easy-to-use fashion. Statistics have always been frightening for most people, but after you complete this chapter and try a few of the examples—and some of your own—you'll work numbers like a pro.

This chapter leads you through the following:

- Installing the Analysis ToolPak
- Understanding the Analysis Tools
- Using business tools
- Using engineering tools
- Using statistical tools

The examples given in this chapter should help you get started. Feel free to use them to experiment as you want. If you can't quite master a tool or two right away, don't worry. Find some that you want to work with, and after you have mastered those, you can go back and try the others. The more you use these tools, the easier it becomes. You will soon wonder how you ever managed without them!

With the Analysis ToolPak, Excel can rival—and even rise above—other software packages that are designed solely for statistical analysis. Using the data-analysis tools in the Analysis ToolPak, you can easily perform simple or complex statistical operations with any amount of data. The results of your analysis then can be used as the basis for further calculations, graphed in a variety of ways, or both. Excel's robust features add an extra dimension to statistical analysis by allowing you to merge statistics into spreadsheet calculations or database operations. You can organize your data in separate workbooks or on separate worksheets of the same workbook, and still have access to it all from the data-analysis tools in the Analysis ToolPak.

■ Installing the Analysis ToolPak

If the Data Analysis entry already appears in your Tools menu, skip this section—the Analysis ToolPak has already been installed and activated in your copy of Excel. If you don't see the Data Analysis command in the Tools menu, then use the Add-ins command in the Tools menu to see if the Analysis ToolPak is listed in the Add-ins dialog box. If it is, skip to the next section. If it isn't, use the steps that follow to install the Analysis ToolPak.

NOTE. *Be sure to close Excel before you run Setup. If you do not, Setup will ask you to close Excel before running. You might as well save time by doing it first.*

■ Installing the Analysis ToolPak Add-In

To install the Analysis ToolPak, follow these steps:

1. Using Windows Explorer, change to your Excel directory, then double-click on SETUP.EXE to run the Microsoft Excel Setup program. If you are using Microsoft Office, click on the Office Shortcut Bar's control menu and select Add/Remove Office Programs.

2. Click on the Add/Remove button. A series of check boxes for the available options will appear.

   WARNING. *The items currently installed are already checked: do not uncheck those items unless you are sure you want to remove them from your system.*

3. Double-click anywhere on the word Add-ins or in its check box. The Microsoft Excel Add-ins dialog box will appear, showing a list of add-ins with check boxes.

4. If it's not already checked, click on Analysis ToolPak to select it, then click on OK and proceed with the rest of the Excel Setup, inserting the appropriate disk(s) as prompted.

   NOTE. *If Analysis ToolPak is already checked, the Analysis ToolPak is already present in your system. You can exit Setup (click on Cancel) and go on to the next section.*

Adding the Analysis ToolPak to an Excel Menu

After you have installed the add-in tools, if necessary, you must let Excel know that they now are available. Use the following steps:

1. Select the Tools menu, then select Add-ins. After a moment, the Add-ins dialog box will appear, displaying all the available add-ins, as shown in Figure 9.1.

2. Click on the Analysis ToolPak check box and select OK. The Data Analysis command will then appear in the Tools menu after a brief pause while the ToolPak is activated in Excel.

■ Understanding the Analysis Tools

For clarity, this discussion is split into three parts to cover the three types of analytical tools in Excel: business tools, engineering tools, and pure statistical tools. Although all of these tools are statistical in nature, they are grouped here into categories that describe how they are most commonly employed. Their uses, however, are not restricted to any one field. Histograms, for

Figure 9.1

The available add-ins

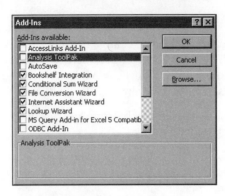

example, are discussed in the "Business Tools" section, but also are used by engineers and statisticians.

Each section explains the use of a particular tool and provides an example of each. Many sections in this chapter contain an introductory paragraph that assumes little or no prior knowledge of statistics. These paragraphs are not intended as complete discussions of each statistical operator, but are instead simple explanations intended to bridge the gap for the uninitiated, leading them into a fuller explanation of each statistical tool in the ToolPak. Tools that require more prior knowledge of statistical terms than an introductory paragraph can dutifully provide do not include such a paragraph.

To use any tool in the ToolPak, select Data Analysis from the Tools menu. The Data Analysis dialog box will appear, as shown in Figure 9.2. Scroll through the list until you find the tool you want to use, and either double-click on it, or click on it and then choose OK. You can also use the up- or down-arrow key to scroll through the list.

Figure 9.2

The Data Analysis dialog box

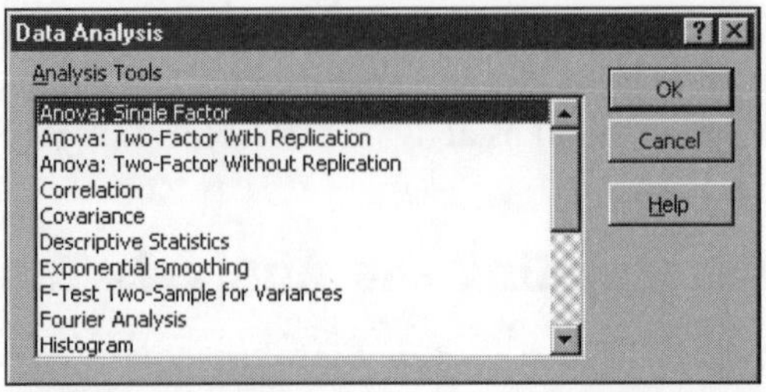

Using Business Tools

The tools discussed in this section are statistical tools used more often in business applications than anywhere else. They include the following:

- Correlation

- Covariance

- Exponential Smoothing

- Histogram

- Moving Average

- Random Number

- Rank and Percentile

These tools are not only used in business applications. Generally, the tools explained in this section are the most basic and easiest to use of the statistical tools in the Analysis ToolPak. It pays to know what each one of them does, regardless of how you might plan to use them.

Most of the dialog boxes for the tools in this section have some common features, including the following:

- **Input Range.** In the Input Range field, enter the range of cells in a spreadsheet where the source data resides. You can enter the range in A1 or R1C1 format—depending on Excel's setting—and you can include external references to other workbooks and sheets. Remember that you can use the Collapse Dialog button to temporarily put aside the dialog, allowing you to select the input range instead of typing it.

- **Grouped By.** If the source data is oriented in columns, select the Grouped By Column option button. For data that is oriented in rows, select the Grouped by Rows option button.

- **Labels in First Row.** If the Input Range includes labels for each column in the first row of the range, check Labels in First Row to indicate that the row does not contain data. If you have labels in the first row of data but do not select this box, Excel will assume that the first row contains data that it can use, and it will try to compute the first row with the rest of the data. This mistake can either throw off your results or generate an error message.

- **Output Range.** The result of the tool appears in the cell location that you indicate in the Output Range. A single-cell reference can be used for an output range to indicate the upper-left corner of the resultant data. Excel will automatically expand the range to include as many cells as necessary.

- **New Worksheet Ply.** Selecting this option lets you send the tool's results to a new worksheet in the same workbook. To do so, you'll need to check the box and supply Excel with a name for the new sheet.

- **New Workbook.** If you want to send the tool's results to an entirely new workbook, check this box.

Correlations

A *correlation* can indicate whether a particular set of data might be related by cause-and-effect to another set of data. For instance, do higher marketing costs relate positively to higher sales? Conversely, you could look for a negative correlation, such as whether higher marketing costs relate to lower sales. The Correlation tool checks each data point against its corresponding data point in the other data set (see Figure 9.3). It returns a positive number if both sets of numbers move in the same direction (positive or negative) throughout the data. Likewise, it returns a negative number if the sets of numbers move in opposite directions (positive or negative). The more closely the sets of values move together, the higher the correlation value. A correlation value of 1 indicates that the values move exactly together, and a value of -1 indicates that they move exactly opposite.

Figure 9.3

The Correlation dialog box

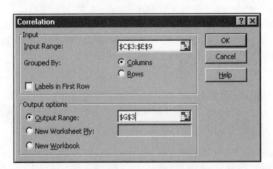

If more than two sets of data are given, correlation values will be returned for each set of data as it relates to every other set of data. The data to be analyzed must be located in adjacent rows or columns.

The example in Figure 9.4 shows three columns from which a correlation is drawn: column 1 is Average Temp, Column 2 is Sales of Ice Cream, and Column 3 is Sales of Donuts. You can see that a high correlation exists between Average Temp and Sales of Ice Cream, and that there is very little correlation between Average Temp and Sales of Donuts.

Figure 9.4

An example of correlation and covariance

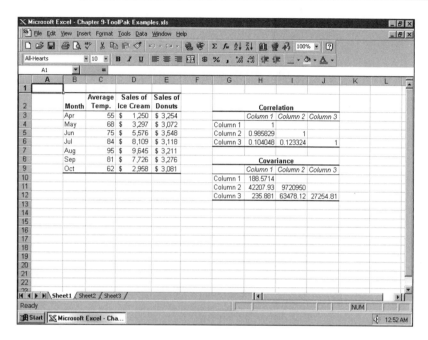

Covariances

Covariance is much like correlation, except covariances aren't restricted to numbers between -1 and +1. Thus, results from covariance analysis can be misleading if different units or widely different data set values are compared. While you might want to use covariance under special circumstances, such as when you are dealing with sets of very similar data or when you need more in-depth statistical analysis, correlation is useful far more often.

In the example, you can see how covariance can be misleading. The covariance of Column 1 (Average Temp) to Column 2 (Sales of Ice Cream) is 36178, but the covariance of Column 2 to Column 3 (Sales of Donuts) is 52487, or greater than that of Column 1 to Column 2. This fact suggests that the sales of ice cream and sales of donuts are closely related, but a look at the correlations for these columns tells you that they are not related. The correlation values are, in this case, the correct numbers—as the temperature goes up, so do ice cream sales.

Covariances can be useful in comparing, for example, two years of sales data for ice cream. The data in this case would be about the same, but would more closely show relationships because of the larger resulting numbers. For in-depth statistical analysis, the covariance results can be more useful when using them in succeeding calculations, because they have not been "normal-ized" to 1.

You use the Covariance dialog box shown in Figure 9.5 in much the same way that you use the Correlation dialog box. The results of both the correlation and covariance examples are shown in Figure 9.4, to better display the relationship between the two tools.

Figure 9.5

The Covariance dialog box

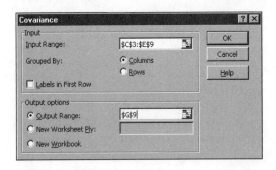

Exponential Smoothing

Exponential smoothing is most commonly used to forecast trends—a forecast is generated that shows the current trend of existing data based on prior performance. You then can tailor a forecast using a "Damping Factor" to smooth out random variations in the data or to detect trends in the data that are delayed from their stimulus (see Figure 9.6).

Figure 9.6

The Exponential Smoothing dialog box

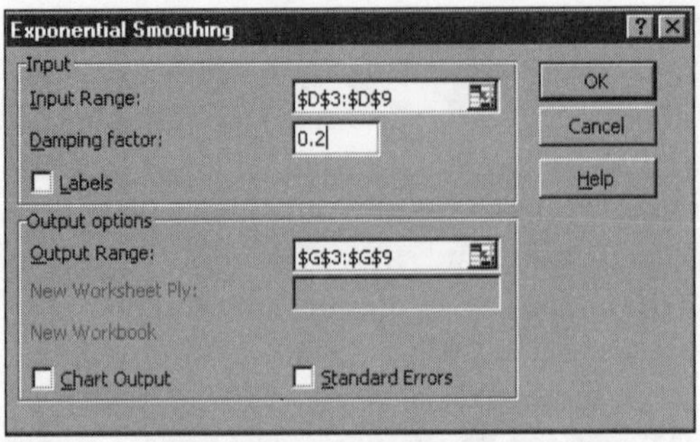

A good example is plotting mortgage applications to determine housing sales. Actual housing sales are delayed from their loan applications because of the time it takes for the lender to process the loan. This results in a delay of about a one month between mortgage applications and the appearance of a housing-sales trend. If mortgage applications suddenly stop, housing sales will still continue for about a month; if applications suddenly abound, however, sales will not start booming for about a month.

The Damping factor field permits you to tune the sensitivity of the smoothed output to any variability of the input data. A larger damping factor provides smoother data. It's recommended that you use a damping factor between 0.2 and 0.3—these numbers are a good balance between highly smoothed output data (greater than 0.5) and output that is very sensitive to changes in the input data (less than 0.1).

In the example in Figure 9.7, if you had data for many years of ice cream sales—and you wanted to know in general if your business was improving or receding—you would want to choose a large damping factor (0.8, for example) to mask the seasonal variation in sales and show you the "big picture." If, however, you wanted to see how your business varied from week to week, you would probably want a small damping factor (0.1, for example) to show those weekly fluctuations in sales. These damping factors are not given as fixed numbers, but as general starting points for analysis. You will probably need to use different damping factors a few times until you get just the results you want. The example in Figure 9.7 shows a lot of detail, and was created with a damping factor of 0.2.

Figure 9.7

Examples of exponential smoothing. Series 1 in each chart is the raw data, while Series 2 shows the smoothed data.

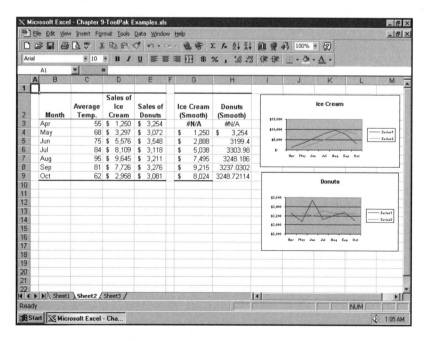

If you select the Chart Output option, Excel automatically generates a chart for the output data. The charts presented in this chapter, however, were generated manually for better appearance in this book. Automatic charts are quick, and usually work well for interactively displaying "pictures" of numerical results.

If you select the Standard Errors check box, Excel will include standard errors for each data point in the output data. *Errors* are measures of how much the smoothed output data is different from the raw input data.

Note the charted result for the Donut Sales data in Figure 9.7, in which the smoothed data makes the sales trend more obvious than does the raw data. The raw data tends to fluctuate up and down, and it is difficult to see from just that line whether sales are growing, declining, or holding steady. The smoothed line clearly shows that sales are on the rise.

Histograms

A *histogram* counts the number of occurrences of a unique piece of information within a set of data. Each unique piece of information is called a *bin*, and the number of times each bin is repeated in a set of data is called the *frequency*.

Excel generates bins by default if you do not enter anything in the Bin Range field. If, however, you want to show only certain bins, or explicitly declare bins, enter the bin you want to show in a specific row or column, then indicate that range in the Bin Range field (see Figure 9.8).

Figure 9.8

The Histogram dialog box

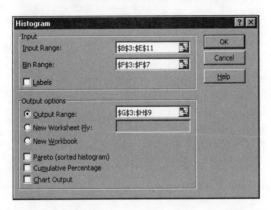

You can get a Pareto histogram (not shown) by selecting the Pareto check box under Output options. A *Pareto histogram* uses the same data as a standard histogram, but the bins are presented in descending order of frequency, rather than simply in order of bin numbers. The first (left-most) bar in a Pareto chart is always the tallest bar, and the chart proceeds in order from left to right, concluding with the shortest bar on the far right.

If the Cumulative Percentage check box is selected, cumulative percentages will be included in the output data. The *cumulative percentage* is the percentage of data covered from the first bin to the current bin. A cumulative percentage is most useful with Pareto histograms, because it indicates the percentage of the total that the largest bins occupy. In the example, a cumulative percentage of the 10-minute bin would equal the number of times the employee was 10 minutes late for work, or 14+6+6=26 times.

Check the Chart Output check box if you want Excel to automatically generate charts for the output data. The chart presented in the example in Figure 9.9 was, however, generated manually. The entries for each day have been arranged in multiple columns so that you can see all of the data upon which the histogram is based; normally the data would be arrayed in a single column or row.

Figure 9.9

A histogram example

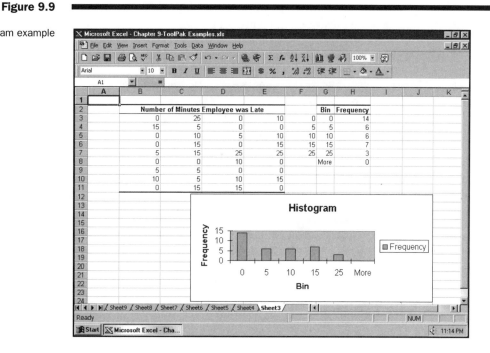

Moving Averages

A *moving average* is the average of a range of data taken from within a set of data. Moving averages are typically used in forecasting, as shown in this example, where we want to see the trend in donut sales and make some guesses from it about future sales. The input data points, which are used to generate the output data points, overlap. For example, if three input data points are used to generate one output data point (an *interval* of 3), output data point No. 2 is generated from input data points Nos. 2, 3, and 4. Output data point No. 3 is generated from input data points Nos. 3, 4, 5, and so on.

In our donut-sales example, you can see how variations in sales are averaged into one generally increasing line. Notice how the average flattens out around the fifth and sixth months. This is the result of averaging the previous three months' sales, two of which were somewhat sluggish.

Another explanation of moving averages can be made by taking a year-long set of data, using only three months worth of data for each data point in a forecast. The total set of data fell significantly, but then returned to its original value. A total average in such a case would indicate a zero trend, because the beginning and the end will be at the same point—in other words, a flat trend. A moving average, however, will show a true upward trend, because only the most recent data points are used for the last few output data points.

The Moving Average dialog box is shown in Figure 9.10; some examples are illustrated in Figure 9.11.

Figure 9.10

The Moving Average dialog box

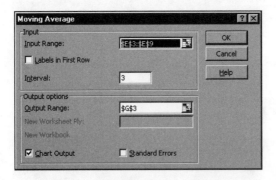

The Interval field indicates the number of data points from the input data Excel should use to create each data point in the output data.

NOTE. *The total number of output data points is determined by the following formula:*

```
Number of input points - Interval + 1
```

Check the Chart Output check box if you want Excel to automatically generate a chart for the output data.

Figure 9.11

Moving average examples

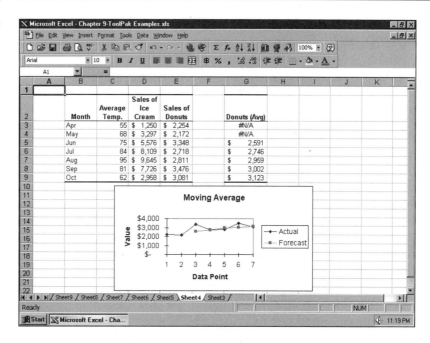

Use the Standard Errors check box to include standard errors for each data point in the output data. These errors are the result of the differences between the raw input data and the averaged output data.

Random Numbers

Excel can generate a set of random numbers that fit certain criteria you specify in the Random Number Generation dialog box (see Figure 9.12). The most important of these criteria is *distribution*, or the chance that any random number will fall within certain limits. If you are not familiar with distributions, you might want to use the Uniform Distribution option at first, then experiment later with others. A *uniform distribution* simply generates random numbers between given upper and lower limits. There is not as much tailoring of the data available within those limits as there is in other distributions.

NOTE. *More accurately, these numbers should be called* pseudorandom, *because the numbers are not truly random (instead, they are generated mathematically), but their distributions can be tailored somewhat for a specific use.*

The Number of Variables field allows you to tailor the distribution of the random data by using more than one random variable to generate the

Figure 9.12

The Random Number
Generation dialog box

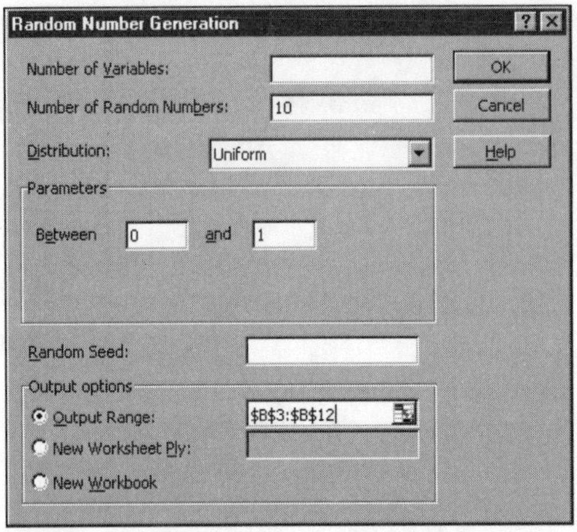

random numbers. If you leave this box blank, Excel assumes one variable, and will return one set of values to the output table.

The Number of Random Numbers field is where you indicate how many random numbers you want Excel to generate. If you do not specify a number, Excel fills all of the cells you establish as the output range. In the Parameters box, your entry will vary according to the selected Distribution. If you use Uniform distribution, however, numbers can be given for the upper and lower limits (see the Between and text boxes) of the output data; all random numbers generated will fall between the limits you specify.

Use Random Seed for any set of random numbers. Random Seed is the number Excel uses to initiate the mathematical process of generating pseudo-random numbers. Normally, Excel uses its own seed number, but you can enter a different number. Because the numbers are generated mathematically and are not truly random, the numbers on rare occasions may follow a pattern. The pattern, if any does exist, might not be obvious, and would certainly defeat the purpose of using "random" numbers. Entering your own seed number can sometimes ward off unwanted repetition of certain numbers or sequences of numbers. Establishing your own seed also makes it possible to generate the same set of random numbers again.

Two separate columns of random numbers are presented in the example to illustrate the use of the Parameters in the Uniform distribution (see Figure 9.13). The first list is a Uniform distribution set between 0 and 1; the second is a Uniform distribution set between 0 and 10.

Figure 9.13

Two sets of random
numbers with different
parameters

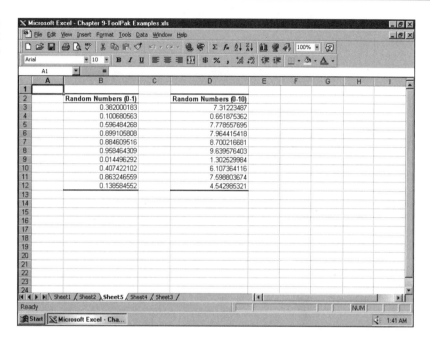

Ranks and Percentiles

Rank and Percentile generates a list of all values within a set of data, assigns
each a rank from greatest to least, and generates the percentile of each data
point to the top data point in the data set. This tool is commonly used in
schools and universities to calculate each student's class rank (for example,
8th out of 92 in the class) and the student's percentile in the class (84 percent, or in the top 16 percent of the class). The Rank and Percentile dialog
box is displayed in Figure 9.14.

Figure 9.14

The Rank and Percentile
dialog box

In the example in Figure 9.15, a Rank and Percentile calculation is performed on the Donut Sales column. The sales figures are ranked from highest sales volume to lowest sales volume, so you can see at a quick glance how high and how low sales were at their most extreme points during the period of time plotted. Each point is also ranked in order, and assigned a percentage value from the current highest value.

Figure 9.15

A Rank and Percentile
example

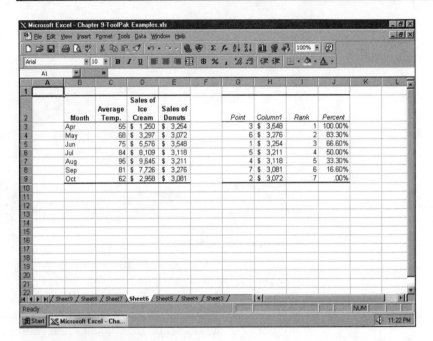

Using Engineering Tools

The tools discussed in this section are statistical tools used most often in engineering applications. These tools include the following:

- Fourier analysis

- Sampling

As in the previous section, these tools are not dedicated to engineering use only. Although Fourier analysis is rarely used outside of engineering circles, Sampling is a useful tool in many areas, especially where a great deal of data is analyzed.

The dialog boxes for these tools have some common features, including the following:

- **Input Range.** In the Input Range field, enter the range of cells in a spreadsheet where the source data resides. You can enter the range in either A1 or R1C1 format—depending on Excel's setting—and you can include external references.

- **Grouped By.** If the source data is oriented in columns, select the Grouped By Column option button. For data that is oriented in rows, select the Grouped by Rows option button.

- **Labels in First Row.** If the Input Range entered above includes labels for each column in the first row of the range, check Labels in First Row to indicate that the first row does not contain data. If you have labels in the first row of data but do not select this box, Excel will assume that the first row contains data that it can use, and will try to compute the first row with the rest of the data. This can either throw off your result or generate an error message.

- **Output Range.** The result of the tool will appear in the cell location that you indicate in the Output Range. A single-cell reference can be used for an output range, to indicate the upper-left corner of the resultant data. Excel will automatically expand the range to include as many cells as necessary.

- **New Worksheet Ply.** Selecting this option permits you to send the tool's results to a new worksheet in the same workbook. To do so, you'll need to check the box and supply Excel with a name for the new sheet.

- **New Workbook.** If you want to send the tool's results to an entirely new workbook, check this box.

Fourier Analysis

Fourier analysis is most often used by engineers to translate a set of time-dependent (*time-domain*) data into a set of complex constants (*frequency-domain*) that more clearly show the frequencies of certain data. The Fourier Analysis dialog box is shown in Figure 9.16.

Figure 9.16

The Fourier Analysis
dialog box

Excel requires that the number of input data points be a factor of 2 (2, 4, 8, 16, and so on).

An *inverse Fourier* transform is available by selecting the Inverse check box. This procedure converts frequency-domain data into time-domain data.

Two different sets of time-domain data are presented in the example to illustrate different frequency-domain outputs produced by Excel's Fourier transform (see Figure 9.17).

Figure 9.17

Two separate examples of Fourier analysis

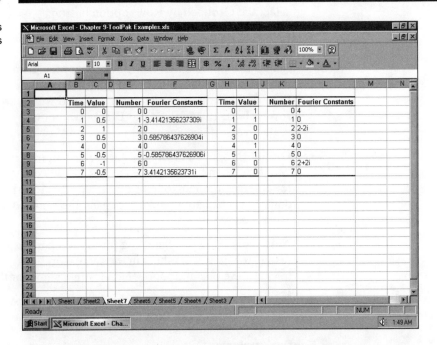

Two standard wave forms are shown in the preceding figure. The first is a triangle wave of amplitude Vpk=2v and period t=8 milliseconds.

The "Number" column is the harmonic number of the frequency output. Harmonic 0 is DC, harmonic 1 is the fundamental frequency (in this case, 125 Hz), harmonic 2 is the second harmonic (250 Hz), and so on. The Fourier Constants column is the amplitude of the given harmonic, presented as a complex number.

Sampling

Sampling extracts a selected number of values from a set of data. Sampling helps to reduce the size of a large set of data, while changing its overall qualities as little as possible. It is most useful with larger sets of data.

Two sampling methods are available in Excel. The first method, Periodic, moves down the data in order and returns every *interval* number of input data points as an output data point. You specify the interval in the Period edit box. An interval of 3, for instance, samples every third data point. The second method is termed Random. Use it to generate a specified number of output data points randomly chosen from the input data. These methods can be chosen from the Sampling dialog box, displayed in Figure 9.18.

Figure 9.18

The Sampling dialog box

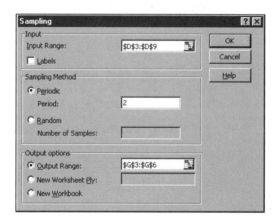

Both sampling methods are shown in this Figure 9.19. The ice-cream sales data was periodically sampled, and the donut-sales data was randomly sampled.

Notice that periodic samples ("Ice Cream Sales") might not include the true peak and low sales, even with a large volume of data. This can be especially true if the sample interval is high and only a few data points are taken for a lot of data. The data order is retained, however, and you can draw a general trend from the sampled data.

Random samples ("Donut Sales") can include the peak sales and low sales values, even if only a few samples are taken. Data order is lost, however—you will have no way to track back and find out at what time each of the data points occurred. Thus, you cannot draw general trends from this sampled data. Random sampling, however, is more effective than periodic sampling when used with distribution and average statistics.

Figure 9.19

The results of the
different types of
sampling

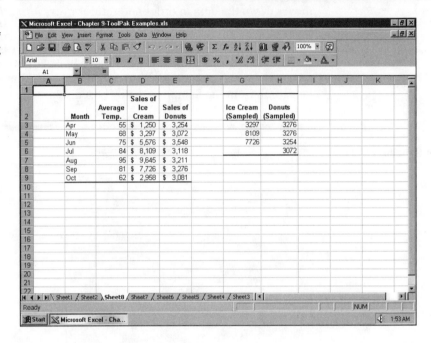

Using Statistical Tools

The tools discussed in this final section are generally used only for statistical analysis. The tools in this group include the following:

- Anova

- Descriptive Statistics

- Regression Analysis

- Sampling Tests

These tools are not necessarily useful just to statisticians. Some (like the sampling tests) *are* better suited for those who are somewhat experienced in statistics. Descriptive statistics, however, can be very useful in many areas, as they offer easy access to such basic calculations as means (averages) and standard deviations.

The dialog boxes for these tools have some common features, including the following:

- **Input Range.** In the Input Range field, enter the range of cells in a spreadsheet where the source data resides. You can enter the range in either A1 or R1C1 format—depending on Excel's setting—and you can include external references.

- **Grouped By.** If the source data is oriented in columns, select the Grouped By Column option button. For data that is oriented in rows, select the Grouped by Rows option button.

- **Labels in First Row.** If the Input Range entered previously includes labels for each column in the first row of the range, check Labels in First Row to indicate that the row does not contain data. If you have labels in the first row of data but do not select this box, Excel will assume that the first row contains data that it can use, and it will try to compute the first row with the rest of the data. This can either throw off your result or generate an error message.

- **Output Range.** The result of the tool appears in the cell location that you indicate in the Output Range. A single-cell reference can be used for an output range, to indicate the upper-left corner of the resultant data. Excel will automatically expand the range to include as many cells as necessary.

- **New Worksheet Ply.** Selecting this option allows you to send the tool's results to a new worksheet in the same workbook. To do so, you'll need to check the box and supply Excel with a name for the new sheet.

- **New Workbook.** If you want to send the tool's results to an entirely new workbook, check this box.

Anova Analysis of Variance

An analysis of variance, or *Anova*, generally examines the mean values of multiple sets of data (assuming that all means are equal) to determine if the mean values of samples taken from these sets also are equal. Three types of Anova tools are available in Excel, as follows:

- **Anova: Single-Factor.** Performs a single-factor analysis of variance (see Figure 9.20). Data sets of different sizes can be used with this tool. A single-factor analysis of variance tests the effect of a single factor (one column on the sample), as shown in Figure 9.21.

- **Anova: Two-Factor With Replication.** Performs a two-factor Anova, including more than one sample for each group of data. Data sets must be the same size.

  A two-factor Anova classifies input data by two different factors. The total variation is partitioned into the part that can be attributed to each factor (each row), and the interaction of each factor.

Figure 9.20

The Anova: Single Factor dialog box

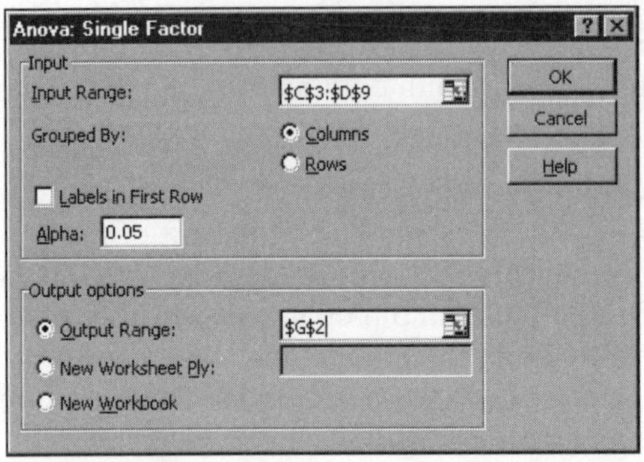

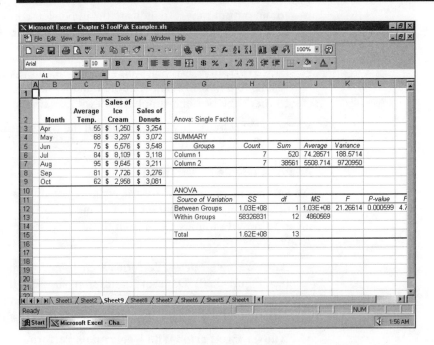

Figure 9.21

Single-factor Anova results

- **Anova: Two-Factor Without Replication.** Performs a two-factor Anova, but does not include more than one sampling per group.

  Enter the Anova alpha factor in the Alpha box. The *alpha factor* is the significance of the fit as a whole. It is the significance level of the ratio of the regression mean square value to the residual (error) mean square value.

The Anova: Two-Factor With Replication dialog box is shown in Figure 9.22. It is very similar to the Anova: Single Factor dialog box. You can use data from multiple rows as a single data point by indicating the number of rows to use in the Rows Per Sample box.

Figure 9.22

The Anova: Two-Factor With Replication dialog box

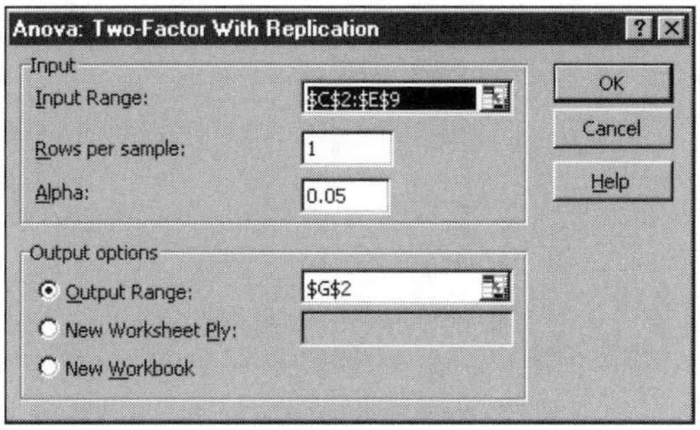

Figure 9.23 illustrates the results of the sample data.

Figure 9.23

Two-factor Anova with replication results

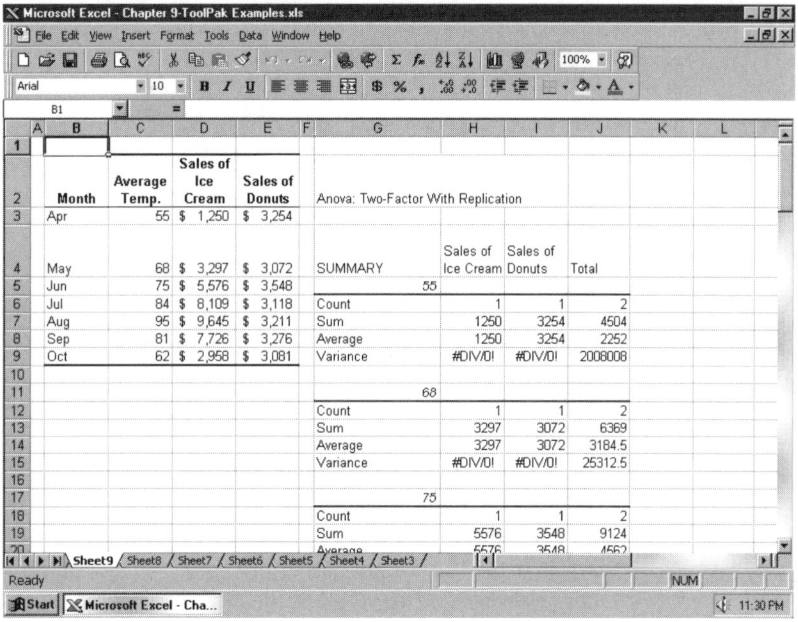

Row	B	C	D	E	G	H	I	J
2	Month	Average Temp.	Sales of Ice Cream	Sales of Donuts	Anova: Two-Factor With Replication			
3	Apr	55	$ 1,250	$ 3,254				
4	May	68	$ 3,297	$ 3,072	SUMMARY	Sales of Ice Cream	Sales of Donuts	Total
5	Jun	75	$ 5,576	$ 3,548	55			
6	Jul	84	$ 8,109	$ 3,118	Count	1	1	2
7	Aug	95	$ 9,645	$ 3,211	Sum	1250	3254	4504
8	Sep	81	$ 7,726	$ 3,276	Average	1250	3254	2252
9	Oct	62	$ 2,958	$ 3,081	Variance	#DIV/0!	#DIV/0!	2008008
11					68			
12					Count	1	1	2
13					Sum	3297	3072	6369
14					Average	3297	3072	3184.5
15					Variance	#DIV/0!	#DIV/0!	25312.5
17					75			
18					Count	1	1	2
19					Sum	5576	3548	9124

Figure 9.24 shows the Anova: Two-Factor Without Replication dialog box, which works in much the same way as the other two Anova dialog boxes. The results of Figure 9.24 are illustrated in Figure 9.25.

Figure 9.24

The Anova: Two-Factor
Without Replication
dialog box

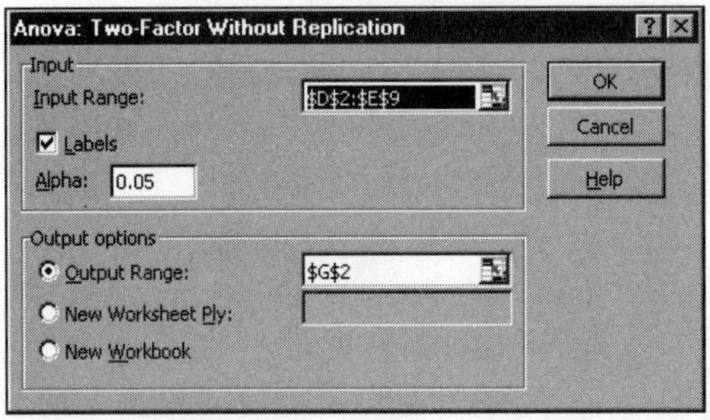

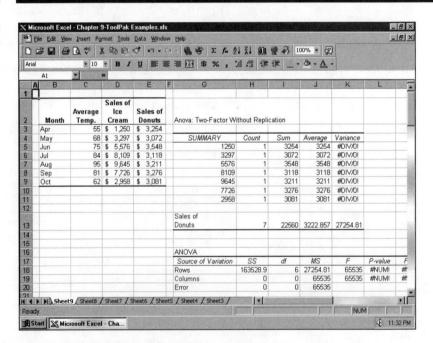

Figure 9.25

Two-factor Anova without
replication results

Descriptive Statistics

Descriptive statistics generate various numbers that describe properties of a data set, such as mean, standard deviation, and so on. The Descriptive Statistics dialog box is shown in Figure 9.26.

Figure 9.26

The Descriptive Statistics
dialog box

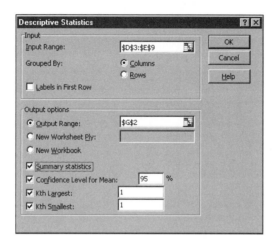

Enter the desired confidence level in the Confidence Level for Mean box. The confidence level, 95 percent in this example, means that 95 percent of the time a given data point will be contained within a certain range (interval) about the mean value.

The Kth Largest and the Kth Smallest boxes let you exclude a number of data points from either the largest of the data points or the smallest—or both. Often, when you have large amounts of data a few data points will be wildly different than the rest, and this difference can introduce error into your descriptive statistics. If you want to exclude, for example, the largest two values from your analysis, enter **3** in the Kth Largest box: the analysis will then start with the third-largest data point and proceed to the smallest. If you then wanted to exclude the smallest value as well, enter **2** in the Kth Smallest box. The analysis will then range from the third-largest to the second-smallest data values.

You can also ask Excel to provide Summary statistics, which are shown in Figure 9.27.

The descriptive statistics produced are as follows:

1. **Mean.** The average between the Kth largest and the Kth smallest values.

2. **Standard Error.** The standard error of the data.

3. **Median.** The middle value.

4. **Mode.** The mode of the data.

5. **Standard Deviation.** A measure of the data spread.

6. **Sample Variance.** Another measure of the data spread.

Figure 9.27

Examples of descriptive
statistics for both
columns

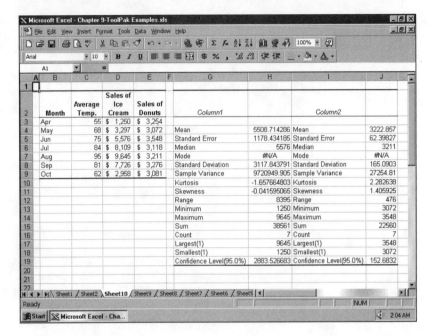

7. **Kurtosis.** A measure of the "tails" of a distribution, or how much of the data is far away from the mean.

8. **Skewness.** A measure of how the distribution of the data is "balanced" around the mean.

9. **Range.** The largest value used minus the smallest value used.

10. **Minimum.** The smallest value used.

11. **Maximum.** The largest value used.

12. **Sum.** The total of all data points.

13. **Count.** The number of data points used.

14. **Confidence Level.** The interval (range) within which a given data point can be found 95 percent of the time.

Regression Analysis

Regression fits a smooth line (not necessarily a straight line) to a set of otherwise jagged data. This statistical tool is most often used graphically, where a straight or smooth line is superimposed on rough data. Regression permits you to more easily see a trend, in situations where the trend may not be obvious from the raw data. Statistical data is given for each data point.

Regression is also useful for reducing raw data to a mathematically simple function.

The Regression dialog box is shown in Figure 9.28. Use the Input X and Y Range fields to indicate where the X and Y data resides within the spreadsheet.

Figure 9.28

The Regression dialog box

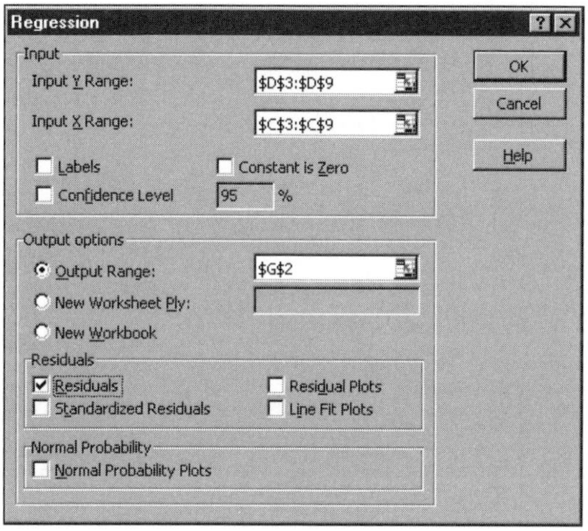

Regression uses a series of x-y values—coordinates of each data point—to calculate its results, so both the Input Y Range and the Input X Range must be entered.

The confidence level is the same as that described in the Descriptive Statistics section.

You have a variety of options for choosing results to be displayed in addition to the standard expression results. You can display the Residuals (errors), the Standardized Residuals, or both. You can choose to have the Residuals plotted for each independent variable. A plot of the central data with the regression line also drawn on the same graph is available when you select Line Fit Plots. You can also specify the display of a Normal Probability Plot.

The statistical result will be placed in the range indicated (the single reference points to the upper-left corner of the result table). You also can select Summary statistics.

The results of the example are partially shown in Figure 9.29.

Figure 9.29

Portion of the Regression
summary results

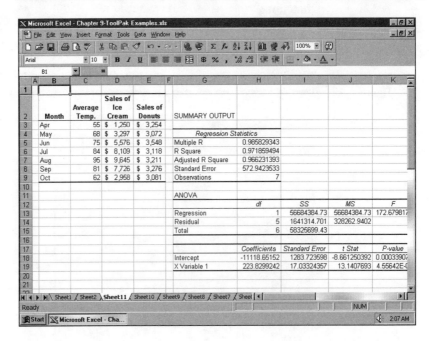

Sampling Tests

The *sampling tests* compare certain properties of two sets of data. Five varieties of this tool are available:

- **Two-Sample for Variances F-Test.** Compares the variances between two sets of data.

- **Paired Two-Sample for Means t-Test.** Compares the means between two paired sets of data. The data should show a natural pairing of data points, such as running the same experiment twice, and must contain the same number of data points. The variances between the two sets of data are not assumed to be equal.

- **Two-Sample Assuming Equal Variances t-Test.** Determines whether the means of two samples are equal, based upon the assumption that the variances of the two samples are equal.

- **Two-Sample Assuming Unequal Variances t-Test.** Determines whether the means of two samples are equal, based upon the assumption that the variances of the two samples are not equal.

- **Two-Sample for Means z-Test.** Tests the probability that a sample was drawn from a certain population.

The F-Test: Two-Sample for Variances dialog box appears in Figure 9.30. Enter the data range in the Input Variable 1 and 2 Range fields. Enter the alpha factor in the Alpha edit box. The Output options section is identical to those discussed earlier in this chapter.

Figure 9.30

The F-Test Two-Sample for Variances dialog box

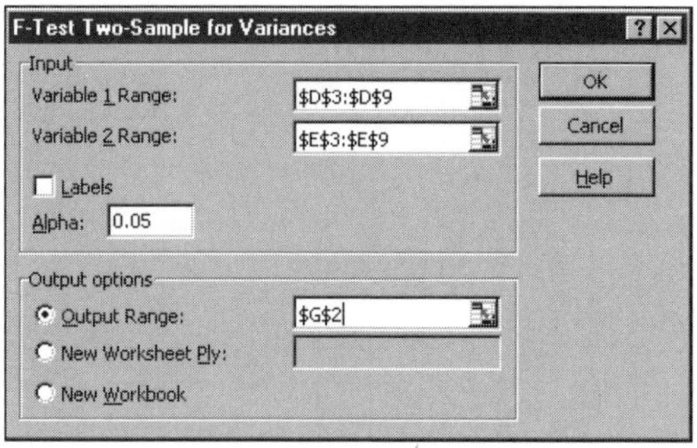

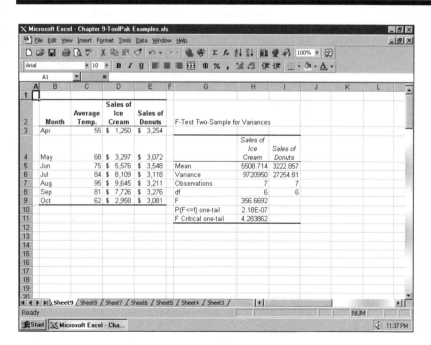

The dialog boxes for the remaining sampling test tools are all very similar, and are used in much the same way. Study Figures 9.31 through 9.35 to see the difference between the results returned by each of these tests.

Figure 9.31

Two-sample for variances F-test results

Figure 9.32

Paired two-sample for
means t-test results

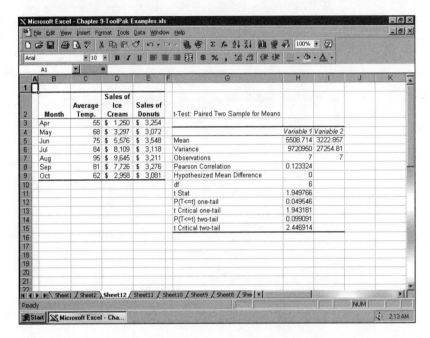

Figure 9.33

Two-sample assuming
equal variances t-test
results

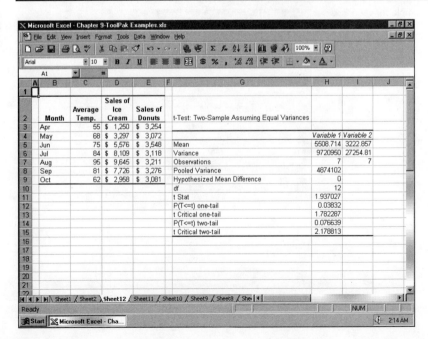

Figure 9.34

Two-sample assuming
unequal variances
t-test results

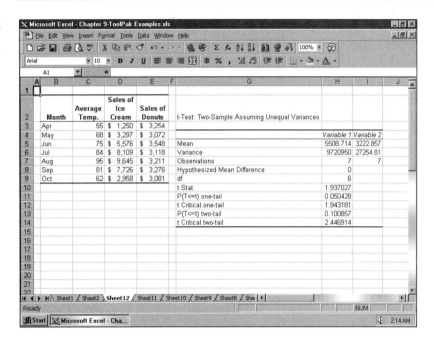

Figure 9.35

Two-sample for means
z-test results

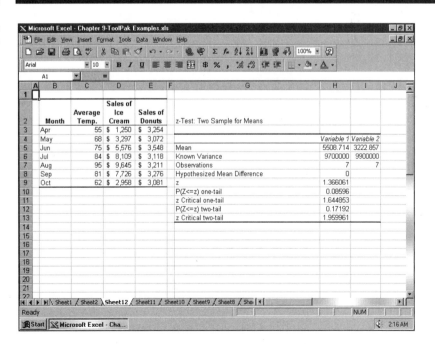

P A R T

2

Databases

- *Database Terminology*

- *Using Spreadsheets as Database Tables*

- *Basic Design Elements*

- *Designing a Database: A Case Study*

- *Filtering Data in a List*

- *Using AutoFilter*

- *Advanced Filters*

- *Advanced Sorting and Filtering Features*

- *Using the Excel Data Form*

- *Merging an Excel Database with a Microsoft Word Document*

- *Knowing When to Use a Real Database Program*

10

Excel Database Basics

Excel's excellent data-management features are quite powerful. Although Excel worksheets are most often used to manipulate numeric data, your worksheets can also be used as a database to store and retrieve text and other non-numeric information.

This chapter presents the following information:

- Introducing database terminology
- Using spreadsheets as database tables
- Designing a database list in Excel
- Using Excel's data filters
- Sorting data in a list
- Using an Excel database in a Word merge operation
- Knowing when to use a "real" database system

As you will see, Excel 97 for Windows provides interactive, visual methods for sorting, filtering, and searching the data stored in Excel worksheets. This chapter shows you the basic technology you must master to use Excel spreadsheets as databases.

Businesses run on data. Customer lists, inventory control, employee records, and sales histories are all examples of common business data-management needs.

In many ways, Microsoft Excel is the ideal data-management tool for small to medium businesses, and for many personal data-management needs as well. You can use Excel spreadsheets to store and retrieve data, in the same way that you can use sophisticated, specialized database-management systems. Excel also is more forgiving and easier to learn than database systems like Microsoft FoxPro or Borland dBASE.

Excel has many functions specifically designed to help you sort and filter the data that is stored in your worksheets. This chapter covers sorting and filtering, as well as general design considerations for the novice database user.

■ Database Terminology

The first step to learning how to use databases is becoming familiar with the specialized terminology that database experts use. The following list is by no means complete, and it is somewhat Excel-specific. Nevertheless, it is intended to provide you with a basic understanding of common database terms that are used in Excel and elsewhere.

- Database. The term "database" is used in several different ways, depending on what database system is being used. In Microsoft FoxPro and Borland dBASE, for instance, a database is a collection of table files that are part of a database application. A Microsoft Access database, on the other hand, includes all of the tables, forms, and other objects that make up the application in one file.

- Table. A database table is just like an Excel worksheet. An Excel database table contains rows and columns (these are called records and fields, respectively) of data contained in the worksheet cells (which might be empty). A table is usually referred to as a list in Excel.

- List. In Excel terms, list is another name for a database table. Based on certain design elements (discussed later in this chapter) and the way in which it is used, Excel automatically recognizes a list on a worksheet.

- Field. A field is a column of data in a database table. A field contains a specific category of data, which might be entered as alphanumeric or numeric text. The fields in a table might include "Name," "Address," and "Phone Number."

- Record. A record contains all of the fields of data for a particular person or entity. In other words, it is a set of related data that corresponds to a single row in the database table. A record in a database table might be a person's name, address, and phone number.

- Query. A query is a request sent to a database for the purpose of retrieving data. Normally, a query only retrieves specific information from the database table, based on parameters (called "criteria") that you define.

  In Excel terms, a query definition is all the information needed by Microsoft Query (an Excel add-in discussed in Chapter 11) to extract data from a source of data (like an external database). This information includes the table names, field names, and specific search criteria needed to complete the database search.

- Query criteria or search criteria. Because a query returns specific information from a database table or Excel list, a method must exist for specifying which data to extract from the table. The expressions "query criteria" and "search criteria" both apply to the set of information that specifies the data to be retrieved from the Excel list.

- Query design. When using Microsoft Query, query design refers to the tables, relationships between tables, and other elements included in the query criteria used to extract data from an external database.

■ Using Spreadsheets as Database Tables

Whatever the underlying database system, a table (or list, in Excel) consists of rows and columns of data. A Microsoft Excel worksheet is perfectly analogous to a database table in FoxPro, Access, or dBASE.

Because Excel is designed primarily to handle financial or other numeric data, however, certain principles apply differently to Excel than to most other database systems.

Guidelines

Because many Excel features can be applied to only one list on a worksheet at a time, it is generally a good idea to put only one list on a worksheet. It also is a good idea to dedicate a single worksheet to maintaining a single list of data.

Surround the list with blank rows above and below and blank columns to the left and right. This arrangement makes it easy for Excel to distinguish your list from other things on the worksheet.

As you soon learn, filtering a list hides rows that are excluded from the list, leaving only those records meeting the selection criteria. If you have important information on the left or right of your list, it might be hidden when you filter the list.

Using the Data List

An Excel data list can be used interactively or through macros and other automation techniques. Excel provides a number of menu options that enable you to quickly and easily filter the data contained in lists. Several macro functions can also greatly enhance your ability to utilize data in Excel lists and external databases. These techniques are discussed later in this chapter.

■ Basic Design Elements

As mentioned previously, when you build Excel data lists, worksheet columns become fields and worksheet rows serve as database records. Several other important concepts should be kept in mind, however, as you design and build Excel data lists.

Designing a Database Worksheet

As an example of a common database, consider the address and phone directory you carry in your briefcase. This phone directory is correctly thought of as a database of contact information. Most often, these directories are pre-printed with areas for a person's name, an address, and phone numbers.

Columns Become Fields

Each of these areas is a field in the directory database. If you are designing an Excel worksheet to use as a phone directory, you should add fields for the name, address, and phone number information.

TIP   *Depending on how you plan to sort and search your data, some fields could be broken down into smaller units of data. For example, "Name" could become "FirstName," "MiddleInitial," and "LastName." However, don't carry*

*this practice too far—breaking up "Date" into "Month," "Day," "Year," will
serve no useful purpose.*

*Consider also adding fields that provide flexibility, such as "Prefix" (Mr.,
Mrs., Ms.), "Area Code," or "Record Number." If you assign a sequential
record number to records as you enter them into your database, you'll be able
to return the records to their original entry order by sorting on the "Record
Number" field—this is a neat trick to know if you're trying to recover from a
"bad sort day."*

Each row in the worksheet will serve as a database record, and will contain
all of the contact information for one person.

Allow Enough Fields

Very often, people design databases without enough fields. You'll want to include a field for each type of information that you might want to access. As
you will soon see, it is much easier to search for a person's last name if it appears in a field of its own, rather than being included with the first name in
the "Name" column. Most databases function more efficiently if only one category of data (such as the first or last name) is stored in a field.

Figure 10.1 shows an Excel worksheet containing a data list that serves
as a simple address book.

Figure 10.1

A data list on an Excel
worksheet

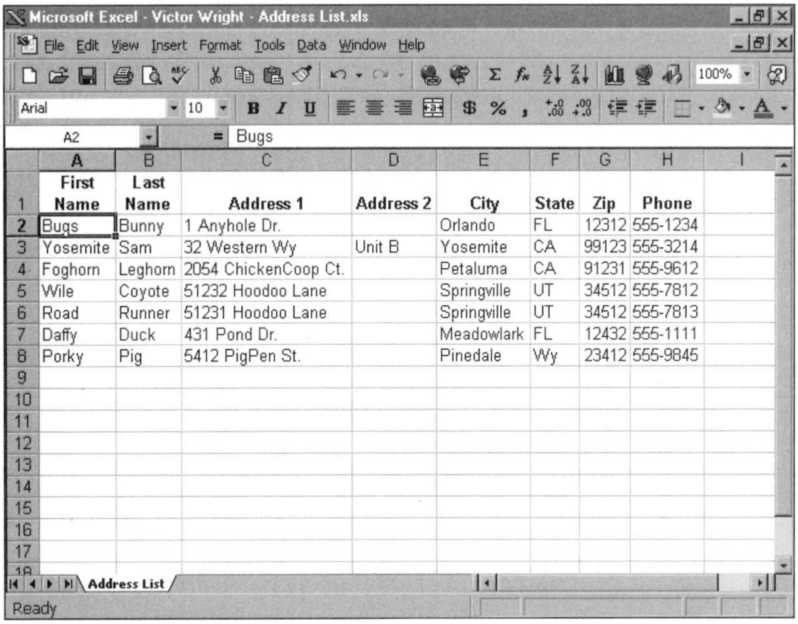

NOTE *If you plan to export your Excel database to a non-Microsoft database, spaces in the label names could cause problems.*

Use Field Labels

It is generally a good idea to use field labels on the list. Excel uses field labels when finding data in the list, and for creating reports from the data.

Field labels should appear in a different font or typeface than the data stored in the column. Most often, field labels will appear in a bold typeface. It's enough to use a pattern or cell border to distinguish the field labels from the data in the columns.

If you want to visually separate the field labels from the data in the field, use a border along the bottom of the labels rather than empty cells. If the field labels aren't contiguous with the data in the fields, Excel won't know that the field labels belong to the list.

TIP *Another way to visually separate field labels from the data is to increase the height of the first row containing data.*

Entering Data into Cells

When entering data into the cells of an Excel data list, don't put blank spaces at the beginning of a cell. Any extra blanks will be used by Excel when sorting the list, and this might cause unexpected results.

Some Windows fonts (for instance, Arial) are proportionally spaced, which means that spaces take up less room than wide characters like "m" or "w." When extra spaces are inadvertently entered at the front of cells displayed in a proportionally spaced font, they can be difficult to see.

Font Formatting in Cells

Use the same font characteristics (bold, size, and so on) for all of the cells containing data in a field. Arbitrarily mixing typefaces can lead to unnecessary confusion.

Name the List and its Major Elements

After you have the basic list in place, assign a name to the entire list. This will make it easier to refer to the database in formulas. If you plan to use the worksheet only to hold the data list, assign the list name by highlighting all of the fields in the list. Otherwise, select only the cells containing the field labels and data. Choose Name from the Insert menu. The cascading menu shown in Figure 10.2 will appear.

When you choose Define from the cascading menu, the Define Name dialog box will appear (see Figure 10.3). Enter the name you want to assign to your data list in the Names in workbook text box, and then click OK.

Figure 10.2

The Name cascading menu

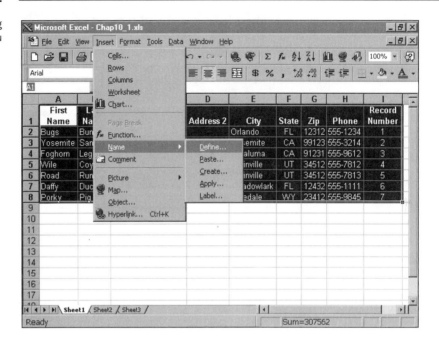

TIP *There are rules to follow when you name your list or major elements. Defined names can contain up to 255 characters. The first character of a name must be a letter or an underscore character (_), the rest of the name can be a combination of letters, numbers, periods, and underscores—but NO SPACES! You cannot use cell references such as A$100 or R2C2. You can use uppercase and lowercase letters, just remember that Excel doesn't distinguish between the two. For example, if you've defined a name Tax and then define a name TAX, TAX would replace Tax—they're the same name, as far as Excel is concerned.*

Figure 10.3

The Define Name dialog box

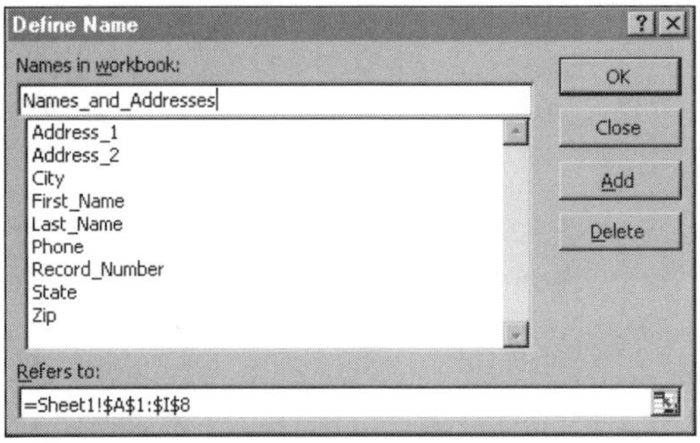

Each of the fields can be named by highlighting the column, and then entering appropriate names in the Define Name dialog box. Later, these fields and the list can be referenced by the names assigned to them.

It's easy to find the names assigned to the list or parts of the list. Click on the down-arrow next to the names box on the Formatting toolbar to reveal the list of named items in the list (see Figure 10.4).

Figure 10.4

The names of elements of the data list

Name List

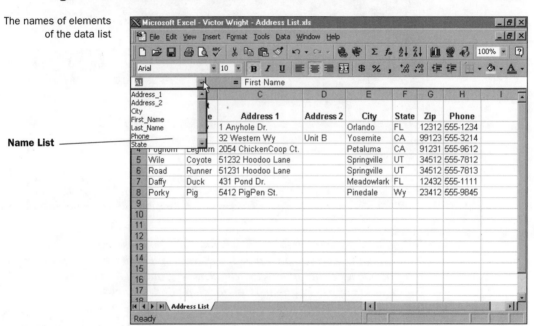

Although it isn't necessary to name the items in the list, you can use the appropriate element name any time Excel requires a reference to data in the list. For instance, when sorting the list by the values in the "Last Name" field, you can use the name assigned to that field ("Last_Name") rather than a range or other reference.

■ Designing a Database: A Case Study

Designing a database table is a rather straightforward exercise. A little advance planning can make it much easier when it comes time to lay out the list in an Excel worksheet.

Determining the Structure

The first step is deciding what data you want the database list to manage. Expanding somewhat on the address-book analogy, consider the case of Sarah Wood, the manager of a busy shoe store, who is building an Excel database to manage the commissions paid to her salespeople.

Sarah's data-management needs are similar to those of most businesspeople. Dissimilar information (employee names, sales figures, and commission rates) will all be contained within the Excel data list. Calculations will be applied to the data in the worksheet to determine sales commissions and bonuses (Sarah's shoe store pays a monthly bonus to the top-grossing salesperson). Finally, summary reports can be used to determine which salespeople are showing the most improvement in their sales figures.

Sarah Wood's Data List

Sarah's first iteration of her worksheet is shown in Figure 10.5. The names of the 10 salespeople are listed in the field labeled "Employee Name," and the gross sales made by each employee for the first six months of 1996 are in the six fields to the right of the Employee Name field.

Figure 10.5

Sarah Wood's worksheet

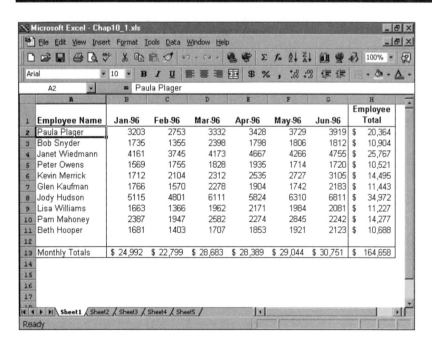

Employee Name	Jan-96	Feb-96	Mar-96	Apr-96	May-96	Jun-96	Employee Total
Paula Plager	3203	2753	3332	3428	3729	3919	$ 20,364
Bob Snyder	1735	1355	2398	1798	1806	1812	$ 10,904
Janet Wiedmann	4161	3745	4173	4667	4266	4755	$ 25,767
Peter Owens	1569	1755	1828	1935	1714	1720	$ 10,521
Kevin Merrick	1712	2104	2312	2535	2727	3105	$ 14,495
Glen Kaufman	1766	1570	2278	1904	1742	2183	$ 11,443
Jody Hudson	5115	4801	6111	5824	6310	6811	$ 34,972
Lisa Williams	1663	1366	1962	2171	1984	2081	$ 11,227
Pam Mahoney	2387	1947	2582	2274	2845	2242	$ 14,277
Beth Hooper	1681	1403	1707	1853	1921	2123	$ 10,688
Monthly Totals	$ 24,992	$ 22,799	$ 28,683	$ 28,389	$ 29,044	$ 30,751	$ 164,658

There is a wide disparity in gross sales, because most of the Top Shoes employees are employed only part-time. The full-time employees have much higher gross sales figures than the part-time employees.

Sarah is interested in the monthly sales totals for each month, so she added a simple formula (=SUM(B2:B11)) in column B, a couple of rows below the last row of data. Then, using the data fill handle at the bottom right corner of the active cell, she copied this formula into the other cells in row 13, below each column of monthly data. She also added a field to the right of the list containing the total sales of each employee over the six-month period.

Being new to Excel, Sarah isn't sure what to do next. The data in the worksheet in Figure 10.5 is somewhat difficult to work with. The records and fields are in no particular order, so not much information can be derived.

Sarah does understand, however, that her worksheet qualifies as an Excel database list. In any field, all the cells contain the same category of data. Each row is the sales record for one employee, so each cell in a row is related to the other cells in the same row. Sarah assigns the name "Sales96" to the range of cells from A1 to H11. Excel recognizes the field labels at the top of each column, because Sarah has set their typefaces to Bold and put a thick single-line border at the bottom of each cell in the top row.

Sorting the List Alphabetically

First, Sarah wants to sort the list alphabetically. This arrangement will make it easier to enter employee data.

Sorting the list by the Employee Name field is easy. All she needs to do is to click on any cell within the "Sales96" area (she chose the Employee Name field label) to inform Excel that she intends to work with the "Sales96" data list.

Next, she selects the Sort option from the Data menu. The Sort dialog box appears (see Figure 10.6). Notice that the Sales96 list is highlighted while the Sort dialog box is open: this lets you know that Excel understands what area is about to be sorted.

TIP   *Here's a quicker way to sort the list by employee name (or any one field for that matter). Position the cell pointer anywhere in the employee name field then click on the Ascending button on the Toolbar—it works for descending sorts as well.*

If Sarah wanted to sort the list by a field other than Employee Name, she could display the Sort by dialog box and then select the appropriate field name. Because Excel recognizes "Sales96" as a data list, each field name will automatically be added to the Sort by list.

Figure 10.6

The Sort dialog box

What Ascending and Descending Mean

Notice that you can select Ascending and Descending for each sort option. An Ascending sort (the default) reorders the list from the smallest number (including negative numbers) to the largest number on numeric fields. If the field is alphabetic, an Ascending sort follows alphabetic order (A to Z). Fields containing date or time data are sorted from earliest date or time to latest. Remember, because all of the data within a field is of the same type (numeric, alphabetic, or date/time), Excel won't become confused when data types change during a sort. A Descending sort reorders the list from largest to smallest, highest to lowest, and latest to earliest.

Using Field Headings During Sorting

At the bottom of the Sort dialog box in Figure 10.6 is an area (labeled My list has) in which you can tell Excel how to treat the first row in your list. If your list has field labels, but Excel didn't find them for some reason (most likely because you did not use a different typeface for the field labels), the "No Header Row" option button will be selected. If you click on the "Header Row" option button, Excel will use the top row of the list as field labels and exclude the row from the sort operation.

TIP   *If Excel thinks your list does not have field headings, the top row of your list will be included in the sort. This can lead to unexpected changes to the list order. Always check the results of a sort. If the field headings (also called the field labels) have been included in the sort, undo the sort by selecting the Undo option in the Edit menu, then check to make sure the field headings look different than the items in the list.*

When Sarah clicks on the OK button, the Sales96 list is instantly sorted alphabetically by Employee name, as shown in Figure 10.7. If Sarah wanted the list to be sorted by the employees' last names, she probably should have put the names into the list as "Last Name, First Name." As it is, the list is nicely sorted by the employees' first names.

Figure 10.7

The list sorted by the Employee Name field

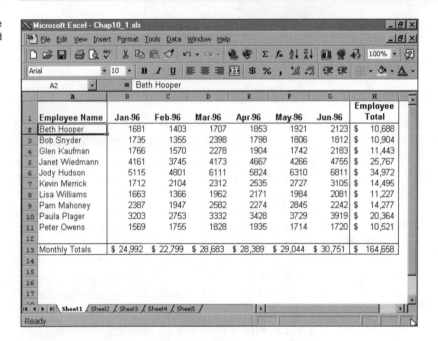

Sorting the List Numerically

Working with a sorted list is easier than dealing with rough, unorganized data. Although the alphabetically sorted list is easier to use, it still doesn't indicate which employees are Sarah's top performers. She sorts the list once more, this time choosing "Employee Total" as the Sort By field. She also clicks on the Descending button. The results of this sort are shown in Figure 10.8.

From this list, it is easy to see that Jody Hudson was, by far, the highest-grossing employee for the first half of 1996 (although a case could be presented that, in such a small list, it is easy to pick out the highest number from the Employee Total field). Consider for a moment how different the situation would be if there were several hundred rows and dozens of fields in the data list. It is very difficult to pick out the highest (or lowest) number if the list spans across many screens.

More advanced sorting options are discussed later in this chapter.

Figure 10.8

The list sorted by
Employee Total

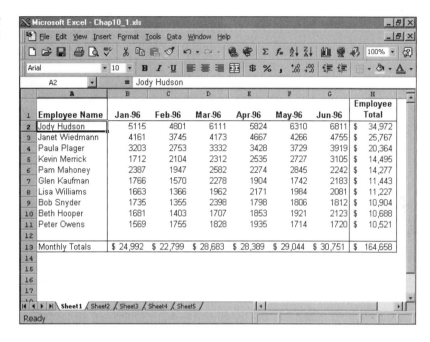

■ Filtering Data in a List

So far, Sarah Wood has sorted her list by both alphabetic and numeric data. Excel's built-in sorting routines have made these tasks quick and easy.

Her next step is experimenting with filtering the data in the list. Bonuses in the Top Shoes store are only paid to employees who exceed their monthly sales quotas. Any full-time employee bringing in more than an average of $3,000 in sales is eligible for a tidy bonus every six months. Sarah wants to filter out employees who didn't make their quota.

■ Using AutoFilter

Obviously, Sarah wants to exclude employees with gross sales of less than $18,000 for the six-month period covered in her list. Excel makes simple filters like this easy to create. Again, Sarah's first step is clicking on a cell in the Sales96 data list. She then chooses Filter from the Data menu to reveal the Filter cascading menu (see Figure 10.9).

Initially, Sarah just wants a quick and easy filter, so she selects the Auto-Filter option. AutoFilter places drop-down arrows on each field in the data list (see Figure 10.10).

Figure 10.9

The Filter cascading menu

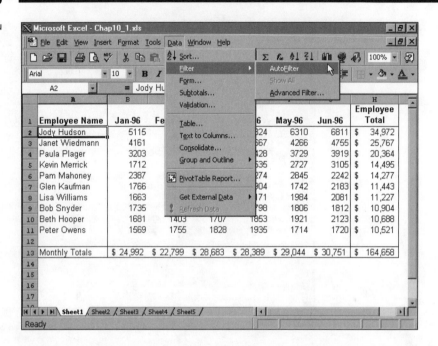

Figure 10.10

The AutoFilter drop-down
arrows on the data list.

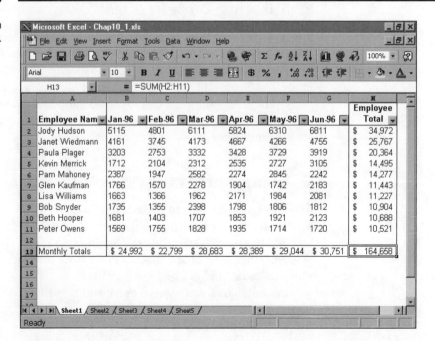

Specifying AutoFilter Criteria

When you click on the drop-down arrows, a list of filter criteria is revealed, as shown in Figure 10.11. This drop-down list contains all of the unique value in the field. By clicking on a value in this list, Sarah could quickly exclude all rows except for those that contain the value she selected.

Figure 10.11

The filter criteria list

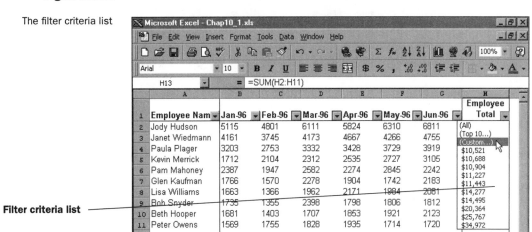

Filter criteria list

This approach, however, does not help her determine which employees have met their quotas. Instead, she selects the Custom option from the list, which opens the Custom AutoFilter dialog box (see Figure 10.12). This dialog box contains fields for specifying which data should be included in the filtered data.

Figure 10.12

The Custom AutoFilter dialog box

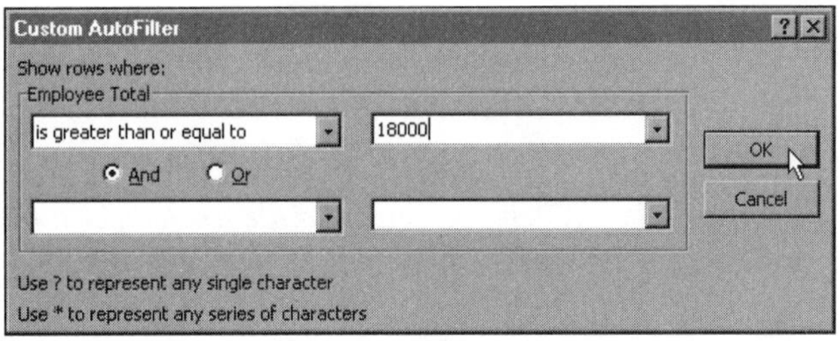

Because she wants to identify all employees who brought in $18,000 or more in gross sales, Sarah selects "is greater than or equal to" from the first drop-down box, enters 18000 in the text box to the right, and clicks on the OK button (see Figure 10.12). The list instantly changes to the result shown in Figure 10.13.

Figure 10.13

The result of the custom AutoFilter

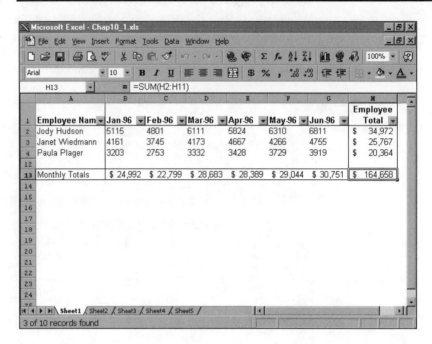

Although at first glance it appears that a lot of rows have been deleted from the list, look at the row numbers at the far left in Figure 10.13. These row numbers indicate that all of the rows from 5 through 11 have been hidden, rather than deleted. When you filter data in an Excel database list, the rows excluded by the filter are simply hidden from view.

How Filters Affect List Operations

Many list operations, such as printing, copying, and charting, work only on displayed data. The fields hidden by a filter will not be printed or copied along with the displayed fields.

TIP   *To remove the AutoFilter, choose Filter from the Data menu and click on AutoFilter. When you return to the worksheet, all of the drop-down arrows will disappear, and previously hidden rows will be displayed.*

Summing Across Hidden Rows

A couple of things are worth noting here. For instance, notice that the grand total in the lower-right corner of Figure 10.13 is the same as it was when all data was displayed (see Figure 10.10). The formula for the grand total is =SUM(H2:H11), which includes rows that are hidden from view.

Even when rows are hidden from view, Excel continues to correctly display summary data based on the hidden values.

■ Advanced Filters

January and February were particularly difficult months for Top Shoes. Bad weather kept away many customers, and a few employees called in sick for several days during this period. Sarah is interested in knowing which employees had been able to make their quotas during the bad weather, indicating a willingness to tough it out when things got bad.

Although AutoFilter is easy to use, Sarah will face limitations if she tries to create criteria that involve the "or" operator on more than one field of data. This more-complex filter criteria will require Excel's Advanced Filter capabilities.

TIP   *AutoFilter can be used to create criteria that involve the "and" operator on more than one field. For example, if Sarah wants to identify employees who sold more than $3,000 in January and more than $3,000 in February, she could define custom criteria for both months to select values greater than $3,000.*

The Advanced Filter feature requires a certain amount of setup before selecting the Advanced Filter menu option. First, Sarah must specify the criteria she wishes to use for the filter. The criteria was quite simple: for the months of January and February, she needs all rows with values greater than 3,000.

The Advanced Filter option requires Sarah to build an area on the worksheet with this information (see Figure 10.14). Just below the data list, Sarah puts exact duplicates of the field labels for the January and February data, and below each label she places the value for which she wants to search. The field labels and criteria make up the criteria range for the advanced filter.

TIP   *If you anticipate that your to list will grow (and most do), consider placing your criteria area to the right of and slightly below the list. That way, when you add records or fields to your list, the criteria area will be unaffected.*

TIP   *The labels for the criteria range must be exactly like the labels on the fields you want to filter. The best way to get exact duplicates of the field labels is to copy and paste them into the criteria range.*

Next, Sarah selects the Advanced Filter option from the Filter cascaded menu (see Figure 10.15). It is important to note that you must have the criteria range established before invoking the Advanced Filter option.

The Advanced Filter dialog box then opens (see Figure 10.16). The List Range box is automatically filled in by Excel with the range for the Sales96 data list. Sarah has to fill in the Criteria Range box herself, however, either by typing the range or by using the mouse to select it.

Figure 10.14

The criteria range for the Advanced Filter operation

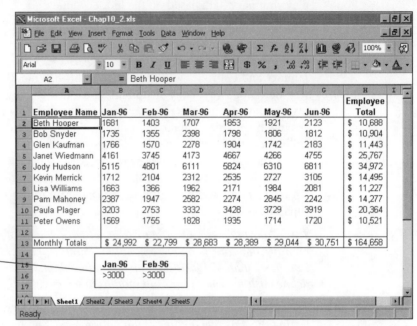

Criteria range

Figure 10.15

The Advanced Filter option in the Filter cascaded menu

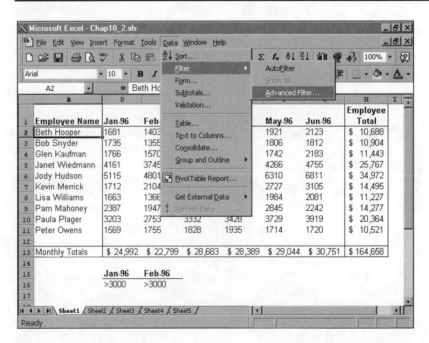

Figure 10.16

The Advanced Filter
dialog box

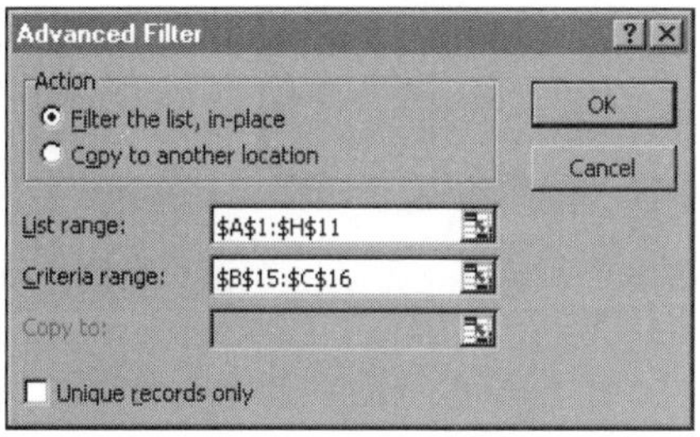

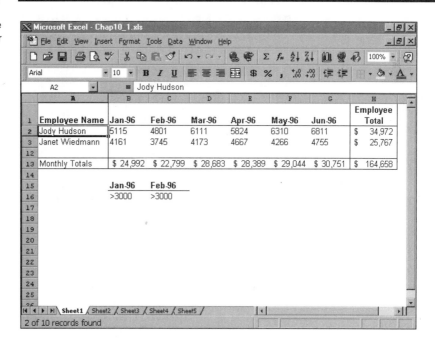

When Sarah clicks on the OK button, the data in her list is instantly filtered according to the information specified in the criteria range (see Figure
10.17). Only those rows with values above 3,000 in January or February appear.

By default, the filter results will be displayed in place of the original list
of data. If Sarah wanted the results copied to another location in the active
worksheet, she would have clicked on the "Copy to another location" action
from the Advanced Filter dialog box (see Figure 10.16). Sarah would also
need to enter the "Copy to:" range.

Figure 10.17

The result of the
advanced filter

TIP   *To remove the Advanced Filter, select the Show All option in the Filter cascade menu under the Data main menu. The Show All option is available only when an Advanced Filter has been applied to a data list.*

■ Advanced Sorting and Filtering Features

In addition to the basic sorting and filtering operations described earlier in this chapter, Excel 97 for Windows has a number of advanced features that extend your ability to manage lists that are used as databases.

Custom Sort Order

The default sort orders are Ascending and Descending. When Sarah Wood wanted to see who the highest-selling employee was, she simply sorted the list by the "Employee Total" field. As you read this chapter, it might have occurred to you that it was not entirely fair to her part-time employees to include them along with the full-time employees during this sort.

Since part-time salespeople have less opportunity to sell shoes, their sales figures are naturally lower than those of full-time workers. With the current Sales96 list design, it is not possible to easily include information indicating employment status in a sort or filter.

Even a field added to the list indicating FT (for full-time) and PT (for part-time) does not provide a full solution. "PT" will always fall after "FT," because it comes after "FT" when sorted in alphabetical order. Sarah Wood wants to be able to sort by more than just FT and PT, however. She'd like to be able to use FT (full-time), TQ (three-quarter time, or 30 hours a week), and HT (half-time, 20 hours or less per week). Sorting this field alphabetically puts the half-time people at the top of the sorted list.

What Sarah needs is a "custom sort order" that appropriately sorts or filters FT, TQ, and HT fields. She first adds a new field to the list to contain the employment status, as shown in Figure 10.18.

Next, Sarah needs to add the custom sort order to her Excel 97 for Windows installation. She simply opens the Options dialog box by choosing Options in the Tools menu and clicks on the Custom Lists tab (see Figure 10.19).

The left half of the Custom Lists page displays the current set of custom lists. Excel has pre-installed lists for sorting by months of the year and by days of the week.

To add a list, simply enter it in the List Entries box to the right of the Custom Lists area, separating each list item by pressing Enter, and then click on Add. Figure 10.19 shows the Custom Lists page after Sarah has entered the employment status items. When Sarah clicks on the OK button, she will return to the Sales96 list.

Figure 10.18

The Sales96 list with the new field added

	A	B	C	D	E	F	G	H	I
1	Employee Name	Jan-96	Feb-96	Mar-96	Apr-96	May-96	Jun-96	Employee Total	ES
2	Jody Hudson	5115	4801	6111	5824	6310	6811	$ 34,972	FT
3	Janet Wiedmann	4161	3745	4173	4667	4266	4755	$ 25,767	FT
4	Paula Plager	3203	2753	3332	3428	3729	3919	$ 20,364	TQ
5	Kevin Merrick	1712	2104	2312	2535	2727	3105	$ 14,495	TQ
6	Pam Mahoney	2387	1947	2582	2274	2845	2242	$ 14,277	HT
7	Glen Kaufman	1766	1570	2278	1904	1742	2183	$ 11,443	QT
8	Lisa Williams	1663	1366	1962	2171	1984	2081	$ 11,227	HT
9	Bob Snyder	1735	1355	2398	1798	1806	1812	$ 10,904	HT
10	Beth Hooper	1681	1403	1707	1853	1921	2123	$ 10,688	QT
11	Peter Owens	1569	1755	1828	1935	1714	1720	$ 10,521	QT
12									
13	Monthly Totals	$ 24,992	$ 22,799	$ 28,683	$ 28,389	$ 29,044	$ 30,751	$ 164,658	

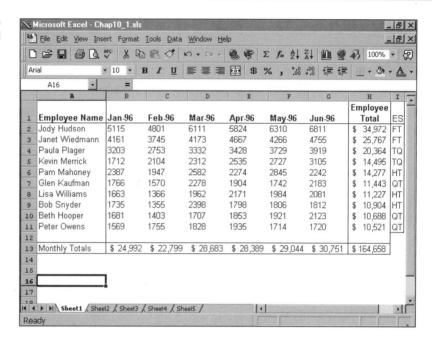

Figure 10.19

The Custom Lists page in the Options dialog box

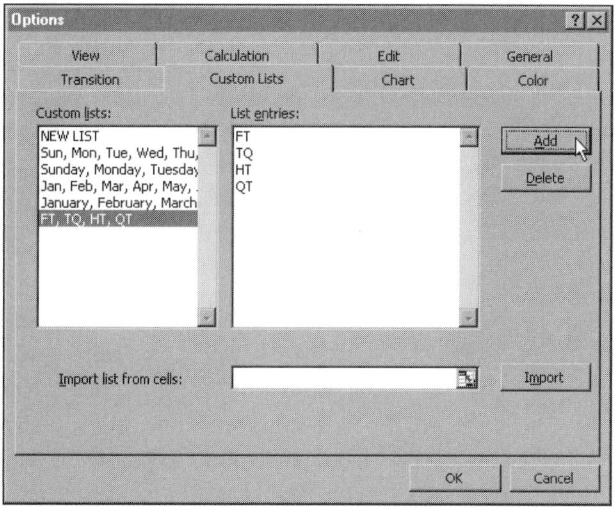

Sorting the list by the Employee Total and ES fields is easy. When Sarah chooses Sort in the Data menu, the Sort dialog box will appear, as shown in Figure 10.20.

Figure 10.20

The Sort dialog box

Sarah enters the new ES field in the Sort By box and enters the Employee Total in the Then By box. This sequence ensures that employees will be grouped together by their employment status and then, within the employment status group, by the Employee Total field.

With the Sort by box highlighted, Sarah makes sure the new custom list is used to sort the ES column by clicking on the Options button in the Sort dialog box to open the Sort Options dialog box (see Figure 10.21).

Figure 10.21

The Sort Options dialog box

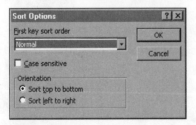

When open, the First key sort order drop-down list box shows the names of all of the custom lists that are known to Excel (see Figure 10.22). Sarah selects her custom list (FT, TQ, HT, QT) from this list and then clicks on the OK button.

The results she obtained after sorting her list are shown in Figure 10.23.

Figure 10.22

The custom orders that
can be used for sorting

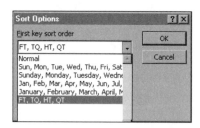

Figure 10.23

The sorted list

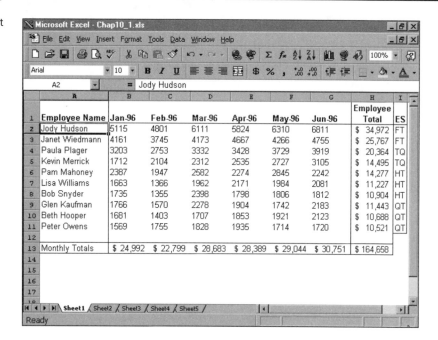

A quick look at the Employee Total field shows Sarah that she has one
quarter-time employee (Glen Kaufman) who has out-performed two half-
time people (Bob Snyder and Lisa Williams). Either Glen Kaufman is an ex-
ceptional salesperson, or Bob Snyder and Lisa Williams need a little training!

Sorting More Than Three Fields

Only three fields can be sorted at a time. If you need to sort by four or more
fields, perform your sort in stages. Sorting rearranges the rows in the list; unlike filtering, this rearrangement is permanent (unless you immediately undo
the sort, of course). Therefore, you should sort by the least-important fields
in the first pass and by the more-important fields in the last pass. Sorting by

the most-important fields last allows those fields to wield the most influence on the arrangement of the rows within the list.

TIP   *If you don't have a record number field, it's a good idea to create a temporary "sort order" field, numbering each record quickly by creating an incremented number series, to establish the original sort order of the records. That way, if something goes wrong with the sort, you can quickly get back to square one by sorting on the temporary sort order (or record number) field. Once the sort has been accomplished and is deemed satisfactory, the temporary sort order field can be removed.*

If you don't have a record number field or temporary "sort order" field, remember that if the sort goes wrong, you can always close the file without saving it.

Sorting multiple fields makes sense when one of the fields is likely to contain multiple entries with the same value. The Top Shoes example is not a good candidate for a multiple-field sort, because each field contains unique values.

Sorting Selected Parts of Records or Fields

It is possible to sort selected (contiguous) records or fields in the list. Simply highlight the records or fields you want to sort, then proceed as if you were sorting the entire list.

WARNING   *Keep in mind that sorting selected parts of records or fields could result in scrambled data. Proceed cautiously if you elect to use this feature.*

Figure 10.24 shows the Sales96 list with the middle five rows marked for sorting. Rows from 4 through 8 were highlighted by clicking the mouse on the row heading for Row 4, and then dragging the mouse down to Row 8.

Figure 10.25 shows the Sales96 list after it has been sorted alphabetically by the Employee Name field. As you can see, Bob Snyder has been moved to Row 4, the top of the area marked in Figure 10.24.

You can also sort parts of one or more fields. First, select the part of the field or fields you wish to sort. Next, click on the Options button in the Sort Dialog box. Then choose the "Sort left to right" orientation, and click OK. The fields you selected will be sorted in the order you have specified.

Sorting Fields Rather Than Records

You also can sort fields of data rather than records. As an example, suppose you want to rearrange the order of dates to Jun-96 through Jan-96. First select the Fields you wish to sort. In this example Jan-96 through Jun-96 have been selected (see Figure 10.26). Next, display to the Sort Options dialog box (see Figure 10.27), by clicking on the Options button at the bottom of

Figure 10.24

The Sales96 list
prepared for a partial sort

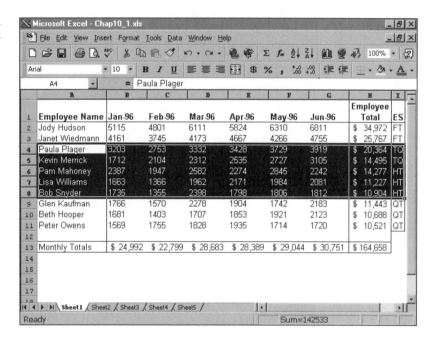

Figure 10.25

The Sales96 list after
sorting Rows 4 through 8

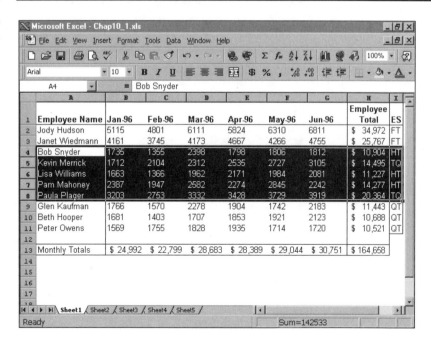

the Sort dialog box. Remember that the Sort dialog box will appear when you choose Sort from the Data menu.

Figure 10.26

The Sales96 list with date fields Jan-96 through Jun-96 marked for sorting

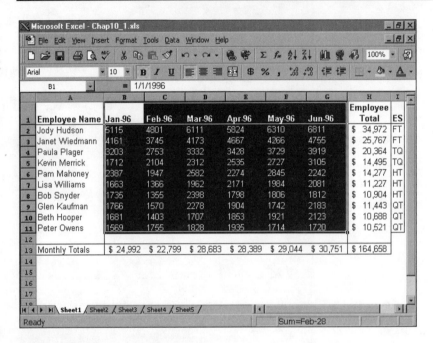

Figure 10.27

The Sort Options dialog box with Sort Left to Right orientation chosen

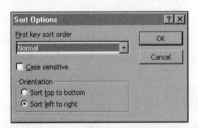

In the lower left corner of the Sort Options dialog box is an area labeled Orientation. By default, the Sort top to bottom option button is selected, meaning that sorts will rearrange the order of the rows in the list. When the Sort left to right option is enabled, the fields of data will be sorted instead.

When you return to the Sort dialog box choose Descending as the sort order for Row 1 (see Figure 10.28). Click the OK button to sort the fields. Figure 10.29 shows the results of the sort. Notice that the order of the date fields is now Jun-96 through Jan-96.

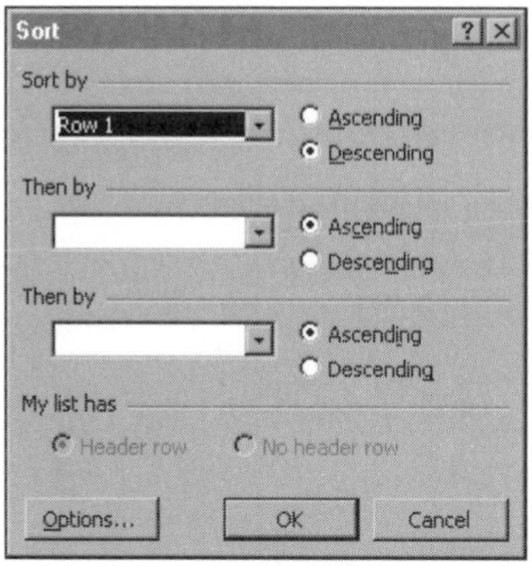

Figure 10.28

Sort Dialog box with
Descending Field Order

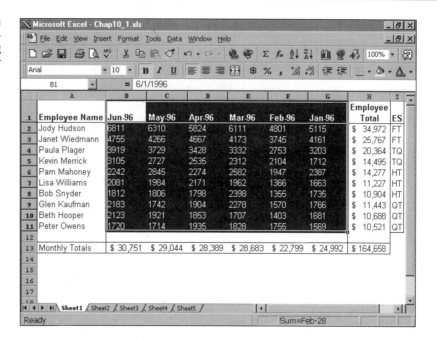

Figure 10.29

The Sales96 list with
fields Jan-96 through Jun-
96 sorted in descending
order

Copying Filtered Data to Another Location

Occasionally, you will want to copy filtered data to another worksheet location. Advanced filtering occurs "in place" by default. The rows that are filtered out of the data by the information in the criteria range are hidden from
view, leaving only the selected rows on display.

If you want to leave the original data list intact and make another copy of the filtered data somewhere else, click the Copy to another location option button in the Advanced Filter dialog box (see Figure 10.30).

Figure 10.30

The Copy to another location option button

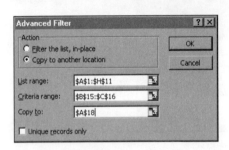

When this option is selected, the Copy to text box becomes active (it normally is grayed out). All Excel needs is the worksheet cell in which you want the upper left corner of the filter results to appear. In Figure 10.30, this location is cell A18. When you click on the OK button, Excel will immediately copy the filter results to the location specified in the Copy to box.

Figure 10.31 shows the result of the advanced filter that is illustrated in Figure 10.30. The Excel toolbars have been turned off in Figure 10.31 to permit more vertical viewing space, and the overall dimensions have been scaled to 90 percent. The filtered data has been copied to the area beginning with cell A18.

WARNING   *Be careful when using the advanced filter Copy to option. Any data already in the area specified in the Copy to will be overwritten without warning!*

Copying Filtered Data to Another Application

If you want to copy filtered data to another Windows application, be sure to leave the filter criteria in place before the copy operation. Records excluded by the filter criteria are hidden and are not copied.

NOTE   *When you copy a list from Excel to Word for Windows, the list becomes a table in Word.*

■ Using the Excel Data Form

Excel provides an incredibly easy-to-use tool for entering new data into lists. The Excel data form displays the data from one record in a list and permits you to add, delete, or otherwise modify the field information in the list.

Figure 10.31

Copying the result set to a different location

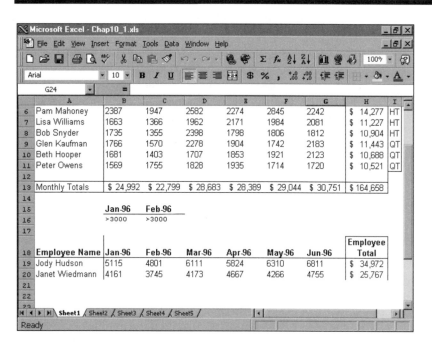

To open the data form for a list, put the insertion point anywhere inside the list and choose Form in the Data menu. The data form opens with the first record of the data list already displayed (see Figure 10.32).

Figure 10.32

The Excel data form

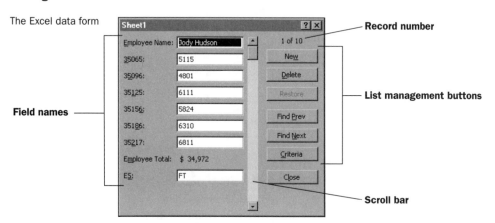

The data form contains all the fields in the record, arranged vertically. In Figure 10.32, the field labels containing dates are expressed as the numbers that Excel uses internally to store dates. If this bothers you, consider converting your date labels to their text equivalents. For example, enter " 'Jan-96" instead of "Jan-96" in the cell. Jan-96 would now appear in the form.

The data form also contains all the items needed to add, delete, or modify records in the data list. The data form can also be used to search for a particular record based on specific criteria entered in the form.

Notice that the Employee Total field cannot be changed in the data form. The information in this field is calculated—it is the sum of all of the "month" fields in the record. Therefore, its value is dependent on other fields in the record, and it cannot be changed directly by the user.

Adding New Records Via the Data Form

A new record can be added to the list by clicking on the New button. All the fields in the form will be blanked out, as shown in Figure 10.33, and "New Record" will appear in the upper-right corner of the data form. Any data written in the fields on the data form will be added to the data list when either the Close button or New button is selected.

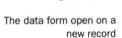

Figure 10.33

The data form open on a new record

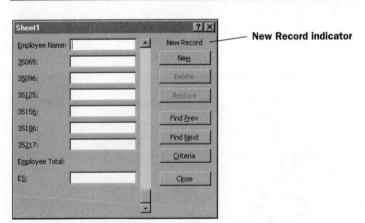

New Record indicator

Deleting a Record Via the Data Form

The record that appears on the form will be deleted when the Delete button is clicked. The record deletion is permanent and cannot be undone.

If any data in an existing record displayed in the form is changed, the Restore button becomes active (by default, the Restore button is grayed out as it appears in Figure 10.33). When clicked, the Restore button will revert all changes back to the original condition of the record. After you move on to another record, however, all changes will become permanent, and you will not be able to restore the record or undo changes to it.

Navigating Records With the Data Form

The Find Prev and Find Next buttons simply move up and down the data list, displaying records one at a time. As you move through the records, you can make changes to the displayed record or you can delete it using the list management buttons.

TIP   *The scroll bar can also be used to view the records in a list.*

Searching for Records With the Data Form

The Criteria button enables you to search for a particular record based on information you enter in the fields on the data form. After the Criteria button is pressed, the form will clear and the scroll bar will become inactive (see Figure 10.34). The word "Criteria" will appear in the upper-right corner of the form to indicate the form is ready to accept search criteria.

Figure 10.34

The Excel data form that is prepared to accept criteria

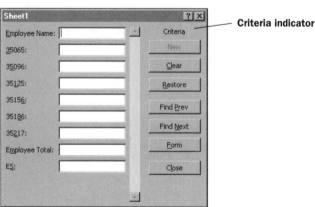

To perform a search, enter your search criteria in the appropriate field and click the Find Next or Find Prev buttons to find the next or previous record (respectively) that meets the criteria entered in the field.

Figure 10.35 illustrates a search using the Criteria button.

In Figure 10.35, <15000 has been entered in the Employee Total field. When the Find Prev or Find Next buttons are pressed, Excel will look for the previous or next record (respectively) with a value of less than 15,000 in the Employee Total field, as shown in Figure 10.36.

Figure 10.35

The data form with search criteria inserted

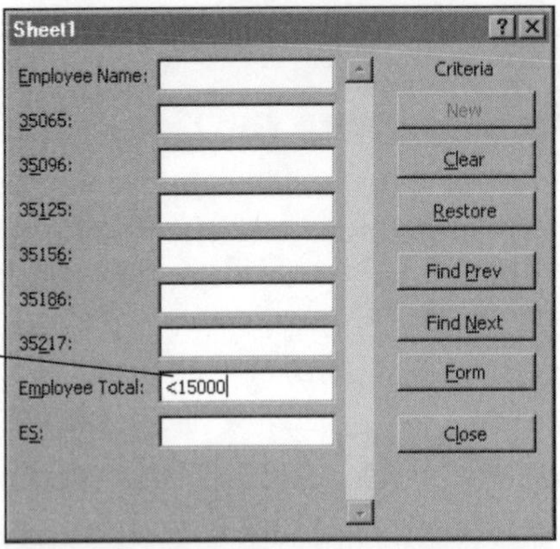

Search Criteria ——

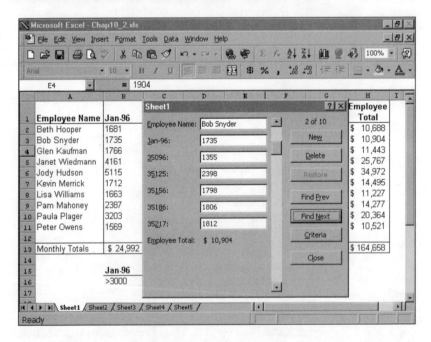

Figure 10.36

The next record in which Employee Total is less than 15000 (<15000)

Criteria can be entered in more than one field, if desired. Complex criteria can be built to narrow or broaden the search. An AND condition is implied between the criteria in multiple fields. For example if you were to enter >3000 in the Jan-96 field and >3000 in the Feb-96 field the results of the search would include all records with January sales >3000 AND February sales >3000.

If no records meet the search criteria, no error message will be generated. Instead, the form will simply display the current record. Always check the results of the searches you conduct through the data form to be sure you've retrieved the information you intended to find.

NOTE   *The data form can display as many as 32 fields. If the list contains more than 32 fields (Excel worksheets can contain as many as 256 columns),only the left-most 32 fields will be shown.*

■ Merging an Excel Database with a Microsoft Word Document

Data from an Excel database can be merged with a Microsoft Word document to create form letters, mailing labels, or any other merged document. The procedure for merging an Excel database and a Word document consists of three basic steps:

1. Create the Excel database.

2. Create the Word document.

3. Merge the Excel database with the Word document.

Create the Excel Database

You must create the Excel database before you can merge it with a Word Document. The database must include field labels and contain no empty records. Before you save and close the workbook, define a name for your database. Naming your database will simply the merge step later.

In our example (see Figure 10.37) a database of donors has been created in the cell range A3:H7. Notice the field names in the first row and the database name "DonorList" in the Name Box.

Create the Word Document

You can use an existing Word document or create a new document to merge with the Excel database. In our example we've opened an existing document (see Figure 10.38).

Merge the Excel Database with the Word Document

To merge an Excel database with a Word document, use Word's Mail Merge feature. From the Tools menu, click on Mail Merge. When the Mail Merge Helper dialog box appears, click on the Create button and select the type of document you wish to create. In our example we choose Form Letters. Next, select Active window if you're using an existing document or select New Main Document if you wish to create a new document.

Figure 10.37

A donors database

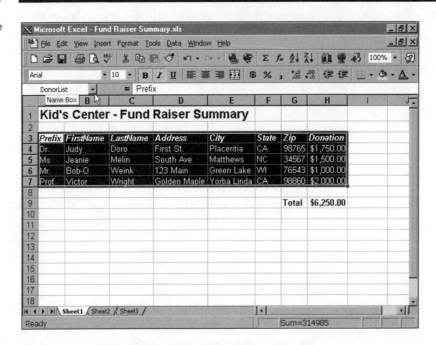

Figure 10.38

Merging a Word document and an Excel database

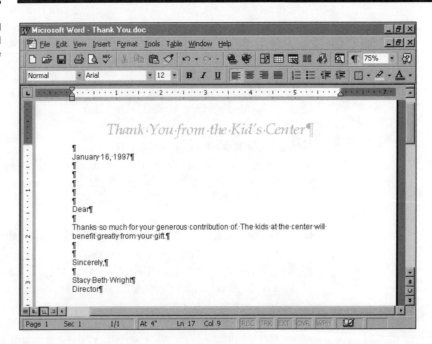

Now specify the Excel database as the data source by clicking on the Get Data button then clicking on Open Data Source. In the Open Data Source dialog box, open the folder that contains your Excel workbook. In the Files of type box, click MS Excel Worksheets (*.xls). Double-click on the workbook that contains your database. In the Microsoft Excel dialog box, select the named range, or type the cell references that identify the data you want to use, then click the OK button. In our example, we've selected the database name "DonorList" (see Figure 10.39). When Word displays the next message, click on Edit Main Document if you have an existing document open or Set Up Main Document if you're creating a new document. In our example, we selected Edit Main Document.

Figure 10.39

Selecting a database to merge with a Word document

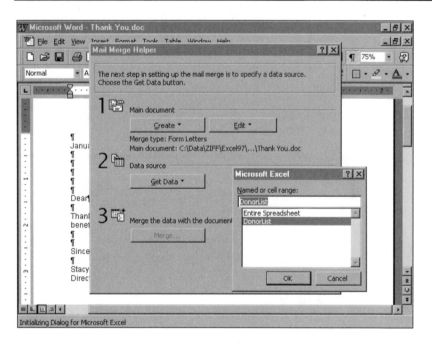

If you're creating a form letter, use the Insert Merge Field list on the Mail Merge toolbar (which is now displayed) to insert your database fields into the document. Include spaces and punctuation marks between merge fields as necessary. Figure 10.40 shows the list of merge fields. Notice that the list of merge fields match the field names from the Excel database.

To view the merged data click on the View Merged Data button on the Mail Merge toolbar or from the Mail Merge Helper dialog box, click Merge, and select the option you want. Figure 10.41 shows a database record merged with the Word form-letter document.

Figure 10.40

List of merge fields

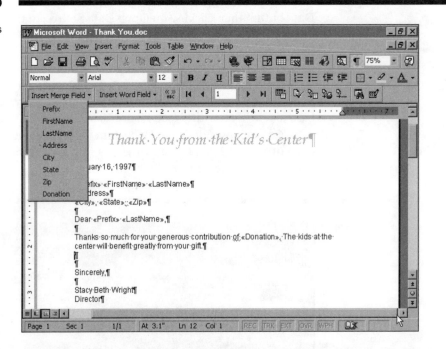

Figure 10.41

The merged data

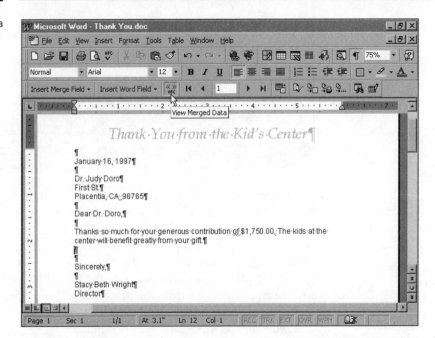

NOTE *Complete step-by-step instructions on how to merge an Excel database with a Word document can be found in Excel's on-line help. In the Help Index box type "merging," then double-click on "mail merge in Microsoft Word."*

■ Knowing When to Use a Real Database Program

Although Excel offers some very powerful list-management options, it does not qualify as a full-fledged database-management system. If your data-management needs are complex, or if you are working with large data sets, a full-fledged, relational database system like Microsoft Access, Microsoft FoxPro for Windows, Borland Paradox, or Borland dBASE for Windows might be more appropriate for your needs.

The Advantages of Relational Databases

First and foremost, Excel does not offer relational database capabilities. In a relational database system like FoxPro or Access, items in a table can be "tied" to items in another table through a relationship maintained and managed by the database system.

In other words, a table that contains employee names, addresses, and other employment information can be related to another table that contains payroll information. Each record in the employee table has many connections to the payroll table (one connection for each paycheck that has been issued to the employee). After the employee name or other identifier has been determined, a lookup in the payroll table is very fast and efficient.

The same example in Excel would require a very large table of employee data. Each record would contain all the employment information plus payroll data for an employee. Each time a payroll check is issued, a new record will be added to the table for each employee. The new record will contain all of the employee data plus the new payroll information.

Alternatively, a new field could be added onto the end of the table for each new payroll period. That wouldn't be very practical, though, since Excel only provides 256 columns.

In either case, a simple table approach to managing complex data quickly becomes unmanageable. Relational database systems like FoxPro, Access, Paradox, and dBASE contain all the features and utilities necessary to efficiently manage many links between tables.

Databases Provide Powerful Query Capabilities

The query capabilities of relational database systems are formidable and permit rapid performance of very complex queries on large data sets. A database system built of a number of Excel tables just cannot compete with the vast capabilities of modern relational database systems.

You Can Build Powerful Forms Using a Database

Although the Excel data form (discussed earlier in this chapter) is extremely easy to use, it lacks many of the features of a true forms-oriented database system like Microsoft Access or Borland Paradox for Windows.

Forms produced by Access, Paradox for Windows, and other relational database applications contain field properties and built-in routines for validating input. For instance, if a field is expecting numeric data and a user tries to input text in the field instead, the form will notice the error and informs the user. In Excel, it's not that easy. You must either build validation rules into formulas, or use Visual Basic routines to check for errors and display error messages.

Windows database forms can contain a wide variety of objects, such as text input fields, option buttons (often called radio buttons, because they provide selection between mutually exclusive options, much like the buttons on a radio), check boxes, combo boxes, drop-down lists, and so on.

True database forms are flexible. Because of the wealth of different objects and designs that can be used to construct forms in Access, Paradox for Windows, or FoxPro, the developer is not limited to a fixed size, shape, or appearance of the form. The Excel data form is designed for a few specific tasks and cannot be modified to accommodate more complex functions.

Should You Use a Database Rather Than Excel?

There is no simple answer to the question of whether a true database is better suited to managing your data than Excel 97 for Windows is. The list-management tools in Excel are easy to learn and use. In contrast, a product like Access or Paradox for Windows can take months (or even years) to master completely.

Generally speaking, however, Excel-based lists are well-suited for managing reasonably small sets (less than 1,000 records) of data, and for handling data with fewer than 20 or 30 fields. After you have exceeded the practical limits of Excel's list management tools (for instance, when a simple sort or filter does not yield the information you need), it is time to consider a true database.

The good news is that all contemporary Windows database systems can read and write Excel worksheets. If you discover that you have outgrown

Excel's list-management capabilities after investing a considerable amount of time and effort in building Excel worksheets to contain your data, you can easily migrate to a Windows database system.

NOTE   *Microsoft Access is bundled in the Microsoft Office Professional package. If you own Microsoft Office Professional or another Windows database, you might want to import a worksheet or two in a true database table and experiment. Obviously, however, you should carefully back up your Excel worksheets before experimenting with another data-management system.*

11

Using Microsoft Query

In THIS CHAPTER, YOU'LL LEARN ABOUT THE POWER BUILT INTO Microsoft Query, an add-in program that's included with Excel 97 for Windows. The information in this chapter permits you to directly access data stored in database tables produced with Microsoft Access and FoxPro, Borland dBASE and Paradox, and other database systems.

This chapter explores the following:

- Understanding Microsoft Query
- Installing and starting Microsoft Query
- The Query Wizard
- Mastering the Microsoft Query environment
- Retrieving data with Microsoft Query
- Building query criteria
- Sorting data in Microsoft Query
- Saving and reusing queries
- Transferring data from Microsoft Query to Excel
- (Using the Refresh/Edit External Data Options
- (Canceling Microsoft Query and Returning to Excel

A little practice with Microsoft Query can greatly improve your skill at utilizing the data-access capabilities of Excel 97 for Windows.

Microsoft Excel 97 for Windows provides several different ways to access data stored in external database files. As you learned in Chapter 10, an Excel worksheet is comparable to a database table. Accordingly, you might find it very useful to be able to extract data directly from database files for use within Excel.

Virtually any database can supply information to Excel. Even if Excel does not contain a driver specifically designed for your database (for example, no drivers exist in Excel for Alpha Four or Lotus Approach,) you can export its tables in a common format like dBASE or Paradox or as delimited text.

NOTE. *Although it's not an "official" abbreviation, this chapter uses the expression MSQuery to indicate the Excel add-in application Microsoft Query.*

■ What is Microsoft Query?

Microsoft Query (MSQuery) is a complete, standalone application that lets you retrieve data from a number of external data sources. MSQuery, which includes the Query Wizard, is an optional Excel feature and is *not automatically installed* on your computer. However, once it has been installed, you can find the MSQuery application files in the folder of the same name. This MSQuery folder can be located by following the path C:\Program Files\Common Files\ Microsoft Shared or, if you installed the Microsoft Office Suite, C:\Program Files\Microsoft Office\Office (note that path may vary from PC to PC).

MSQuery help you perform many common database tasks, such as extracting data from database tables, deleting or modifying data in database tables, and adding new data to database tables.

■ Understanding What Microsoft Query Does

When used within Excel, data retrieved from external database sources like Microsoft Access and FoxPro, or Borland Paradox and dBASE, can be added to Excel worksheets. Using Microsoft Query, data can be piped into Excel worksheets directly from the source database tables.

MSQuery is designed for building complex database queries without the aid of the entire database engine. These queries draw data from database tables, and provide a mechanism for adding that data to Excel worksheets.

As this chapter shows, when you start MSQuery you will find yourself inside a complete Windows application. Microsoft Query has its own menu, toolbar, wizard, and other controls. You are able to create, save, and reuse database queries from within MSQuery.

This chapter explains how to use Microsoft Query, and describes what you must do to put MSQuery to work for you.

■ Installing MSQuery

If you installed Microsoft Office 97 using the Typical installation option, then MSQuery was *not* automatically installed along with Microsoft Excel 97. Figure 11.1 shows the message that will be displayed if you attempt to use MSQuery when it is not installed

Figure 11.1

Message displayed if
MSQuery is not installed

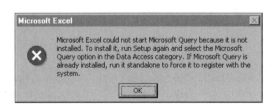

To add MSQuery after Microsoft Excel 97 has been installed, first close any applications you have open—leaving Windows running of course. Click on the Start button, point to Settings, and from the Settings options click on Control Panel. When the Control Panel window opens, double-click on the Add/Remove Programs icon. When the Add/Remove Program Properties dialog window opens, click on the Install/Uninstall tab. From the list of software that appears, pick the Microsoft Office 97 or Microsoft Excel 97 application and click on the Add/Remove button. Then click again on the Add/Remove button when the Microsoft Office 97 Setup dialog window appears. From the "Microsoft Office 97—Maintenance" dialog window, select the Data Access option and click on the Change Option button.

At this point in the installation process the "Microsoft Office 97—Data Access" dialog window is displayed (see Figure 11.2). You can now install MSQuery by clicking in the check box next to the Microsoft Query option and then clicking the OK button.

NOTE. *If you're installing MSQuery from the Excel 97 Setup feature, the instructions are nearly identical. But to be safe, refer to the "Installing MSQuery" instructions from Excel's On-line Help.*

Figure 11.2

Installing Microsoft Query
from Microsoft Office 97
Setup/Maintenance
Feature

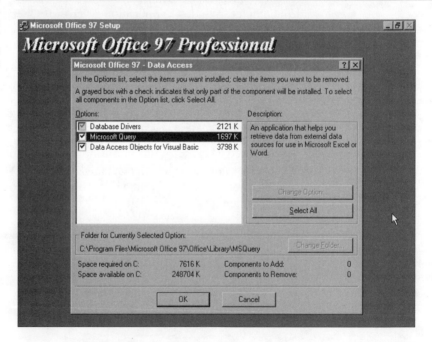

■ Starting MSQuery

The MSQuery add-in is located in the Excel Data menu. When you click on the Get External Data option and then select Run Database Query or Create New Query, Microsoft Query will start up (see Figure 11.3).

Figure 11.3

Use Get External Data to
start MSQuery.

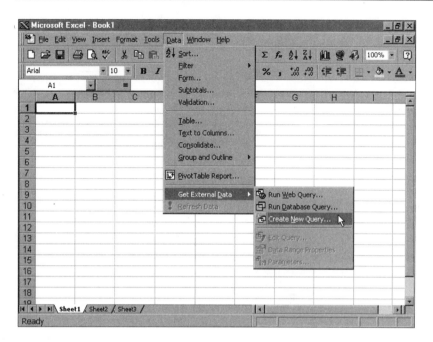

Excel still is running after the MSQuery environment appears—it's hidden just behind the MSQuery window. When started, MSQuery is able to transfer data directly from database files into Excel. Because MSQuery includes the necessary tools and options to extract only the data you are interested in, it's much more efficient to use MSQuery than to import the same files directly into Excel.

Although Excel can directly open only dBASE database files, most database systems can convert their native table formats to dBASE format. Opening a Paradox table inside Excel, therefore, requires two steps: using Paradox to save the table in dBASE-format, and opening the dBASE-format file in Excel. MSQuery allows you to work directly with the Paradox, dBASE, FoxPro, or other database files from within Excel.

■ The Microsoft Query Toolbar

All of your interaction with Microsoft Query will take place through the toolbar and menu options in the MSQuery environment itself. Although a complete description of this environment is not necessary at this point, it might be useful to become familiar with the icons on the toolbar. Figure 11.4 shows the entire MSQuery toolbar. These tools are explained further in Table 11.1.

Figure 11.4

The Query toolbar

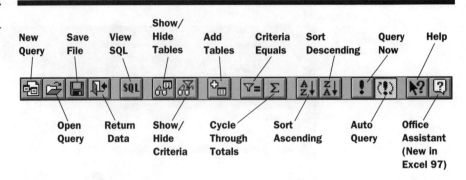

Table 11.1

Microsoft Query
Toolbar Icons

ICON NAME	DESCRIPTION
New Query	Begins the process of building an entirely new database query.
Open Query	Opens an existing query.
Save File	Saves the current query for future use.
Return Data	Returns the data to Excel when your query activity is complete. This button is not on the toolbar when Microsoft Query is started as a standalone application.
View SQL	Queries generated by Microsoft Query are converted to Structured Query Language (SQL) by Microsoft Query, even when the database you are querying does not require the use of SQL. You might want to use this button to view the SQL statement during your work.
Show/Hide Tables	Hides the Table pane in Microsoft Query to provide more room for the Query pane.
Show/Hide Criteria	Hides the Query pane in Microsoft Query to provide more room for the Table pane.
Add Tables	Opens the Add Tables dialog box so that you can add another table to the query.
Criteria Equals	Automatically selects records that contain the same value as the active cell (the cell containing the insertion cursor).
Cycle Through Totals	Provides access to a number of basic statistics for data retrieved from databases, as discussed later in this chapter.
Sort Ascending	Quickly sorts columns of data in ascending order.
Sort Descending	Quickly sorts columns of data in descending order.

Table 11.1 (Continued)

Microsoft Query
Toolbar Icons

ICON NAME	DESCRIPTION
Query Now	Activates the query.
Auto Query	Runs the query when the query criterion is complete.
Help	Provides specific help for the objects you see in the MSQuery window.
Office Assistant	A new Excel 97 innovation that offers tips, and provides help for a variety of MSQuery features.

Although most of your work with MSQuery will involve little more than opening a database source, specifying which tables to examine, and building your query criteria, this chapter details each of the options available to you when you are using Microsoft Query.

It is not necessary to memorize the purpose of each toolbar button. As you move the mouse cursor across the buttons, the MSQuery status bar will show you each button's function.

The rest of this chapter deals with using MSQuery to extract data from database tables. Although a Microsoft Access database is used in the example, the principles of data extraction are essentially the same when working with any database source.

■ Using MSQuery to Retrieve Data

The first thing you will see when you open Microsoft Query is the Choose Data Source dialog box (Figure 11.5). This dialog box also appears when you click on the New Query button or select New (query) from the File menu in the Microsoft Query application window.

Figure 11.5

The Choose Data
Source dialog box

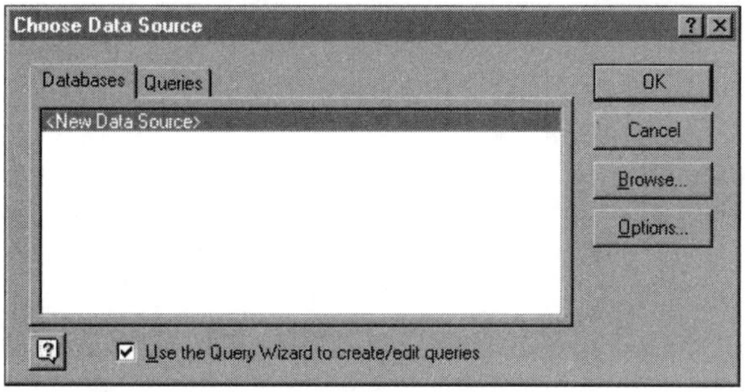

Choosing the Data Source

Microsoft Query needs to know the data source from which you want to get data. The first time MSQuery is opened, the Choose Data Source dialog box will contain one entry: <New Data Source>.

Microsoft Query needs to know what kind of new data source you want to use. Clicking on the OK button opens the Create New Data Source dialog box (see Figure 11.6). The first question you must answer is "What name do you want to give your data source?" Enter a name, then press the Tab key or click in the second text box to continue.

Figure 11.6

Create a new
MSQuery data source.

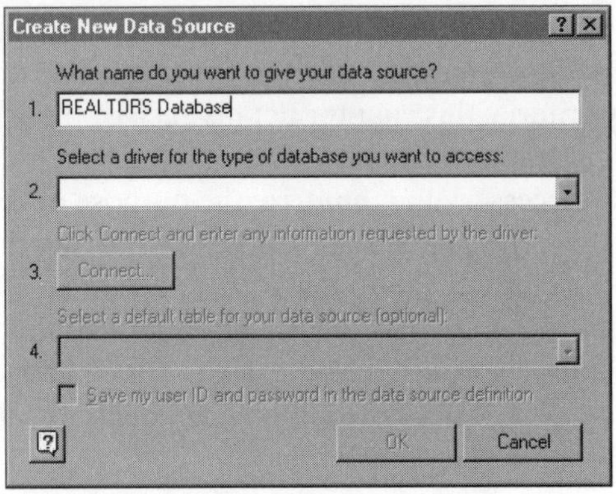

Next, select a driver for the type of database you want to access (see Figure 11.7). For this example, the Microsoft Access Driver (*.mdb) option has been selected.

Figure 11.7

Selecting a MSQuery
database driver

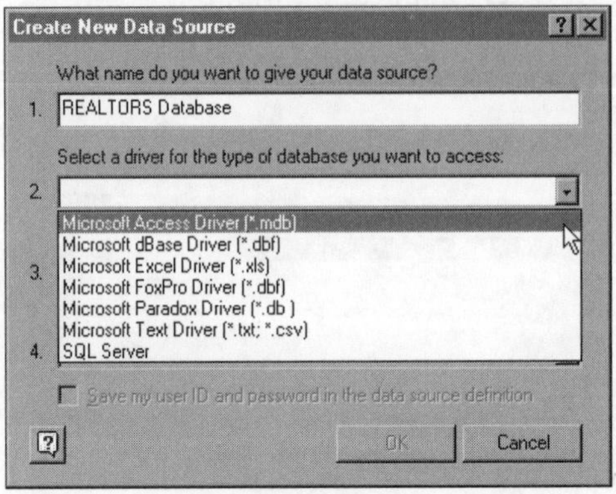

Your system might have more or fewer ODBC drivers than Figure 11.7 displays.

NOTE. *What is ODBC? Microsoft has established the Open Database Connectivity standard for Windows in an attempt to provide a shared application interface for the bewildering variety of database file formats that exist in the world today. Like Microsoft Query, any application that understands ODBC can use ODBC drivers to connect to a wide variety of database files.*

An ODBC driver is usually written by the database vendor, and is distributed as a particular type of Dynamically Linked Library (DLL). DLLs usually are stored in the Windows system directory.

When Microsoft Query is started, it checks to see if ODBC drivers that have been installed on the computer system. When you ask MSQuery to open a particular type of database, such as (Access, FoxPro, or Paradox, MSQuery uses the ODBC driver DLL to find out how to interpret the data stored in the database tables.

Adding/Removing ODBC Drivers

ODBC drivers can be added to or removed from your system by following the instructions available in the MSQuery Help. Click on the Help menu, select Contents and Index from the Index tab, type ODBC Drivers, and click on the Display button. When the list of topics appears, double-click on the topic "Install an ODBC driver so you can access an external data source."

NOTE. *Entirely new ODBC drivers (those not yet located on your system) are installed through the 32-bit ODBC icon in Windows Control Panel.*

Deleting MSQuery Data Sources

If you do not need to use Microsoft Query with one of the data sources shown in the list in the Choose Data Sources dialog box, you can remove the ODBC DSN file from the Data Sources Folder, which is located in the path C:\Program Files\Common Files\ODBC (this path can vary from PC to PC).

NOTE. *While it's possible to remove ODBC drivers, they don't take up much space on your hard disk and you're likely to use them in the future—consider the pros and cons before you uninstall them.*

Connecting to the Data Source

After selecting the driver type, click on the Connect button (see Figure 11.8) and enter any information requested by the driver. In our example (see Figure 11.9), the ODBC Microsoft Access 97 Setup window appears because we selected the Microsoft Access Driver option. To select an existing database, click the Select button.

Figure 11.8

Connect to a
MSQuery data source

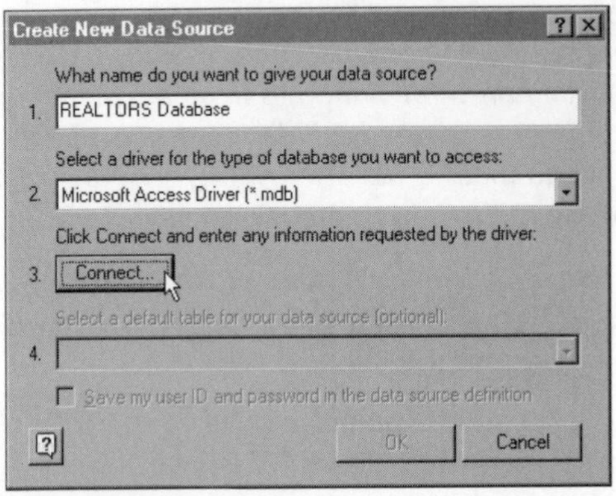

Figure 11.9

Select an existing
database

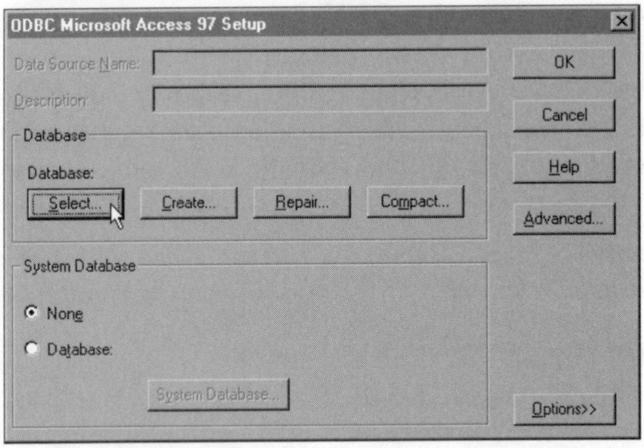

The Select Database dialog box shows all candidate databases in the active directory (see Figure 11.10). Because we selected "Microsoft Access Databases," only Microsoft Access databases appear in the Database Name list. You can use the Drives drop-down list to switch to another storage device, and you can use the folders to browse to another location on a drive, if necessary.

Click on the name REALTORS.MDB in the Database Name list located on the left side of the dialog box, and then click OK.

Figure 11.10

All databases in the
current directory

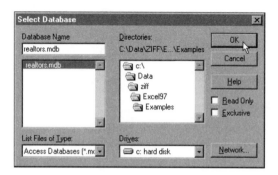

NOTE. *Do not be misled by the List Files of Type combo box in the lower left corner of the Select Database dialog box. Although it might appear that this list lets you select a different type of database file, it is there only in case your database file has a different extension than the default for the type of database selected.*

For instance, the default extension for Microsoft Access database is MDB. If the name of an Access database has a different extension for some reason, its name will not appear in the Database Name list. The List Files of Type combo box allows you to see either the Access Databases with the MDB extension or All Files in the current directory. It does not permit you to select a different type of database file.

When the Microsoft Access database is selected, you are returned to the ODBC Microsoft Access 97 Setup window. The database you selected will appear along with its path statement (e.g., D:\Excel\Chap11\Realtors.mdb). You can confirm your selection by clicking on the OK button (see Figure 11.11), or you can change your selection. You can also, by clicking on the Advanced button, specify User ID and password if the database you plan to access requires them.

The final step in creating a new data source is optional. If you wish, you can select a default table from your data source. This table will appear automatically each time you create a query with the new data source. Selecting a default table does not preclude other tables from being added to the newly created query, nor does it prevent the default table from being deleted from the query. Figure 11.12 shows the Create New Data Source dialog box completed with no default table specified. Click the OK button to go to the next step without establishing a default table.

Figure 11.11

Select an Access
database as a
Data Source.

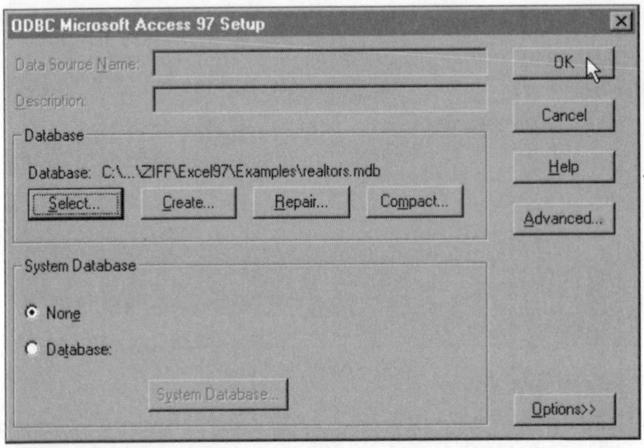

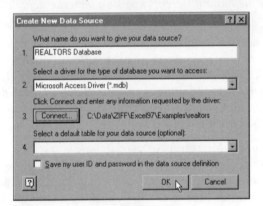

Figure 11.12

Completed Create New
Data Source dialog box

Opening a Database Source

When you first start up MSQuery, or after you click the OK button from the
Create New Data Source dialog box, MSQuery will open the Choose Data
Source dialog box. Figure 11.13 shows the Choose Data Sources dialog box
with the new REALTORS Database selection.

The Query Wizard

MSQuery comes with a feature called the Query Wizard that permits you to
quickly create and edit queries. Notice at the bottom of Figure 11.13 that
placing a check mark next to "Use the Query Wizard to create/edit queries"
summons the Query Wizard to help you when you click the OK button from
the Choose Data Sources dialog box.

Figure 11.13

The Choose Data
Source dialog box

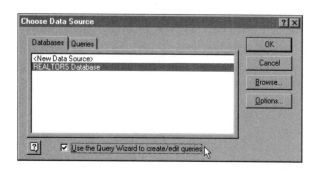

If you choose this option, you will be guided through a series of dialog boxes by the Query Wizard, which will create your query for you. Figure 11.14 shows the first of several dialog boxes presented by the Query Wizard to help you create your queries.

Figure 11.14

The Query Wizard

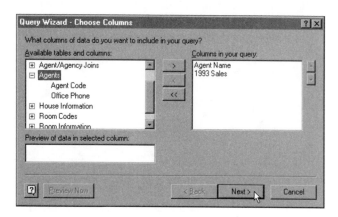

NOTE. *You can cancel the Query Wizard at any time by clicking the Cancel button. However, canceling the Wizard on your first attempt at entering MSQuery will return you to Excel with a message that no data was received from MSQuery.*

In our example, we do not invoke the Query Wizard. Accordingly, make sure you remove the check mark next to "Use the Query Wizard to create/ edit queries" if you're following along.

In the case of REALTORS.MDB, seven different tables (named "Agents," "Agencies," and so on) are in the database. The Add Tables dialog box, which opened automatically upon return to the MSQuery environment, shows the tables in the REALTORS.MDB database (see Figure 11.15).

Figure 11.15

The REALTORS.MDB database contains seven tables.

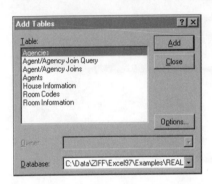

The data in the REALTORS database includes names of and contact information for a number of different Realtors and the real-estate agencies for which they work, plus the sales information for several different homes.

When you select the Agents table and click on the Add button, the Agents table will be added to the current query, as shown in Figure 11.16. To close the Add Tables dialog box, click on the Close button.

Figure 11.16

The Agents table has been added to the query.

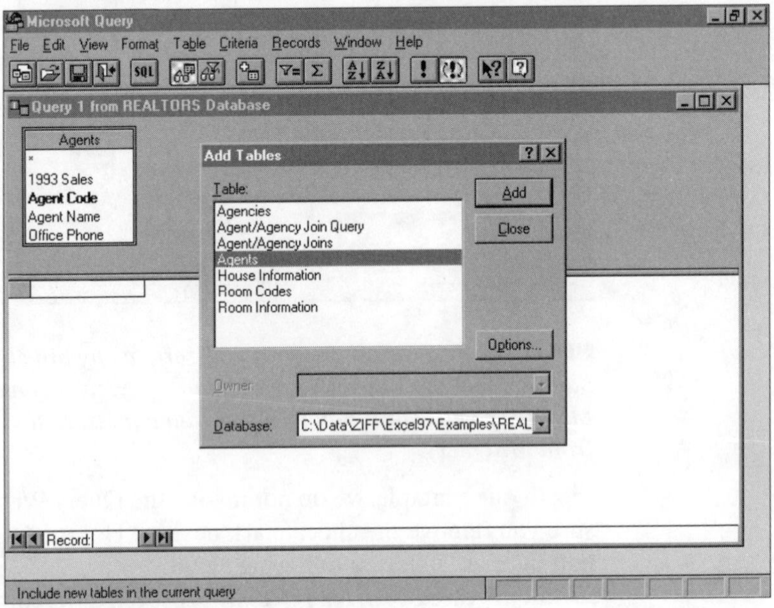

The large window within the MSQuery program window is called the Query window. (MSQuery features a multiple-document interface, which means that more than one Query window can be placed within the MSQuery environment at one time. Normally, however, you'll want to work with only one query at a time.) The section at the top of the Query window is called the Table pane, while the lower section is called the Data pane.

Displaying Data

A list of the fields in the Agents table will appear in the upper pane of the Query window. To include fields in the query, either double-click one at a time on the field names in the field list, or drag them to the Data pane in the bottom half of the Query window. Figure 11.17 shows the Query window after the "Agent Name" and "1993 Sales" fields from the Agents table have been added to the Data pane.

Figure 11.17

Adding fields to the Data pane

Fields can be dragged to the Data pane

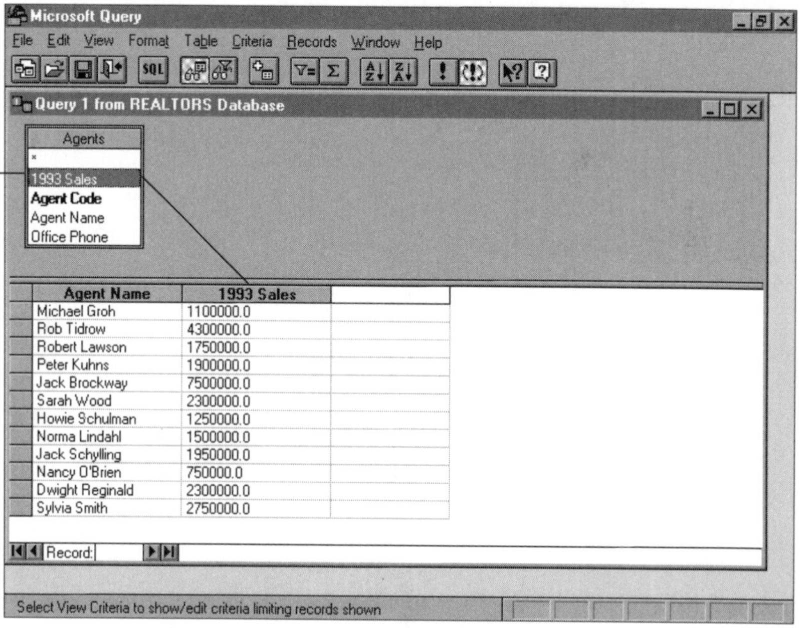

Note that no query criteria have been applied to extract the data in Figure 11.17. All of the data in the Agent Name and 1993 Sales fields are displayed. None of the records in the Agents table have been excluded. The result of this query is similar in function to importing a database table directly into Excel.

Understanding the Query Window

The Query window is rather complicated. It contains all of the information necessary to build complicated database queries, and although it is actually quite straightforward to use, it can look confusing at first glance. Before we proceed with building complicated queries, a quick overview of the Query window's components is necessary.

Initially, the Query window is divided into upper and lower portions. The upper portion contains field lists for all the tables involved in the query, while the lower area contains the data retrieved by the query.

Figure 11.18 explains the default components of the Query window.

Figure 11.18

The default Query window

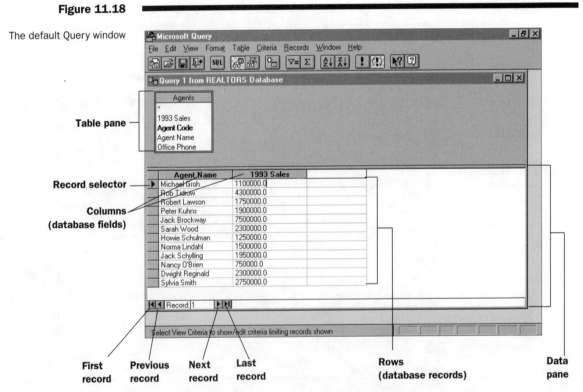

These default components are as follows:

- Table pane. The Table pane contains fields lists for all of the tables included in the query.

- Field List. The boxes representing the tables included in the query. The field lists contain all of the field names for their respective tables. In the case of the Agents table, the fields are named "1993 Sales," "Agent Code," "Agent Name," and so on.

- Data pane. Although currently empty, the Data pane displays the data extracted from the Agents table by MSQuery. The data extracted from the database source is called the result set.

- Record selector. The small button at the extreme left of each record in the Data pane can be used to highlight (or "select") the entire record. The triangle displayed on the first record selector in Figure 11.18 is the "focus." It tells you which record is the active record (the record where the insertion point is located.)

- Navigation ("VCR") buttons. In the lower-left corner of the Data pane are four buttons for moving through the records in the Data pane. Large data sets might have hundreds, or even thousands, of records. The VCR buttons (so named for their similarity to the control buttons on most VCRs) provide a way to quickly move through the records in the Data pane. The four buttons allow you to move to the first record, the next record, the previous record, and the last record.

- Columns (database fields). Each column in the Data pane holds data from a field in the database table.

- Rows (database records). Each row in the Data pane contains the data for one record in the database table.

As you work your way through this chapter, you should become familiar with the various components of the Query window.

NOTE. *Be aware of the difference between the words "field" and "column." A field is the name of a specific category of information in a database table. Database fields normally are displayed as columns of data. In this chapter, the words field and column are used almost (but not quite) interchangeably.*

This chapter strives to use the word "field" when referring to the structure of the database table, and "column" when describing the way in which database fields are displayed.

Similarly, a record is a component of a database table. Database records are normally displayed as rows of data. A record is comprised of all of the categories of information pertaining to one individual or entity—for instance, your name, address, and phone number might make up a record in a database, and could be displayed on the screen in a row within a table.

Selecting Individual Fields

A field is added to the query by dragging it to the Data pane. If you release the field anywhere in the unoccupied area of the Data pane, the field will be added to the first unoccupied column on the far-right side of the Data pane.

If you release the new field on top of an existing column in the Data pane, the new column will be inserted in the existing column's location, pushing the existing column to the right.

Selecting All Fields

Note that in Figure 11.18 an asterisk (*) appears at the very top of the Agents field list. If you drag the asterisk to the Data pane, all fields in the Agents table will be added to the Data pane in the order in which they were created in the Agents database table.

If you want to add all the fields to the Data pane, double-click on the field list's title bar (in Figure 11.18, the field list title bar says "Agents") to highlight all the fields in the list, and drag any of the fields to the Data pane. All fields will be automatically added to the Data pane in the same order they appear in the field list.

■ Specifying Query Criteria

So far, the examples in this chapter have involved working with the complete set of records from the Agents database table. In most cases, however, you do not really want to work with the complete set. Most often you'll want to select only certain records from the database for display or manipulation.

A thorough understanding of constructing and using query criteria is essential to success with Microsoft Query.

What is Query Criteria?

Before you can extract specific records from a database table, you must specify the query criteria that MSQuery should use during its search of the database table.

Perhaps the simplest form of query criteria is something similar to "Show me the names of all real-estate agents who sold more than $2,000,000 of property in 1993." Intuitively, you know that somewhere along the way the mathematical expression "> 2,000,000" must figure into the query criteria.

Furthermore, you must be able to tell MSQuery that you want the criteria to be applied to the "1993 Sales" field, and that you want to see only those records whose "1993 Sales" field contain values greater than 2,000,000.

Query criteria need not be restricted to a single field, as in this simple example. You might, for instance, want to see the real-estate listings for all four-bedroom houses in the database with offering prices between $100,000 and $150,000, attached two-car garages, and at least two full bathrooms. This query involves no fewer than four different fields: "Number of Bedrooms," "List Price," "Garage," and "Number of Bathrooms."

It should come as no surprise that MSQuery is carefully designed to help you construct query criteria exactly like these examples.

The Show/Hide Criteria Button

So far in this chapter, you have not used the MSQuery toolbar's Show/Hide Criteria button. By default, the Show/Hide Criteria button is not enabled, meaning that the Criteria pane of the Query window is hidden from view.

When you click on the Show/Hide Criteria button, the Query window will change, as shown in Figure 11.19, to reveal the Criteria pane. The Criteria pane normally is kept hidden between the Table and Data panes.

Figure 11.19

The Criteria pane

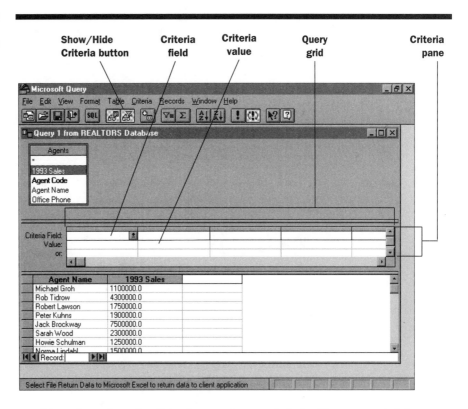

Note that when the Criteria pane is revealed, the Data pane shrinks to accommodate the space required by the Criteria pane.

Using the Criteria Pane

The query criteria area in the Criteria pane appears as a grid, usually called the Query grid. Each column in the Query grid represents one field that is involved in the criteria. The row labeled "Value" is where you enter the expression you want MSQuery to apply to the data in the field when it is searching for records to display in the Data pane.

To add a field to the Criteria field row of the Criteria grid, either drag the field name from the Field List box down to the Criteria field row, or click on the Criteria field cell, click the drop-down list arrow, and then select the appropriate field. Figure 11.20 shows the result of adding a field name to the Criteria pane.

Figure 11.20

Drag fields from the field list to the Query grid

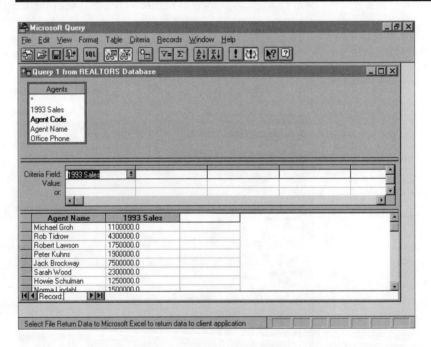

Next, enter the mathematical expression that completes the query criteria. In this case, ">2000000" yields the records of all real-estate agents who sold more than $2,000,000 of real estate in 1993. The expression ">2000000" is entered into the Value row under the name of the field (1993 Sales) in the Criteria pane. The completed query criteria is shown in Figure 11.21.

By default, the query will be triggered as soon as you have completed the query criteria and moved the insertion point to someplace else on the Query window. To test MSQuery's Auto Query capability, after the criteria expression (">2000000") is filled in, press the Tab key to move the insertion

Figure 11.21

The completed query
criteria in the Query grid

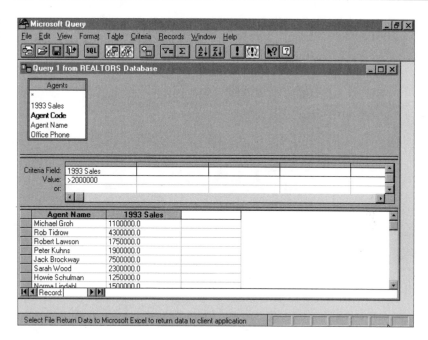

point to the next column in the Query grid. You will see the screen change,
as shown in Figure 11.22.

NOTE. *MSQuery does not accept commas in the expression, although you can
have a space between the ">" and "2000000."*

This Auto Query feature can cause significant delays when the data set is
very large, and can also hinder building the complex queries discussed later
in this chapter. If you don't like it, you can turn it off by clicking on the Auto
Query button.

NOTE. *The Auto Query button remains depressed once it has been clicked.
The Query Now button, however, is a "momentary contact" button—it works
only when you click it.*

After the Auto Query button has been disabled, if you want to see the
most current result set you must explicitly trigger (or "run") the query by
clicking on the Query Now button on the toolbar (the Query Now button
looks like an exclamation mark).

NOTE. *You can have several queries open at one time—which means you can
create a new query without having to close any open ones. However, it's good
practice to save any open queries you plan to use later before you create a new*

Figure 11.22

By default, the query will run automatically after the criteria are complete.

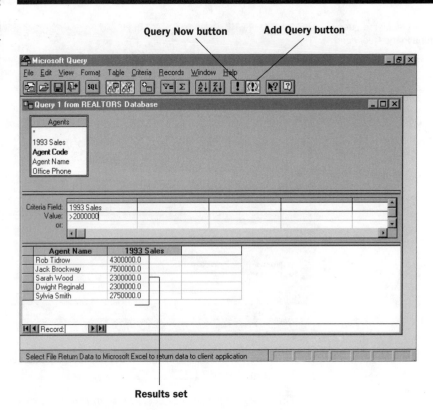

Results set

one. After you save a query, you can close it, minimize it, or just leave it where it is. In our example, we save and then minimize the inactive queries to avoid screen clutter.

Adding Criteria to the Query Grid

Usually, a successful query requires more than simple criteria built from a single field. Most real-world exercises involve multiple fields, or even multiple tables.

Adding a field to the query criteria is simple. The Criteria grid has space for more than one field. Figure 11.23 shows the effect of adding fields to the Criteria grid. In this case, both the List Price and Number of Bedrooms fields are examined, apparently because the user wants to see the MLS numbers and addresses of all houses with three or more bedrooms that also have list prices of less than $150,000.

TIP. *The concept of multiple criteria is easily understood if you keep this analogy in mind. Say you have a long list of persons you're considering for marriage. The list consists of four fields: a Name field, and three Quality fields: Caring, Attractive, and Rich. For each person in the list, you put a "Yes" in the appropriate field if the person has that particular quality. If you're allowed only one criteria with which to choose a mate, then you may end up with someone caring, or attractive, or rich—but not necessarily all three. Having the ability to apply multiple criteria ensures you of finding someone with all three qualities. Ergo, you get to have your cake and eat it too!*

Figure 11.23

A query with two fields in the Criteria grid

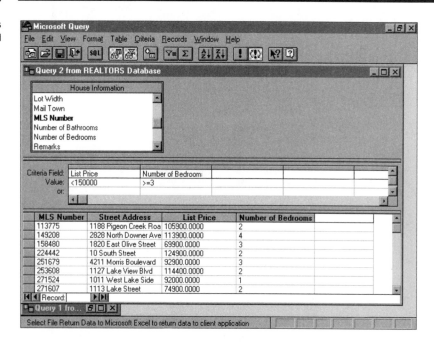

NOTE. *When adding fields to the Query grid, you might find that the Auto Query feature of MSQuery gets in the way. Because Auto Query runs the query every time a criteria set (field and query criteria) is completed (for instance, List Price < 150,000), you might find that Auto Query interrupts your work. After you enter the information for the query in one field and move to another field, Auto Query will run before you can enter the information for the next field.*

In all of the cases illustrated in this chapter, the data sets involved are so small that queries should run quickly. On larger data sets, however—and particularly if the data source is located on a server or another node on a network— you might find that the pause that occurs while queries run is intolerable.

Be sure to disable Auto Query if the delays it causes become too intrusive.

■ Saving the Query

After you have built a query and are satisfied that it will retrieve the data you want from the database table, you might want to save your query for reuse at a later time.

When you click on the Save Query button, the Save As dialog box will open (see Figure 11.24). Note that the default extension for MSQuery files is DQY.

Figure 11.24

Saving the query for future use

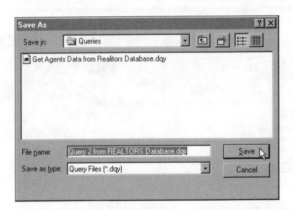

All of the information that MSQuery needs to rebuild the query conditions is saved in the query file: the database type and name, the table name, and the SQL statement.

You can open the query later, and run or modify it as needed.

■ Understanding Expressions

Microsoft Query recognizes a wide variety of different expressions. Simple expressions like ">" (greater than) are easy to understand, but MSQuery can also work with much more complicated expressions.

Using Comparison Operators in Query Criteria

The "greater than" sign (">") is an example of a comparison operator. When you use ">" in the query criteria, you are telling MSQuery that you want to compare the data in a field with the value to the right of the ">." For instance, ">2000000" means "show me all of the records with values higher than 2000000."

MSQuery understands a number of other comparison operators as well:

- Value less than (<). Returns all records with field data less than the named value. "<2000000" returns records with numbers like 1,500,000 and 1,900,000.

- Value less than or equal to (<=). Returns all records with field data smaller than or equal to the named value. "<=2000000" returns 1,500,000 and 1,900,000, as well as 2,000,000.

- Value greater than (>). Returns all records with field values greater than the given value.

- Value greater than or equal to (>=). Returns all records with field data larger than or equal to the given value. ">= 2000000" returns 2,350,000 and 4,300,000, as well as 2,000,000.

- Value equal to (=). Returns only those records with field data equal to value. Be careful with this one, because you might not find any records that meet this criteria. This operator is often used with text that you want to find in the database. For instance, ='Sarah Wood' in the Agent Name field returns all the records in which the agent's name is Sarah Wood.

  Notice that single quotes are used around the text in expressions. Spaces within the quotes are permissible. Also, MSQuery is not case-sensitive. The criteria ='Sarah Wood' and ='sarah wood' will return the same records.

- Value not equal to (<>). Returns all records with field data that are not equal to the named value.

Most of the mathematical comparison operators look like the algebraic symbols you learned in high school. A little practice is all that's necessary to master the use of these symbols in MSQuery expressions.

NOTE. *Always remember that mathematical expressions cannot contain commas. ">2,000,000" is an illegal MSQuery expression.*

Using Logical Operators in Expressions

Another category of operator uses multiple conditions when performing the search. These logical operators (also called Boolean operators) combine the expressions, exclude certain expressions, or use the expressions separately when building the query criteria:

- AND. In "value1 AND value2," the values are combined for the search to narrow the result set to only those records that match both conditions. Figure 11.25 illustrates the use of the And operator.

Figure 11.25

This query criteria returns
only those houses with
list prices between
$120,000 and $150,000.

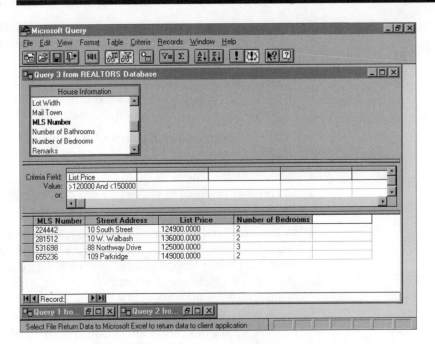

- OR. In "value1 OR value2," the OR operator expands the search somewhat by returning records that match either value1 or value2. In Figure 11.26, The query criteria has returned all houses with three or four bedrooms. (Here, the result set was also sorted in ascending order on the List Price column.)

- NOT value. Returns all records that do not have the named value in the field. Figure 11.27 illustrates a query that returns all houses not in the county of Hendricks. If you're following along, be sure to add the County field so you can check the results of the query.

Esoteric Operators

A few operators are rarely used in expressions, but may pop up in requests from your supervisor or coworkers. Most of these operators are equivalent to other, more commonly used operators, and can be replaced with these equivalents in expressions. They include

- Between value1 and value2. Returns all records with data in the field between value1 and value2. You might want to see all houses with list prices between $120,000 and $150,000, for instance. This operator is easily replaced with comparison operators or the AND operator, as described earlier in this chapter.

Figure 11.26

All houses with three
or four bedrooms

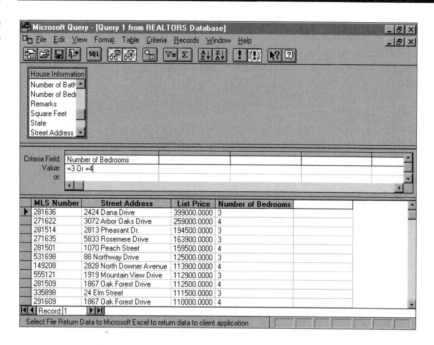

Figure 11.27

All houses not in the
county of Hendricks

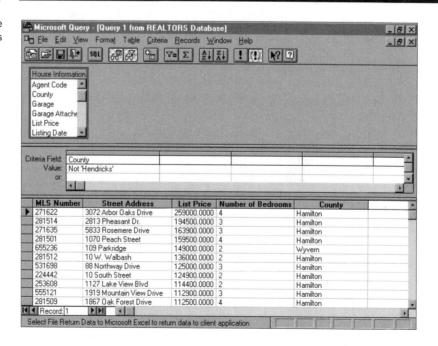

- In (value1, value2, ...). Returns records with values found in a list of values. The list of values must be enclosed in parentheses. An example might be finding the records with Agent Names In ('Sarah Wood', 'Rob Lawson', 'Rob Tidrow'.)

- Is Null, Is Not Null. Determines whether the value in the field is null (has no value) or not null (has a value.) When used with Null, this operator returns all records with empty values in the field.

- Like "value." Returns values that match the named value, where that value contains the wildcard character ("%"). In fact, value must contain the wildcard character. Figure 11.28 shows how the Like operator works. All records with Agent Name fields that begin with "Rob" have been returned in the result set.

Figure 11.28

Using the Like operator to get fields with agent names beginning with "Rob"

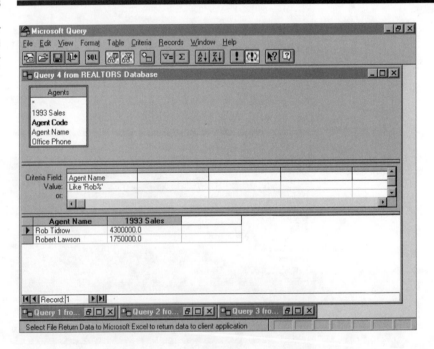

The Like operator is very powerful, and can be used to return records from fairly ambiguous query criteria.

■ Sorting the Result Set

The data displayed in the Data pane is difficult to use in its current condition. The records in the result set are in no order: they appear in the order in which they were entered into the Agents database table.

Sorting the Result Set in Ascending Order

You can understand the results of a query more easily if the data is sorted in alphabetical or numeric order. To illustrate this point let's return to our Agent Sales query—the one that lists Agent Name and 1993 Sales fields. If the query is open but not in view, use the Window menu to redisplay it. If you've closed it, you'll need to reopen it by clicking of the Open Query button on the toolbar or by clicking Open from the File menu.

Perhaps the objective of this query is to determine the best-selling real-estate agent in the database. It is, therefore, useful to sort the 1993 Sales data in ascending order so that the top agent appears at the bottom of the list.

It is not necessary to highlight the entire column before sorting. Simply position the insertion point somewhere within the 1993 Sales column, and click on the Sort Ascending button. Figure 11.29 shows the result of an ascending sort on the 1993 Sales column.

Figure 11.29

The 1993 Sales column sorted in ascending order

Sort ascending button

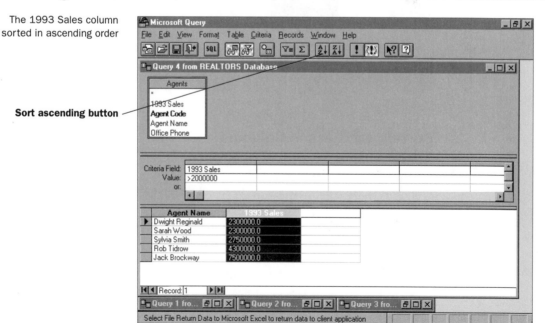

NOTE. *Sorting the data in the result set does not modify the data in the underlying database tables.*

Sorting the Result Set in Descending Order

It looks a bit odd, however, to have the top sales agent at the bottom of the list. To reverse the sort order, click on the Sort Descending button (see Figure 11.30).

Figure 11.30

The 1993 Sales column sorted in descending order

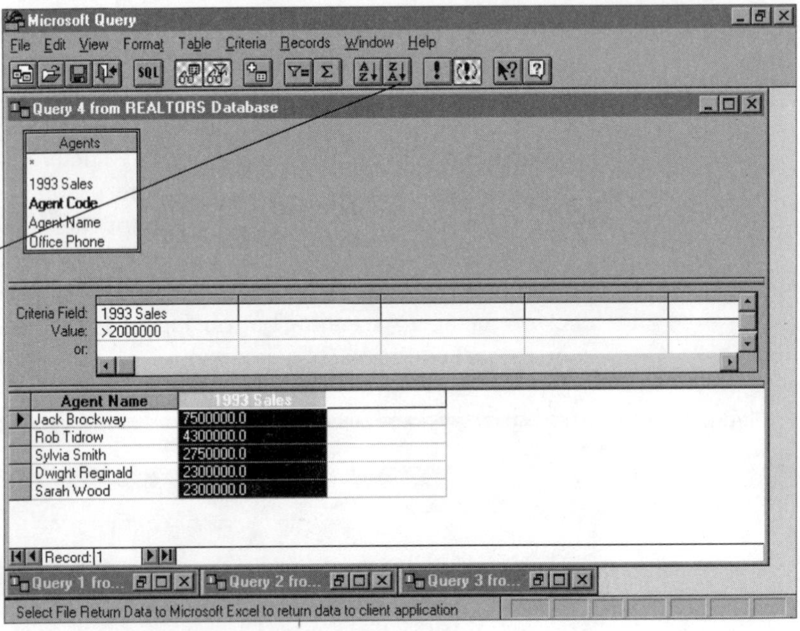

Sort descending button

Sorting on Multiple Columns

You can sort multiple columns at one time. Simply arrange the columns from left to right in the Data pane in the order in which you want to sort them. Drag across the column headings to select the columns you want to include in the sort, and then click Sort Ascending or Sort Descending.

Two methods are available for arranging columns in the Data pane. The first and most obvious method is to arrange the fields you're selecting to place in the Data pane in the order you wish to sort them as you go. That is, the column you want to sort first should be the first (left-most) column, the column you want to sort second should appear to the right of the first column, and so on.

The second method is to arrange the columns after you have placed them in the Data pane. To move a column, select the entire column. Position the mouse pointer on the column heading so that the pointer is pointing left, then drag the column to its new position. Figure 11.31 illustrates this principle. The House Information table was used for this query rather than the Agents table. The Agent Code column was sorted first, and the MLS number column was sorted second.

Figure 11.31

The House
Information table

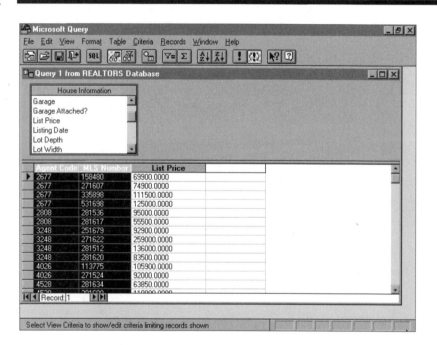

Note that for each agent code, the MLS numbers assigned to that agent are sorted in ascending order.

■ Queries on More than One Database Table

You'll need to use more than one table in a query. So far, the examples in this chapter have used only one table in the Table pane, and all queries have been directed to that one table. More-complex queries require data from two, three, or more tables to provide data. In fact, multiple-table queries are often used to consolidate and filter data before adding it to Excel worksheets.

Adding Tables to the Query

For the moment, return to the query you built earlier in this chapter that extracted all records from the Agents table for agents who had sold more than $2,000,000 of property in 1993.

Suppose you want to see listing information about the houses these agents are currently trying to sell. The only fields in the Agents table are Agent Code, Agent Name, Office Phone, and 1993 Sales. Nothing in the Agents table tells you about the houses in the database. How can you determine which houses each of these agents has listed?

The House Information table in the REALTORS.MDB database contains all the information relating to house listings, including the MLS number, list price, address, and other data. Obviously, the House Information table contains the information you want to see.

Ideally, there ought to be some way to join the Agents table to the House Information table so that you can see just which houses each agent has listed.

Relational databases like Microsoft Access, FoxPro, and Paradox, are the answer. Each table contains one or more key fields that serve as "connectors" to tie the table to the other tables in the database.

Joining Tables

To begin the process of joining the Agents and House Information tables, create a new query by clicking on the New Query button. Microsoft Query will "remember" the database sources that have been used in the past, and it will present them in the Choose Data Source dialog box (see Figure 11.32). Select REALTORS Database, and then click OK.

Figure 11.32

The Choose Data Source dialog box

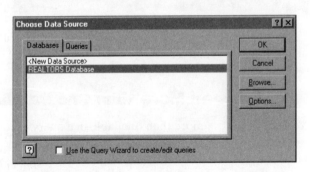

Next, the Add Tables dialog box will open. This time, instead of adding only the Agents table, the House Information table will be added to the Table pane as well.

When the Add Tables dialog box is closed, the Agents and House Information tables will appear in the Tables pane (see Figure 11.33). Note that Microsoft Query has drawn a line to connect these tables.

Figure 11.33

The Agents and House Information tables in the Tables pane

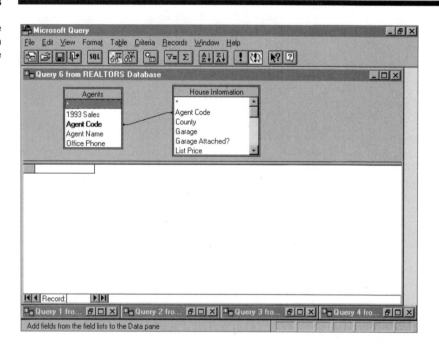

To be more specific, the line joining the Agents and House Information tables is drawn from the Agent Code field in the Agents table to the Agent Code field in the House Information table. In the Agents table, Agent Code appears in bold-face type to indicate that it is a key field for the Agents table. The Agent Code in the House Information is just another field of data contained in this table.

The line drawn between these tables, however, represents a relational join between the Agents and House Information tables. Microsoft Query draws lines between field names that the tables have in common. This relational join means that the Agent Code in the Agents table can be used to find all of the corresponding Agent Code fields in the House Information table. You can, therefore, determine which houses an agent has listed by looking for the agent's code in the House Information table.

Using Joined Tables in Queries

Microsoft Query makes it easy to use joined tables in queries. Start by dragging the Agent Name field from the Agents table to the Data pane. Next, drag the MLS Number, Street Address, and List Price fields from the House Information table to the Data pane. The result will look like Figure 11.34.

Figure 11.34

Adding fields from
multiple tables to
the Data pane

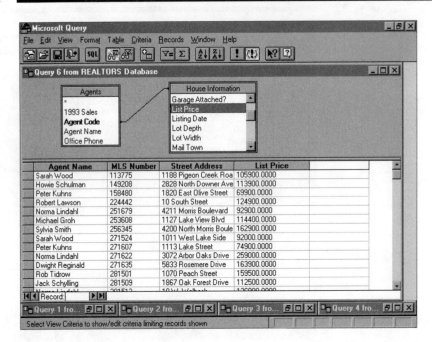

Each row of data in the Data pane represents a real-estate agent's name and some information on one house that the agent has listed.

You do not need to add the Agent Code to the Data pane, because MSQuery understands the relationship between these tables and will bring the related data to the Data pane.

The data displayed in the Data pane is a little difficult to understand. You may have a hunch that each agent has more than one house listed in the database, but at first glance, it looks as though only one house is listed for each agent. If you look more closely at the Agent Name column, however, you'll notice that the names of all of the agents except Dwight Reginald and Sylvia Smith appear more than once, indicating that each of those agents has more than one house listed.

It's easy to clarify the data displayed in the Data pane. An ascending sort can be applied to the Agent Name column, resulting in Figure 11.35.

Figure 11.35

After sorting on the
Agent Name column

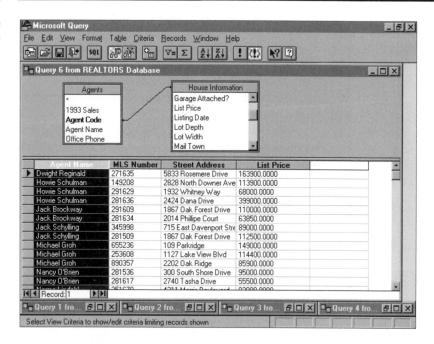

Mission accomplished! Now you easily can see that Dwight Reginald has
only one house listed, while Howie Schulman has three different houses in
the database.

Although more-complicated multiple-table queries are possible, the principles involved will be the same as those presented in this example: open the
database source, add the tables to the Table pane, and drag the desired fields
to the Data pane. Often sorting or other manipulation is required to make
sense of the data as it is drawn from the database tables.

Automatic Joins

Microsoft Query calls the lines drawn between related tables *automatic joins*
to indicate that it automatically recognizes the relationship between the
joined tables. Sometimes MSQuery needs you to perform a *manual join* to
help it understand relationships between tables.

Manual Joins

From time to time, no automatic relationship exists between tables in the
Table pane. In the example described earlier in the section, the Agent Code
field in the Agents and House Information tables defined a relationship

between these tables. The relationship was formed in Microsoft Access at the time the tables were created.

But consider a situation in which one table comes from an Access database, while another comes from a dBASE application. Although the data in the tables might be related (for instance, the Access application could contain customer names and addresses, and the dBASE table might contain invoice information,) no direct link exists between the tables because they came from different applications.

Microsoft Query lets you specify relationships between tables manually, even though the tables were created in different applications. You can create manual joins only if the tables share common field names.

Add the tables to the Table pane using the techniques discussed earlier in this chapter. Then, use the mouse to drag a common field from the primary table to the field list of the other table. Microsoft Query will now understand the relationship between the tables, and it will build the relational join between them.

■ Returning Query Data to Excel

To return the results of a query to Excel, start by running the query. Then click on the Return Data button from the MSQuery toolbar (see Figure 11.36).

Figure 11.36

Returning Query Data to Excel

Return Data button

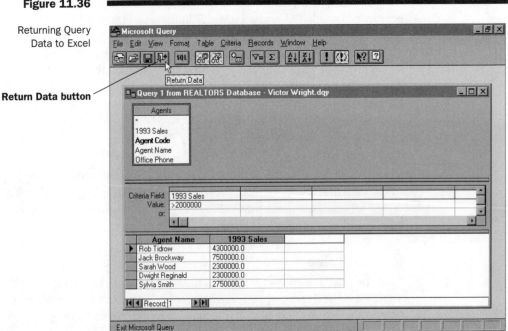

When the Returning External Data to Microsoft Excel dialog box appears, identify where you want to put the data in the workbook. You may place the data in an existing worksheet, create a new worksheet in which to place the data, or place the data in a Pivot-Table Report. Position the cell pointer in the upper-left corner of the destination range before you click the OK button.

In the example shown in Figure 11.37, the data being returned from MSQuery will be placed in "sheet1," beginning in cell A1.

Figure 11.37

The Returning External Data to Microsoft Excel dialog box

Cell pointer in upper-left corner of the destination range

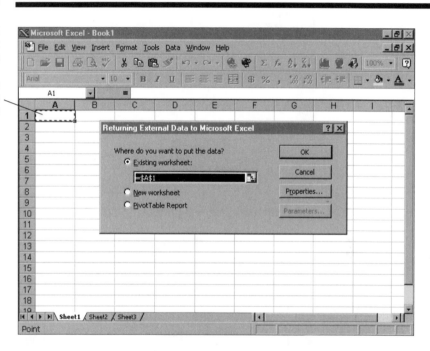

Figure 11.38 shows the data returned from MSQuery. Note that the data returned to Excel matches the results of the query from MSQuery (see Figure 11.36). Also note the appearance of the External Data toolbar. This toolbar allows you to perform MSQuery operations from inside the worksheet. If the External Data toolbar is not displayed, open the View menu in Excel, point to Toolbars, and from the list of toolbars click on External Data.

Refreshing/Editing External (Query) Data

Data extracted from MSQuery can be refreshed or edited. When you save the workbook containing the external data, Excel establishes a link to the source of that data—in our example, this is a query. If you wish to refresh the data

Figure 11.38

External (Query) Data in
Excel Worksheet

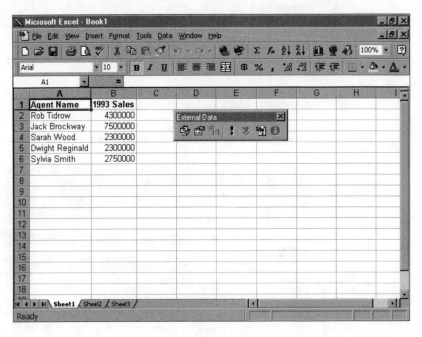

(or to run the query again,) position the cell pointer anywhere in the external data range, then choose Refresh Data from the Data menu (see Figure 11.39).

You can also edit the query that created the external data. With the cell pointer in the external data range, open the Data menu, point to Get External data, and click on Edit Query (see Figure 11.39). MSQuery will automatically start with the query opened.

■ Canceling MSQuery and Returning to Excel

You may cancel your work in MSQuery and return to Excel by opening the File Menu and clicking the Cancel and Return to Microsoft Excel option (see Figure 11.40). You'll be prompted to save any unsaved queries before MSQuery will close.

■ Running Saved Queries from Excel

Queries that you saved in MSQuery can be run directly from Excel. Position the cell pointer in an empty cell, open the Data menu, point to Get External Data, and click on Run Database Query (see Figure 11.41).

Figure 11.39

Refresh/Edit Query Data

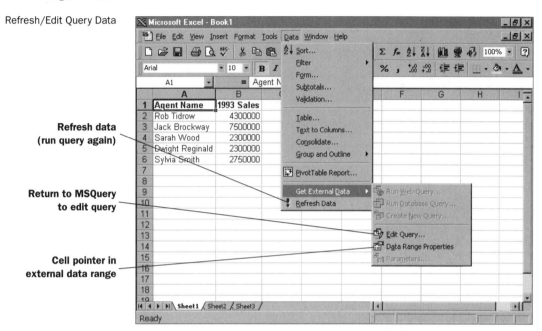

**Refresh data
(run query again)**

**Return to MSQuery
to edit query**

**Cell pointer in
external data range**

Figure 11.40

The Cancel and Return
to Microsoft Excel
option in MSQuery

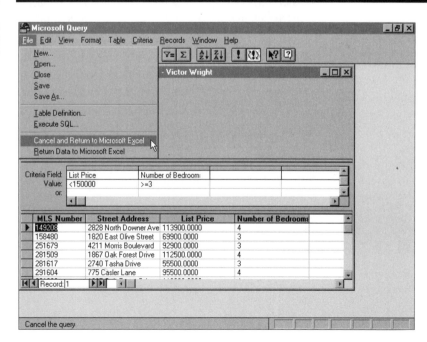

Figure 11.41

The Run Database
Query option

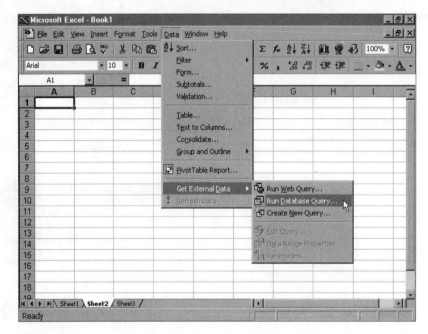

NOTE. *If the cell pointer is anywhere in an external data range, the Get External Data option will appear to be disabled or gray (see Figure 11.39).*

Figure 11.42 shows the Run Query dialog box that appears when you select the Get External Data option. The queries in the list were saved in the MSQuery application. To run a query from the list, select it, click the Get Data button, specify the output range, and then click OK.

■ Some Closing Thoughts on MSQuery

Whether you're new to Excel or an Excel "power user," MSQuery offers a unique combination of features for accessing a wide variety of external data sources. With a little practice and a click of your mouse, you'll be importing data from all over the world (assuming, of course, that you're on a network or have access to the Internet). As trite as it sounds, you're only limited by your imagination!

Figure 11.42

The Run Query dialog box

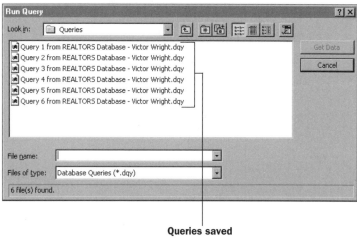

Queries saved
in MSQuery

3

Charts

- *Understanding Charts*
- *Introducing the ChartWizard*
- *Changing Charts*
- *Guided Tour of Excel Charts*

12

Complete Guide to Charts

O<small>NE OF THE MOST VALUABLE PARTS OF EXCEL IS ITS CHARTING</small> function. This feature makes it easy to prepare a wide variety of charts that can help you communicate or assist you in analyzing the information contained in your worksheets. Whether your need is based on analyzing data or presenting information, Excel's powerful charting function will most likely suffice. In this chapter, you will learn the following:

- Charting terminology

- Creating charts using the ChartWizard

- Editing and changing charts

- Embellishing your charts using legends, text, arrows, and graphics

- Determining which types of charts are better for presenting or analyzing your data

Despite the wide variety of choices available for generating charts, Excel makes creating and formatting charts easy. You can use this chapter to help you understand all the fundamentals of making and using charts.

Excel 97 for Windows has one of the most complete charting functions of any spreadsheet. In fact, it's so good that you will have little need for dedicated charting programs—even for making difficult technical charts. It can produce not only standard charts, like bar charts and line charts, but also complex, attractive charts that have a three-dimensional appearance.

Excel also contains many tools for embellishing your charts, including features that give you the ability to add legends, text, arrows, and graphic images to your charts. You'll also have full control over the symbols and colors that Excel uses on your charts, and you can use a graphic image rather than colors in certain types of charts (for example, a chart showing auto sales might use bars made up of stacked cars, as you've seen in many newspapers and magazines).

Microsoft has also made creating attractive, effective charts in Excel fairly easy. A function called the ChartWizard can walk you through all the steps required to quickly create a chart, previewing the eventual results at each step.

■ Understanding Charts

Before you begin, you'll need to understand the terminology used to describe the different parts of each chart. Please examine Figure 12.1.

Data Points

The *data points* are the individual points on each series of a chart. You can control the way the data points are represented by using different symbols (squares, circles, triangles, and so on) to make your chart more readable. This idea is particularly important when you are presenting black-and-white charts instead of color charts.

As you will learn in this chapter, certain types of charts allow you to move data points manually. When you are finished, Excel will actually change the worksheet data to match your changes to the chart—a marketing person's dream!

Figure 12.1

A sample line chart

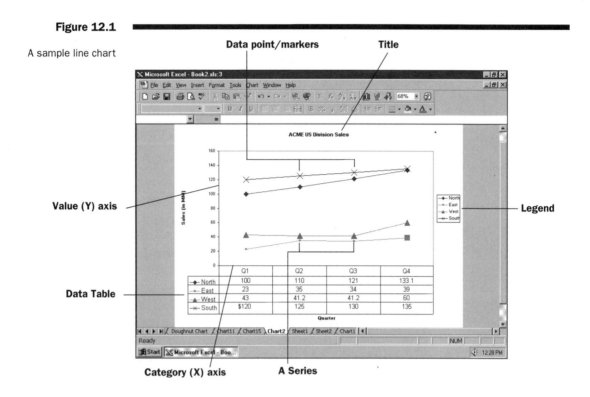

Series

A *series* is a group of data that forms one part of the data shown on a chart. In the sample chart in Figure 12.1, each line represents a series of data. Each series of data is made up of a formula that you can see when you click on the series. If you click on the North line, for example, you'll see the series formula appear in the formula bar. The series formula in this case is as follows:

```
=SERIES(Sheet1!$C$2,Sheet1!$D$1:$G$1,Sheet1!$D$2:$G$2,1)
```

Understanding and editing series formulas is covered in Chapter 14, "Advanced Charts for Business and Science."

Axes

The *axes* are the vertical and horizontal lines that show what is being charted. Excel offers many features for controlling these axes, including formatting, manual control of the scale shown, and double y-axes (the vertical axis).

Most charts have two axes: the *x-axis*, also known as the *Category* axis, and the *y-axis*, typically called the *Value* axis. Some charts also can contain a second Value (Y) axis. Certain three-dimensional charts can be formatted to contain a z-axis (a 3D chart can show categories along two dimensions, with the z-axis normally showing the categories or values from the front of the 3D chart to the back).

NOTE *See Chapter 14 for more information on creating dual Value (Y) axis charts.*

Legend

The *legend* defines what each series represents. In Figure 12.1, the boxed legend explains that North is represented by diamonds, East by squares, West by triangles, and South by Xs. Legends can be formatted in many different ways, and you can place them anywhere in your chart.

Markers

The *markers* are the symbols (squares, diamonds, and so on) used at each intersection of the plotted data on a line chart. The markers show what the actual data is; the lines between each marker are generated by Excel simply to "connect the dots." You can control the color, type, and style of markers in Excel.

TIP *You can rest your mouse pointer briefly on a chart marker to see a ChartTip that shows you the range of data being referred to by the marker and the actual value of the marker. This feature, new to Excel 97, also works with bar-chart bars and pie-chart slices.*

Tick Marks

Tick marks are the incremental marks that appear along each axis to measure or designate the data. The chart shown in Figure 12.1 shows eight tick marks along the value axis to show exactly where each value falls. Excel lets you control the degree of detail that the tick marks show, and lets you decide if they will be shown at all. You could, for example, show a tick mark for each $20 MM and also for each $5 MM, with the two ranges of tick marks formatted differently.

Grid

Figure 12.2 shows the same sample chart as Figure 12.1, but a grid has been added. *Grids* help the reader see more easily where the chart markers line up with the axis references.

NOTE *Be careful when using gridlines. Sometimes they don't really add anything to the chart, and they can actually make it more difficult to read. The sample chart with gridlines shown in Figure 12.2 is a good example. The gridlines make the chart too busy, and don't really help the reader of the chart. It was easy to see where the data markers lined up with the sales figures and categories without the gridlines.*

Figure 12.2

A sample chart with gridlines

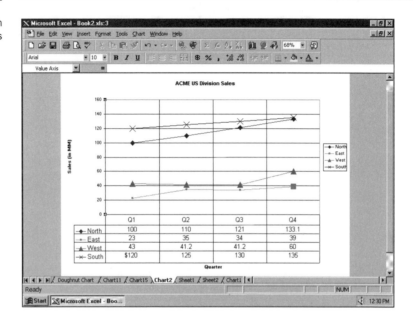

Titles

Titles are lines of text you use to label or identify elements of a chart, or to name the chart itself. The sample chart has a main title at the top ("ACME US Division Sales") as well as titles attached to each axis ("Quarter" and "Sales (in MM)").

■ Introducing the ChartWizard

Excel includes a powerful utility that walks you through each step of the chart-creation process. This utility is called the *ChartWizard*, and it makes creating charts in Excel a snap. Not only can you use the ChartWizard to create new charts, but you also can use it to change existing charts.

Selecting Chart Data

To use the ChartWizard, you begin by selecting the data you want to plot:

1. Click and drag, or click and Shift+click, on the range of cells you want to chart. Select noncontiguous ranges by holding down the Ctrl key as you select each range.

2. The first Chart Wizard dialog box now appears, shown in Figure 12.3.

Figure 12.3

Step 1 of the ChartWizard

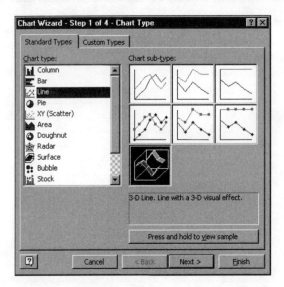

Using ChartWizard Dialog Boxes

Each ChartWizard dialog box uses the buttons described in Table 12.1.

Table 12.1

ChartWizard Dialog
Box Buttons

BUTTON	FUNCTION
Help	Get help on the current step in the ChartWizard
Cancel	Cancel the chart
Back	Go back to the previous steps to change your choices
Next	Move to the next step in the ChartWizard
Finish	Complete the chart-creation process using Excel's standard chart and default chart settings

Selecting the Chart Type

The first step of the ChartWizard (see Figure 12.3) lets you select the Chart type and the Chart sub-type. Click on each type of chart in the left-hand list, and the available sub-types will appear to the right. When you select a sub-type, you can also click on the Press and hold to view sample button to preview the chart using the data you've selected.

There are also a number of customized chart types, which you can access with the Custom Types tab in the dialog box (see Figure 12.4). You can choose from a number of built-in custom chart types, or you can create your own, selecting them from this dialog-box page with the User-defined button.

Figure 12.4

Selecting a custom
chart type

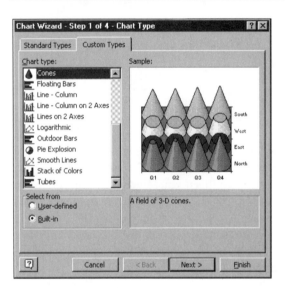

For this example, select the Line chart type from the Standard Types tab, and then the 3-D effect sub-type. Then click Next to continue.

Selecting the Chart Source Data

The second step of the Chart Wizard lets you confirm the source data upon which the chart is based, as shown in Figure 12.5. The chart using the selected data is previewed in the window shown.

Usually you can create a chart by simply choosing a "block" of data. Excel then figures out which cells contain data to be plotted, and which cells

Figure 12.5

Confirming or selecting
the chart source data

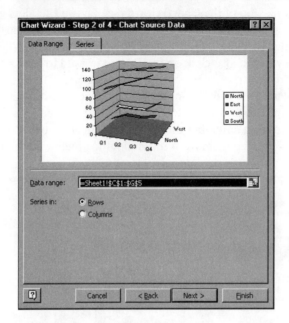

contain labels for the data. You simply select the block of data with the Data Range field shown in Figure 12.5, and you're off and running. And you don't even need to do this if you selected the chart data before you clicked on the Chart Wizard button: in that case, the field will have already been completed for you.

However, sometimes you need to exert finer control over how Excel looks at the data. In such cases, use the Series tab in Chart Source Data dialog box, which you can see in Figure 12.6.

In the Series tab, you can select each series of data individually, by first selecting the series in the Series window, and then selecting the title and data in the Name and Values fields. You can add new series in this dialog box with the Add button, or remove existing series with Remove. Finally, you can select the chart labels data with the fields provided.

In this example nothing needs to be changed, so you can click Next to continue to Step 3 of the Chart Wizard.

Choosing Chart Options

The third step of the Chart Wizard (see Figure 12.7) lets you set all of the options that control how your chart is displayed. The Chart Options dialog box

Figure 12.6

Selecting chart data
in detail

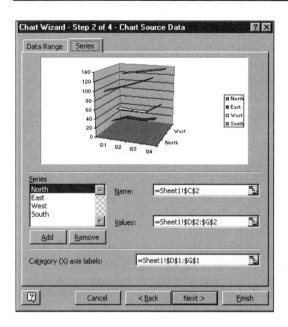

is tabbed into six different pages, each one controlling a different aspect of
your chart formatting. As you make changes to any of the pages, your change
will be previewed in the window to the right of the different options.

Figure 12.7

Setting Chart Options
with the Chart Wizard

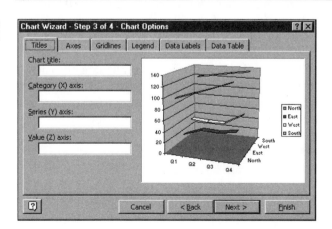

Adding Titles

The Titles tab of the Chart Options dialog box lets you insert titles for your chart, and for the different axes used. Figure 12.8 shows some titles added in this fashion for the example chart.

Figure 12.8

Adding titles to charts

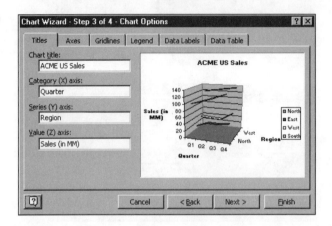

TIP *If the preview window doesn't quite show the formatting the way you want it to appear, don't worry; Excel previews the chart as best as it can in the small window. Once you have finished the chart and it's displayed at full size, the appearance of your formatting choices typically improves. For example, notice how the Sales label in Figure 12.8 wraps, which doesn't look very attractive. In the complete chart, this problem disappears because Excel has more room in which to display the label.*

Controlling Axes

The Axes tab of the Chart Options dialog box shown in Figure 12.9 lets you control which axes are displayed with the different axes option boxes. Also, you can choose from different formatting options for the Category (X) axis, forcing it to assume that the axis is category-based or time-scale-based.

Selecting Gridlines

Many charts are improved by the addition of gridlines that make the chart easier to read. You can control the inclusion of gridlines with the Gridlines tab shown in Figure 12.10. Simply use the check boxes shown to choose where you want gridlines placed in your chart.

Figure 12.9

Controlling axes on
your chart

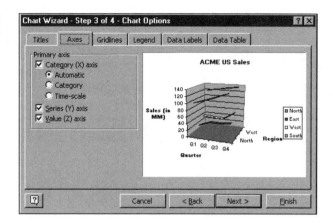

Figure 12.10

Adding gridlines to a chart

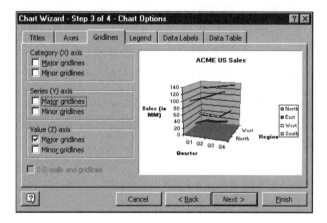

Adding a Legend

Legends are another tool that can improve the readability of a chart, and
they are often necessary to convey what is being plotted. The Legend tab
shown in Figure 12.11 lets you choose whether or not a legend is included,
and where on the chart the legend is placed.

Figure 12.11

Controlling legend inclusion and placement

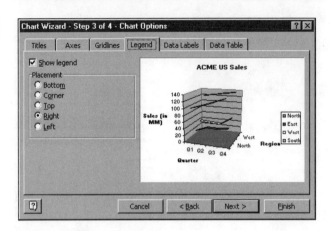

Data Labels

On some charts, you will want to include data labels next to each charted point so that the reader can easily see the detailed number or label (or some other detail) upon which the point has been placed. These data labels can be controlled with the Data Labels tab shown in Figure 12.12. You can choose to include no label, values, percentages, a label, a label and a percentage, and bubble sizes. Certain choices are only available for certain chart types: for instance, percentages are available for pie charts alone.

Figure 12.12

Adding data labels to your charts

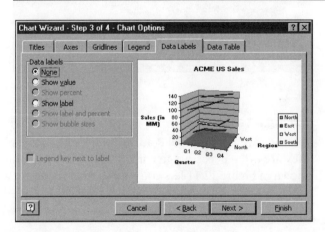

Including Data Tables

New to Excel 97 is the ability to automatically create data tables in your charts that show the data on which the chart is based next to the chart (see Figure 12.13). These tables can also display the legend keys, obviating the need to include a legend on charts with such data tables. You control these options with the Data Table tab of the Chart Options dialog box. Choosing either of the available options previews the data table next to the chart.

Figure 12.13

Adding a data table to your chart

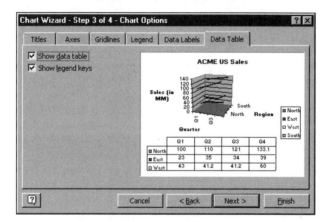

Determining the Chart Location

After selecting all of the chart options in the tabbed dialog box, clicking the Next button takes you to the final step of the Chart Wizard, in which you decide where the resulting chart will be placed. You can choose to create a chart as a new sheet, within which it takes up all of the room on a special "chart sheet," or you can include it as an object floating above a regular Excel worksheet. Figure 12.14 shows the Chart Location dialog box, while Figures 12.15 and 12.16 show the completed chart located in both places.

■ Changing Charts

Creating charts is only half the battle. Even with the ChartWizard, you will often have to format and reformat charts until you achieve the exact results you want. This section teaches you to format all of the elements of your charts.

Figure 12.14

Determining chart location

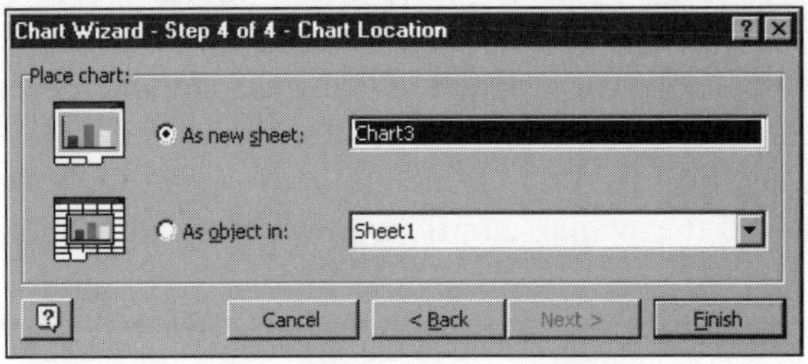

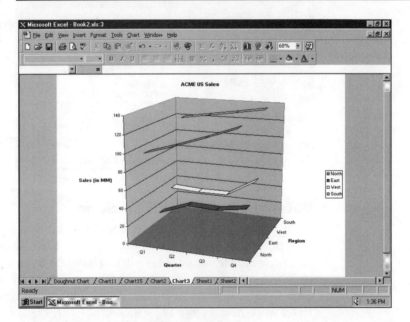

Figure 12.15

The completed chart
created in a chart sheet

Selecting Areas of the Chart

You can select each element of a chart simply by clicking on it. Alternatively, you can press the right-arrow key repeatedly to cycle through all the selectable chart elements. You might want to try this on a couple of charts to see which parts of the chart you can select individually.

Excel 97 improves on the program's previous method for selecting chart elements when a chart is embedded on a worksheet. Called *single-click selection*,

Figure 12.16

The completed chart
created as an object on
a worksheet

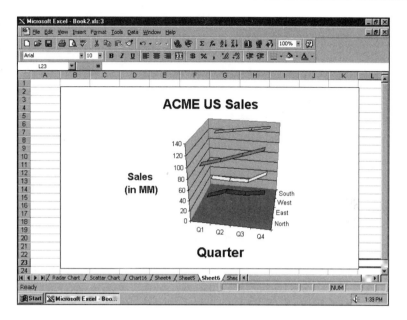

this new feature lets you choose a chart element with one click. Earlier
versions of Excel made you double-click the chart to put it in editing mode,
and then required an additional click to choose the element you wanted to
work with.

TIP *To select an individual data point, click once on the point to select the
entire series. Click a second time on the point to select just that data point.
Alternatively, click on the series to select it, and then press the right-arrow key
to cycle through each data point.*

Adding a New Series to a Chart

Figure 12.17 shows a chart that was created before the Europe data line was
added to the table.

To add the new line of data to the chart, follow these steps:

1. Access the Source Data command in the Chart menu.

2. Move to the Series tab in the Source Data dialog box.

3. Click the Add button.

4. Use the Name field to select the cell that contains the name of the series.

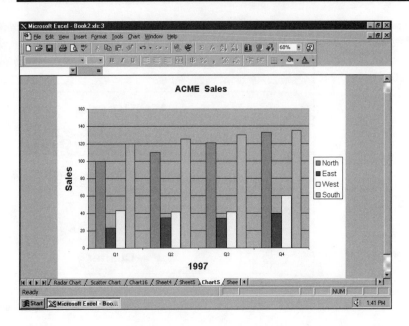

5. Use the Values field to select the range of data to be plotted.

6. Click the OK button.

   Figure 12.18 shows the new chart with the added series.

Removing a Series from a Chart

To remove a data series from a chart, simply click on the series you want to
remove so that it is selected, and then pick one of these options:

- Press the Del key.

- Click the right mouse button on the series you want to remove, then
  choose Clear from the pop-up menu.

- Pull down the Edit menu and choose Clear. This displays a cascading
  menu from which you can choose All (clear all series), Series (clear
  only the selected series), or Formats (which removes any formatting
  you have applied). Select Series from the cascading menu to remove
  the selected series.

Figure 12.18

The new data series
added to the chart

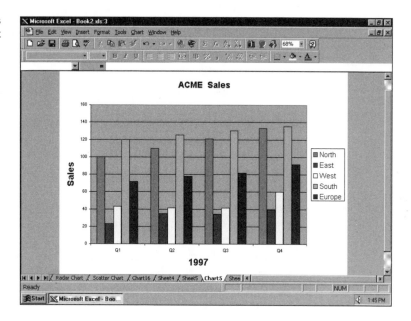

Moving and Sizing Chart Elements

Many elements of the chart can be moved, including text and legends. To move a chart element, just select it and drag it to its new location. In the case of text objects in the chart, select the text object, then grab the border of the text box and drag it to a new location.

You can also resize many parts of a chart, such as the plot area or text boxes. To do so, select the object. Grab one of the small boxes in the corner, which are called *handles*. You can then drag the handle to a new position. When resizing an element by dragging one of the handles, hold down the Shift key to force the element to retain its original proportions.

Changing the Appearance of Chart Elements

Excel provides you with virtually unlimited possibilities for formatting your chart, allowing you to make it as pleasing and effective as possible. To format any chart element, select that chart element and click the right mouse button on the selected element. From the pop-up menu, choose Format *x*, where *x* is the name of the element you want to format. Also, rather than using the pop-up menu, you can pull down the Format menu and choose Selected Object.

The actual name of the menu item will change depending on which object you have selected when you access the Format menu.

TIP *To instantly pull up the formatting dialog box, press Ctrl+1 after selecting the object you want to format.*

Each type of object presents a different formatting dialog box, depending on what can be formatted for the selected object. For example, if you pull up the formatting dialog box with an axis selected, you will see a page to change the axis scale.

The following sections show you each dialog-box page, and explain which types of objects apply to the dialog-box page.

Patterns

Depending on what type of element you are formatting, the Patterns page makes different choices available. Sometimes these choices are subtle, like adding a check box called Smoothed line if you are formatting a series in a line chart. Other times the differences might be obvious, such as a section on the page for choosing tick-mark styles when you are formatting an axis.

The Patterns page of the formatting dialog box is used to control the following formatting tasks:

- **Borders.** You can control the style, color, and weight of the line used to border the object. With some objects, you also can choose a *drop shadow*, which gives the box the appearance of depth.

- **Area fill.** Some objects allow you to control their fill colors and patterns. You can, for example, control the color and pattern of each bar in a bar chart or each slice of a pie chart. Also, with some charts you can select a check box called Invert if Negative, which tells Excel to reverse the color for any parts of the series that represent negative numbers.

- **Lines.** Some objects—notably gridlines and axes—let you control the style of the line with which they are drawn. You can control the color, style, and weight of these lines. Also, if you are formatting a series in a line chart, the Patterns page has a check box that allows you to select smoothed lines. On a line chart you can use the Patterns dialog-box page to select the style of the markers used for each plot point.

One example of the Patterns dialog-box page is shown in Figure 12.19.

Font

If the object you are formatting is a text box or has text associated with it, such as an axis, you can use the Font page in the formatting dialog box to change the characteristics of the font used. Figure 12.20 shows the Font page.

Figure 12.19

The Format Data Series
dialog box showing the
Patterns page

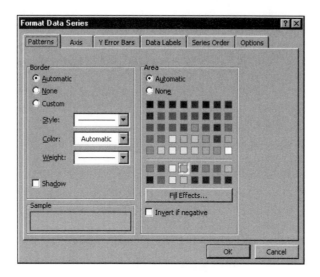

Figure 12.20

The Format Axis dialog
box showing the
Font page

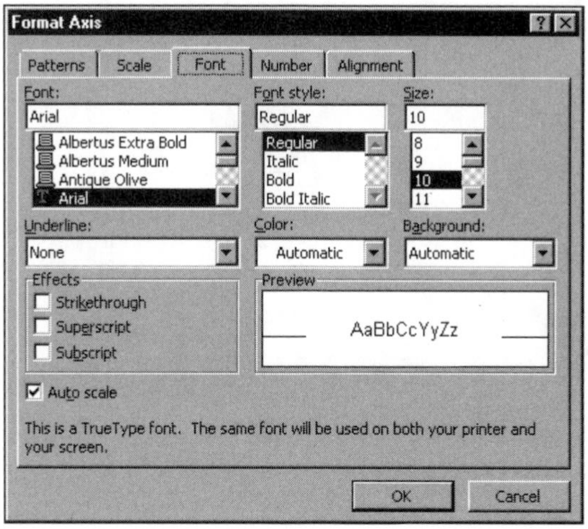

Using AutoFormat

If you want to use a chart format again, Excel permits you to store your formatting choices as a custom chart type. You can select this chart type in the future, and avoid having to repeatedly make the same formatting choices. Custom chart types also help you reduce error in cases where you constantly produce charts that you want to format in the same way: there'll be no need to worry that you forgot to change some font to a particular size, or neglected to select a particular color or gridline arrangement, when using your own custom chart type.

To add a chart type to the user-defined chart types, follow these steps:

1. Start with a chart selected that contains all the formatting you want to store.

2. Pull down the Chart menu and choose Chart Type. The Chart Type dialog box will appear, and you should select the Custom Types tab (see Figure 12.21).

Figure 12.21

The Custom Types
dialog box

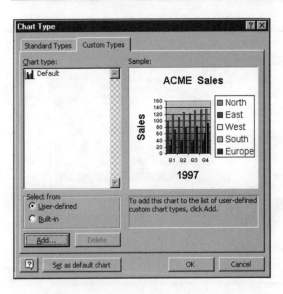

3. Click on the User-defined button to show chart types you've created.

4. Click on the Add button. You'll see the Add Custom Chart Type dialog box shown in Figure 12.22.

5. Complete the Add Custom Chart Type dialog box and click OK. Then click OK to close the Chart Types dialog box.

Figure 12.22

Add Custom Chart Type
dialog box

NOTE *You also can select an existing format by selecting it and clicking the Remove button.*

You can distribute your custom chart types to other people. To do so, simply have them open the workbook that contains your custom chart and select the chart. Then, have them follow the procedures shown in the preceding list. The new custom chart type will be added to their Excel Chart Types menu, and they'll be able to select it even without the workbook available.

Adding Text

Excel charts can use several types of text: axis labels, attached labels, attached text, and unattached text. *Axis labels* indicate what each point on the axis represents; this type of text cannot be moved. *Attached labels* are titles, axis titles, and data labels. *Attached text*, although it is created in certain predefined locations, can be moved freely around the chart. Finally, you can create *unattached text* that you also can place anywhere you want to within the chart.

Creating Unattached Text

To create unattached text in an Excel chart, deselect any selected chart elements and simply start typing. Your text will appear in the formula bar. After you press Enter, the text will be placed in the center of the chart area. You can click on the text to select it, format it, and move it.

Changing Text Alignment

Most of the text on the Excel chart, with the exception of legend text, can be realigned or rotated to help you fit more data onto the page at very little cost in readability. To try these options, select the text you want to align and press Ctrl+1 to bring up the formatting dialog box for that text. Click on the Alignment page, which is shown in Figure 12.23. These options are self-explanatory.

Figure 12.23

The Alignment formatting page

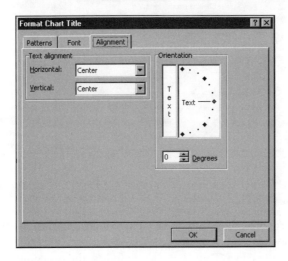

Controlling Legends

You can decide whether to include a legend on your Excel charts. To delete an existing legend, select the legend and press Del, or click on the Legend button in the Chart Toolbar. To create a new legend, pull down the Insert menu and choose Legend. A default legend will be created, which you can then format as you wish using the techniques covered earlier in this chapter.

You also can change the way a legend is arranged by dragging any of its handles. As you drag the handle, an outline previews the way your legend will be arranged, from a straight vertical arrangement of legend items, to multicolumn legends, to a straight horizontal arrangement.

Controlling Axes

Controlling the axes of your charts can play a powerful role in the impact of the information you convey. For example, consider Figure 12.24, which shows a line chart. Note that it is virtually impossible to tell what the chart is saying, because so many lines are grouped together closely at the top of the chart. While the Chart Wizard attempts to compensate for the range of displayed values, Excel will sometimes show zero as the bottom Value axis entry.

Figure 12.24

A line chart with closely grouped data

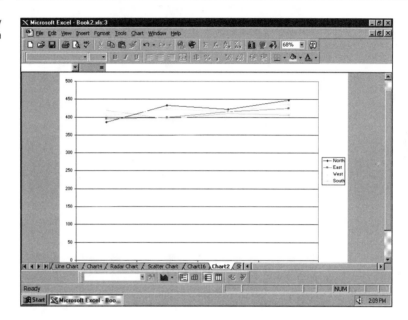

You can solve this problem by changing the Value axis scale:

1. Click on the Value (Y) axis to select it.

2. Pull down the Format menu and choose Selected Axis. The axis-formatting dialog box appears.

TIP *After you have selected the object you want to format, either press Ctrl+1 to instantly pull up the formatting dialog box for that object, or click the right mouse button and choose Format object.*

3. Click on the dialog-box tab labeled Scale. The Scale dialog-box page is shown in Figure 12.25.

Table 12.2 shows the different settings available on the Scale dialog-box page.

Figure 12.26 shows the sample line chart with the Minimum value set to 370. As you can see, the chart is now much more readable, and you can see how each region is doing with respect to the other regions. You can also discern an overall upward trend in the numbers. Although this trend is somewhat

Figure 12.25

The Format Axis dialog
box showing the
Scale page

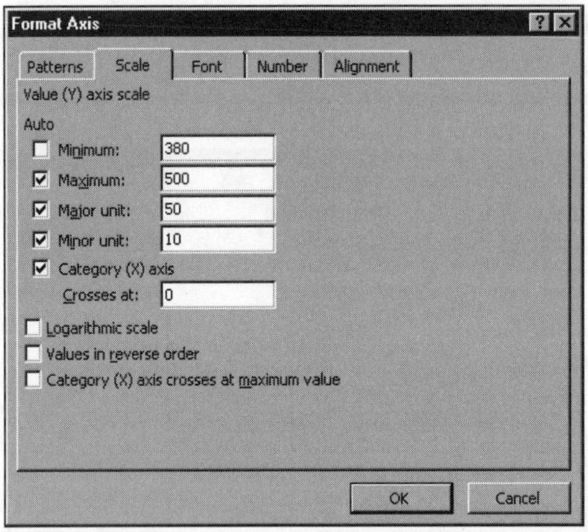

Table 12.2

Scale Dialog Box Page

SETTING	PURPOSE
Minimum	Defines the minimum point on the scale. If the check box in this field is selected, Excel uses the default value (0 or the lowest data point on the chart, whichever is lower). Entering a minimum value automatically deselects the check box.
Maximum	Defines the maximum point on the scale. If the check box is selected, Excel will automatically use the highest data point on the chart, rounded up to the next-highest major axis number.
Major Unit	Defines the Major Unit used for gridline control. You can choose to display gridlines at each major unit on the axis. You also can control the tick marks used to denote the major unit. See the following section on controlling tick marks for information about how this page and the tick marks relate.
Minor Unit	Defines the Minor Unit used for gridline control. You can choose to display gridlines at each minor unit on the axis. You can also control the tick marks used to indicate each minor unit on the axis.
Category (X) axis crosses at:	Allows you to tell Excel where on the Value axis you want the axis to intersect. You could, for example, enter the number used in the Maximum field, which would cause Excel to place the Category axis along the top of the chart.
Logarithmic Scale	Causes Excel to use a logarithmic scale for the axis.

**Table 12.2
(Continued)**

Scale Dialog Box Page

SETTING	PURPOSE
Values in Reverse Order	Forces Excel to reverse the default order for the Value axis, so that the lower numbers are at the top of the axis, and the higher numbers are at the bottom of the axis.
Category (X) Axis Crosses at maximum value	If you select this check box, Excel places the Category axis wherever the maximum value of the Value axis is. In the example chart, this would cause the Category axis to be displayed at the top of the chart.

difficult to see, you can observe it far easier than you could when all the lines were grouped very tightly together.

Figure 12.26

Value axis with an
adjusted scale

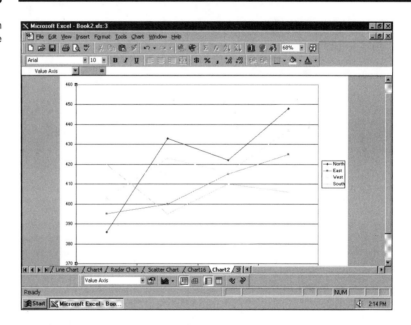

NOTE *Although being able to adjust the axis measurements on your charts is a valuable tool for analysis and presentation, I have to admit that I really dislike it when newspapers make economic data more alarming or positive than it really is by making it unclear that they are changing the Value axis in the charts they show. Some charts that purport to show steep economic increases or declines actually say very little (or show only very small changes) after the values used in the Value axis are considered.*

Changing 3D Perspective

Excel contains a number of 3D charts. Using a 3D chart, however, presupposes that you can change your viewing perspective. Fortunately, Microsoft did not forget to include this capability. Being able to rotate 3D charts can be critical in showing information that might otherwise be hidden, and it can also be used to change the impact that a chart has. All else being equal, viewing a chart as if they are looking up at it rather from viewing it from above looking down can have a subtly different impact on your audience.

Figure 12.27 shows a 3D bar chart with the hindmost series being somewhat obscured by the other bars. You can fix this problem simply by rotating your viewpoint of the chart to the left by about one-eighth of a turn. You can accomplish this feat using a dialog box or the nifty wireframe feature.

Figure 12.27

A 3D chart with an obscured series

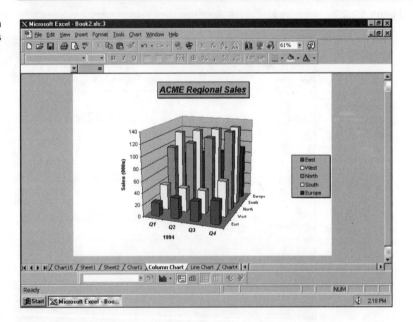

To change the perspective of the chart using the dialog box, follow these steps:

1. Pull down the Chart menu and choose 3D View. You'll see the dialog box shown in Figure 12.28.

2. Adjust the Elevation, Rotation, and Perspective to the new viewpoint. The viewpoint fields are accompanied by convenient buttons that help

Figure 12.28

The 3-D View dialog box

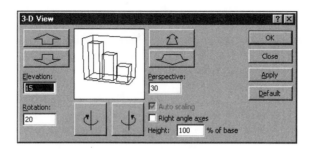

indicate their functions. See Table 12.3 for a breakdown of all the choices offered by the 3-D View dialog box.

Table 12.3

Format 3-D View Dialog Box Settings

FIELD	FUNCTION
Elevation	This field controls the height of your viewpoint, and is expressed in degrees (from -90 degrees, looking up at the chart, to 90 degrees, which is looking down onto the chart). Pie charts and bar charts have different limits. The elevation for pie charts is limited to 10-80 degrees; bar charts are limited to 0-40 degrees.
Rotation	Rotation also is given in degrees, from 0 to 360 degrees. Bar charts are restricted from 0 to 44 degrees.
Perspective	Perspective controls the perceived depth of the chart. This value controls the ratio of the size of the front of the chart to the size of the rear of the chart. Perspective can range from 0 to 100.
Right Angle Axes	When this check box is selected, the axes always are displayed at right angles (90 degrees, 180 degrees, 270 degrees, and 0 degrees). Otherwise, the axes are free to be displayed at varying angles called for by the chart perspective.
Auto Scaling	This choice is available only if Right Angle Axes is selected. When Auto Scaling is selected, the chart will be scaled proportionally to take up as much of the chart area as possible.
Height % of base	This field controls the percentage of the height of the chart in relationship to the Category axis. If you set this number to 300, for example, the chart will be three times taller than the Category axis is wide.

Table 12.3 (Continued)

Format 3-D View Dialog Box Settings

FIELD	FUNCTION
Apply	This button applies your changes without exiting the dialog box, so that you can see your changes before you commit to them. You might need to move the dialog box off to the side to see the chart, however. Note that when you apply your changes, they will not be canceled by exiting the dialog box. Instead, the Apply button lets you adjust and view your changes, permitting you to quickly readjust and view them until the chart view is to your liking.
Default	When clicked on, this button returns the chart to Excel's default settings for 3D view.

3. Click on the Apply button to look at your changes. If you are not happy with the result, continue to adjust the values in the dialog box, and click on the Apply button until you see what you want.

4. Click on the OK button to finalize your changes and exit the dialog box.

Excel also allows you to change the 3D view more directly by dragging handles on the chart itself, as follows:

1. Select the chart by clicking on it. Handles will appear at each corner of the chart. Click on one of these handles and hold down the mouse button to begin dragging. As you drag, you will see a *wireframe* (three-dimensional outline) image of your chart, as shown in Figure 12.29.

2. When the wireframe indicates the view you want, release the mouse button to have Excel redraw the chart based on the new perspective.

Changing Data from the Chart

In most Excel charts, you can change the value of a particular data marker directly by simply dragging it. When you do this, Excel automatically adjusts the values in the original worksheet data so that they correspond to the new data-marker position.

NOTE *If you are going to be adjusting a chart in this way, you should consider making a copy of the worksheet data upon which the chart is based before manipulating the chart and changing the data.*

Consider the chart and worksheet example in Figure 12.30. It's a simple line chart graphing two data series. The second data series is based on the first, with 40 percent added to the original data.

Figure 12.29

A wireframe of a 3D chart is displayed when you drag a corner.

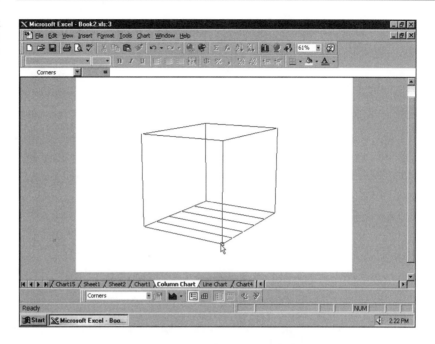

Figure 12.30

A sample line chart

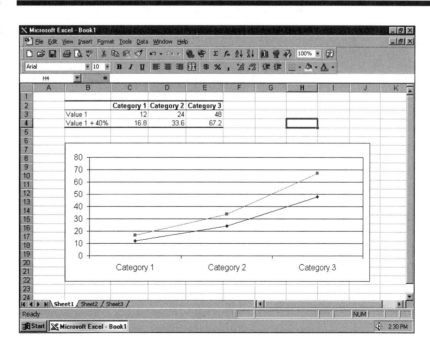

To directly change the middle data point in the first series, follow these steps:

1. Click on the left data marker of the lower series once to select the series, then again to select the individual data point. After the individual data point is selected, your pointer changes to a small double-headed arrow that points up and down.

2. Drag the data point to a new position and release the mouse button to complete the change. As you are dragging the data marker, a small cross will appear in the Value axis to help you select the new value more accurately. A ScreenTip will display the exact value that will be placed in the worksheet data as you drag the data marker.

When the change is finished, the sample chart will look similar to Figure 12.31. As you can see, the data in the worksheet has changed automatically to be consistent with the chart data.

Figure 12.31

Moved data marker

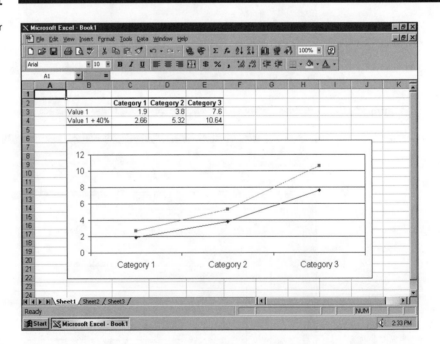

If you move a data marker that represents the result of a calculation, Excel will automatically update the data. In this example, moving one of the markers in the top data series would also have to change the number in the lower data series, because the top data series is dependent on the lower data series.

When you move a dependent data marker, Excel automatically invokes its Goal Seek feature so that it can reverse the change to the cells that make up the formula. Figure 12.32 shows the Goal Seek dialog box as it appears when you have moved one of the dependent data markers.

Figure 12.32

The Goal Seek dialog box

The Goal Seek dialog box has three fields. The Set Cell field shows the cell on the worksheet that you have changed with the data marker. The To Value field shows the new value for the cell associated with the moved data marker. The final field, By Changing Cell, prompts you for the cell that should be changed in order for all the calculations on the worksheet to remain consistent. This field must be set to a cell that provides a constant value (in this case, cell D4 is the cell that must be changed in order for cell D5 to remain consistent). If the cell being changed is based on many constant values, the Goal Seek Status dialog box lets you choose which one to manipulate to reverse the calculations. Select the appropriate cell by making the By Changing Cell field active and then clicking on the cell to change. Click on the OK button to initiate the Goal Seek process.

If Goal Seek is not able to find a solution that fits all the formulas involved, it will display an error message indicating that the Goal Seek process has failed. If it finds a solution, it will show you the message in Figure 12.33.

Figure 12.33

The Goal Seek Status dialog box

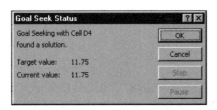

NOTE *The Goal Seek function works by trying many different values in the target cell, zeroing in on a solution until it finds one that works perfectly. Note that you might not be able to solve some formulas with the Goal Seek*

function. Also, if more than one solution exists, Excel might not choose the solution you want. Examine the results carefully before you accept the change.

■ Guided Tour of Excel Charts

The remainder of this chapter shows you examples of each major type of chart in Excel, along with suggestions about how best to use each chart and notes about special features particular to that chart.

The variety of charts supported by Excel are not included for mere aesthetic reasons. Rather, each chart is specialized for showing different types of information.

NOTE *The chart you choose to present your data can have a subtle but profound impact on your audience. Different charts prompt different questions about the information, and can influence your audience to come to different conclusions. Take some care in choosing the right chart for the job and in anticipating the questions that your chart might prompt.*

Area Charts

Area charts work best when you want to show the relationship of different series of numbers and to examine how each series contributes to the total of all series. If Figure 12.34 were a line chart, you would have to add a line to represent total sales to easily see the sum of all series in a given category. Even then it would be difficult to see how each one contributed to the whole.

Area charts emphasize change across the categories, particularly relative change between different series.

Area charts can show error bars and standard deviations. Access these features by selecting a particular series, pulling up its formatting dialog box (double-clicking on the series), and using the Y Error Bars page in the dialog box.

Bar Charts

Bar charts emphasize comparison of the different categories rather than comparison across time, unlike column charts. Several different subgroups of bar charts exist, including the stacked bar and 100-percent stacked bar. The *stacked bar* shows the relationships between the different series more accurately, whereas the *100-percent stacked bar* shows the percentage of the whole for each series. Figure 12.35 shows a sample bar chart.

NOTE *Bar charts, along with column charts, are an excellent place to use error bars. Typically,* error bars *are used to show the standard deviation on technical charts. To add error bars to a bar chart, select the series to which you want to add the error bars, pull down the Insert menu, and choose Error bars. On the*

Figure 12.34

A sample area chart

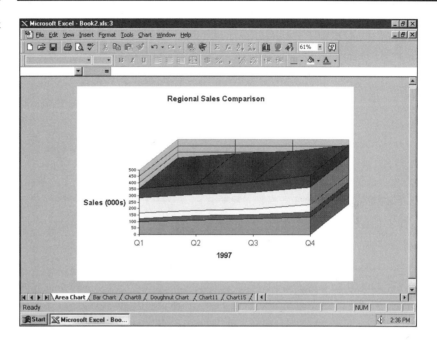

Figure 12.35

A sample bar chart

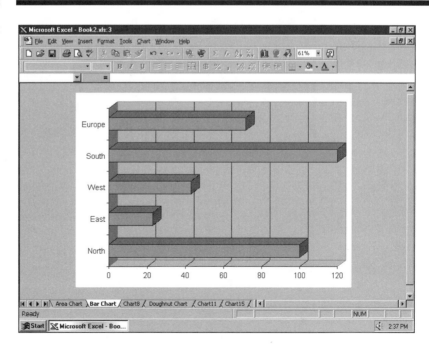

dialog box page that appears, choose the style of error bars you want and define the amount of error to be shown in the Error section of the page. See Chapter 14, "Advanced Charts for Business and Science," for more information.

Column Charts

Column charts are best at illustrating the way values change over time, and they also help the reader compare different values by placing them side by side. Because time is on the horizontal access, column charts emphasize change over time. Like bar charts, column charts can use error bars, and they can also be produced in a stacked column format and a 100-percent stacked format. Figure 12.36 shows a simple column chart.

Figure 12.36

A sample column chart

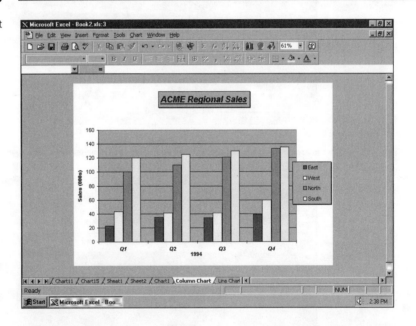

NOTE *One key difference between a column chart and a line or area chart is that the column chart shows only discrete values across time. Line and area charts, on the other hand, suggest activity between each data point because of the lines drawn between each point.*

Line Charts

Line charts emphasize trends in your data. Although line and area charts have some similarities, they also have some big differences. Area charts, for example, easily express the total of all series, but line charts do not, unless you add that total as a separate series. Line charts are designed to show a trend over time, and the Category axis is almost always time-based (months, quarters, years, and so on).

If you need to show a trend using a value on the Category axis, use a scatter chart with the data points connected by lines (this is one of the scatter subtypes: see the following section on scatter charts). Because line charts are designed to use time or other discrete categories on their Category axis, you cannot have a logarithmic scale on the Category axis, as you can with scatter charts.

You also can add trend lines to your charts. See Chapter 14 to learn more.

Figure 12.37

A sample line chart

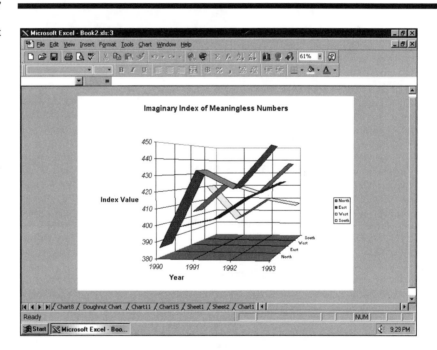

Pie Charts

Pie charts always show percentages of a whole and emphasize a particular part of your data, as the emphasized Europe slice shows in Figure 12.38.

You can rotate the pie chart by selecting the chart, pulling down the Format menu, and selecting Pie Group from the menu. In the dialog box that appears, click on the Options tab. On this page, you can change the Angle of First Slice field, which specifies the degrees of the angle at which the first pie slice appears.

Figure 12.38

A sample pie chart

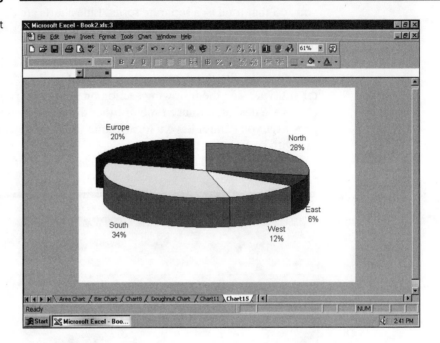

Doughnut Charts

Doughnut charts are very similar to pie charts, because they show the proportion of sections within a whole. The main advantage of a doughnut chart, however, is that it allows you to compare multiple series of data, as shown in Figure 12.39.

Radar Charts

Radar charts show changes between categories (see Figure 12.40). Each radiating axis from the center represents a category, and each line is a series. As you can see in Category 1 (the vertical category at the top of the chart), radar charts also can be formatted to use a logarithmic scale to represent their data. Radar charts are most commonly used in Asia and Europe.

Scatter (XY) Charts

Scatter (XY) charts show the relationship between two or more scales. Generally, both scales are numeric measurements. In fact, the scatter chart is not really designed to show a time series, although it can do so if needed. A scatter

Figure 12.39

A sample doughnut chart

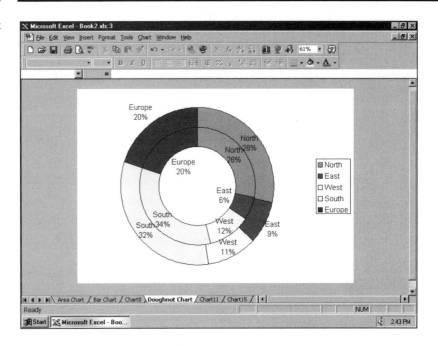

Figure 12.40

A sample radar chart

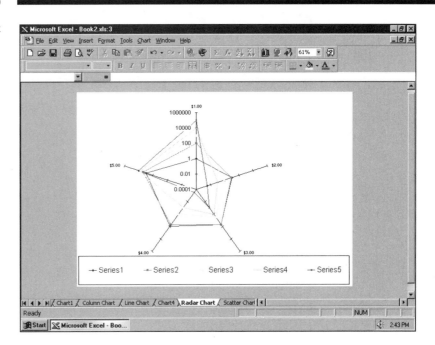

chart often is used for scientific plots, and such charts are often seen with logarithmic scales, as shown in Figure 12.41.

Figure 12.41

A sample scatter (XY) chart

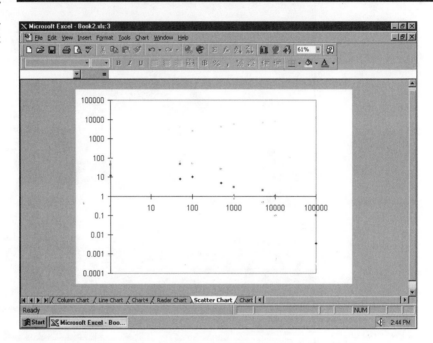

If you need to show the relationship between two number-based axes, but want connecting lines between the data points, you can use the scatter chart, but choose the subtype of scatter chart that connects the data markers.

NOTE *For more information about scatter (XY) charts, see Chapter 14.*

3D Charts

The pie, bar, column, and line charts are also available in a 3D format. Their 3D variants are provided for aesthetic reasons, and the preceding notes for bar, column, and line charts also apply to the 3D versions of these charts.

3D Surface Charts

The *3D surface chart*, as shown in Figure 12.42, is used to help you find the best combination of two sets of data. Using the surface chart can make large sets of data easier to interpret.

NOTE *The colors on the 3D surface chart show different axis ranges rather than different series.*

Figure 12.42

A sample 3D
surface chart

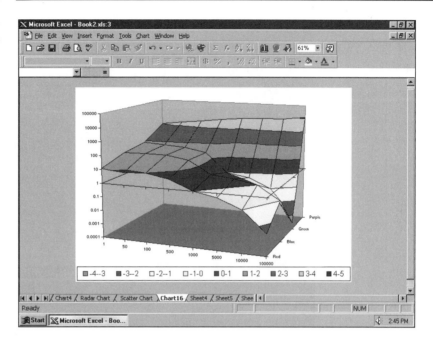

Bar of Pie and Pie of Pie Charts

Excel 97 includes two new variants of pie charts: Bar of Pie and Pie of Pie. Both let you explode a particular pie slice into its constituent parts. Figures 12.43 and 12.44 show, respectively, Pie of Pie and Bar of Pie charts.

Bubble Charts

Another new chart type in Excel 97 is the Bubble chart, as shown in Figure 12.45. This chart is like a scatter chart that shows the intersection of two values, but it adds a new element: the size of the bubbles. Bubble charts can make three-dimensional data easy to understand quickly. For example, in Figure 12.45 the bubbles indicate where the data points intersect, and the data labels indicating the size of the bubble show the strength of the interception point.

Figure 12.43

An example Pie of
Pie chart

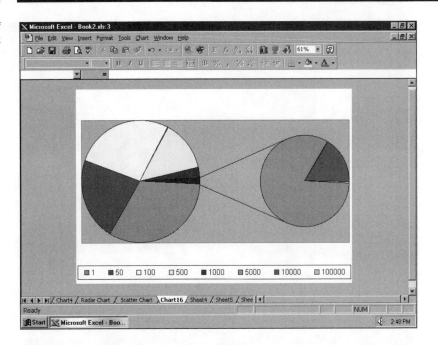

Figure 12.44

An example Bar of
Pie chart

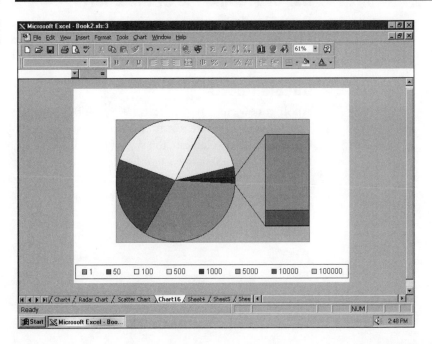

Figure 12.45

An example Bubble chart

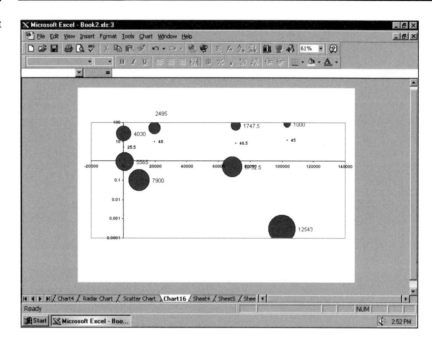

- *Enhancing Your Documents Using the Drawing Tools*

- *Importing Graphics Images*

13

Drawing and Adding Graphics to Documents

Not only can you use the graphics capabilities of Excel to annotate your worksheets and charts, you also can use its graphics tools to create more complex drawings, such as organizational charts, on-screen sketches, and flow charts. In this chapter, you will learn the following tasks:

- Drawing and controlling graphics on your Excel documents

- Linking an Excel macro to a graphics object

- Incorporating pictures from other programs into your work- sheets and charts

- Using a graphic image as your charting symbol

Not only do they provide you with the basic ability to annotate your charts and worksheets with graphics, but the drawing tools in Excel are actually as good as those in many dedicated drawing packages. Unless you have complex needs, you will find that most drawing tasks can be accomplished easily and quickly in Excel.

Now more than ever before, spreadsheet programs are being used not only for analyzing and automating the processing of numerical data, but also for presenting the results of these calculations. Some people might feel that graphics capabilities are more like toys than serious business tools, but you can make a strong case for their use.

In addition to preparing complete presentations with Excel, you can use its graphics capabilities to make your spreadsheets more clear to the people who need to read them. Pointing out a particular number with an arrow, placing borders around parts of the spreadsheet, or even illustrating a point graphically are all functions that have a very serious purpose—not merely to show results, but to truly communicate. Communicating complex information more effectively is, in one sense, the very purpose of spreadsheets.

Spreadsheet programs like Excel can be thought of as *decision support tools* rather than as software for simply crunching numbers. Because Excel plays a role in helping people make decisions, the ability to communicate your information is an integral part of the tool.

As you will discover in this chapter, Excel 97 for Windows has a wealth of features that you can put to work immediately to help convey your information more concisely, accurately and, most important, compellingly.

■ Enhancing Your Documents Using the Drawing Tools

This chapter makes extensive use of the Drawing toolbar. To see the Drawing toolbar on-screen, pull down the View menu and choose Toolbars, and then choose Drawing from the sub-menu. Alternatively, click on the Drawing tool icon on the Standard toolbar to display or hide the Drawing toolbar. Yet another way to access the Drawing toolbar is to right-click anywhere on the visible toolbars, then select Drawing from the pop-up menu.

The following sections show you ways to use the tools built into Excel to add drawings to your charts and worksheets.

NOTE *The drawing tools work the same way on both charts and worksheets. Although this chapter shows most of the drawing tools on a worksheet, they work in the same manner and equally well on a chart sheet.*

Although each drawing tool is somewhat different, they have many common characteristics. To use any of the drawing tools, simply click on the tool you want and then drag in the document to begin drawing with it.

TIP *Normally, when you click on a drawing tool and then draw something with it, the tool is immediately deselected when you have finished drawing the object. To make a tool "stick" on, so that you can draw several items of the same object type, double-click on the tool. It will then remain selected until you click on it again to deselect it, or until you click on another drawing tool.*

Drawing Tools Summary

Table 13.1 shows you each of the drawing tools and discusses features specific to each tool.

Table 13.1

Drawing Toolbar Icons

ICON	NAME	DESCRIPTION
	Draw	The Draw button displays a menu from which you can choose a number of commands that will affect a selected drawn object.
	Select Objects	Use the Select Objects button to "grab" drawing objects that are on your sheets, after which you can move or manipulate them in various ways.
	Free Rotate	The Free Rotate button, which you can select after you've selected a drawn object, lets you drag the corners of the object and rotate the object to any angle.
	AutoShapes	New to Excel 97, the AutoShapes button lets you choose from a wide variety of pre-drawn objects that you can quickly add to your sheets. Figure 13.1 shows a worksheet with several AutoShapes.
	Line	The Line tool draws straight lines. You can take a line drawn with the Line tool and make it into an arrow by bringing up the Format AutoShape dialog box (just right-click on the line) and then using the Arrows section of the Colors and Lines tab. Figure 13.2 shows a line that has been bent using the Edit Points command on its short-cut menu.

**Table 13.1
(Continued)**

Drawing Toolbar Icons

ICON	NAME	DESCRIPTION
	Arrow	Instead of using the line object to draw arrows, use the Arrow object. Lines drawn with the Arrow object will have an arrowhead at the end of the line you draw. Figure 13.2 shows an arrow line.
	Rectangle	Use the Rectangle tool to draw rectangles and boxes. You can see a drawn rectangle in Figure 13.2.
	Oval	The Oval tool draws ovals and circles. The Patterns page of an ellipse's formatting dialog box has a check box called Shadow, which gives the ellipse a drop shadow. See Figure 13.2 for an example of an oval created with this tool.
	Text Box	The Text Box tool allows you to draw rectangles that contain text.
	Insert WordArt	Excel can use the WordArt tool to insert nifty presentation-quality text into your sheets. Clicking on the Insert WordArt button brings up the WordArt Gallery dialog box, from which you can select a number of text styles.
	Fill Color	Use this button to fill an object with a chosen color.
	Line Color	Use this button to change the color of the lines that make up an object.
	Font Color	This button lets you quickly choose a color for selected text on your sheet, or for text in a Text Box.
	Line Style	After selecting a drawn line, click on this button to display a menu from which you can choose different line thicknesses.
	Dash Line	After choosing a line, use the Dash Line button to choose from a number of different dash schemes.
	Arrow Style	After selecting a line, this button lets you quickly choose a style for the arrowheads on the line.

Table 13.1
(Continued)

Drawing Toolbar Icons

ICON	NAME	DESCRIPTION
	Shadow	Use this tool to add a drop shadow to an object without opening the Formatting dialog box.
	3-D	This button displays a menu offering a number of three-dimensional viewpoints from which you can display your object. It automatically converts the drawn object to a 3D object — choose a circle and use this tool, and you will create a cylinder, for example. Figure 13.1 shows one of the AutoShapes modified by the 3D button: the "explosion" drawing in the upper-left corner.

TIP *After selecting an object, click on the Shadow button in the Drawing toolbar to turn its shadow on and off.*

Figure 13.1

Several AutoShapes

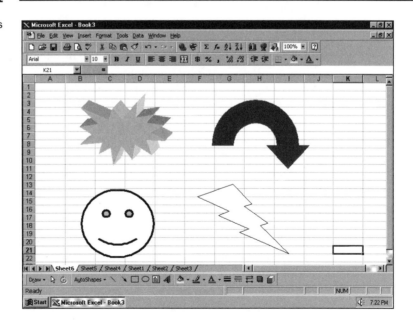

Figure 13.2

Basic drawing shapes

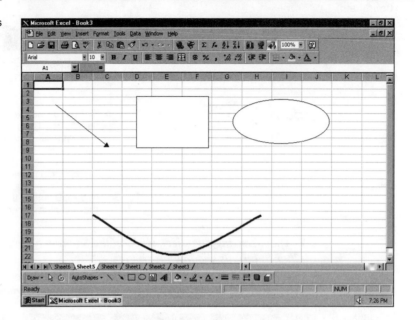

After you've drawn an object, such as a rectangle, an oval, or an Auto-Shape, you can use the Fill Color button to fill the object with the color you choose or the Line Color button to choose its line color. You can then choose the style of its lines with the Line Style tool, choose from a variety of dashed lines with the Dash Style tool, control the arrows on a line with the Arrow Style tool, add or remove a shadow with the Shadow tool, or give the object a 3D perspective with the 3D tool. Figure 13.3 shows a drawing created using a combination of lines and filled objects.

When you draw objects, the object will extend from where you first click to begin the drag operation to the current location of your mouse pointer. You can change this, though, by holding down the Ctrl key as you draw objects. Doing this forces the object to be drawn centered on the point at which you first started dragging. To position an object properly, you will sometimes need to do this instead of drawing from corner to corner.

Formatting Objects

Once you have drawn an object, you can format it by choosing the Format AutoShape command in its shortcut menu. This activates the dialog box shown in Figure 13.4.

Figure 13.3

The house that Excel built

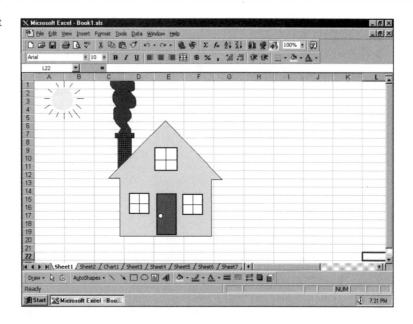

Figure 13.4

The Format AutoShape
dialog box

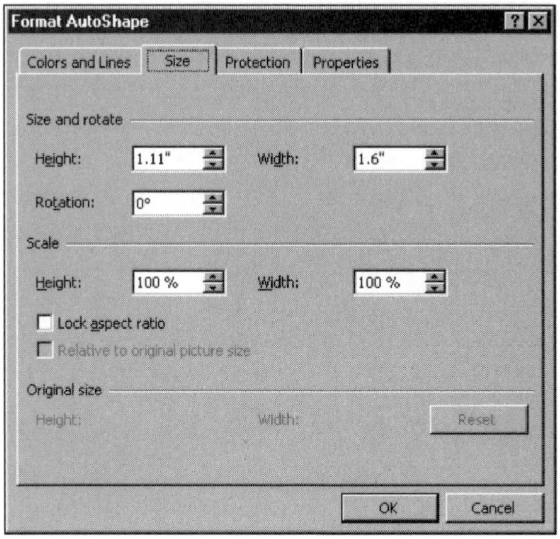

The Format AutoShape dialog box has four tabs:

- **Colors and Lines.** Use this tab to set the object's fill color, line styles, colors, and weight, and any arrow styles that may apply to the object. You can also choose the Semitransparent check box to make a filled color partially transparent.

- **Size.** When you need to control the size and rotation of drawn objects, use the Size tab. You can set the object's height and width, determine its angle of rotation, and choose the scale of height vs. width. Choose the Lock aspect ratio check box to force the object to always maintain the same proportions, even if it is resized.

- **Protection.** By default, the Locked check box is set on all objects. This has the effect of making the drawn objects unchangeable once the sheet is locked using the Protection commands in Excel's Tools menu.

- **Properties.** You can choose from these three properties to control how the selected object moves on the worksheet: Move and size with cells, Move but don't size with cells, and Don't move or size with cells. The first option is the default, and means that the object will "follow" changes in the cells upon which it sits. You can also choose the Print object check box, which controls whether or not the object prints when the worksheet on which it resides is printed.

Editing Points on Lines and Arrows

Lines and Arrows let you insert points at which these objects can then bend or curve. To do so, select the object, click the right mouse button, and then choose Edit Points from the shortcut menu. You can then perform a variety of actions on the line.

Drag a part of the line to bend the line in that direction. Doing this creates a point in the line at the position at which you dragged. You can then edit the point you've created.

Right-click on a point in the line (indicated by the small black handles) and choose one of the commands on the shortcut menu that let you control the point:

- **Auto Point** forces the point to follow the curve of the surrounding segments.

- **Smooth Point** calls up white point-control handles on the point at the end of a blue line intersecting the point. You can drag the white handles to reshape the point's curve. The two handles are always balanced between the point, and so only smooth curves are possible.

- **Straight Point** functions similarly to Smooth Point, but the white handles for controlling the point can be unbalanced, creating more complex point curves.

- **Corner Point** also calls up the white handles: drag one of them, and you will create a corner at the point rather than a bend.

Figure 13.5 shows a line being edited with the Straight Point command.

Figure 13.5

Editing a line's point with the Straight Point command

Point handles

Point control handles

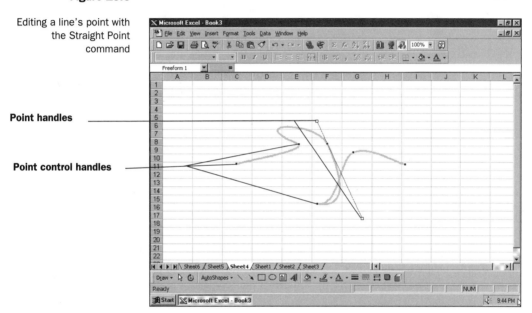

You can add and delete points with the appropriate commands on the point's shortcut menu. You can also choose Close Curve on the shortcut menu to cause a line to appear from one end of the line to the other, "closing" the line into a shape. Figure 13.6 shows the shortcut menu for the points on a line.

You can also control whether line segments (the portion of a line between the points) are straight or curved. Right-click on a section of the line, and then choose Straight Segment or Curved Segment from the shortcut menu to make that segment either straight or curved.

To stop editing the points and segments of a line, right-click on the line and choose Exit Edit Points from the shortcut menu.

Figure 13.6

The point shortcut menu

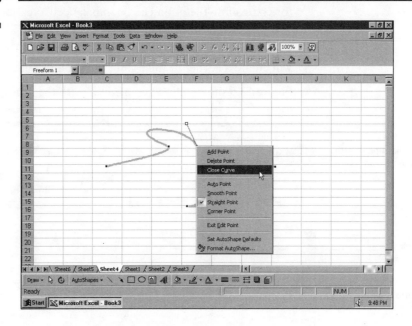

Understanding Constrained Drawing

Most of Excel's drawing tools support a feature called *constrained drawing*. This feature is activated when you hold down the Shift key as you draw the object. Constrained drawing is used to ensure that lines are at perfect 15-degree angles, that a rectangle is perfectly square, or that an oval is perfectly formed.

TIP *When you resize a drawing with the Shift key held down, Excel will ensure that the drawing retains its original proportions. Also, you can select multiple objects by holding down the Shift key when you click on each object. Then, after they all are selected, hold down the Shift key while you resize one object. All of the objects will be resized proportionately at the same time.*

Linking Actions to Objects

Any objects you draw can be linked to macros, allowing them to perform actions when they're clicked on. To edit an object with an attached macro, you must right-click or Ctrl+click on the object to select it, because a left-click will execute the macro.

NOTE *Macros are normally linked to button objects you create using the Button tool, although they can be attached to any graphic object on your worksheet or chart.*

To attach an existing macro to a graphics object, follow these steps:

1. Draw the object to which you want to attach the macro.

2. Click the right mouse button on the object to bring up the shortcut menu. From the shortcut menu, choose Assign Macro to access the Assign Macro dialog box shown in Figure 13.7.

Figure 13.7

The Assign Macro
dialog box

3. Choose the macro you want to assign by clicking on it in the list box. Click on the OK button to store your choice.

TIP *You can also edit or record a macro from the Assign Macro dialog box. Click on the Edit or Record button to do so.*

To detach a macro from a graphics object, bring up the Assign Macro dialog box, clear the field titled Macro Name/Reference, and click on the OK button.

Controlling a Graphic Object's Order

Sometimes you need to control whether a particular graphic object is in front of or behind another graphic object. For instance, if you have two intersecting shapes, you probably want one to be in front of the other where they intersect. At times, you will have several graphic objects that intersect, and you'll need to control the order in which they appear.

You can accomplish this with the Order sub-menu of the shortcut menu for each object. The Order menu contains four commands:

- Bring to Front. This command causes the selected object to be on top of any other objects it intersects with.

- Send to Back. This command takes the selected object and sends it behind all other intersecting objects.

- Bring Forward. This command brings the selected object one layer up from its present position. If an object is at the fourth layer down—with three other objects on top of it—choosing this command will bring it up to the third layer.

- Send Backward. The reverse of Bring Forward, Send Backward moves an object one layer down.

Figure 13.8 shows four intersecting rectangles, with the number in each one indicating its layer. The rectangles are filled with color so that you can see how these layers, or levels, work.

Figure 13.8

Four rectangles at
different levels

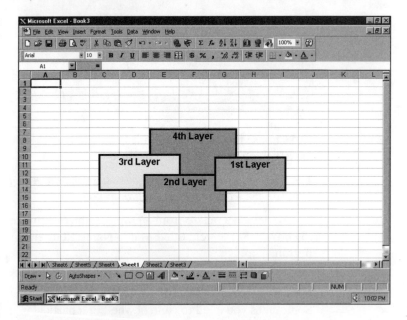

Grouping Objects

When you're building complex drawings, you will sometimes need to move or reformat a number of objects as a group. To do so, select all the objects together by Shift-Clicking each one before reformatting any one of them. Now any changes will be applied to all of the selected objects. However, if you need to do this often it may become cumbersome to constantly reselect all of the objects. Instead, you can group the objects so that they behave as a single object when you reformat them. It's almost like you're "merging" a number of distinct objects into one, except that you can break them apart into individual objects again if you wish.

The grouping can be broken into different levels if you wish. Returning to the example shown in Figure 13.8, you could group the 3rd and 4th Layer objects by Shift-Clicking each one so that they're both selected. Then, you could access a shortcut menu by right-clicking on either object. From this menu, choose Group from the Grouping submenu. The two objects will now move and format as one. Shift-Click the new 3rd/4th Layer object and the 2nd Layer object, and then choose Group again. When you select the new grouped object and choose Ungroup from the shortcut menu, the three-object grouping won't be completely dissolved into all of the individual objects. Instead, you can just reverse one level of grouping so that the 2nd Layer object is again separate from the 3rd/4th Layer grouped object. To completely ungroup the objects, you would have to choose Ungroup a second time.

To reverse an ungrouping, choose Regroup from the Grouping submenu of any of the previously grouped objects.

■ Importing Graphics Images

Excel can import and display many different types of graphics images, including images in the following formats (the common extensions for the different formats are shown in parenthesis):

- Windows Enhanced Metafile (EMF)
- Windows Metafile (WMF)
- JPEG File Interchange Format (JPG)
- Portable Network Graphics (PNG)
- Windows Bitmaps (BMP, DIB, RLE)
- Encapsulated PostScript (EPS)
- WordPerfect Graphics (WPG)
- Macintosh PICT (PCT)
- AutoCAD Format 2-D (DXF)
- Computer Graphics Metafile (CGM)
- Corel Draw (CDR)
- Micrografx Designer/Draw (DRW)
- Tagged Image File Format (TIF)

- PC Paintbrush (PCX)

- Kodak Photo CD (PCD)

- Graphics Interchange Format (GIF)

You can import graphics directly as long as they are stored in one of these formats. Pull down the Insert menu and choose Picture, and then choose From File. You will see the dialog box shown in Figure 13.9.

Figure 13.9

The Insert Picture
dialog box

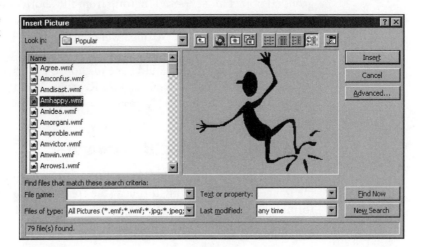

Use the Insert Picture dialog box to locate the file you want to open. By default, you'll be in Preview mode, allowing you to browse files that you select from the Name pane of the dialog box.

Inserting Graphics with the Paste Special Command

You can insert graphics created with virtually any Windows-based drawing program by using the program's Cut or Copy option. After the object is in the Windows Clipboard, use Paste Special in Excel to insert the object. When you do this, the Paste Special dialog box will appear, as shown in Figure 13.10.

You can choose between the two option buttons on the left of the dialog box: Paste and Paste Link. Paste simply pastes the image in the format you select, but Paste Link creates a DDE link back to the application that created the drawing (in this case, Microsoft Photo Editor). When you Paste Link a drawing, changing the drawing in the source application will automatically update the same drawing in your linked Excel document. Also, you can double-click on a drawing that has been pasted using Paste Link to automatically load

Figure 13.10

The Paste Special
dialog box

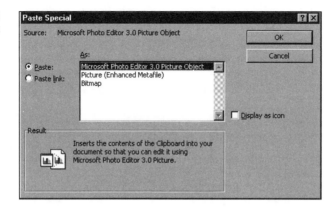

the source application with the drawing ready for editing. Similarly, you may also double-click on a Windows bitmap picture to activate the Paint program for editing, even though it was inserted using the Paste option only.

NOTE *DDE stands for* Dynamic Data Exchange, *one of the methods that Excel can use to communicate with other Windows programs. Excel also uses OLE, which stands for* Object Linking and Embedding. *For a complete discussion of DDE and OLE, see* Inside Windows 95, *also from New Riders Publishing.*

In the As list box, various options for pasting the data are listed. Click on each choice to see the comments about that type of graphics discussed in the Result box at the bottom of the dialog box. The type of image being pasted determines the choices you will see in the As list box.

If you select the Display as Icon check box, the graphic will not appear on the worksheet. Instead, an icon will appear that represents the image's source application. Use this feature to conserve space and reduce memory requirements in complex documents. Although the image does not appear, the worksheet user can click on its icon to easily open the image in its source application.

Changing Imported Images

You can resize and move imported pictures just like any other graphics objects in Excel. Because imported images are likely to be more complex than the other objects you work with, however, remember to hold down the Shift key as you resize the pictures to constrain the object to its original proportions. Failing to do so can ruin the quality of the image by stretching it to abnormal proportions.

Using an Image for Chart Patterns

Excel will also permit you to use an imported image as a chart pattern. Consider the chart shown in Figure 13.11. This chart could be improved and made more interesting to the audience by replacing the bars in the bar chart with an appropriate symbol. One possibility is shown in Figure 13.12.

Figure 13.11

A recycling chart

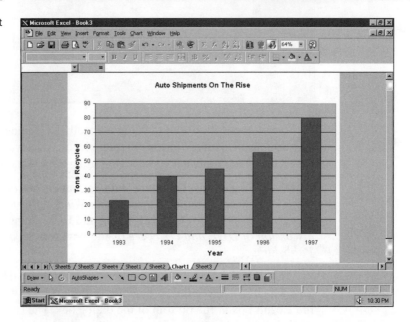

You can replace chart markers (for Line, Radar, and Scatter charts) or area fills (for Bar and Column charts) with graphic images using either of two methods. One option is copying the image to the Clipboard in the source application, switching to your chart, selecting the data series you want to change, and choosing Paste from the Edit menu.

You can also import the images directly. To do so, follow these steps:

1. Select the series you want to modify.

2. Pull down the Insert menu and choose Picture and then From File. You will see the Picture dialog box shown in Figure 13.13.

3. Use this dialog box to find the picture file you want to use. After you have found it, click on the Insert button to replace the chart symbol with this graphic image.

Figure 13.12

The recycling chart
using symbols

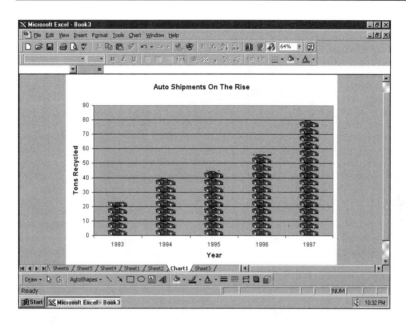

Figure 13.13

The Picture dialog box

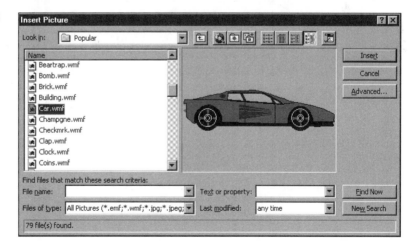

When you replace the symbol in a series with a graphic image, some additional settings will become available through the Fill Effects button on the Patterns tab of the Format Data Series dialog box (see Figure 13.14).

Figure 13.14

The Picture tab of the Fill
Effects dialog box for
chart symbols

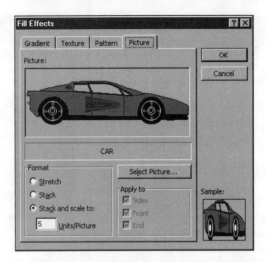

The Picture tab has these settings available:

- **Stretch.** Stretches the image to cover the entire area in the bar or column rectangle. Figure 13.15 shows the graph with this choice selected.

- **Stack.** Keeps the image size the same, but stacks as many images as are necessary to fill up the bar or column rectangle.

- **Stack and Scale.** Allows you to control the number of units of the Value axis that are represented by each chart image. When you select this option button, you can type a number in the Units/Picture field to control the number of axis units represented per picture. Figure 13.12 shows the chart with this option selected and five drawings per unit selected.

Figure 13.15

The Stretch option

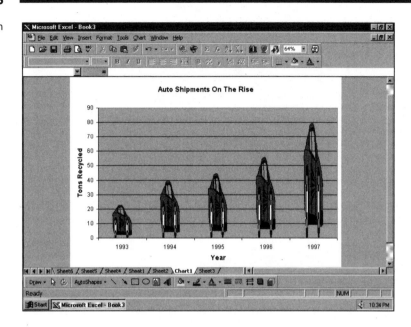

- *Understanding Series Formulas*
- *Changing the Series Using the Format Dialog Box*
- *Plotting or Adding Noncontiguous Ranges*
- *Using Advanced Charts*

14

Advanced Charts for Business and Science

Excel has many advanced charting capabilities that are applicable to projects undertaken by the more advanced business or technical user. In this chapter, you will learn to accomplish the following tasks:

- Editing the series formula for a chart

- Creating stock charts

- Plotting trend lines

- Creating charts that use logarithmic scales

- Plotting missing data

- Creating multi-axis charts with dual x or y axes

- Creating error bars for many Excel chart types

As you will see, Excel has the ability to generate just about any type of chart you could want. After you have mastered the basics of Excel charts from Chapter 12, use the information in this chapter as a reference for these advanced chart types and for complex editing tasks.

At times, you will probably need to generate charts that require something a little more complex than simply grabbing a chunk of your worksheet and hitting the ChartWizard button. Perhaps you want to control which parts of a series of numbers are plotted, or you want to use different category references for different data series. The next sections show you ways to accomplish these tasks.

■ Understanding Series Formulas

When you plot data from a worksheet to a chart, Excel uses a *series formula* in the chart to indicate each series. The series formula is what actually tells Excel how to find the data on which the chart series is based. Although you usually don't have to work directly with this series formula, understanding how to read it and how to change it can be an important step in advancing your charting skills.

The series formula indicates the workbook name, the name of the sheet in the workbook, and the cells that contain the data being charted. To display a series formula for a particular chart series, click on the series. The formula is shown in the formula bar. Figure 14.1 shows a series formula for the bottom chart series. From the formula bar, you can see that the data series is referencing Sheet1. Figure 14.2 shows the data on Sheet1 from which the example chart was plotted.

Figure 14.1

A series formula example

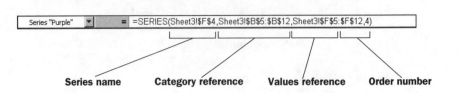

The series formula is divided into four major parameters, each separated by commas. The series-formula parameters are arranged in this order:

1. **Series Name.** This parameter references the name of the series, which you also can see in the legend of your chart. In this case, the reference points to cell F4, giving the series the name "Purple."

Figure 14.2

Data for the
example chart

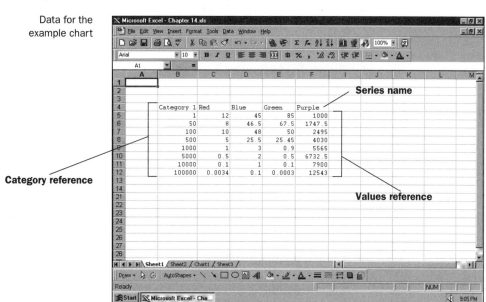

2. **Category Reference.** The second reference in the formula is to the range
   of cells that defines the categories for the plotted data. For this series formula, the reference is to cells B5 through B12—the categories against
   which the data was plotted.

3. **Values Reference.** The Values Reference is the actual data that is plotted—in this case, cells F5 to F12.

4. **Order Number.** The Order Number in the series formula defines where
   the series belongs in the order of the plotted data. The sample series formula is for the fourth data series on the chart.

   You can edit the series formula directly to change the data that the chart
is plotting, but there are easier methods available.

■ Changing the Series Using the Format Dialog Box

You can change the series formula easily via the Format dialog box.

1. Pull down the Chart menu and choose Source Data.

2. Move to the Series tab.

3. Select the series you want to edit by clicking on it in the Series list box. You will see the page shown in Figure 14.3.

Figure 14.3

The Series page of the Source Data dialog box

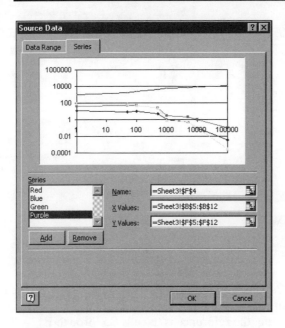

When you click on the Series tab and then choose one of the series listed, you will see definition information for the series in the Name, X Values, and Y Values fields. Once you've clicked in one of those fields, you can edit the information or reselect the appropriate cells.

■ Plotting or Adding Noncontiguous Ranges

You do not necessarily need to arrange your data so that it is contiguous before you create a chart. Excel allows you to plot noncontiguous ranges of data (data not adjacent on the worksheet) or to add data to an existing chart using a range that is not next to the original data. For instance, consider the example shown in Figure 14.4. If you wanted to plot the values for Category 2 and for Purple against the other values (Category 1, Red, Blue, and Green), you would need to follow a procedure such as this one. To try this procedure, follow these steps:

1. Select the first set of data to plot. If the data is not organized so that you can select the set, hold down the Ctrl key as you select each part of the set.

Figure 14.4

A selection of
noncontiguous ranges

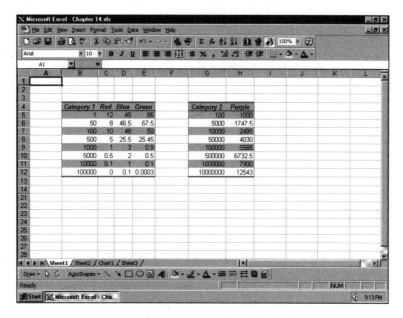

2. Plot the data from the first set.

3. Return to the worksheet and select the second set of data.

4. Use the Copy command on the Edit menu.

5. Switch to the chart and select the chart.

6. Use the Paste Special command in the Edit menu. You will see the dialog box shown in Figure 14.5.

Figure 14.5

The Paste Special
dialog box

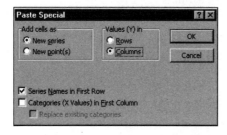

In the Paste Special dialog box, you can choose to add the new data as a New Series or as New Point(s) in existing series. You also can specify whether the values are organized in Rows or Columns. Finally, use the three check boxes at the bottom of the dialog box to define what part of the pasted data should contain the labels for the data. Click Series Names in First Row if the name of the series is in the first row of the range you selected, and Categories (X Values) in First Column if the left-most column of the selected range contains the category labels. Also, if you select Categories (X Values) in First Column, you can also choose the Replace Existing Categories if you want the categories in the pasted data to be used in favor of the existing categories in the chart.

When you click on OK in the Paste Special dialog box, your second set of data will be added to the chart. At this point, you might want to designate a different Value (Y) axis for the second set of data. See the section in this chapter titled "Creating a Dual Y-Axis Chart."

■ Using Advanced Charts

The remainder of this chapter will show you some of the more esoteric charts that Excel can produce, as well as some charting features that are not commonly used, but that can be of great benefit when you need them.

Creating Stock Charts

Excel users can make several special types of charts intended specifically for plotting stock-market data over time. You can choose from the following formats:

- High-Low-Close

- Open-High-Low-Close

- Volume-High-Low-Close

- Volume-Open-High-Low-Close

Each of these formats requires that your data be arranged accordingly. For instance, to plot a High-Low-Close chart, your left-most column should contain the dates being plotted, followed by columns for the high price of each day, the low price of each day, and the closing price of each day.

For this example, you'll see how a Volume-High-Low-Close chart is created. The source data appears in Figure 14.6.

NOTE *Many online services can download stock data in formats that Excel can import. Look for services that can download files in comma-separated-values (CSV) format, for example, or ones that provide fields for stock history that match the fields you want to chart, so that you can copy and paste the data to Excel. Also, don't overlook the Web queries that come with Excel in the Data, Get External Data sub-menu, which can also provide stock data.*

Figure 14.6

Stock market data

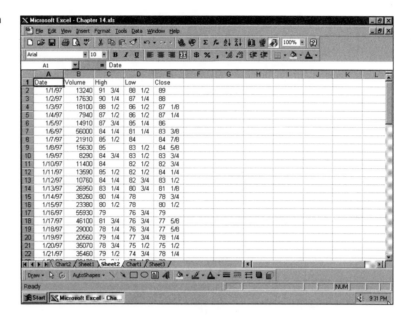

To create the chart, start with your active cell within the table and click the ChartWizard. Choose the Stock chart type and the appropriate sub-type (in this case, Volume-High-Low-Close), as shown in Figure 14.7. The resulting chart is shown in Figure 14.8.

Creating a Dual Y-Axis Chart

When you need to compare two sets of data that are based on different scales, you can do it with a dual Y-axis chart. Generally, this type of chart is used to look for correspondence between two sets of data. A dual Y-axis chart shows one set of data against values on the left axis of the chart, whereas the second set of data is shown against the right axis of the chart.

Examine the chart shown in Figure 14.9. The top line of the chart contains numbers that are dramatically higher than the rest of the series (in fact, if the Value axis wasn't already set to Logarithmic scale, you wouldn't even be able to see all the series). When this sort of spread happens, you lose the ability to discern some of the detail in both sets of data, because the chart must cover a much larger range.

In cases like this one, you might want to consider plotting the series that are different against another value category. To plot a second Y-axis, follow these steps:

1. Select the series that you want to plot against the second Y-axis.

Figure 14.7

The Volume-High-Low-Close chart type

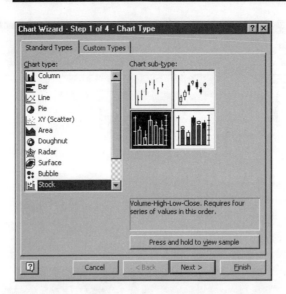

Figure 14.8

The Volume-High-Low-Close chart

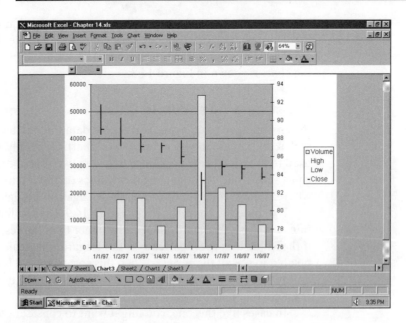

Figure 14.9

A line chart with a broad range of values

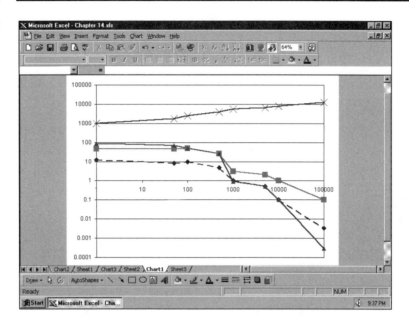

2. Pull up the formatting dialog box for that series by pressing Ctrl+1 or double-clicking on the series.

3. Click on the Axis tab. The Axis page is shown in Figure 14.10.

Figure 14.10

The Axis page

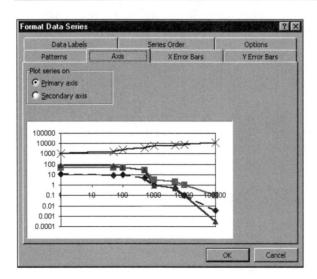

4. Click on the option marked Secondary Axis. The change can be previewed on the Axis page.

5. Click on OK to save your changes and return to the chart. The results are shown in Figure 14.11.

Figure 14.11

The dual Y-axis chart

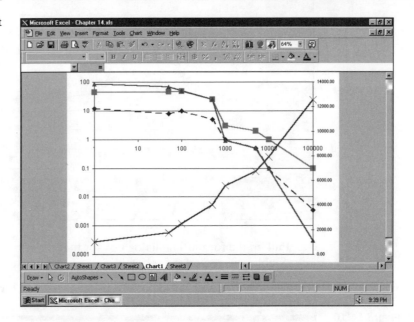

To demonstrate the power of this approach for certain graph-analysis problems, carefully examine Figure 14.9, looking for a correlation between the values plotted for the top series as compared to the three other series that contain much lower numbers. You really can't see much of a correlation, if any. Now examine Figure 14.11, and note that you can now see an inverse relationship between the three series plotted against the first Y axis and the series plotted against the second Y axis. Understanding the meaning of the relationship depends on the data being examined, but careful analysis of the charted data reveals that at least a relationship exists between the series, and can now be explored.

Working with Error Bars

Excel has a robust error-bar feature that can give you the ability to plot error bars easily.

Error bars are used to visually demonstrate the amount of uncertainty—or error—in plotted data. Excel permits you to calculate the amount of error in a number of ways, as follows:

- Fixed value that you enter
- Percentage that you enter
- Calculated Standard Deviation based on the mean of the plotted values
- Calculated Standard Error
- Calculated cell-by-cell error values from a worksheet

You can add error bars to area, bar, column, line, and scatter charts only. In addition, scatter charts can contain both Y-axis error bars and X-axis error bars.

WARNING *If you change the chart type of a chart containing error bars from one of the allowed chart types to a different chart type, the error bars will be deleted from the chart.*

To add error bars to a chart, follow these steps:

1. Create the chart using one of the allowed chart types.

2. Select the series for which you want to show error bars.

3. Access the Format Data Series dialog box for the series (press Ctrl+1 or choose it from the shortcut menu). Move to the Y Error Bars tab shown in Figure 14.12.

4. Set the parameters for the desired error bars, and click on OK to add the error bars.

Table 14.1 details the options on the Error Bars formatting page.

Figure 14.13 shows a chart with error bars calculated to plus or minus 15 percent.

Plotting with Missing Data

If you are using Excel as a technical graphing tool, you will often have to work with charts in which some of the data is missing. Excel provides three different methods for accounting for missing points of data:

- Don't plot them at all.
- Assume that the missing data are zeroes.
- Interpolate the missing data.

Figure 14.12

The Y Error Bars
formatting tab

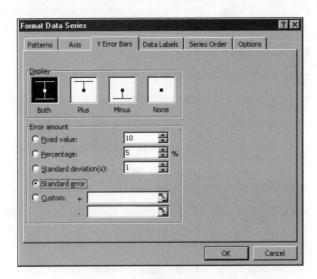

Table 14.1

Error Bars Settings

SETTING	DESCRIPTION
Display	In the Display section, you can choose whether you want error bars to be shown in both the positive and negative direction, in either direction alone, or not at all.
Fixed Value	Enter an amount here to force all the error bars to be shown based on the entered number. Fixed error amounts are often given with various types of testing equipment, for example.
Percentage	Enter a number in the Percentage field to show what percentage of each value to use as the error amount.
Standard Deviation	This choice calculates the standard deviation based on the plotted series, which is then multiplied by the value you enter in the field next to the Standard Deviation option.
Standard Error	Select Standard Error to calculate the standard error for the plotted values using a least squares method.
Custom	Use the Custom setting to define the error amount based on values stored in the worksheet. Click on either the + or - field, then select the range in the worksheet that contains the appropriate error values. You must select the same number of error values as the plot contains. You also can use an array formula in these fields, such as {12,15,3,4.5,12.1}.

Figure 14.13

Percentage-based
error bars

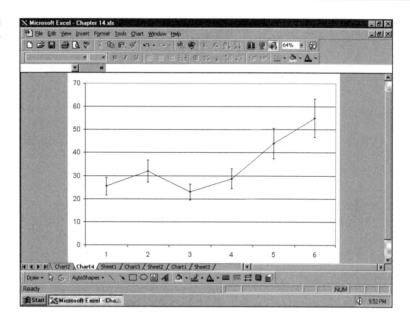

You can control the way Excel handles missing data through the Options
dialog box. Access the Options dialog box by selecting the Options command in the Tools menu, then click on the Chart page of the dialog box. The
Chart page is shown in Figure 14.14.

Table 14.2 discusses the three methods of plotting empty data points.

Creating Trend Lines

Trend lines can be used to smooth fluctuations in the plotted data, or to predict values forward or backward. You can base the trend lines on a number
of different statistical models.

NOTE *Trend lines are calculated using* regression analysis. *Regression analysis
uses the values provided to predict the relationship between the values. After
the relationship is known, it can be used to display the data in a "smoothed"
fashion, or to predict values that aren't given.*

*Note that the Moving Average trend line is not a regression-based trend line: it
is used only for data smoothing, and cannot be used for prediction.*

To create a trend line, select the series upon which you want to base the
trend line. Then right-click on the series and choose Add Trendline from the
shortcut menu. The Add Trendline dialog box is displayed in Figure 14.15.

Figure 14.14

The Chart page of the
Options dialog box

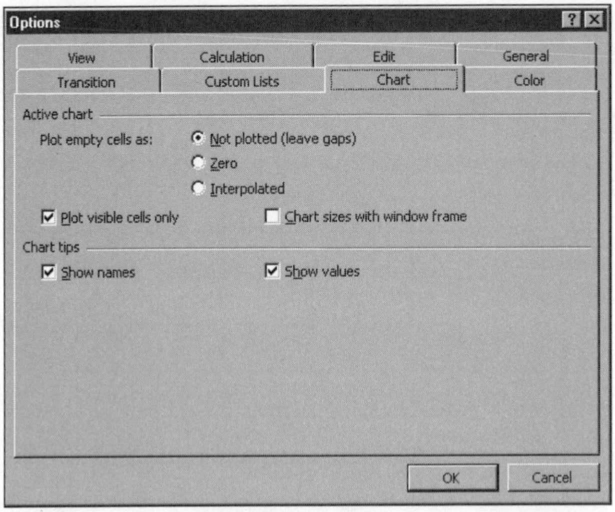

Table 14.2

Missing Data Settings

SETTING	DESCRIPTION
Not Plotted	Often the most appropriate choice for bar charts or column charts, Not Plotted simply leaves the data out of the chart. If this option is selected on line charts, two segments of the line will be missing in the chart—the line before the missing data point, and the line from the missing data point to the next data point. For that reason, avoid this setting when working with line charts, because it can make it hard to determine which lines should match up with which other lines: sometimes you can't easily connect them visually.
Zero	This choice assumes that the missing data are set to zero. This choice is rarely appropriate, because it can mislead the reader of the chart into thinking that data was collected, and that zero is the actual value.
Interpolated	For line charts and for scatter charts that use lines to connect the data points, Interpolated is often the most appropriate choice. Excel will continue the line through any missing data points. The point itself is not plotted for missing data, and there will be no data marker displayed for the missing data.

In the Type tab, choose the regression method that best suits your data. You might need to try different methods, depending on the data you are using. To find out how well the regression method fits your data, look at the R-Squared value, which is set on the Options page of the dialog box. The closer the R-Squared value is to 1, the more accurate the trend line will be.

Figure 14.15

The Add Trendline dialog
box's Type tab

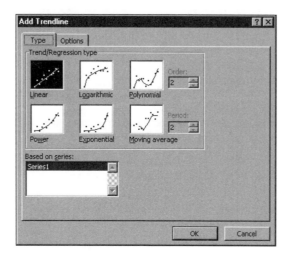

The Options page also includes a variety of other settings for controlling the trend line. Figure 14.16 shows the Options page. Table 14.3 details these settings.

Figure 14.16

The Options tab for the
Add Trendline dialog box

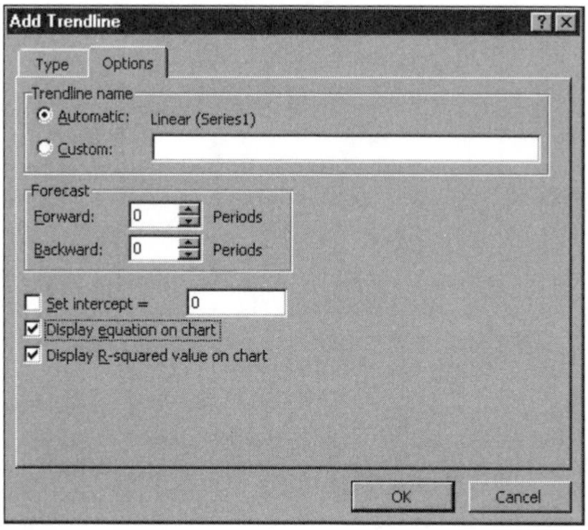

Table 14.3

Trend Line Options
Settings

SETTING	DESCRIPTION
Trend line Name	Use this area to define the name of the trend line, which is used for the legend on the chart.
Forecast	The Forecast section can contain the number of periods to forecast the data either Forward or Backward.
Set Intercept	Enter a value here to force the first location of the trend line against the Y-axis.
Display Equation on chart	Select this check box to place the formula used for the regression calculation on the chart, as shown in Figure 14.17.
Display R-Squared value on chart	Select this check box to display the R-Squared value on the chart. An R-Squared value close to 0 indicates that the regression is not matching the curve closely, while an R-Squared value close to 1 indicates increasing accuracy in the trend line. The R-Squared value is displayed in the chart in Figure 14.17.

Figure 14.17

A chart with the trend
line, showing the
Equation and R-Squared
values

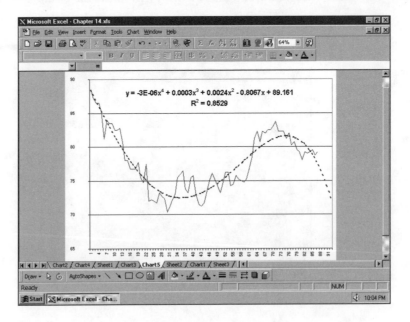

4

Programming Excel

- *Recording a Simple Macro*

- *Playing a Macro*

- *Using the Visual Basic Toolbar*

- *Changing Macro Properties*

- *Relative and Absolute Selection*

- *Classifications of Macros*

- *Understanding Macro Code*

- *Streamlining Macro Selection*

15

Understanding and Using Macros

Macro programming can save you a great deal of time and effort. After you have completed the examples in this chapter, you'll be able to record and execute macros that automate repetitive tasks.

In this chapter, you'll learn how to do the following simple operations:

- Recording a macro to repeat keystrokes, menus, and dialog-box operations

- Assigning a macro to a shortcut key

- Creating macros for use with every workbook

- Printing macros

- Editing existing macros

- Deleting macros

- Understanding Excel's macro languages

- Assigning macros to toolbar buttons

Macros make your work with Excel faster, more efficient, and even more fun! In fact, the more frequently you create and use macros, the more uses you will find for them. One day you'll wonder how you ever got along without them.

Despite Excel's impressive power, you may still find yourself performing some operations over and over. You might begin several worksheets with the same column and row headings, or apply the same series of formats to cells time and time again. Macros automate these repetitive tasks for you. A *macro* contains a series of keystrokes, menu selections, or formulas. After you have created a macro, you can repeat all the operations stored within it by pressing a shortcut key combination, or by selecting the macro from a list. You can even customize a toolbar to run a macro by clicking on a toolbar button.

NOTE. *You might not realize it, but you've been taking advantage of the power and flexibility of macros all along. You use a macro every time you press a key combination, such as Ctrl+B to turn on boldface, and each time you click on a toolbar button. Key combinations and toolbar buttons run macros that Microsoft has already written for you. These macros perform the most frequently used Excel and Windows functions. When you record or write your own macros, you're customizing Excel for the way you work.*

Macros also help you design consistently formatted worksheets. You probably want each part of a multipage worksheet to have the same overall appearance, for example. If you apply the formats manually, you might accidentally format one page of the worksheet differently from another. By recording the formats in a macro, you can apply the same formats to common elements on different pages or in different worksheets.

The Excel macros you record and play back are built behind the scenes, using a programming language called Visual Basic for Applications, also known as VBA. VBA is built into most Microsoft Office applications, such that once you learn to use VBA in one application, using VBA in other applications follows the same consistent rules and methods. While you don't need to learn to program in or read VBA programming code to use macros, you can easily access the macros should you wish (and, indeed, you learn how to get at them in this chapter and make minor changes).

Learning about using macros is the key to becoming proficient in Excel. However, you should understand that the VBA language built into Excel is much more powerful and can be used for much more than simply automating certain actions. It is a complete programming language with which you can build sophisticated applications using Excel—along with the rest of the Office suite if necessary—as the underlying application. Learning to write programs in VBA from scratch is beyond the scope of this book, but many good books dedicated to VBA programming exist to help you if you wish to learn more along these lines.

NOTE. *Excel macros are actually programs. The term* macros *generally refers to an ability to record certain actions in a software program and then play them back at will. Since that is what you mostly learn about in this chapter, the term macro is used. Understand, though, that the macros you record are actually complete programs for Excel and can be extended to do more if you learn how to program using Excel's programming language, Visual Basic for Applications.*

■ Recording a Simple Macro

The easiest way to create a macro is to record it. When you record a macro, Excel saves each of the keystrokes or mouse actions that you perform so that you can quickly repeat the steps another time. Macros are recorded "live," meaning that Excel performs the instructions you are recording. If you are recording a macro that prints a selected portion of a worksheet, for example, Excel will actually print that portion of the worksheet as you record the macro.

NOTE. *If you want to create a macro without performing the actions, you'll have to do so by typing all of the macro commands into the Visual Basic Development Editor window.*

Before you record a macro, make sure that Excel, Windows, and your worksheet are set up exactly as you want them to be. Otherwise, you might have to stop recording the macro, change your settings, then record the macro again. If you want to print a worksheet, for example, make sure your printer is set up properly in the Windows environment before you start recording the macro.

To record a macro, select Macro from the Tools menu, then choose Record New Macro. The dialog box shown in Figure 15.1 will appear.

Figure 15.1

The Record Macro
dialog box

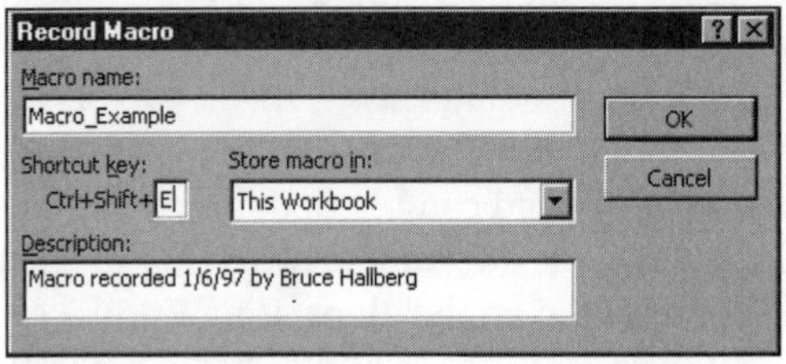

Macro Names

Enter the macro's name in the Macro Name text box. Excel will suggest the name Macro1 for the first macro you record, Macro2 for the second, and so on. You can accept these suggested names, or create names of your own. It's a good idea to enter a name that clearly illustrates the macro's function. Several months from now, you might forget the function that Macro1 performs, but you will know exactly what task is performed by the macro named Print_Worksheet.

NOTE. *Excel reserves some special macro names for automatically executing macros. If you record a macro named Auto_Open, for example, it will run as soon as you open the workbook that contains the macro. If you usually start Excel and change to full-screen display, name the macro Auto_Open, then record the menu command View, Full Screen. Other reserved macro names are Auto_Close, Auto_Activate, and Auto_Deactivate.*

Macro names must start with a letter, and cannot contain any spaces or punctuation marks other than the underline character. Use uppercase letters or the underline character to designate separate words, such as Print_Worksheet or OpenBudget.

WARNING. *Excel will display a warning message if you try to use a macro name that already exists. You can select Yes to replace the existing macro with a new macro or select No to enter another macro name.*

Completing the Record Macro Dialog Box

Type a brief description of the macro in the Description box. By default, the description will include the date you recorded the macro and the user name inserted when Excel was installed. If you don't care about maintaining that information, you can press the Del or Backspace key to delete the default entry. Otherwise, place the cursor at the end of the default description and add your own comments there. Later, if you can't remember the function of the macro by its name, you can use the description to help you determine which macro you want to run.

You can also assign a shortcut key to the macro. After you record the macro, you can press this key combination indicated to play the macro instantly. Enter a letter or other keyboard key (such as F1 or a symbol, if you wish) into the Shortcut key field. Excel will ensure that you don't use a key in this dialog-box field that conflicts with a predefined shortcut key. It does this by changing the state keys for the shortcut key you enter. For instance, when this field is blank, you can see that the shortcut key will be Ctrl plus whatever letter, number, or other key you type. If you enter in the letter B, the field will change to show Ctrl+Shift plus the letter B. Excel automatically adds Shift to this macro, because otherwise its shortcut key would conflict with Ctrl+B, which is already defined as the built-in macro for bold character formatting.

In the Store macro in field, you can choose where the recorded macro will be stored. You can store it in the default location, which is This Workbook, or you can choose New Workbook and Personal Macro Workbook. Choosing New Workbook causes a new workbook to be created during the recording process that will store the macro — this is an excellent choice when you're recording an AutoOpen macro that should execute when a new workbook is opened. You can also choose Personal Macro Workbook, which is an Excel workbook that you designate to hold all of your macros. You'll learn more about macro locations later in this chapter.

After you have completed the Record Macro dialog box fields, click on OK to begin recording the macro. Follow these steps to record a macro that prints a worksheet:

1. Make sure your printer is on.

2. Select Tools, Macros, Record New Macro to display the Record Macro dialog box. The Macro Name text box will automatically be selected.

3. Type **QuickPrint** as the macro name, replacing Excel's suggested name, Macro1.

4. Select the Description text box and type **Prints an entire worksheet**.

5. Enter the letter Q in the Shortcut key field (which will change to show Ctrl+Shift+Q).

6. Choose Store macro in This Workbook.

7. Click OK.

8. Select File, Print, then select OK.

9. Because your worksheet is empty, a warning box will now report that there is nothing to print. Select OK to close the warning box without affecting the macro.

10. To stop recording, click on the Stop button or select Tools, Macro, Stop Recording.

NOTE. *You cannot stop recording a macro while you are entering text in the formula bar — the options in the Macro submenu will be dimmed. Click on the Enter box to accept your entry or press Esc to cancel it, then select Stop Recording.*

TIP. *If you press an arrow key or press the Enter key to move to another cell, and then stop recording, the selection of that cell will be recorded in the macro. When you later run the macro, Excel will make the same selection. If you want to stop recording without moving to another cell, click on the Formula toolbar's Enter box to accept the text you just entered, then stop recording.*

Do not forget to either click on the Stop button or select Tools, Macro, Stop Recording to stop recording your actions. If you forget, Excel will continue to record all of your operations until you finally do one of these things.

■ Playing a Macro

To play a macro, select Tools, Macro, Macros to display the dialog box shown in Figure 15.2. Double-click on the name of the macro in the list, or choose the macro and click on Run.

When you select a macro in the list, its description will appear in the Description box. Make sure you have selected the proper macro before you run it.

Excel will beep and display a message box if it encounters an error in the macro. This beep should not occur if you recorded the macro properly. Do not confuse an error beep with the normal system beep that sometimes occurs when computing is complete.

Most of your macros will run so quickly that they will appear to perform their tasks almost instantaneously. However, should you need to stop a longer macro while it is running, just press Esc. A dialog box will appear, offering you the option to end the macro, continue running it, debug the macro to locate errors, or go to the cell where the macro stopped. Select End to stop the macro, or select Continue to continue from the last stopping point. Debugging macros is discussed in later chapters.

Figure 15.2

The Macro dialog box

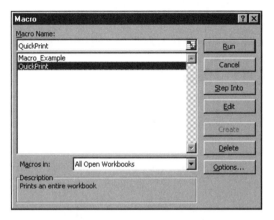

When you run a macro, Excel repeats the keystrokes, menu, and dialog-box actions you recorded. The pull-down menus and dialog boxes you used to record the macro do not appear, however—only the results of selecting them are repeated. Suppose, for example, that you use the Font dialog box to record a macro that formats a number of cells. When you run the macro, the fonts will be applied to the cells, but the Font dialog box will not appear on-screen.

■ Using the Visual Basic Toolbar

You can streamline your work with macros by displaying the Visual Basic toolbar, shown in Figure 15.3. To do so, select View, Toolbars, click on Visual Basic, and select OK.

Figure 15.3

The Visual Basic toolbar

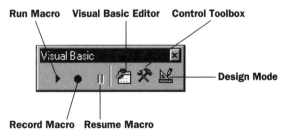

For fundamental work, you will only need the Run, Stop, and Record buttons. The other buttons are used for more advanced programming tasks.

NOTE. *The toolbar is called Visual Basic because macro instructions are recorded in the* Visual Basic for Applications (VBA) *language.*

Macro Locations

You can store a macro in any of three locations. By default, your macros will be stored with the current workbook. You can use these macros whenever you open that workbook.

Since Excel 5.0, global macros are no longer being stored in the global macro sheet. If you have macros from Version 4.0, however, you can still use them.

If you want to use the macro with every workbook, store it in the Personal Macro Workbook, a file called PERSONAL.XLS in the EXCEL\XL-START directory. Each time you start Excel, this workbook will open automatically, making its macros available for use.

NOTE. *If you have just installed Excel, don't bother looking for the PERSONAL.XLS file. This file does not exist until you create a macro and ask to save it to the Personal Macro Workbook.*

You can also record the macro in a new workbook. If you select this option, Excel will open another workbook just to record the macro. If you store your macro in a workbook other than the Personal Macro Workbook, you must open the workbook to access the macro—Excel will not open it automatically.

You might want to create individual workbooks for categories of macros. If you have several macros you use just to create budget worksheets, for example, you can store them together in one workbook. When you need to create a budget, just open the workbook to access the macros.

NOTE. *It might seem more convenient to store all of your macros in the Personal Macro Workbook so that you can use them without opening a workbook first. The use of other workbooks to divide your macros into logical groups makes sense for several reasons, however. A workbook crammed with rarely used macros takes up needed system memory and other resources. In addition, you will quickly run out of unique key assignments, and then you'll have to spend time scrolling through a list of macro names to locate the one you want to run.*

Use the Personal Macro Workbook for macros that you use on a regular basis. Use other workbooks for macros you use only periodically.

Running Macros from Workbooks

You can run a macro in any worksheet of the workbook. You might, for example, use the Title macro created later in this chapter to add headings to any worksheet in the same workbook. Keep in mind, however, that any text, numbers, or formulas entered by the macro will replace contents already in the cells.

To use a macro in another workbook, you must open the workbook first. Macros in any open workbook are available for use. You can run macros from the Personal Macro Workbook in any workbook.

WARNING. *Before you run a macro, make sure that the worksheet you want to run the macro against is active. Do not run a macro that sets up standard headings, for example, when the active worksheet already has headings.*

If the macro you want to run is not listed in the dialog box or does not run when you press its shortcut key, the workbook in which it is located is not open. Use the File, Open command to open the correct workbook.

Macro Language

Excel gives you two language options for recording your macros. By default, macros are saved in the Visual Basic for Applications language. Microsoft uses this powerful programming language in many of its application programs and as a standalone development tool.

■ Changing Macro Properties

Excel makes it easy to change the name, shortcut key, or menu assignment of an existing macro:

11. Select Tools, Macro, Macros.

12. Click on the name of the macro you want to modify, then click the Edit button to display the selected macro in the Visual Basic Development Environment (VBDE), as shown in Figure 15.4.

13. In the window that contains the macro code and definition (in this example, you see **Sub QuickPrint()**), change the name of the macro. Then pull down the File menu in the VBDE, and choose Close and Return to Microsoft Excel.

■ Relative and Absolute Selection

When you want to record a macro that includes cell selection, you can do so in two ways. By default, Excel records cell selections on an *absolute* basis. If

Figure 15.4

The Visual Basic
Development Environment

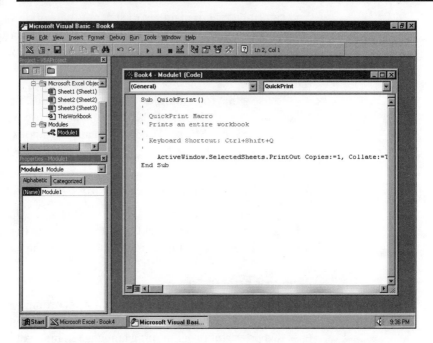

you select a cell when recording the macro, the same cell will be selected when you execute the macro later on. Suppose you begin recording a macro when you are in cell A1, for example. You click on cell B2 to select it, then continue recording your macro instructions. When you later run the macro, cell B2 will be selected, no matter where in the worksheet you are when you run the macro. If you are in cell C5, cell B2 will still be selected when you run the macro.

Alternatively, you can choose to select cells using a relative reference. When you select a cell *relatively*, the macro selects a cell in relation to the currently active cell. If you start in cell A1 and select cell B2 using a relative reference, Excel will select the cell one column over and one row down from whichever cell is currently active when you later run the macro. If you run the macro when cell C5 is active, for example, cell D6 will be selected. You can select the preferred method with the Relative Reference button in the Stop Recording toolbar, which appears while a macro is being recorded. Click the button—it will stay selected—to ensure that references are recorded as being relative, then click the button again to record cell references absolutely.

In the following steps, you will record a macro that enters standard row and column headings using a relative reference. You should be in Excel with a blank worksheet. Record the macro in your Personal Macro Workbook.

1. Start with cell A1 as your active cell.

2. Select Tools, Macros, Record New Macro. Enter the name **Relative_Example**, and choose to store the macro in the Personal Macro Workbook. Enter the letter **r** as the shortcut key before clicking the OK button to start recording.

3. On the Stop Recording toolbar that appears next, click on the Relative Reference button to select it.

4. Select cell B1.

5. Type **1st Qtr**. Do *not* press Enter.

6. Drag the fill handle in the lower right corner of cell B1 to cell E1.

7. Select cell A2 and type **Sales**.

8. Select cell A3 and type **Rentals**.

9. Select cell A4, type **Total**, and press Enter.

10. Click on the Stop button, or select Tools, Macros, Stop Recording to stop recording your actions.

The cell selections were recorded using a relative reference. When you later run this macro, Excel will insert the text **1st Qtr** in the cell to the right of the active cell, and use AutoFill to complete the series in the next three cells. The row headings will appear in the three rows below the starting cell position.

NOTE. *To change back to absolute cell selection for further macro recording, deselect the Relative Reference button on the Stop Recording toolbar.*

Displaying the Personal Macro Workbook

Unlike workbooks, modules, and other windows, Excel does not normally display the Personal Macro Workbook on the screen—it is hidden. However, to edit or delete macros in the Personal Macro Workbook, the workbook must be unhidden. To open the Personal Macro Workbook, select Window, Unhide to display a dialog box listing the names of hidden windows. Click on PERSONAL.XLS, then select OK. Excel will display the personal workbook that contains your macros.

Printing Macros

Although the macro instructions might not mean much to you, they can serve as an excellent source of reference, particularly when you record a large number of operations.

As your macros become longer and more sophisticated, you should print a hard copy of the macro list as a reference. You can study the hard copy, writing notes where you'd like to make changes.

To print a copy of your macros, access the Tools, Macro, Macros command. Then choose the macro you want to print and click the Edit button. The VBDE displays with the macro you selected. Use the File, Print command in the VBDE, choose Current Module in the Range area of the Print dialog box, and click OK. This will print a copy of all macros in the current workbook.

Hiding and Saving the Personal Macro Workbook

If you close the Personal Macro Worksheet when it is unhidden, its macros will not be available, and you will have to open it again. Rather than closing it, hide it again. This removes the workbook from the Window menu, but keeps its macros accessible. To hide the worksheet, make it active and select Window, Hide. If you don't hide the Personal Macro Worksheet, it will appear on-screen the next time you start Excel.

NOTE. *Remember to display and select the Personal Macro Workbook before you select Window, Hide. If you don't, the active worksheet window is hidden.*

Deleting a Macro

You can delete a macro if you change your mind after recording it, or if you just want to remove unused macros from a workbook.

To delete a macro, select Tools, Macro, Macros, click on the macro name in the list box, then select Delete.

To delete all your personal macros, delete the file PERSONAL.XLS from your hard drive. Excel will create a new one the next time you save a macro using that option.

■ Classifications of Macros

Excel's macro language is a powerful tool for automating worksheets. Recorded macros, however, only touch on the possibilities for power and versatility that macros bring to your spreadsheets. When you record a macro, you are creating a command macro, which is just one of two types of macros you can create. The other type of macro is called a function macro.

Command Macros

A *command macro* performs some action on the worksheet. It repeats keystrokes or selections from menus or dialog boxes. Command macros save you from repeating the same series of operations.

Macros that you record are always command macros. You can also write a command macro without actually performing the instructions. By writing macros, you can repeat a series of steps, make decisions based on the contents of cells, and even create interactive macros that accept input from the keyboard.

Function Macros

A *function macro* creates a user-defined function. These macros operate the same way as Excel's built-in functions do when they perform a calculation and return a value. They do not perform any action on the worksheet, except to insert a value into a cell.

Some complex calculations that you perform might require formulas in several cells. Each formula is actually another step in the overall calculation. If you add the formulas directly in the worksheet, they could occupy a considerable amount of space. By adding all of the formulas into a function macro instead, you can perform the calculation using a single worksheet cell.

NOTE. *You cannot record an entire user-defined function macro. You have to write the entire macro, or perform extensive editing on a recorded macro.*

■ Understanding Macro Code

Unless you decide to record macros in the Excel 4 format, your macros will be constructed using the Visual Basic for Applications (VBA) language.

A *keyword* is a word that represents a macro language command or instruction. Every macro begins with the keyword Sub followed by the macro name and ends with the keyword End Sub. The macro instructions are called *statements*. Each statement tells Excel to perform a specific action. VBA instructions are combinations of objects, methods, properties, and variables.

NOTE. *Technically, the Sub and End Sub commands indicate a subroutine. This is one of the basic VBA concepts discussed here.*

The VBA statement to select cell D9, for example, looks like this:

```
Range("D9").Select
```

Range is a VBA object that represents a cell or a range of cells. The range object, however, requires an argument that further identifies the object being referred to, specifying the cell or range of cells. In this case, the object is cell D9.

The VBA statement also must specify the *method* of dealing with or using the object. The keyword *Select* is the method. It tells Excel what action to perform on the object—in this case, to select the cell. In the statement *Range("D9:G9").Select*, the object to be selected is the range of cells D9 through G9.

The statement for entering contents into a cell looks like this:

```
ActiveCell.FormulaR1C1 = "Profit"
```

The object is the currently active cell. In this case, however, you are not performing a method on the cell, but defining its properties. A *property* explains the conditions or state of the object. In this statement, the property is *FormulaR1C1*, and it indicates that the following text will be contained in the object.

In some cases, the object has a number of properties. For example, the command to format a cell in a particular font is as follows:

```
Selection.Font.Name = "Arial"
```

Selection is an object that refers to the currently selected object in the worksheet. *Font* also is an object to be applied to the selections. But the Font object needs a property (*Name*) to explain how it should be applied. In this case, the selected cells are assigned the font named Arial.

NOTE. *Recorded macros are not simply a record of your keystrokes. Instead, they are translations of your keystrokes into the VBA commands that the commands you executed represent. For instance, the VBA command to change a font has no reference to the Format Cell selection that's needed to display the Font dialog box.*

A definite pattern exists for performing Excel tasks. Usually, a cell (or range of cells) is selected, then one or more properties are assigned to the selection. Suppose, for example, you record the instructions that use AutoFill to complete a series of entries. Here is a typical process:

```
Range("D9").Select
ActiveCell.FormulaR1C1 = "1st Qtr"
Selection.AutoFillDestination:=Range("D9:G9"),Type:=xlFillDefault
```

These VBA statements select a cell, enter the starting value ("**1st Qtr**") and then assign properties to the cell that complete the series.

When you select items from a dialog box, any number of properties can be included in the VBA statement. For instance, when you use the Font dialog box, you can select a font name, size, and various other character attributes. Rather than repeating the object names for every property, Excel places them in a **With** structure, as follows:

```
With Selection.Font
    .Name = "Arial"
    .FontStyle = "Regular"
    .Size = 10
    .Strikethrough = False
    .Superscript = False
    .Subscript = False
    .OutlineFont = False
    .Shadow = False
    .Underline = xlNone
    .ColorIndex = xlAutomatic
End With
```

The statement **With Selection.Font** indicates that all of the following properties refer to the same object. **Name**, **FontStyle**, **Size**, and so on are properties of the **Selection.Font** object.

You can use a similar technique to format the position of text within a cell. In the following example, the five properties are applied to the **Selection** object:

```
With Selection
    .HorizontalAlignment = xlCenter
    .VerticalAlignment = xlBottom
    .WrapText = False
    .Orientation = xlHorizontal
    .AddIndent = False
End With
```

■ Streamlining Macro Selection

If you use a macro often, you can add it to a toolbar or to a graphics object. This procedure makes the macro visible on-screen, so that you don't have to remember its shortcut key or select it from a list.

Adding a Macro to a Toolbar

Pressing the shortcut-key combination is a quick way to run a macro. Still, it's easy to forget which keys you have assigned to the macros you've created. Also, as you build a large library of macros, you may run out of unique keys to assign.

Rather than trying to remember the shortcut keys or scrolling through the Run Macro dialog box to locate a macro every time you need to run one, you can assign your favorite macros to a toolbar. You can then run the macro of your choice by clicking on the toolbar button. You can even create your own toolbars to contain your macros.

Follow these steps to create a new toolbar, which will contain a single button that runs the Relative_reference macro you recorded earlier:

1. Choose the Tools, Customize command. You will see the Customize dialog box shown in Figure 15.5.

Figure 15.5

Use the Customize dialog box to create and edit toolbars.

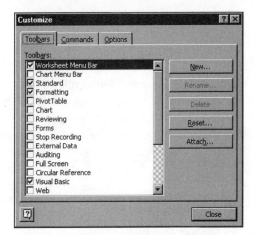

2. On the Toolbars tab, click the New button to create a new toolbar. You will see the New Toolbar dialog box, which will prompt you for the name of the new toolbar. Use the name **My Macros,** and click the OK button. An empty toolbar will appear on the screen.

3. Move to the Commands tab of the Customize dialog box, and choose Macros in the Categories list box. Your screen should look like Figure 15.6.

4. Drag the Custom Button icon in the Commands list box to your new toolbar. The icon will now appear on the toolbar, and the Modify Selection button on the Commands tab will become available.

5. Click the Modify Selection button (see Figure 15.7) to set the options for the toolbar button. Minimally, you should set the following options:

   • **Name.** Choose the Name field to assign the toolbar button a name. For this example, you can use **Relative**.

   • **Change Button Image**. You can choose from a number of predefined button images with the Change Button Image command, which displays a submenu of available choices.

Figure 15.6

The Commands tab in the
Customize dialog box

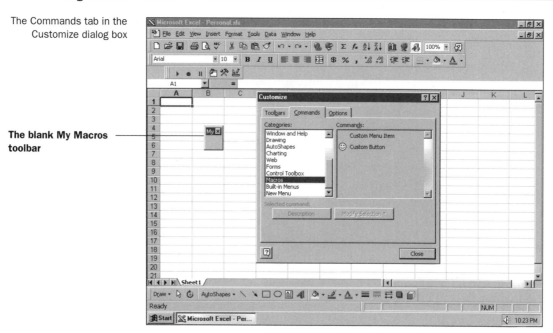

**The blank My Macros
toolbar**

Figure 15.7

The Modify Selection
button options

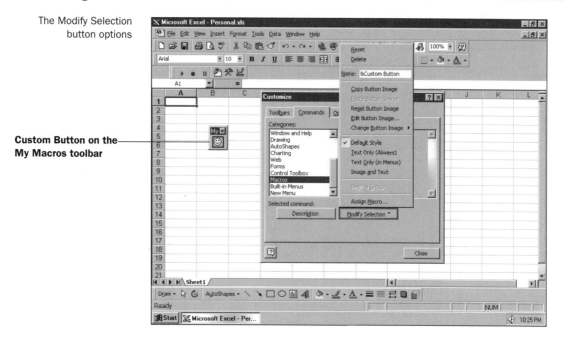

**Custom Button on the
My Macros toolbar**

- **Assign Macro**. Choosing this command brings up the Assign Macro dialog box shown in Figure 15.7. Choose the macro that you want the toolbar button to execute, and click OK.

After setting these options, click the Close button in the Customize dialog box to save your selections and finish creating the toolbar.

Using this procedure, you can create multiple toolbars, each containing a number of your personal macros.

5

Excel and the Internet

- *What Are the Internet and the World Wide Web?*

- *Browsing Internet Pages with Excel*

16

Browsing Web Pages with Excel

IN THIS CHAPTER YOU WILL LEARN HOW EASY IT IS TO GET ON THE Internet with Excel 97. You will learn about the Internet, and about how to access World Wide Web pages via Excel. Excel's Internet features make it simple to browse Web pages, as well as to open workbooks on the Web.

■ What Are the Internet and the World Wide Web?

The Internet is a worldwide network that is itself made up of thousands of computer networks. Millions of commercial, educational, governmental, and personal computers are part of the Internet. Computers that are connected to the Internet can share information with other linked computers.

The technology for the Internet came out of research funded by the US Department of Defense. The Advanced Research Projects Agency (ARPA) conducted pioneering studies on long-distance network technology for the military. Its research culminated in the creation of a network, ARPANET, which consisted of individual packet-switching computers interconnected by leased lines. ARPANET was the predecessor of today's Internet. It served as a test bed for early networking research, and was central to the development of today's Internet.

Network technology permits computer users connected to the Internet through corporations, nonprofit organizations, government agencies, educational institutions, and dial-in Internet service providers to communicate with each other. Users can exchange messages, transfer files, and remotely log on to other systems. The Internet is mainly composed of local and wide-area networks that use the same network protocols to communicate and share information between computers. The primary protocol used on the Internet is TCP/IP (Transmission Control Protocol/Internet Protocol).

One of the tools included within the TCP/IP protocols is a protocol for sharing files. It is known as FTP (File Transfer Protocol). It allows you to find files on the Internet and transfer them to your system, as well as to transfer files from your system to the Internet. In order to post a file on the Internet, you must have access to storage space on the Internet. You can use FTP to post an Excel spreadsheet, chart, or data-gathering form to another computer over the Internet.

The World Wide Web (WWW) is a system of hypertext-based documents that are linked across the Internet. Most hypertext documents are created using HyperText Markup Language (HTML). This language allows creators to tag different parts of a document so that browsing software will know how to display the document's links to other files, text, graphics, and attached media. Users can access linked documents by just clicking on a highlighted word or graphic. Document links on the World Wide Web are non-linear and unrestricted, and can be represented on-screen by the address of the site, or by words or graphics that represent that address. This seemingly endless web of hypertext links ("hyperlinks") makes it easy to explore information on the Internet. HTML documents can also be posted on Intranets: networks within a single institution that, like the Internet, support Internet protocols like

HyperText Transfer Protocol (HTTP, the protocol used to present hypertext information online) and FTP.

Because Excel can save files in HTML format, you can easily post Excel files on your company's Intranet or on the publicly accessible Internet.

Other Internet Terms

A URL is a "Uniform Resource Locator." Just as the post office uses your address to deliver your mail, the World Wide Web uses URLs as a standardized address system to identify the location of documents and other Internet sites. For example, the URL for Microsoft Corporation on the World Wide Web is:

```
http://www.microsoft.com.
```

This address begins with an abbreviation for the type of site it identifies ("http" for World Wide Web sites, "ftp" for FTP sites, and so on), and then identifies the exact computer on the Internet that holds the information in question. In the example above, that computer has been named "www.microsoft.com." This segment of a URL typically includes a three-character extension that indicates the type of organization that owns the computer. Sample extensions include:

com   commercial business

gov   government agency

edu   educational institution

org   non-profit organization

After the name of the computer, the path to a document is delineated with a series of slashes. For example, the imaginary URL "http://www.example.com/~possibilities/bingo.html" would take you to the Web page called "bingo" on the "www.example.com" Web server.

■ Browsing Internet Pages with Excel

Depending on how you prefer to access Web pages, you can either activate Excel's built-in Active Web capabilities and view pages from within Excel, or you can launch your favorite Web browser and load a specific Web page.

When you type a Web page's URL into Excel's Open dialog box, Excel will use its internal Active Web browser to load the page. However, Active Web will not display many graphic elements of Web pages correctly, and the Web pages will generally not appear as they were designed. Typically, you will want to use the Open dialog box to access a Web page only when the Web page contains a table of data that you want to work with in Excel.

Oddly enough, when you do browse a Web page using Excel's Active Web browser and then click on one of the page links, your destination will be loaded into whatever Web browser you have identified as your default instead of Excel's Active Web browser. When you use the Address box in Excel's Web toolbar, your Web browser is also used to display the page.

NOTE *In order to access most of Excel's Internet and Web features, the computer on which Excel is installed must have a modem and must have Internet access through Windows 95. It should also have a Windows 95-compliant browser installed, such as Microsoft Internet Explorer or Netscape Navigator 3.0.*

You must also have an account with an Internet service provider (ISP). The ISP may be a small, local company, or a large, all-inclusive service like America Online or CompuServe. In addition to giving you the ability to surf the Net, an ISP gives you access to e-mail and other tools.

Using the Web Toolbar

One of the new toolbars included in Excel 97 is the Web toolbar (see Figure 16.1). It contains icons and commands that make it easy to access and browse the Internet.

To display the Web toolbar:

- On the Standard toolbar, click the Web Toolbar button.

  or

- Pull down the View menu, point to Toolbars, and then choose Web. Table 16.1 discusses the various buttons on the Web toolbar.

TIP *The Back button can be very helpful when browsing the Internet. Since clicking a hyperlink moves you to another Web page, it is easy to jump to a different location. If this location doesn't have a hyperlink to return you to the previous location, the Back button can be used to do so.*

Setting a New Start Page

When you use the Start Page command in the Web toolbar's Go menu, your browser software will display the same location on the Internet or on your company's Intranet. This location is known as your "Start Page." From this location, you can set out to explore the World Wide Web. Exploring hyperlinks may sometimes take you to unfamiliar territory. Clicking the Start Page button once returns you to your normal starting location.

Figure 16.1

The Web toolbar

Web toolbar

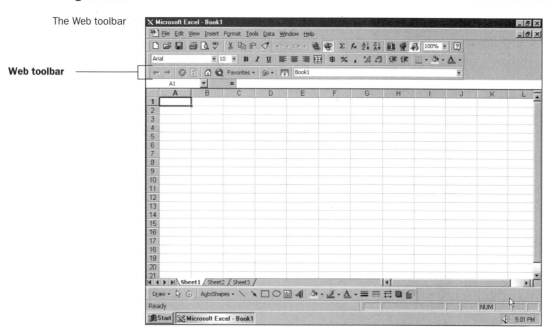

Table 16.1

Web Toolbar Icons and
Commands

NAME	DESCRIPTION
Back	Opens the previous file or item in the list of the last 10 files or items you jumped to.
Forward	Opens the next file or item in the list of the last 10 files or items you jumped to.
Stop Current Jump	Halts the jump to a new location that is in progress.
Refresh Current Page	Reloads the currently selected page.
Start Page	Jumps to the Start Page set in your Web browser. Use the **Set Start Page** command on the **Go** menu of the **Web** toolbar to specify a new Start Page.
Search the Web	Opens a Web-search screen, so that you can search for words or phrases.

IN THE FAVORITES MENU:	
Add to Favorites	Found in the Favorites button menu, allows you to add URLs to the Favorites folder in the **Look in** box.
Open Favorites	Opens a favorite location selected from the Favorites folder in the **Look in** box.
IN THE GO MENU:	
Open	Opens a location/hyperlink that you have selected.
Back	Same as the "Back" icon on the Web toolbar.
Forward	Same as the "Forward" icon on the Web toolbar.
Start Page	Same as the "Start Page" icon on the Web toolbar.
Search the Web	Same as the "Search the Web" icon on the Web toolbar.
Set Start Page	Lets you specify a new Start Page.
Set Search Page	Lets you specify a new Search Page.
Show Only Web Toolbar	Hides all currently visible toolbars except the Web toolbar. Click it again to view the hidden toolbars.
Address	Enters the Web address (URL) you want to go to, or selects an address from the drop-down list of previously visited Web sites.

If you want to change the Start Page location in your Web browser to an Excel file, it's easy. To change the Start Page in your browser software, follow these steps:

1. Navigate to the Web page that you want to have serve as your new Start Page.

2. On the Web toolbar, select the Go menu button.

3. From the **Go** menu, choose the Set Start Page command.

4. A dialog box appears (see Figure 16.2) that asks if you wish to use the current page as your new Start Page.

5. Click the Yes button.

Setting a New Search Page

The Search the Web command in the Go menu on Excel's Web toolbar takes you to a search page located on Microsoft's Web site, from which you can

Figure 16.2

Excel's Set Start Page
dialog box

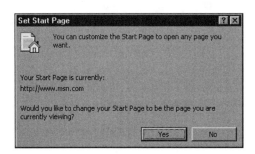

access the most popular search engines on the Internet. A *search engine* is a
program that lets you enter keywords or questions to search an index of Web
pages and other Internet sites. Using search engines, you can find information that interests you or that addresses a topic you're researching. There are
quite a few search engines available, each with somewhat different search capabilities and features. Figure 16.3 shows the default search page that the
Search the Web command takes you to.

Figure 16.3

Excel's default Search
the Web page

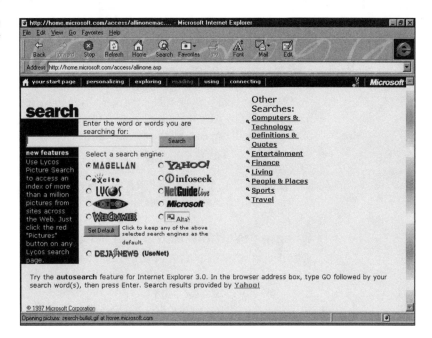

To change the default search page to the Yahoo! search engine or another favorite Web-searching site, use Excel's File Open command. Type in the address of the search page you want to use in the Filename text box. For instance, you might type in **http://www.yahoo.com**. Then click on the Go menu on the Web toolbar in Excel, and choose Set Search Page. You will see the Set Search Page dialog box shown in Figure 16.4. Click Yes to save your selection.

Figure 16.4

Excel's Set Search Page dialog box

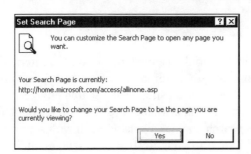

After you have made this change, clicking Search the Web in the Web toolbar will open your Web browser to the search page you selected.

Adding a Favorites Entry

You can add favorite Web pages to the Web toolbar's Favorites menu. Enter the URL to which you want to link into the File Open dialog box's Filename text box, and then click the Open button. The page will load into Excel's Active Web internal browser. Next, access the Favorites button in the Web toolbar, and choose Add to Favorites from the menu. The Add to Favorites dialog box will appear, as shown in Figure 16.5, with the URL you selected in the File Name text box. Click on the Add button to save this URL to your Favorites list.

Once you have added a URL to your Favorites list, you can use the Favorites menu to quickly access that site from within Excel.

Opening Workbooks on the Web

With Excel 97, you can open workbooks over the Web. You may want to do this through your company's Intranet. Workbooks may be posted on your Intranet network by your company's IS department, or end users (including you) may have permission to post workbooks to the Intranet on their own. You can then open those workbooks from any Intranet-linked workstation, as long as you know the correct address, with the Open command in the File menu. In the File Name field, you can type the URL for a workbook, such as

Figure 16.5

The Add to Favorites
dialog box

HTTP://www.mycompany.com/index_of_policies.xls. The workbook will then open in Excel normally after being transmitted to your computer.

You can communicate the addresses of Intranet-based workbooks to others by creating Web pages that have hyperlinks to these Excel documents, by making them available on known FTP sites, or by sending out addresses to the intended users via e-mail.

You should work closely with your company's IS department to make sure that anything you are making available on your Intranet follows corporate policies and procedures. Your IS pros can instruct you on how to set up FTP sites for transferring Excel workbooks, templates, and data files among employees, for example, and can also help you troubleshoot any Internet-related problems that may crop up.

Excel workbooks can also be placed on the public Internet and opened by Internet users with the same commands and procedures. The applications for doing so are few as of now, but this capability may prove valuable in the future. Currently it is used primarily to make data available to employees working at remote sites, such as mobile salespeople and home-based workers, or to communicate research results in a spreadsheet format to a selected online audience.

Querying Web Pages

The ability to query Web pages directly is a powerful addition to Excel 97. You can access this feature by choosing Data, Get External Data, Run Web Query. When you do so, you see the dialog box shown in Figure 16.6, which displays the built-in Web queries that come with Excel.

Figure 16.6

The Run Query dialog box shows Web queries included with Excel 97.

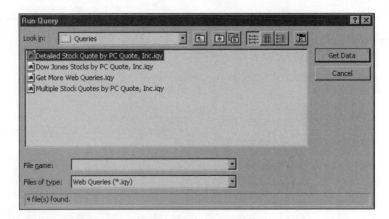

NOTE *Excel Web queries are actually stored on the Web, not on your computer. If you open the Web-query files directly, you will only see HTTP addresses, along with any parameter data the query stored on the Web needs. It is possible to create your own Excel Web queries; for examples, see the collection available through the Get More Web Queries query discussed below.*

Among these built-in Web queries are three that let you get stock-quote information in various ways. Somewhat more interesting is the query Get More Web Queries, as shown in Figure 16.6. When you execute this query, you will see a Web page that lists a number of other queries you can perform. These queries will be updated over time, so the ones you see in Figure 16.7 aren't necessarily the ones you'll see when you perform this query—you will most likely see additional queries.

For instance, using the results of the Get More Web Queries query and then clicking on one of the queries, such as DBC Best Credit Cards, will take you to that page. In this case, you will see a page that compares credit-card interest rates and terms offered by different banking institutions, as shown in Figure 16.8.

Figure 16.7

When you run Get More
Web Queries, a Web-
based worksheet will
open in Excel that
contains a number of
other queries that you
can run.

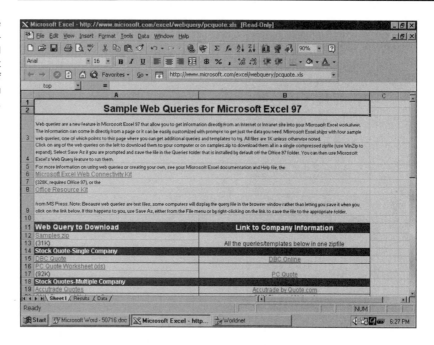

Figure 16.8

Clicking on the DBC Best
Credit Cards link takes
you to the list of current
credit-card deals. See
this link yourself to
receive current data on
credit cards, as the
information returned by
this query changes
rapidly.

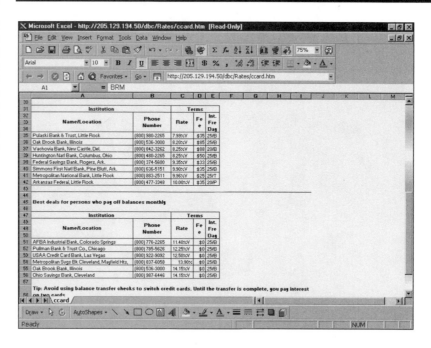

- *Creating Hyperlinks*
- *Creating Web Pages*

17

Creating Hyperlinks and Web Pages with Excel 97

Excel CONTAINS SOME IMPORTANT FEATURES THAT LET YOU create Web pages, or even just simulate how the Web works using existing Office files on your computer or on a company network. In this chapter, you will learn how to accomplish both of these tasks.

Excel 97 can create *hyperlinks*, links in worksheets that, when clicked, instantly activate a destination document. This destination document could be an Excel workbook, a Word document, a Web page on the Internet, or even a blank message form that lets you pen a note for delivery to an e-mail address.

Excel 97 can also save both data and charts as pages formatted with HTML (HyperText Markup Language) for use on the Internet or an Intranet. This tool is designed to make it easy to publish your Excel information on the Web.

■ Creating Hyperlinks

New in Excel 97 is the ability to create hyperlinks in your Excel worksheets. Once created, the user of the workbook has only to click once on the hyperlink to instantly activate the destination of the hyperlink. Hyperlinks can point to many different destinations, such as:

- Other Excel workbooks, or even sheets and locations within a workbook

- Internet-based Web pages

- FTP sites

- Any file on the system or in a network folder

- E-mail recipients

Hyperlinks can appear in worksheets as text references, or they can be attached to drawn objects. Figure 17.1 shows a worksheet with a couple of different hyperlinks embedded.

Hyperlinks are extremely useful when you are using Excel to publish data for viewing or use by others. By providing hyperlinks to additional workbooks, Web pages, e-mail addresses, and so on, you make it easy for the person browsing the information to quickly jump between different resources associated with the information you're publishing.

Understanding Hyperlink References

Hyperlinks can contain two main types of references: Uniform Resource Locators (URLs) and Universal Naming Conventions (UNCs). URLs are used to identify Internet resources, such as Web pages, FTP sites, and e-mail addresses. UNCs are used to identify files on Intranets or other defined networks, or on local disk drives.

As discussed in the previous chapter, URL addresses follow the form: *url_type://url_address*

Examples of valid URLs are:

```
http://www.microsoft.com
ftp://ftp.mcp.com
mailto://bruce_hallberg@msn.com
```

Figure 17.1

An Excel worksheet with
embedded hyperlinks

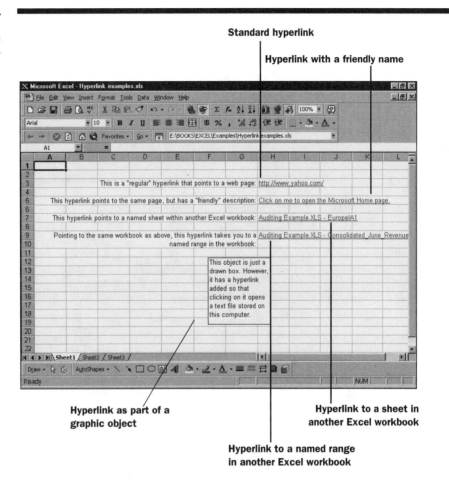

Standard hyperlink

Hyperlink with a friendly name

Hyperlink as part of a graphic object

Hyperlink to a sheet in another Excel workbook

Hyperlink to a named range in another Excel workbook

Respectively, these URLs refer to a Web site, an FTP site, and an e-mail address.

UNCs are used to identify files stored on a local hard disk or on a network to which you directly connect, such as one using Novell NetWare or based on a Windows NT server. DOS or Windows pathnames and filenames, such as **C:\CONFIG.SYS** or **D:\My Documents\Workbook Example.XLS**, can be valid URLs.

UNCs also refer to network files. These UNCs describe a network path that must be followed to access the file. For instance, if you wanted to use a UNC to refer to a file called "My Workbook.XLS" located on the "Public" area on the server named "Curley," the correct UNC would be **\\Curley\Public\My Workbook.XLS**.

Fortunately, you rarely have to type UNCs or URLs, as you can generally simply select them automatically by browsing for the file to which you want a hyperlink to point.

Inserting Hyperlinks

With all of their flexibility, hyperlinks are remarkably easy to create. The easiest way to create a hyperlink is to select the cell in which you want the hyperlink to be located, and then access the Hyperlink command in Excel's Insert menu. This brings up the dialog box shown in Figure 17.2.

Figure 17.2

Using Excel's Insert Hyperlink dialog box

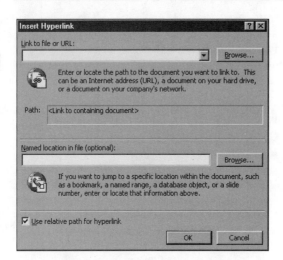

In the Link to File or URL text box, you can type the URL or UNC to which you want the hyperlink to point. You can also click on the Browse button, which activates the Link to File dialog box. You can then locate the file you want to link to, as shown in Figure 17.3.

When you link to an Office file that has a named range or sheet (such as an Excel workbook) or bookmark (such as a Word file), you can also reference that named range, sheet, or bookmark to further refine the location where the person clicking the hyperlink will be taken. To do so, first select the appropriate file in the Link to File or URL text box, and then either type the sheet name, named range, or bookmark name into the Named Location in File text box, or click on the Browse button to the right of the text box. When you click on the Browse button, you see a further dialog box depending on what type of file you're linking to. In Figure 17.4, you can see the dialog box

Figure 17.3

Click on Browse in the Insert Hyperlink dialog box to locate a file using the Link to File dialog box.

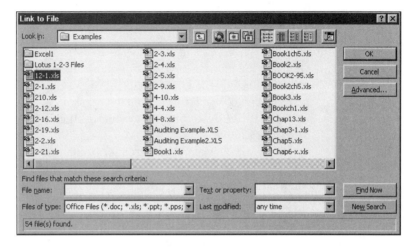

that appears when you're selecting a sheet name or named range in an Excel workbook. Click the appropriate option button, and then choose the sheet name or named range in the window shown. Also, if you're linking to a sheet name, you can specify the cell reference to which the hyperlink refers.

Figure 17.4

You can link to sheet names or named ranges in Excel files, or to bookmarks in Word files (not shown).

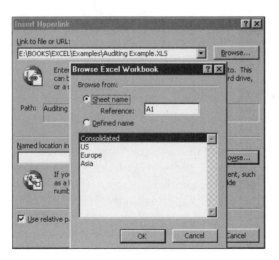

Creating Friendly Hyperlinks

Creating a hyperlink with the Insert Hyperlink dialog box is quick and easy. However, the inserted hyperlink only appears as the text of the URL or UNC you're using. Sometimes, however, you will want a hyperlink to include more descriptive text. You can accomplish this with the HYPERLINK function in Excel.

The HYPERLINK function takes two arguments, each surrounded by quote marks. The first is the URL or UNC to which you are linking. The second is the "friendly name" you want to appear instead of the UNC or URL. Omitting the optional second argument causes the HYPERLINK function to simply display the URL or UNC. An example HYPERLINK function that you could type into a cell on a worksheet is:

=HYPERLINK("http://www.microsoft.com","Click here to go to Microsoft's home page.")

In the above example, the reader of the workbook will only see "Click here to go to Microsoft's home page." When they click on the hyperlink, they will be transported to the URL given in the first argument.

Adding Hyperlinks to Graphics

Just as you can cause graphic objects drawn in Excel workbooks to run Excel VBA macros, you can also cause them to activate hyperlinks. To do so, start with a graphic object you've drawn using Excel's drawing tools. Then, select the object. While it's still selected, access the Insert Hyperlink command. You can then specify the hyperlink in the Insert Hyperlink dialog box. The graphic object doesn't look any different once you've done this. However, when you move your mouse pointer over the object, the pointing hand will be displayed instead of the movement cursor, and if you let the mouse rest for a moment, a ScreenTip will appear that shows you the destination of the hyperlink. In Figure 17.1, the box drawn on the screen has had some text added to it to tell the viewer what will happen when the object is clicked on.

Using Absolute vs. Relative Hyperlinks

By default, the hyperlinks created by the Insert Hyperlinks dialog box use *relative addresses* for the hyperlinked files you link to. In this context, a relative address is one that uses the locational relationship of the file being referred to as regards the workbook that contains the hyperlink.

Consider this example: Imagine you have a folder on your C drive called DOCUMENTS—its address would be C:\DOCUMENTS. In this folder there is a sub-folder called DATA C:\DOCUMENTS\DATA. In C:\DOCUMENTS you have a workbook called BUDGET_OVERVIEW.XLS. In it, you create a hyperlink to a file called OPERATIONS.XLS, which can be located by following the path C:\DOCUMENTS\DATA. When you use a relative reference to the OPERATIONS.XLS file, the hyperlink would simply specify "DATA\OPERATIONS.XLS," or the relative pathname to the file.

The advantage to using a relative reference such as this one is that you can move the hyperlinked documents to different folders. So long as OPER-ATIONS.XLS is contained in a sub-folder called DATA, it doesn't matter where the BUDGET_OVERVIEW.XLS file is stored. You could, for instance, move BUDGET_OVERVIEW.XLS to a folder on the network called \\Accounting\Budgets\. So long as there is also a network folder called \\Accounting\Budgets\Data that contains OPERATIONS.XLS, your hyperlink will continue to function just as you expect it to.

You can also create hyperlinks that use *absolute references* to the hyperlinked documents. As you would expect, this means that no matter where the document is located that contains the hyperlink, it will always refer the person clicking on the hyperlink to the same file, in the same location.

So, when would you want to use relative references instead of absolute references, or vice versa? It depends on how you intend to use the workbook that contains the hyperlink. If you will always store the related documents as a coherent whole, use relative references so that you can move their location without having to re-create the hyperlinks. A good application for an absolute reference would be when you want to distribute a workbook to multiple people, each of whom will store his or her copy in a different location, but you want them all to have a hyperlink that refers to a single, centrally located file.

To use relative or absolute references for hyperlinks, simply select or clear the Use relative path for hyperlink check box in the Insert Hyperlink dialog box. You can see this check box in Figure 17.2.

Modifying Hyperlinks

You will sometimes have to modify the location to which a hyperlink points. You can simply create a new hyperlink in place of the old one, but you can also edit existing hyperlinks if you observe a simple trick.

When you click on a cell containing a hyperlink, you activate the hyperlink. This means that if you want to select a cell containing a hyperlink in order to edit it, you cannot do so by clicking it with your mouse without also activating the hyperlink. Instead, click on an adjacent cell to select it, and then use an arrow key to move to the cell that contains the hyperlink. You can then press F2 to edit the data, and you can edit the hyperlink just as you would the contents of any other cell, pressing Enter when done to save your change.

You can also right-click on a hyperlink, and then choose Hyperlink from the shortcut menu, and Edit Hyperlink from the cascading menu. This activates the Edit Hyperlink dialog box, which functions just like the Insert Hyperlink dialog box. The shortcut-menu approach does not work for hyperlinks created using the HYPERLINK function; instead, use the previous method to edit such hyperlinks.

Changing Hyperlink Appearance

By default, hyperlinks in Excel documents will appear in a 10-point Ariel font, and with blue coloring (for unfollowed links) or reddish-purple coloring (for followed links). You can change these selections, but only if you want to change all hyperlinks at once.

To change the appearance of hyperlinks, access the Style command from the Format menu. In the Style dialog box, you can choose two Style Names: Hyperlink and Unfollowed Hyperlink. For each of these styles, you can choose new display formats using the Style dialog box. Your changes will instantly affect all of the hyperlinks in the current workbook.

Copying and Deleting Hyperlinks

When you right-click on a hyperlink to activate its shortcut menu, you can also copy the hyperlink to another location, or delete it.

To copy a hyperlink, right-click on it, choose Hyperlink from the shortcut menu, and then choose Copy Hyperlink from the cascading menu. Move to your destination cell and use the Paste command to insert the hyperlink copy.

To delete a hyperlink, right-click on it, choose Hyperlink from the shortcut menu, and then choose Delete Hyperlink from the cascading menu.

■ Creating Web Pages

Consider a situation in which you need to regularly publish data that you generate for others in your company, or to others over the Internet. Your data and charts are in Excel. You could cut and paste the data from Excel into a Web-page authoring tool, such as Microsoft FrontPage. However, unless you need to format your data with features (such as frames) that Excel doesn't yet support, it is much easier to create such pages directly in Excel using the Save as HTML command in Excel's File menu.

When you use the Save as HTML command in the File menu, you will see the Internet Assistant Wizard for Excel shown in Figure 17.5. This wizard will walk you through several steps that lead to publishing your Excel data to a Web page. Before starting the wizard, it is best to select the initial data range to be included in the HTML document. If you simply leave the cell pointer on a worksheet cell, Excel will assume that this cell is the initial data range, and it will include it in the list of items to be included in the HTML document.

Figure 17.5

The Internet Assistant
Wizard is invoked when
you use the Save as
HTML command from
Excel's File menu.

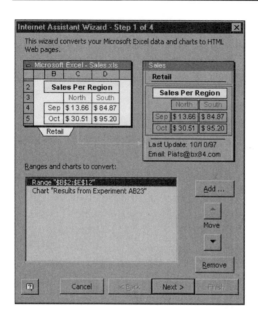

In the first step of the Internet Assistant Wizard's procedure, you will select the data and charts that you will put on your new Web page. The data
and charts you create will be placed on a single Web page, organized in the
order shown in the dialog box. For instance, as you will see in the final result,
the example shown in Figure 17.5 will create a Web page that contains the
range shown, and under it the chart shown. At first, all of the charts in your
workbook will be shown in the Ranges and Charts to convert window. Click
on each chart shown, and remove any charts that you don't want to include
with the Remove button, or use the up- and down-arrow buttons to reorga-
nize the list. After you have your charts arranged, you can click the Add button to choose other ranges of cells to also include in the result page.

NOTE. *You cannot add charts to the list—if you remove a chart by accident,
you should cancel the Internet Assistant Wizard and reselect the Save as
HTML command to restart it.*

Once you have selected all of the worksheet ranges and charts to be included, and have used the up- and down-arrow buttons to arrange the data,
click on the Next button to continue. You will see Step 2 of the Internet Assistant Wizard, shown in Figure 17.6.

Figure 17.6

In Step 2 of the Internet Assistant Wizard, you will choose how the data you selected will be formatted.

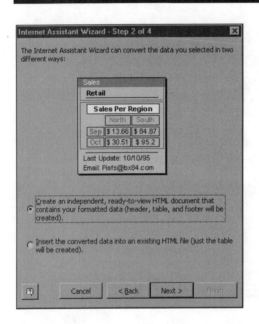

There are two ways to format files created with the Internet Assistant Wizard:

- You can create an HTML file that can be independently viewed by a Web Browser over the Internet.

- You can create a table of data in a file that you can subsequently cut and paste into an existing Web page.

For this example, you will create an independently viewable page, so confirm that this option is selected and click Next to continue.

You will now see Step 3 of the Internet Assistant Wizard (see Figure 17.7), in which you can add titles, headers, and such to your Web page. Fill in the fields you wish to add, remembering to check the two horizontal-line options if you want them to be included. Click Next to continue.

The fourth and final step of the Internet Assistant Wizard process lets you control where the created page is to be placed (see Figure 17.8). Generally, you will store it on your local machine before placing it on the Internet—choose Save results as an HTML file, and ensure that the path and filename shown are correct. If you use Microsoft FrontPage, you can also add the page to your FrontPage Web-document collection. Click Finish to create the page and return to Excel.

Figure 17.7

Step 3 of the Internet Assistant Wizard lets you add title and header information to your Web page.

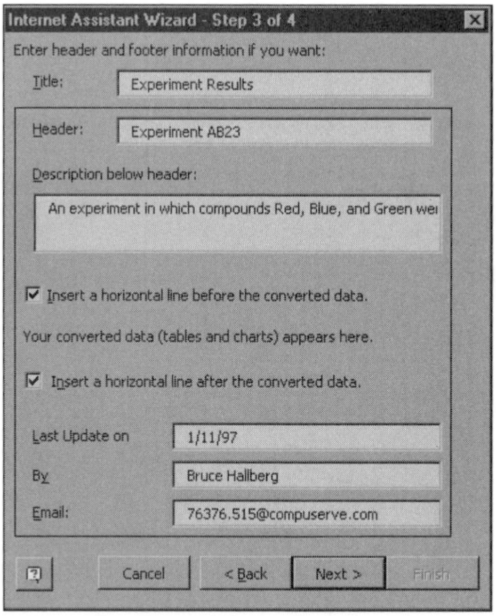

Figure 17.8

Step 4 of the Internet Assistant Wizard lets you control where your Web page is to be stored.

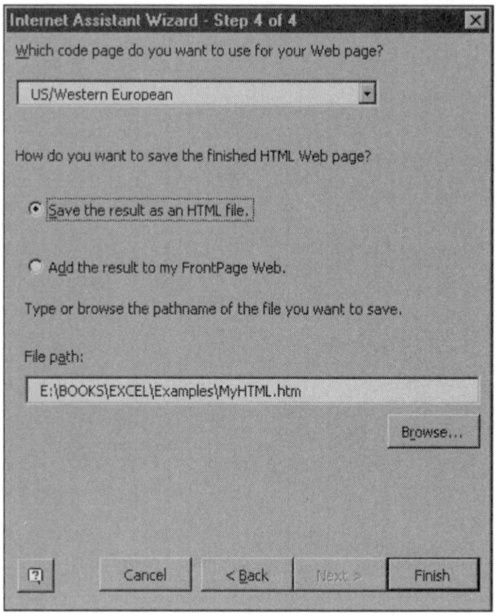

After you've created the HTML file, you can use your Web browser to preview it. Open your browser and use its Open command in its File menu to open the file directly. Figure 17.9 shows the file created in this example, as opened in Microsoft Internet Explorer.

Figure 17.9

The final result of the Internet Assistant Wizard. (Only the very top of the chart is shown at the bottom of the screen.)

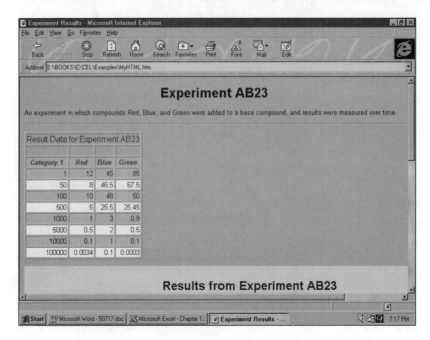

6

Excel Tools

18

Using Excel Add-Ins

Microsoft provides you with some additional tools that, while not part of the basic Excel software, can be added to your repertoire for advanced spreadsheet work. The tools covered in this chapter are known as "add-ins," and you can choose to enable and use them if you want. These tools add a variety of added capabilities, including the following:

- Examining Excel's additional financial, statistical, and engineering functions using the Analysis Toolpak

- Saving workbooks automatically

- Using the Conditional Sum Wizard

- Finding table intersection values with the Lookup Wizard

- Exploring an add-in tool called Solver, which performs more advanced What-If functions than does the built-in Goal Seek

- Converting multiple files from a different spreadsheet format into Excel 97 format using the File Conversion Wizard.

Getting the most out of these tools is an important aspect of mastering Excel. Solver, for example, is a powerful tool that can be used to solve difficult problems. Likewise, the additional financial, statistical, and engineering functions available as add-ins are invaluable for performing various types of analysis in Excel, and enabling the AutoSave add-in frees you from worrying about saving your workbooks regularly.

Excel 97 for Windows contains many additional features that are not part of the core Excel program. You can add these additional capabilities to Excel selectively, so that you use only the features you want. This chapter shows you how to add, remove, and use several of the add-ins that Excel provides.

■ Installing Excel Add-ins

You can install the optional add-in tools at the same time you install Excel. If you did not choose to install them at that time, however, you can make them a part of Excel by using the Microsoft Office Setup program in your Office 97 folder.

■ Using the Add-in Manager

After the add-ins are installed on your computer using Excel's (or Office's) setup program, you can incorporate them into Excel so that they appear on the Excel menus just like any other command. You can control the status of the add-ins by using the Add-in Manager. Access the Add-in Manager by pulling down the Tools menu and choosing the Add-Ins command. The Add-Ins dialog box is shown in Figure 18.1.

In the dialog box, select or deselect the check boxes to control which add-ins appear on the Excel menus.

NOTE *Depending on the speed of your computer, accessing the Add-ins menu might take a brief while. Also, selecting new add-ins might take several moments when Excel installs them after you click on the OK button from the Add-ins dialog box.*

Analysis ToolPak

The Analysis ToolPak is a collection of Excel functions that perform various financial, statistical, and engineering functions. Many of these functions appear

Figure 18.1

The Add-Ins dialog box

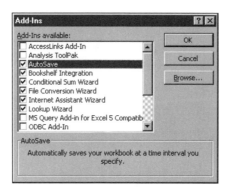

automatically in the Paste Function dialog box when you activate the Analysis ToolPak Add-in, while others can be accessed through the Data Analysis command that appears in Excel's Tools menu. Choosing the Data Analysis command displays the Data Analysis dialog box shown in Figure 18.2.

Figure 18.2

The Data Analysis dialog box

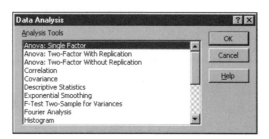

To use any of the analysis tools, select a tool from the list and then click on the OK button. This procedure causes the dialog box for that tool to appear on your screen. For example, selecting Random Number Generator brings up the dialog box in Figure 18.3.

The data-analysis tools contained in the Analysis ToolPak are very extensive. They are covered in detail in Chapter 9, "Mastering Excel Analytical Tools."

AutoSave

Nothing is more frustrating than spending lots of time on a workbook, only to lose your unsaved work because your computer crashes for some reason or the network goes down, or you lose power in a storm. Although you can

Figure 18.3

The Random Number
Generation dialog box

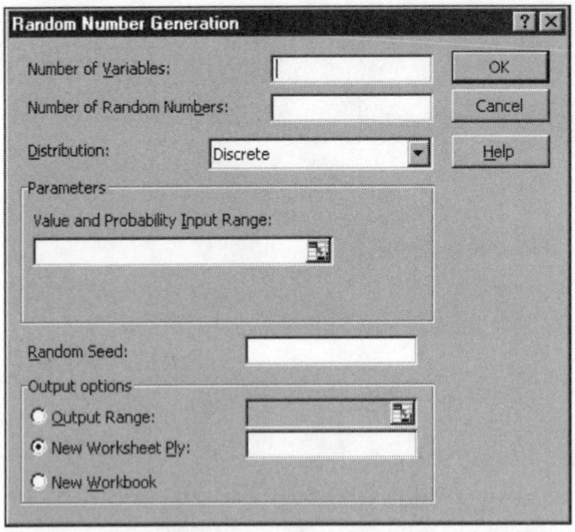

help prevent this problem by remembering to do frequent saves of your work, you can also use the AutoSave add-in to save your work at regular intervals automatically.

Access the AutoSave function by pulling down the Tools menu and choosing AutoSave. You will see the dialog box shown in Figure 18.4.

Figure 18.4

The AutoSave dialog box

From within this dialog box, you can control several functions, as follows:

- **Whether to perform the automatic save.** Select or deselect the check box marked Automatic Save.

- **The number of minutes between automatic saves.** Change the value in the Minutes field.

- **Whether to save the active workbook or all open workbooks.** Use the two option buttons in the Save Options box to make your choice. If you have many workbooks open but are not modifying more than one of them at a time, you can speed up the AutoSave process by choosing to save only the active workbook. If, however, you are using a single workbook that modifies the other workbooks (by means of a macro, for instance), choose to save all open workbooks to ensure that all of your work is saved.

- **Whether you are prompted before every automatic save.** Select or deselect the check box marked Prompt before saving in order to control this option.

Conditional Sum Wizard

There are certain times when you want to sum a column of numbers, but you want to do so conditionally. For instance, imagine you have a list of employees that are both hourly and salaried. The column reports their total pay, but you want to examine the totals for the salaried personnel versus the hourly personnel. This is an example you'll examine here, but there are literally hundreds of different ways to perform a conditional summation.

There are a number of ways to perform such conditional sums. First, you could sort your list by the hourly/salary column, and then do a quick summation on just the ranges that represent the hourly or salaried people. However, this is clumsy, because you may not want to keep your list in that order. Another alternative would be to write a formula in which you manually pick out the hourly pay cells and the salary pay cells, such as in **=C3+C5+C9[ellipses]** (or whatever cells contain the information you want). But this is also clumsy, time-consuming, and may not work for very large lists of data. You could write a series of **IF** formulas to the right of the table, which bring the totals you're interested in into a new column, which can then be summed, but this is also clumsy and can take up a lot of space. Yet another alternative is to write an array formula in Excel, but these can be difficult to write correctly.

Excel 97 adds a tool that helps you perform conditional sums, and it does so by writing an array formula for you, walking you through the process quickly and painlessly. This tool is called the Conditional Sum Wizard, and it's one of the add-ins included with, and new to, Excel 97. You need to first activate it using the Add-ins dialog box, after which you can access it by using the Tools, Wizard, Conditional Sum command.

For this illustration, consider the example worksheet shown in Figure 18.5.

At the bottom of the table, you wish to look at the sum of the dollars paid each month to the hourly and salaried employees. However, you want to keep the table sorted by the employee ID numbers assigned, because you also use this worksheet for other purposes that require that sorting method. So, you decide to use the Conditional Sum Wizard to create your conditional sums.

Figure 18.5

An example worksheet
showing monthly pay
for hourly and
salaried personnel

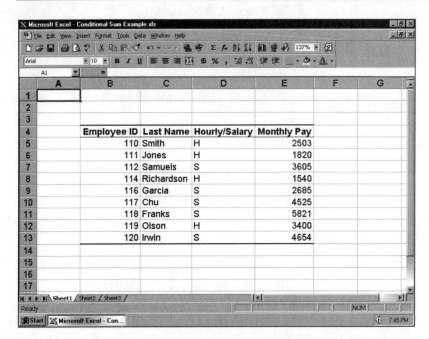

First activate the wizard by accessing the Tools, Wizard, Conditional Sum command. You see the dialog box shown in Figure 18.6 appear. In this dialog box, you choose the range of cells that contain both the cells that will be summed and the cells that contain the criteria you want to use. In this example, cells B4:E13 contain these data (select the range so that any column heading is included).

After you've selected the cells, the Next button takes you to the second step of the Conditional Sum Wizard, in which you define the criteria that will result in the sum you want. In this case, the sum you'll create will total all hourly employees' pay. As shown in Figure 18.7, were you using this worksheet, you would make the following choices:

- Set Column to sum to **Monthly Pay** using the drop-down list box.

- Set Column to **Hourly/Salary** using the drop-down list box.

- Set Is to the operation you want (=, >, <, >=, <=, or <>) using its drop-down list box. In this example, you would choose equals (**=**).

- Set This value to **H** from the drop-down list box.

Figure 18.6

The first step of the
Conditional Sum Wizard
prompts you for the range
of cells to be summed.

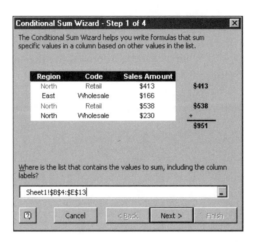

Conditional Sum Wizard - Step 1 of 4			✕

The Conditional Sum Wizard helps you write formulas that sum
specific values in a column based on other values in the list.

Region	Code	Sales Amount	
North	Retail	$413	$413
East	Wholesale	$166	
North	Retail	$538	$538
North	Wholesale	$230	+
			$951

<u>W</u>here is the list that contains the values to sum, including the column
labels?

Sheet1!$B$4:$E$13

| ? | Cancel | < Back | Next > | Finish |

Figure 18.7

Use the second step
of the Conditional
Sum Wizard to define
the criteria for
the summation.

Conditional Sum Wizard - Step 2 of 4		✕

Which column contains the values to sum? Select the column label.

Column to <u>s</u>um: Monthly Pay

Next, select a column you want to evaluate, and then type or select a
value to compare with data in that column.

<u>C</u>olumn: <u>I</u>s: <u>T</u>his value:

Hourly/Salary   =   H

<u>A</u>dd Condition	<u>R</u>emove Condition

Hourly/Salary=H

| ? | Cancel | < <u>B</u>ack | Next > | Finish |

After setting all of the criteria, click the Add Condition button to create
the conditional sum condition. In this case, you tell the Conditional Sum Wizard to prepare a sum using the rows where Hourly/Salary are equal to H.
You can add multiple conditions using this dialog box, clicking on Add Condition for each one. If you make a mistake with a condition, select the condition in the condition pane and click the Remove Condition button. When
you're done defining conditions, click Next to continue.

The third step of the Conditional Sum Wizard asks how you would like the results presented. You can choose from two choices, both shown in the dialog box in Figure 18.8. The top option simply inserts the formula into a cell you select, while the bottom option inserts the formula, and in the cell to the left of formula inserts the criteria label for the formula. Choose the bottom option before clicking Next.

Depending on which of the two choices you use, you have either one or two more steps in the Conditional Sum Wizard. If you choose the bottom option where the label and formula are inserted, you see the dialog box shown in Figure 18.9. Use this dialog box to select which cell will contain the label for the conditional sum. The next dialog box is much the same, but prompts you for the location of the actual sum result. Enter the cell reference into the text box on that dialog box, also, and then click on Finish to complete the conditional sum, as shown in Figure 18.10.

By using the second format in step 3, you can simply type a new value in place of the "H" in cell D14 to see a new conditional sum. In this example, typing an S in cell D14 would instantly yield the sum of salaried workers in cell E14. This is because the Conditional Sum Wizard writes its formula in such a way that it uses the label cell as the lookup reference, rather than hard-coding the lookup you typed into the formula itself.

Lookup Wizard

Related to the Conditional Sum Wizard is the Lookup Wizard, which helps you find, by formula, a value at an intersection of rows and columns in a

Figure 18.9

The final two steps of the
Conditional Sum Wizard
prompt you for the cell
locations of the result
and its label.

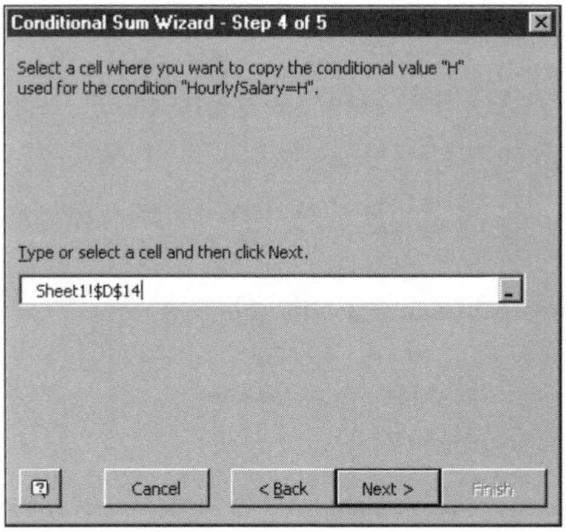

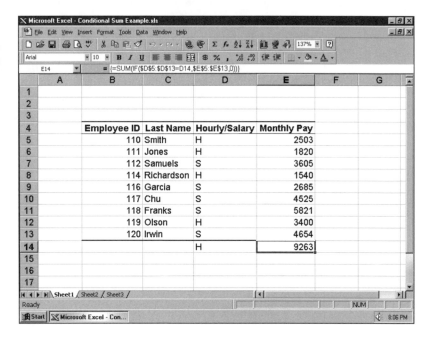

Figure 18.10

The completed
conditional sum.
Examine the formula
bar to see the formula
that the Conditional
Sum Wizard created.

table. Like the Conditional Sum Wizard, a formula is generated by the wizard that can be used to perform quick lookups of the table. It's not the wizard itself that's useful; the results it immediately yields when you run it don't justify its use. However, when you need to repeatedly find a value at different intersections, using the formula created by the Lookup Wizard can yield big benefits, particularly for large tables that would be time-consuming to scan by hand.

Consider the table shown in Figure 18.11. In it, you see a table of temperature readings for a building. In this example, you'll use the Lookup Wizard to create a formula that lets you quickly find values in the table. For such a small table as this, the Lookup Wizard doesn't really make sense, because it's easy to find the value you want manually. However, for much larger tables, the Lookup Wizard really shines.

Figure 18.11

An example table of building temperatures

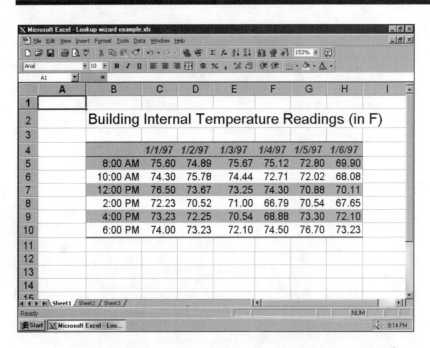

To begin, use the Tools, Wizard, Lookup command, which displays the dialog box shown in Figure 18.12. Select the entire table, including labels, that you want to search for a value.

Next, in the second step shown in Figure 18.13, select the column and row that you want to use for the initial lookup value, using the drop-down lists for each field.

Figure 18.12

In the first step of the Lookup Wizard, you simply select the entire table that you want to search for a value.

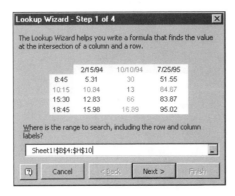

Figure 18.13

In step two, select the row and column that you want to use for the sample lookup.

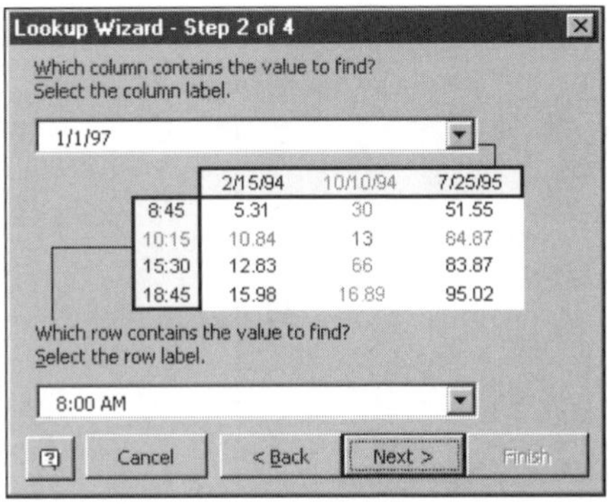

The third step prompts you for how the Lookup Wizard will insert its result. You can choose to insert just the intersection result formula using the row and column you selected in step 2, or you can choose to also include the lookup parameters. Including the lookup parameters (the bottom choice in Figure 18.14) lets you more easily find other intersections in the future.

In the final step (or steps if you choose to include the lookup parameters), you select the cells that will contain the formula result, and the lookup values. Each dialog box prompts you for a cell location. Enter the cell location by typing it or by clicking on the desired cell with your mouse. Figure 18.15 shows one of these final step dialogs.

After selecting the destination cells, click Finish to complete the Lookup Wizard. Figure 18.16 shows the result, with the formula generated by the Lookup Wizard shown in the formula bar.

Figure 18.14

Now you choose how the
results will be inserted
into the worksheet.

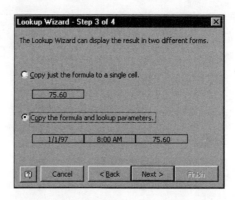

Figure 18.15

In the final step (or
steps), you choose which
cells will hold which
portion of the result.

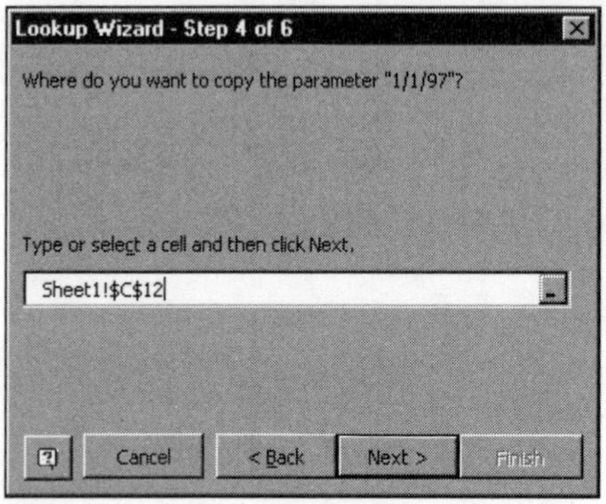

After completing the Lookup Wizard, you can quickly find other intersections by typing a valid row or column heading label into the two cells to
the left of the result. The formula in the result cell recalculates to show the
new intersection value.

The Goal Seek function in Excel will be too limited if you need to solve
problems in which many factors influence the outcome or in which you need
to apply constraints to the solution. Excel contains an Add-in called Solver,
however, that can deal with finding optimal solutions to such problems. Examples of problems to which Solver might be applied include the following:

- Finding optimal schedules for employees

Figure 18.16

The results of the Lookup Wizard generate an INDEX formula that uses MATCH functions to find the information. Change the values in cells C12 or D12, and the result in cell E12 changes.

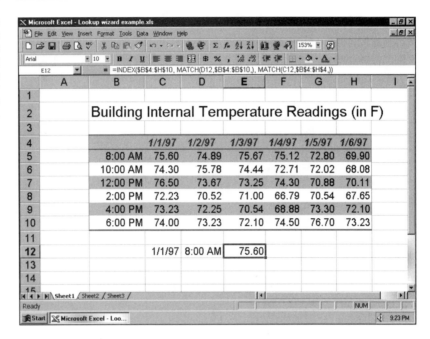

- Maximizing return on investment while keeping within a defined risk in a complex portfolio

- Modeling engine performance, given certain physical constraints and engineering data

- Maximizing profit by choosing product mix

These examples suggest only a few of the uses for Excel's Solver. It is an incredibly powerful tool that you can use to help solve extraordinarily difficult problems. Figure 18.17 shows an example of a problem for which Solver is well-suited.

In order to understand how Solver works, you must understand the structure of the example problem.

Row 7 shows the five warehouses: San Francisco, Denver, Chicago, Dallas, and New York are each are the location of one warehouse. Cells A8:A10 show the three plants. The numbers at the intersection of the plants and warehouses contain the number of packages to ship to each warehouse from each plant. These numbers are *seeded* (or started with "fake" numbers) with

Figure 18.17

An example of an
appropriate problem
for Solver

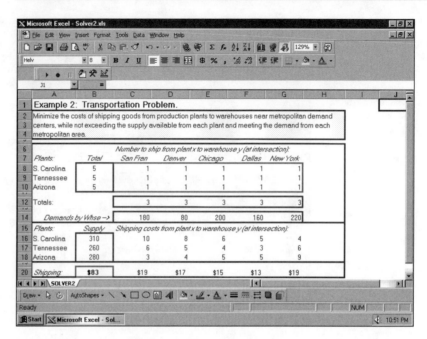

1s to give Solver something to start from. To the left and bottom of the table are the totals shipped from each plant and the totals received from each warehouse. To begin, each warehouse ships five packages, one to each plant.

Below the ship table, cells C14:G14 contain the numbers of packages demanded by each warehouse. One constraint for a successful solution is to find a method that makes certain that each warehouse gets the number of packages it requires.

The bottom table, cells C16:G18, contains the shipping costs from each warehouse to each plant. Cells B16:B18 contain the amount available to ship from each plant.

The bottom line in the worksheet contains the total shipping cost for each warehouse, with the total of all shipping costs shown in cell B20.

The totals in cells B8:B10, C12:G12, and B20:G20 are simply that: totals of the actual data based on the number of packages to ship from each warehouse to each plant in cells C8:G10. In Figure 18.5, these totals merely reflect the seed values in cells C8:G10.

At first glance, the worksheet looks somewhat complex, but when you study it, you'll probably realize that it really is quite simple. It contains no complex math, and should be understood easily.

The problem for Solver can be stated as follows:

- Minimize total shipping costs
- Meet the demands of each warehouse
- Do not exceed the supply available from each plant

NOTE *This worksheet is perfect for illustrating this discussion of Solver. In real life, however, you are likely to need to add timing constraints, along with production rate at the plants, and so forth. Models such as this one can always be made more complicated, however! The real trick in modeling a complex problem is finding the least complicated way for you to meet your goals.*

After you have set up your own worksheet (you don't need to duplicate the one shown here—it's just an example to illustrate how Solver works), you can access Solver by pulling down the Tools menu and choosing Solver. This operation brings up Solver's main dialog box, as shown in Figure 18.18.

Figure 18.18

The Solver Parameters dialog box

Table 18.1 discusses the settings in the Solver dialog box.

Table 18.1

Solver Dialog Box Settings

SETTING	DESCRIPTION
Set Target Cell	The key goal to be met by Solver, it indicates a single cell on the worksheet. In this case, it indicates cell B20, the total shipping costs.
Equal to	The Equal to box allows you to tell Solver what you want it to do with the target cell. You can choose to find the maximum value possible by choosing the Max button, the minimum value possible by choosing the Min button, or a set goal amount defined in the Value field. In this example, you want to minimize shipping costs, so the Min button is selected.

SETTING	DESCRIPTION
By Changing Cells	Indicate in this field which cells on the worksheet should be changed in an attempt to find the optimal solution, or click on the Guess button.
Guess	Click on the Guess button to cause Solver to determine which non-formula cells go into the cell indicated in Set Target Cell. These cells will be automatically entered into the By Changing Cells field by clicking the Guess button. When you choose Guess, Excel will examine the target cell, and then move back through all calculated cells until it finds the cells that do not contain formulas, but that are part of the target cell's solution.
Subject to the Constraints	This list box lists all of the constraints in the problem. As you can see, three are set already. The first constraint, **B8:B10 <= B16:B18**, indicates that the cells in B8:B10 (the total shipped from each plant) must be less than or equal to the values in cells B16:B18 (the amount each plant has available). The second constraint, **C12:G12 >= C14:G14**, indicates that the total amount shipped to each warehouse must be greater than or equal to the amount required by the warehouse. The final constraint, **C8:G10 >= 0**, tells Solver that the amount shipped to each warehouse must be greater than or equal to zero for each plant. This constraint (obvious to you and me, but not to a computer program like Solver) keeps Solver from suggesting solutions that include some negative shipments to certain plants but still meet the other constraints.

To define a constraint, click on the Add button. The Add Constraint dialog box will appear, as shown in Figure 18.19.

Figure 18.19

The Add Constraint dialog box

Indicate the cell reference for the constraint in the field provided. Then select a constraint type by clicking on the down arrow in the middle of the dialog box. Possible constraints are **>=, =, <=**, and **Int**. Int requires that the values in the cell reference cells be full integers (if you are trying to find optimal schedules, for example, you can't very well schedule part of a truck, or part of a person!). After you have chosen the constraint, enter its value in the Constraint field. Click OK to return to the Solver dialog box, or click on Add to store the constraint but keep the Add Constraint dialog box on-screen to define additional constraints.

You can control the behavior of Solver with the Options dialog box, accessed through the Options button. Figure 18.20 shows the Solver Options dialog box, and Table 18.2 shows its settings.

Figure 18.20

The Solver Options dialog box

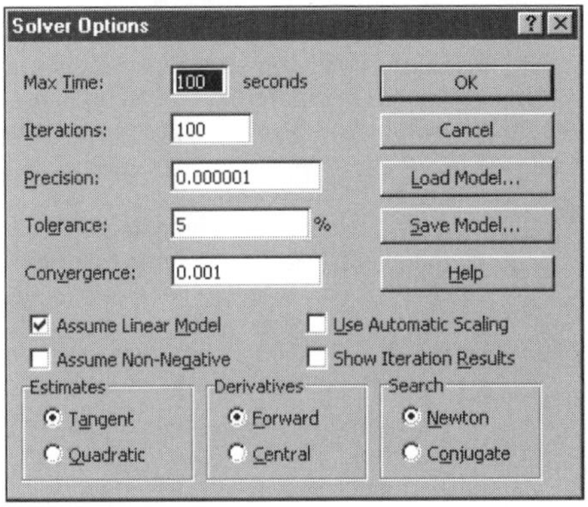

Table 18.2

Solver Options Dialog Box Settings

SETTING	DESCRIPTION
Max Time	Sets the maximum amount of time that Solver can use to solve the problem. You can enter a value as high as 32,767 seconds in this field.
Iterations	Limits the maximum number of iterations that Solver can take. You can enter up to 32,767 in this field.
Precision	This field controls the precision that Solver uses to find solutions. You can enter a value here between 0 and 1. A smaller number (fewer decimal places) indicates greater precision. This value controls the tolerance used for constraints.
Tolerance	The Tolerance settings are used when you solve problems that have integer constraints. When you add integer constraints, you require Solver to solve many subproblems in order to find the answer to the larger problem. The value you enter in this field controls the percentage of error allowed in the optimal solution. Use this field to speed up Solver for problems with integer constraints. Higher tolerance percentages make Solver run faster.
Assume Linear Model	If all of the relationships in a particular problem are linear, selecting this check box can make Solver run faster.

**Table 18.2
(Continued)**

Solver Options Dialog
Box Settings

SETTING	DESCRIPTION
Show Iteration Results	If this check box is selected, Solver stops on each iteration to show you the results in progress. This option can be useful for learning why Solver is arriving at solutions that do not seem to be correct, and it can also suggest additional constraints that might keep Solver on the track toward a correct solution.
Use Automatic Scaling	When you solve a problem where the inputs and outputs have order-of-magnitude differences (such as percentage yield on very large dollar investments,) you can get more accurate results by enabling this check box.
Estimates	The two choices in the Estimates box tell Solver how to come up with the initial estimates used for the problem-solving process. Choose Tangent for Solver to use linear extrapolation from a tangent vector. Choose Quadratic for Solver to use Quadratic Extrapolation.
Derivatives	You can choose between Forward differencing and Central differencing for estimating partial derivatives for the target and constraints. Use Central differencing when Solver gives you a message saying that it cannot improve on the results already obtained.
Search	When Solver comes up with an estimate during an iteration, it must decide which direction to search in order to proceed toward the optimal solution. Newton searching is the default method, but it can consume large amounts of memory for complex problems. In such cases, use Conjugate searching, which is slower but requires less memory.
Save Model	Click on this button to save the Solver parameters for the problem to a cell range. This operation saves the information on the main Solver dialog box, such as the target cell and constraints, but not the options set in the Options dialog box. To work on a Solver problem over multiple sessions with Excel, use this option to save your parameters, and then use the Load Model option to reload the parameters when you return to your workbook.
Load Model	Click on this button to load a model from a cell range.

After changing the Solver options, click on the OK button to return to the main Solver dialog box. To solve for the optimal solution, click on the Solve button. When Solver has finished calculating, it will show you the results, as you can see in Figure 18.21.

In the Completion dialog box, you can choose to view reports of the actions taken by Solver. Click on each type of report you want to see in the Reports box before clicking on OK to complete the Solving process. The results of the example worksheet are shown in Figure 18.22.

As you can see in Figure 18.22, all of the demands by each warehouse are being met. You can also see, in part, that Solver has found an optimal

Figure 18.21

The Solver Results
dialog box

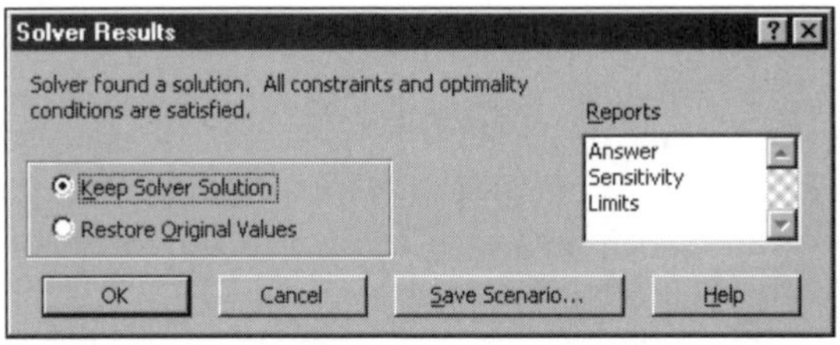

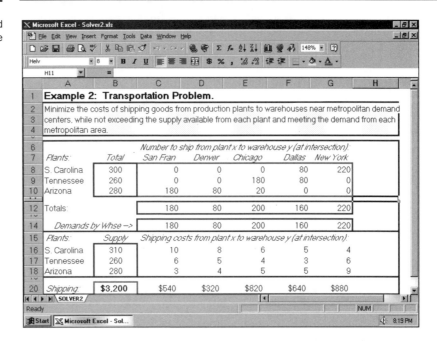

Figure 18.22

The completed
Solver example

solution that meets all of your criteria and the demands of each warehouse. For instance, notice that the supply in South Carolina (300 units) fulfils all of New York's demands (220 units) and then partially fills Dallas's demands (80 units.) Then, when you look in the shipping costs section, you can see that the cheapest shipping route is between the South Carolina plant and New York, followed by South Carolina and Dallas. By looking at certain of these factors in the result, you can help assure yourself that Solver has found the optimal solution to your problem. Moreover, it is important to undertake this step yourself to ensure that you have properly defined all of the constraints for the problem (for example, one of the constraints in this example prevented negative shipments from a plant, which Solver will otherwise suggest if that constraint isn't defined).

Solver is an extraordinarily powerful tool that can be applied to many real-life problems that are otherwise difficult, if not impossible, to solve by hand, or even with the aid of a powerful spreadsheet program like Excel. Even with an effective worksheet defined, there's a limit to how many possible solutions a person can try in a given period of time, and Solver fills such needs handily.

If you would like to play with Solver some more, you might consider trying to solve some personal-finance problems with it. For instance, if you receive a sum of money from a tax refund and want to pay down some credit cards, you can create a Solver worksheet that optimizes which credit cards you should pay off, solving either for best cash flow in the result, or least interest paid. Since all credit cards have different interest rates, methods for computing interest on balances, and so forth, using Solver in a complex case like this one can make finding the optimal solution much easier.

File Conversion Wizard

If you are converting to Excel from another spreadsheet program, or you are given a number of files all stored in another spreadsheet format and want to convert them en masse into Excel format, you can use the File Conversion Wizard to take the drudgery out of performing all of the conversions manually. In order to use the File Conversion Wizard, all of the files in the source directory must be in the same format; for example, Lotus 1-2-3 .WK1 format.

To start the File Conversion Wizard, use the Tools, Wizard, File Conversion command. This brings up the first of three steps for the wizard, shown in Figure 18.23.

Next, you are presented with a list of files that are available to be converted. You can choose files individually by clicking on the checkbox to the left of the filename, or you can click on the Select All button to choose them all with a single click, as shown in Figure 18.24.

In the third step of the File Conversion Wizard (see Figure 18.25), you choose the destination folder that will contain the converted files. Typically, you will choose a different folder than the one where the original files are located so that you don't accidentally use the older version. Enter the name of the folder in which you want to store the new files, use the Browse button to locate it by browsing, or click New Folder to create a new folder into which the files will be placed.

Clicking on the Finish button performs the conversion. Depending on the number and size of the files, the conversion may take quite a bit of time.

Figure 18.23

In the first step of the File
Conversion Wizard, you
choose the directory that
contains the files to be
converted, as well as
their source format.

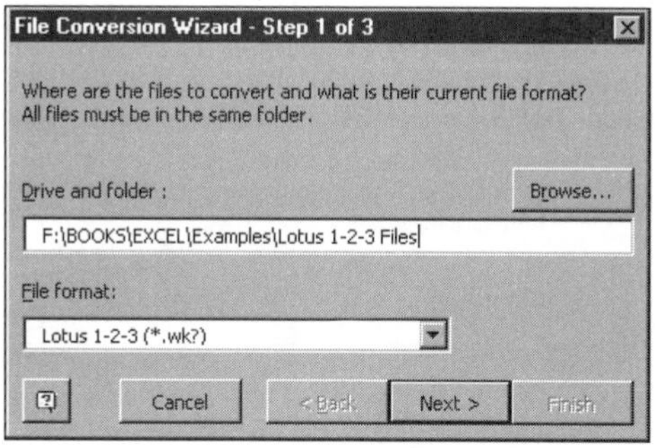

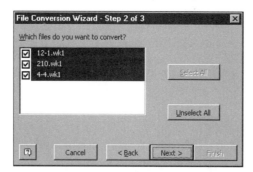

Figure 18.24

Click on each file that
you want to convert,
or choose the Select
All button.

Figure 18.25

In the last step, choose
the destination folder into
which the converted files
will be placed.

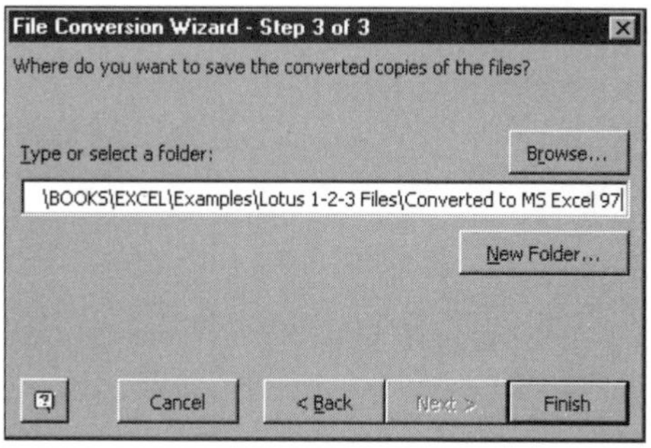

When the conversion is complete, you will be shown a report of the conversion process, detailing the conversion activities and notifying you of any problems that occurred during the conversion (see Figure 18.26).

Figure 18.26

At the end of the conversion, you see this report screen to see if any problems developed during the conversion.

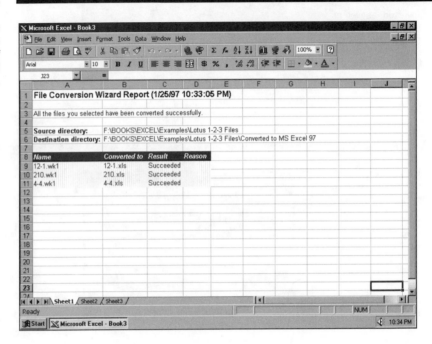

- *Sharing Files on a Network*
- *Using Excel's Shared Workbooks*
- *Tracking Changes to Workbooks*
- *Merging Workbook Changes*
- *Setting Document Properties*
- *Routing Files*
- *Maintaining Security*

19

Excel in Workgroups

Many people use microsoft excel at work, and consequently interact with others in the company who also use Excel. Wouldn't it be nice if Excel helped you work more collaboratively within your organization? What if it let you more effectively manage shared files, for example? What if it provided tools to keep your files secure within a shared network directory? What it if could show you who made what changes to a file, and when they made them? Fortunately, it does all this and more.

In this chapter, you will learn about the following Excel features and capabilities:

- Sharing Excel files on a network

- Tracking changes made to workbooks

- Tracking control information for shared files

- Preserving the security of your files

- Using Shared Workbooks in Excel

- Merging Workbook Changes

One of the biggest benefits that networks bring companies is the ability to rapidly share and process information within workgroups. Taking advantage of the features shown in this chapter will increase your efficiency, and that of your Excel-using peers.

In most companies, tightly knit groups that use networks set up and use shared areas on a common file server. Everyone in a workgroup can access and save files on this server. Workers find it much easier to get their jobs done with this sort of structure, particularly in organizations that ask every worker to get more done with less. Taking advantage of the power of your network to help your peers work more smoothly together can pay large, if occasionally subtle, dividends.

Excel supports this model of information sharing. It has features that make working together more manageable.

■ Sharing Files on a Network

If you often work with files that are stored in areas to which many others have access, you may sometimes try to open a file that someone else is already working on. Other times, someone else may try to open the file that you are using and changing. Dealing with these common occurrences is important if you want to make sure that confusion doesn't ensue.

Unless a file is set up as a shared workbook (see the following section about shared workbooks), Excel warns you when you try to open a file that someone else is already using. When someone first opens a file for editing, that file becomes "locked" on the file server, making it impossible for another user to modify it. Excel helps you deal with this gracefully by warning you with the dialog box shown in Figure 19.1.

You have four ways of dealing with the dialog box shown in Figure 19.1: you can select Cancel and try again later, hoping that the file is free then; you can call the other person up on the phone (if you know their extension: their name is shown on the dialog box) and ask them to close the document so

Figure 19.1

When you try to open a file that someone else is using, you will see this dialog box.

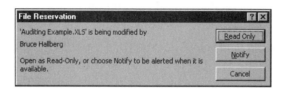

you can use it; you can select Notify and have Excel tell you when the other person is finished working with the file; or you can click on the Read Only button and open the document in read-only mode, in which changes you make must be saved to another filename.

When you open a workbook in Read Only mode, whatever is saved to the server's hard drive at that moment will be loaded into your computer, with the indicator (Read-Only) appearing after the file name in the title bar of the application. If the user who has the original file open makes additional changes while you are working on your Read-Only copy, you won't know about them. You can then freely edit the file. However, you cannot save changes back to the original file. You must instead save any changes to a new workbook filename using the Save As command in the File menu.

If you choose the Notify feature, the file will also be opened for Read-Only viewing and use. When the other person finishes working with the file, you will be told via the dialog box shown in Figure 19.2. Choosing Read-Write will then let you save your changes to the original workbook file.

Figure 19.2

When you choose Notify and the document becomes available, you will see this dialog box.

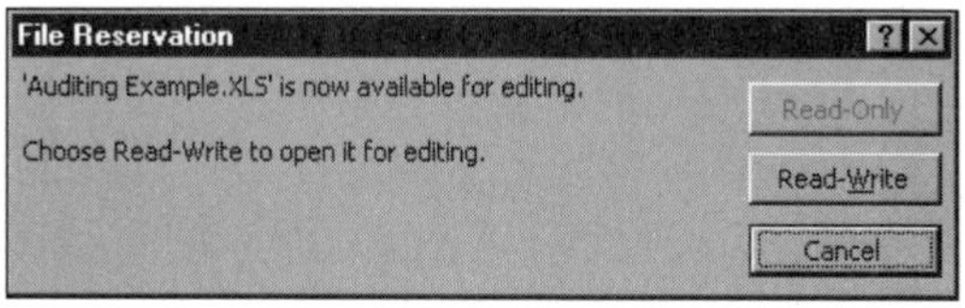

Now, consider this sequence of events:

1. Someone else opens a file and starts editing it.

2. You subsequently open the file, using the Notify option, and start editing it.

3. The other person changes something: the value of cell A1, for example.

4. You change cell A1 to a different value than the one they entered.

5. The other person closes the file, saving their changes.

6. You are notified that the file is now available in Read-Write mode, and you elect to open it that way.

At this point there's a conflict, because the last-saved file from the other person contains a different value for cell A1 than the one you entered and have on your screen, and this conflict must be resolved by you. You can choose to accept their change and lose your own, or to force your change to cell A1 to override theirs. Excel will show you the dialog box in Figure 19.3 when situations like this one arise.

Figure 19.3

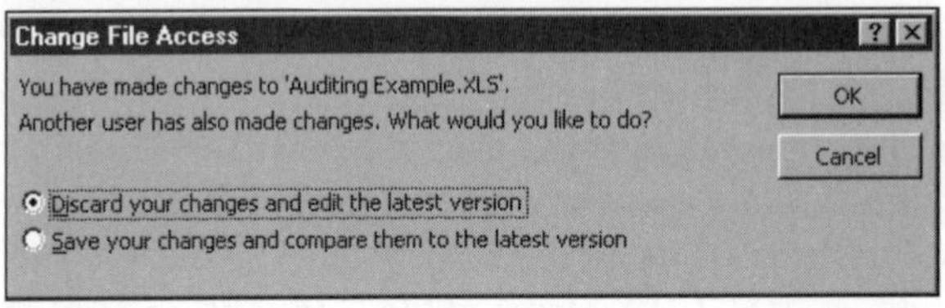

When you are notified that a file can be opened in Read-Write mode and then do so, if there are conflicting cells in the workbook you see this dialog box for resolving the conflict.

■ Using Excel's Shared Workbooks

In Excel 97 you can share workbooks, so more than one person can access and modify the same workbook simultaneously. You can choose to update changes from each user on a periodic basis, or to update changes every time the shared workbook is saved.

Sharing workbooks isn't a panacea for providing multiuser access to workbooks, however, as important limitations exist for shared workbooks:

- Blocks of cells can't be inserted or deleted: only entire rows or columns can be inserted or deleted while the workbook is shared

- Cells can't be merged

- Conditional formats can't be added or changed (although those that existed before the workbook was shared will still function)

- Data tables can't be created

- Data validation rules can't be added or changed (although those that were set up before the workbook was shared will still work)

- Dialog boxes and menus can't be modified

- Excel's automatic subtotals won't function

- Excel's drawing tools can't be used

- Macros can't be changed in the shared workbook (although macros stored in another open workbook can still be used normally)

- PivotTables can't be created or modified, although PivotTables created before sharing is started will continue to work

- Scenarios can't be used

- The shared workbook data can't be outlined or grouped

- Workbook or worksheet passwords can't be applied

- Worksheets can't be deleted

- You can't insert or modify charts, hyperlinks, objects, or pictures, although you can insert normal Excel links

These are significant limitations. However, when it comes to letting many people see and update data, the utility of shared workbooks is still great. Therefore these limitations must be considered in context. For certain types of jobs, such as the examples provided below, shared workbooks can be an important tool:

- Members of a workgroup may keep a schedule of their shared "to-do" items in Excel (an accounting department's period-closing schedule would be a good example). Shared lists let all the members maintain the list simultaneously, adding and deleting items as needed.

- You may have some kind of group database that you keep in Excel workbooks. Perhaps it is a list of people who have requested information from different people in the group. Each person in the group could add and review these requests simultaneously. The person who is responsible for sending the information out could also access the file to see what they have to do.

Enabling the Shared Workbooks Feature

Excel workbooks are not shared by default: you first have to enable this feature using the Share Workbook command in the Tools menu. Accessing this command displays the dialog box shown in Figure 19.4.

To enable sharing, simply select the check box named Allow changes by more than one user at the same time. You can also turn off sharing by deselecting this check box.

The Advanced tab of the Share Workbook dialog box (see Figure 19.5) lets you control how changes to the shared workbook are tracked, how changes are updated to the file, how conflicting changes are handled, and whether or not print settings and filter settings will be stored for each user.

Figure 19.4

Use the Share Workbook dialog box to turn on the sharing feature.

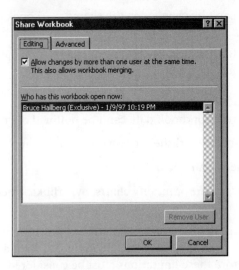

Figure 19.5

The Advanced tab of the Share Workbook dialog box

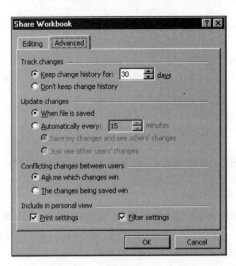

When you choose Keep change history for and choose a number of days, all changes made to the shared workbook will be stored along with the workbook in question. The next section discusses how this works in detail. You can also choose not to store a change history.

When multiple people access a shared workbook at the same time, you may want to control how changes one person makes are reflected to the other users. By default, When file is saved is selected. When each user saves his or her copy of the shared workbook, updates that others have saved will also be on view. The alternative to this method is choosing Automatically every, and selecting a number of minutes. When you choose this, you will automatically see others' changes at the time intervals specified, or you can determine that your changes are saved at the same time as other changes are updated on your screen.

Handling conflicts between changes is important with shared workbooks, and you can choose the simplest method for doing so in the Share Workbook dialog box. More complex methods are discussed in the next section. You can choose to be asked which changes win when changes you've made conflict in some way with those made by others. Or, you can choose to let the most recently saved copy automatically "win," thereby automatically overwriting any conflicting changes.

The final two check boxes on the Advanced tab of the Share Workbook dialog box control how personal settings are saved. Each individual can save his or her own print settings and filter settings (filter settings are those made with the Filter submenu in the Data menu). Select either or both of these check boxes to save individual settings.

NOTE *Once you have designated a workbook as a Shared Workbook, the settings persist until you turn off this feature, even after everyone has closed the file.*

After turning on the Shared Workbooks feature for a workbook, Excel saves the file immediately so that the file on the shared network drive is also saved right away with the Shared Workbook setting enabled. This first save after enabling sharing is required so that others may access the file in a multi-user fashion.

NOTE *When you need to perform one of the actions that aren't allowed in shared workbooks, first turn off sharing, make the changes, and then re-enable sharing.*

Understanding Shared Workbooks

The key to understanding shared workbooks is knowing how conflicts within a file are adjudicated—some are sorted out automatically, while others will require intervention when you save the file.

Let's look at both cases. First, say that two people are working on a single workbook. One person inserts a row of data and saves her copy of the file. The other person has not inserted that new row. What happens when the second person saves his version of the file? The answer is that the new row added by the first person is automatically inserted into the second person's workbook during their save. Inserting a row of data would not generally cause a conflict with any work the second person has done, so it's updated automatically. Excel does tell you when it does this, however, by bringing up the dialog box shown in Figure 19.6.

Figure 19.6

Changes that don't present a conflict are updated automatically at the time of saving the file.

When a change that the first user makes conflicts with something the second user has done within the file, the case is trickier. For example, how does Excel handle it if the first person changes the text in a cell in one way, while the second person makes a different change to the same cell?

When the second person tries to save his copy of the workbook and Excel finds that there is a conflict like the one presented in the previous paragraph, the person trying to save will see the Conflict Resolution dialog box shown in Figure 19.7.

Figure 19.7

Trying to save information that conflicts with what another user has done brings this dialog box to your screen.

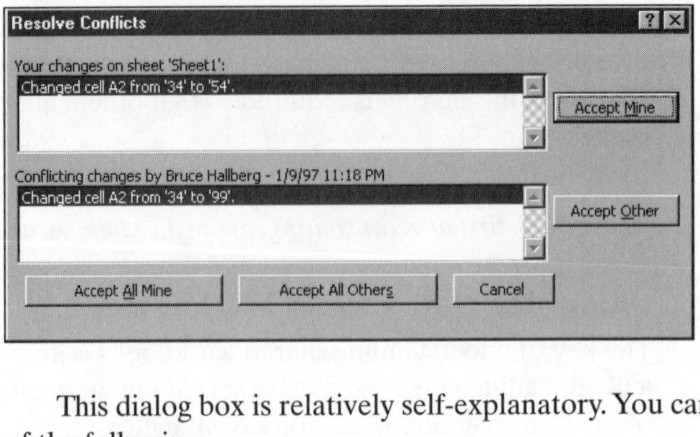

This dialog box is relatively self-explanatory. You can choose to do one of the following:

- Make your change succeed (click Accept Mine), in which case the first person's conflicting change will be overwritten.

- Use the other person's change (click Accept Other), in which your conflicting change will be overwritten by theirs.

- Save the file with your changes to a new file name that doesn't conflict with the main file. (Cancel the Resolve Conflicts dialog, then save your version to a new filename.) This is a good strategy when you're not sure which change should prevail, or when you simply want to save your changes for reference at some other time, but want to accept the other person's changes for the time being.

You can also click on the two bottom buttons in the dialog box in which you elect to resolve all conflicts with the other person's changes or with your own changes.

Managing Shared Workbooks

Excel offers you two tools that let you more easily manage Shared Workbooks: the ability to view who is using the file at any given time, and the Conflict History sheet.

Any time you're working on a shared workbook, you can see who else is working on it by accessing the Share Workbook command in the Tools menu. The Editing tab will show you who has the file open for editing, and when they opened it (see Figure 19.8).

Figure 19.8

The Share Workbook dialog box shows you who else is using the file.

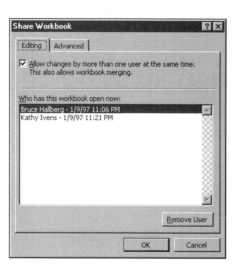

If necessary, you can forcibly disconnect another user of the file. Use the Editing tab of the Share Workbook dialog box, click on the user you want to disconnect from the file, and then click on Remove User. When you do this, the disconnected person will see the message box shown in Figure 19.9 when they attempt to save the file.

Figure 19.9

If you get disconnected
from a shared workbook
by another user, you will
see this message.

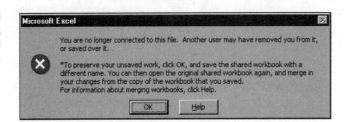

If someone else disconnects you from a shared workbook, follow the instructions in the message box to save your copy of the workbook to a new filename. Later, you can reopen the actual shared workbook and merge any changes you've made into that file (see the following section on Merging Workbook Changes).

■ Tracking Changes to Workbooks

An extremely welcome addition to Excel 97 is the Track Changes feature, which lets you audit changes made to a shared workbook (tracking changes requires that a workbook be shared first). Track Changes keeps a record of modifications to workbooks so you can easily see who has changed what in the workbook, and when they made their changes.

The limitations that apply to shared workbooks also apply to workbooks in which you are tracking changes. Moreover, Excel doesn't track certain types of changes, such as:

- Cell results that change because another cell is changed (the actual cell that is changed is tracked, but any formulas that rely on that cell will not show a change)

- Changes to formatting

- Comments

- Hiding and unhiding rows or columns

- New or deleted worksheets

- Worksheet tab-name changes

If you've used Word's Track Changes feature, you'll find that Excel tracks changes differently. First of all, a workbook must first be shared to have its changes tracked, and its changes are only tracked for the period of time you specify (the default is 30 days). Within that time, all changes (except those listed above) made by all users are tracked. When you want to see highlighted changes, you decide which changes you see by choosing the time period of the changes, who made the changes, and where in the workbook the changes exist. You can choose to see changes highlighted on the screen, or listed in a separate worksheet in the workbook.

The Highlight Changes dialog box controls what tracked changes you can see. Open the Tools menu, click Track Changes, and then click on the Highlight Changes command. You'll see the dialog box shown in Figure 19.10.

Figure 19.10

The Highlight Changes dialog box controls what changes you see.

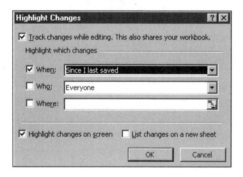

The top check box, Track changes while editing, will automatically be selected when you share a workbook. If the workbook isn't shared and you select this option, the workbook becomes shared. The next three options—When, Who, and Where—control what changes you will see.

The default choice for When is Since I last saved. Any changes made since the last time you saved the file will be shown when you save the file again when you make this choice. You can also choose All, Not yet reviewed, and Since date (which lets you then choose a date).

By default, Who is not checked, indicating that you will see changes from everyone. You can also explicitly choose to see changes from Everyone, from Everyone but Me, and for the specific names of people who are currently editing the shared workbook.

The Where option, also not checked by default, lets you choose to only see changes made to a particular range of cells. Turn on the check box, then click in the field and choose the range of cells for which you want to see the changes.

By combining settings for these three options, you can zero in on the particular changes you're interested in seeing.

The final two check boxes control how you see the changes made to the workbook. You can choose to see them highlighted on the screen, and also on a separate workbook. Figure 19.11 shows you how an on-screen change is highlighted, while Figure 19.12 shows you an example of the special sheet used to list changes.

Figure 19.11

Position your mouse pointer over a cell with a highlighted change, and the comment box will shows you the information pertaining to the change.

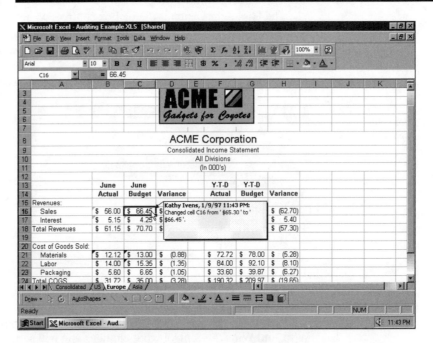

One nice feature of the History workbook is that you can filter the changes. Each category shown has a filter button to the right of the column name. Click on the down arrow to restrict the listing on the History sheet so that it only displays the values you select for each filter.

■ Merging Workbook Changes

Sharing workbooks and tracking changes made to those workbooks is all well and good, but what if you don't have a network over which to share the workbooks? Or what if someone needs to travel and work on a shared

Figure 19.12

The History workbook lets you see a listing of the changes.

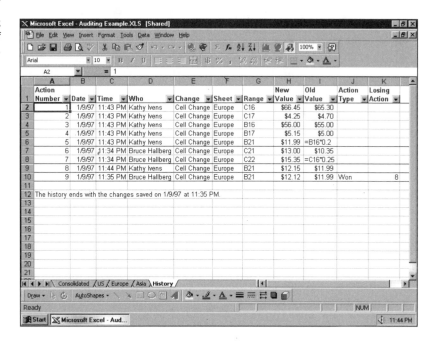

Action Number	Date	Time	Who	Change	Sheet	Range	New Value	Old Value	Action Type	Losing Action
1	1/9/97	11:43 PM	Kathy Ivens	Cell Change	Europe	C16	$66.45	$65.30		
2	1/9/97	11:43 PM	Kathy Ivens	Cell Change	Europe	C17	$4.25	$4.70		
3	1/9/97	11:43 PM	Kathy Ivens	Cell Change	Europe	B16	$56.00	$55.00		
4	1/9/97	11:43 PM	Kathy Ivens	Cell Change	Europe	B17	$5.15	$5.00		
5	1/9/97	11:43 PM	Kathy Ivens	Cell Change	Europe	B21	$11.99	=B16*0.2		
6	1/9/97	11:34 PM	Bruce Hallberg	Cell Change	Europe	C21	$13.00	$10.35		
7	1/9/97	11:34 PM	Bruce Hallberg	Cell Change	Europe	C22	$15.35	=C16*0.25		
8	1/9/97	11:44 PM	Kathy Ivens	Cell Change	Europe	B21	$12.15	$11.99		
9	1/9/97	11:35 PM	Bruce Hallberg	Cell Change	Europe	B21	$12.12	$11.99	Won	8

The history ends with the changes saved on 1/9/97 at 11:35 PM.

workbook: you want to incorporate their changes when they return, but you also need to let others use the shared workbook during their absence?

The answer to these problems is the Merge Workbooks command in the Tools menu. This command lets you merge copies of shared workbooks back into the original file. The copies can be used on remote computers, and then their changes can be merged back into the original.

To set this process up, you first must set the workbook as shared. Then, on the Advanced tab of the Share Workbook dialog box, make sure that the number of days over which changes are tracked is high enough so that the other copies of the workbook will be merged before the time expires. You must do this: if you're only tracking changes for 30 days, you can't merge a copy of the work into a workbook created 31 days ago.

After you've done this, you can save copies of the shared workbook using the File, Save As command. Save the shared workbook to a file with a different name, and then that new file can be used and modified remotely while the original stays in use.

When you receive the remote copy back and need to merge its changes into the main workbook, follow these steps:

1. Open the original workbook.

2. Choose Merge Workbooks from the Tools menu. The original workbook will be saved, after which you will see the Select Files to Merge into Current Workbook dialog box (it's identical to the File Open dialog box).

3. Select the copy of the shared workbook that you want to merge and click the OK button.

4. All of the changes in the merged workbook will be merged into the original automatically at this point. If any conflicts arise, you'll see the normal conflict-resolution dialog box and can use it to resolve them.

■ Setting Document Properties

One of the tricks to making effective use of Excel in a shared environment is using the file properties to track information about a particular file. With these properties, you can track items such as the following:

• Author

• Subject

• Keywords

• Comments

• Custom properties, such as editor, client name, and a host of other choices

To access the file's properties, pull down the File menu and choose Properties. The Summary tab will contain the main tracking information, as shown in Figure 19.13.

Fill in the information in the Properties tab, which can be referred to later when you need to understand details about the file.

Excel also includes a host of custom file properties. These are found in the Custom tab of the Properties dialog box (see Figure 19.14). Some of these can be quite useful.

Access the custom properties using the Name list box—there are more than 25 different properties available to you. After choosing a custom property, choose its data type from the Type drop-down list (choose from Text, Number, Date, or Yes/No). Next, type the information into the Value field. Finally, click on the Add button to store the property. Existing properties appear in the Properties window.

Figure 19.13

You can save summary information about the files you work on in the Summary tab.

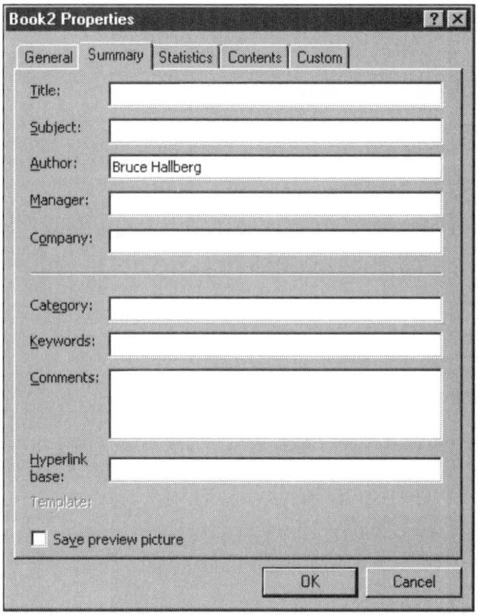

Figure 19.14

Use custom properties to track more detailed information about your files.

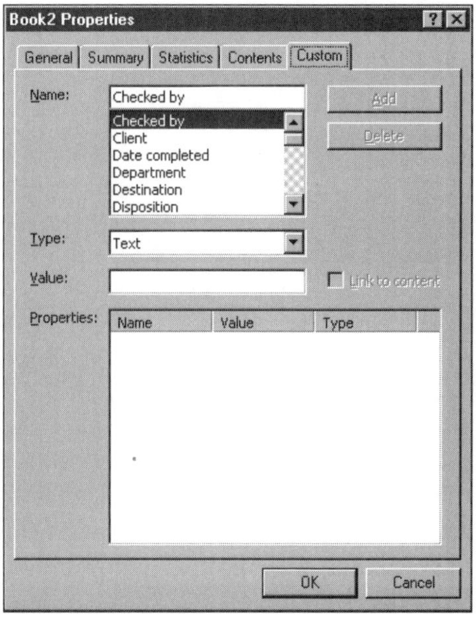

You can develop some more complicated mechanisms using the Link to Content check box. When it is selected, you can link a property to data contained in the file itself. For example, you can reference named cells in Excel, or bookmarks in Word. You must define the named cells or bookmarks first, however. By linking a custom property to a named cell in Excel, for instance, you can then use the advanced search function in the File Open dialog box to search for the custom property, which contains the data found in the named cell. So, if you had a number of workbooks, each one with a different value in a named cell that is then referenced by a custom property, you could search for all of the workbooks that, say, have that cell's value set to a certain range of values.

■ Routing Files

If you use Microsoft Exchange or a similar, compatible e-mail system, you can route your Excel files to others via e-mail. You can access this feature by using the File, Send To, Routing Recipient command. You'll see the Routing Slip dialog box shown in Figure 19.15.

Figure 19.15

Use routing slips to easily distribute Excel files to others in the company.

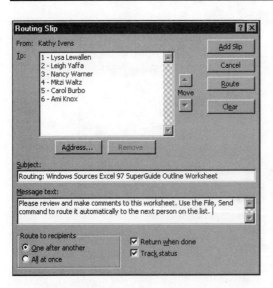

Add recipients using the Address button. Type a subject and a message text so that the recipients will know why they are getting the file, then, choose your routing method. You can choose to send the file to All at once or One after another. Selecting the Track Status check box causes an e-mail message to be automatically sent to you each time a recipient forwards the file on to the next person. You can also choose to have the file automatically sent back to you once the last person is finished with it.

After filling in the Routing Slip, choose the Add Slip button to store it, or the Send button to put the file into your e-mail outbox.

■ Maintaining Security

When working in a shared environment, protecting the security of your documents can be important. You can do this with your Excel files by using file-specific passwords.

To add a password to an Excel file, simply choose the Save As command from the File menu. Then, click on the Options button to reveal the dialog box shown in Figure 19.16.

Figure 19.16

Use the Save As Options dialog box to add password protection to your files.

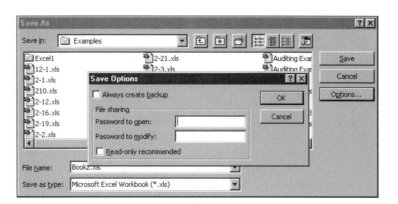

You can set two different passwords: Password to open and Password to modify. Password to open denies access to the file entirely unless the individual knows the password you have chosen. Password to modify lets anyone open the file in Read-only mode, but they can only make changes to the file if they know the proper password.

You can also specify that a file be Read-only recommended. If you select this check box, Excel will warn anyone who accesses the file to open it in Read-only mode. While they could go ahead and open it with full write access, this check box is a reminder from Excel to be careful in doing so.

■ Appendix A

■ Getting Excel Help

When you are learning and using Excel 97 for Windows, questions will inevitably arise, and your work will come to a screeching halt until you find answers. As a general rule, you should become familiar with where and how to find information before you really need it. This appendix uncovers all those places you can go for help, including the following:

- The Excel program (particularly the Office Advisor)
- Reference materials
- Online help
- Microsoft support

If you know where to look, you can get fast relief and proceed with your work as planned.

Experts estimate that as many as 98 percent of the people who call for software support already had the answers to their questions, either in the manuals that came with their programs or in their on-line help.

Why do so many people call for software support, then? With a large, complex program like Excel 97 for Windows, sometimes it's hard to know where to start looking for answers. In this appendix, we'll discuss various alternatives that are open to you for advice or help with Excel.

■ Getting Help for Excel

There are a number of places to turn for quick and easy answers to your Excel questions. Before calling (and paying for) telephone support, explore these options first. You'll save yourself time and money.

Using the Office Assistant

Office 97 includes a powerful new help tool called the Office Assistant. The Office Assistant uses artificial intelligence to help you more efficiently. By default, the Assistant is available whenever you start an Office application, although you can close it with its Close button. To open the Assistant when it's not visible, click on the Office Assistant button of any Office application's toolbar. You can see the default Assistant in Figure A.1.

Figure A.1

The default Office
Assistant

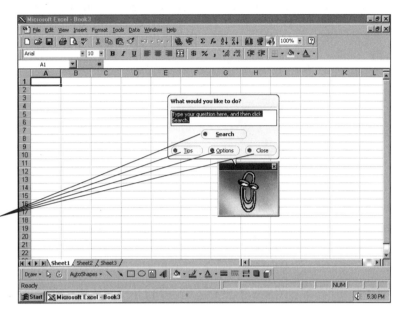

**The Office Assistant
button**

You can enter queries into the Office Assistant. To do so, simply click on the Office Assistant character, and the search window you see in Figure A.1 will appear. Type your question, and then click the Search button to see if relevant help topics pop up. You can phrase your question any way you like. Some examples of valid questions for the Office Assistant are:

- "Tell me about column widths"

- "How do I change column widths?"

- "Column widths"

- "I want skinny columns"

- "What about scrunching columns?"

All you really need to include in your query is the key word or phrase that describes what you want help with. If you don't receive help on the topic you want, try choosing a different word or phrase to describe what you want to do, or try typing something more specific. Normally, though, the Office Assistant is quite adept at figuring out what you want to know about from your query.

When you're using Excel with the Office Assistant open and you perform some action that it has a tip for you about, you'll see a light bulb appear near the Office Assistant character, as shown in Figure A.2. Clicking on the light bulb will bring up the tip.

Figure A.2

When the Assistant has a tip for you, a light bulb will appear.

TIP *The Office Assistant remembers the tips you've seen, and doesn't display them again. You can reset your tips by accessing the Office Assistant and choosing Options, and then choosing Reset my tips from the Options page of the Office Assistant dialog box.*

Choosing Your Assistant

A number of different Assistants are available for use with Excel 97. You can choose one that suits your personality and needs. To choose a new Office Assistant, access the Assistant by clicking on it, and then choose the Options button from the dialog bubble that appears. You'll see the Office Assistant dialog box appear. The Gallery page of the Office Assistant dialog box is shown in Figure A.3.

TIP *You can see different animations for the selected Assistant by right-clicking on the Assistant and choosing **Animate** from the pop-up menu. A random animation appears each time you do this.*

Scroll through the various Office Assistant choices with the Back and Next buttons. When you see one that you want to use, click the OK button to activate that Assistant. You may need your Excel 97 or Office 97 CD-ROM to install the Assistant you have selected. If so, you will be prompted for it automatically.

TIP *Some Office Assistants are more active then others—and while you may find its level of animation distracting, you may still want to use a particular Assistant. The Office Logo Assistant is the least active, while the Dot and PowerPup Assistants are most active.*

Figure A.3

The Gallery page of
the Office Assistant
dialog box

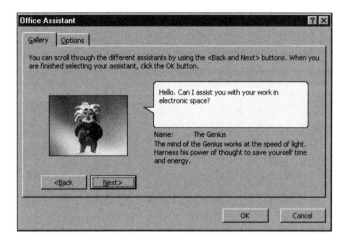

Changing Assistant Help Behavior

There are a variety of settings available to change the way the Office Assistant functions. You can access these settings by clicking on the Assistant, choosing the Options button, and then selecting the Options tab of the Office Assistant dialog box (see Figure A.4).

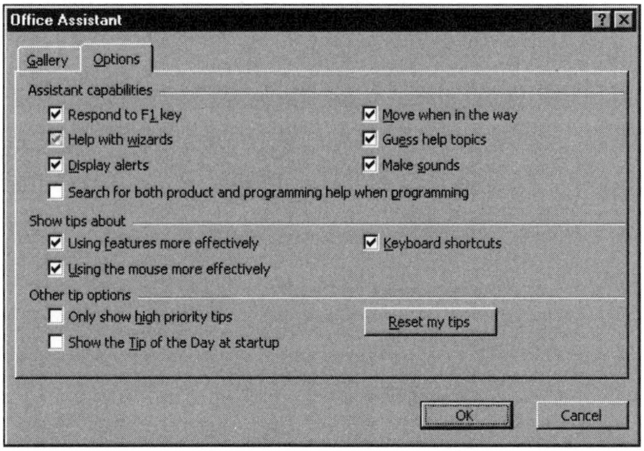

Figure A.4

The Options tab of
the Office Assistant
dialog box

Office Assistant   [?] [X]

Gallery | Options

Assistant capabilities
☑ Respond to F1 key   ☑ Move when in the way
☑ Help with wizards   ☑ Guess help topics
☑ Display alerts   ☑ Make sounds
☐ Search for both product and programming help when programming

Show tips about
☑ Using features more effectively   ☑ Keyboard shortcuts
☑ Using the mouse more effectively

Other tip options
☐ Only show high priority tips   [Reset my tips]
☐ Show the Tip of the Day at startup

[OK]   [Cancel]

The following options are available to you:

- **Respond to F1 key**. Selecting this causes the Office Assistant to appear whenever you press the F1 key (for help) in any Office application.

- **Help with Wizards.** When selected, the Assistant will appear whenever you start using most of the Wizards in Office 97 to offer additional help in using the Wizard.

- **Display alerts.** Causes the Assistant to display any alerts from Office applications.

- **Move when in the way.** This option lets you leave the Assistant on the screen, but keeps it out of your way when you're working. If this option is selected, the Assistant will shrink to a smaller size if not used in five minutes, and it will automatically move out of the way of any dialog boxes that you use.

- **Guess help topics.** If you choose this option, the Assistant will automatically show you help for your recent actions when you access the Assistant.

- **Make sounds.** Gives you additional feedback from the Assistant in the form of sounds. This option only works when you have a sound card installed in your PC.

- **Search for both product and programming help when programming.** If selected, the Assistant will provide help on programming, as well as help on the Visual Basic Development Environment, when you are programming in Visual Basic.

- **Show tips about.** This section of the dialog box lets you select the types of tips that the Office Assistant will display. You can choose tips on using application features more effectively, on using the mouse more effectively, and on keyboard shortcuts that make using Office faster.

- **Only show high priority tips.** Choosing this option causes the Assistant to only show you the most important tips, such as those that might make a large impact on your productivity.

- **Show the Tip of the Day at startup.** This option causes a tip to display whenever you open an Office application.

- **Reset my tips.** The Office Assistant remembers the tips you've seen, and won't display them again. Clicking this button clears its memory of the tips you've seen.

Other Excel Help

You can access help for specific parts of the screen, toolbar buttons, and so on, by clicking on the What's This? command in the Help menu (you can also press Shift+F1). After you choose the What's This? command, your cursor will change into a pointer with a question mark. Point to the part of Excel with which you want additional help, then click on the left mouse button. You can also use this method to choose menu commands to get help.

Using Excel Wizards

In Excel 97 for Windows, Microsoft has included Wizards for various functions. A Wizard (ChartWizard, PivotTable Wizard, Text Import Wizard, Conditional Sum Wizard, and so on) will start up automatically when you begin using the tool it accompanies. Each Excel Wizard is discussed in its appropriate place in this book. They help make Excel more "user-friendly" by walking you through different procedures step by step.

Reading the Manual

The manuals that come with Excel are actually quite good: they are well laid out and reasonably complete, unlike many software manuals. Their only real shortcoming is that some topics are not explained terribly well. The manuals are a great place to look when you have a question about Excel—if you can't find the answer in *this* book, of course!

Reading This Book

Windows Sources' Excel 97 SuperGuide is also a useful resource for you. This book is written and organized to deliver maximum reference value. See the Introduction for organization information, type conventions, and special icons. Whether you are a beginner, intermediate, or advanced Excel user, this book will provide a wide range of helpful information and valuable advice.

Getting Online Help

There are several places you can go online for help with Excel, including Microsoft's Excel Web pages, the Excel forum on CompuServe, and Excel discussion areas on other online services.

Getting Help on the Web

Microsoft provides a number of Internet shortcuts in Excel's Help menu. Access the Help menu, and choose Microsoft on the Web to display a submenu of Web pages that contain Excel help (see Figure A.5).

TIP *You can also use various Internet search engines to locate independently maintained Excel resources on the Internet. Try searching with "Excel 97" or just "Excel" on Alta Vista* **(http://www.altavista.digital.com)**, *Yahoo!*

Figure A.5

Microsoft on the Web submenu in Excel's Help menu provides quick links to Excel-related Web resources.

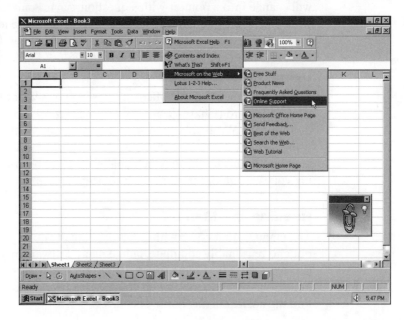

(http://www.yahoo.com), Excite (http://www.excite.com), or other search engines that you like.

Assuming that you have Internet access on your computer, choosing any of the links listed in the Microsoft on the Web submenu will take you directly to the pages listed. For the best help, try Frequently Asked Questions and Online Support. Also, you can find useful Excel files on the Free Stuff page.

Getting Excel Help on CompuServe

If none of the help resources already mentioned answers your questions, do not pick up the phone to call Microsoft's Excel help line just yet. Instead, pick up the phone and call *CompuServe Information Service* (CIS) to get a CompuServe account.

Nearly all large (or even moderately sized) software or hardware companies today provide help on CIS, and Microsoft is no exception. This support is a win-win situation—companies that have their own CIS forums find that it takes far fewer people to support *a lot* more users, and it costs you considerably *less* money to get support on CIS than it does to call the help line.

Understanding CompuServe

If you are not familiar with CIS, take a few minutes to read this section.

You can think of CompuServe as the world's largest computer *bulletin board system* (BBS). A real bulletin board contains messages to specific people and general information for everyone. CIS has everything a real bulletin board has and a whole lot more. In addition to the business-related forums, it has many hobby- and interest-related categories, as well as tremendous databases of information.

The cost to access CompuServe varies with the pricing plan you select, as well as the country in which you reside, but prices are quite competitive with other online services, such as America OnLine and The Microsoft Network.

NOTE *You can greatly reduce your CompuServe costs by using an automatic navigation program. An* autonav *program can go online and offline very quickly, picking up most of the information you need at full speed—because you told it what to get before it went online. Most autonav programs are available for downloading from CompuServe, although they are published independently. Good programs to evaluate include OzCIS, TapCIS, CISOP, and CsNAV, to name a few, although there are other good ones. If you decide to keep and use one of these shareware programs, you need to register it and pay the software company that provided it.*

The best part about CompuServe is that it's usually only a local telephone call away. Every major city, and lots and lots of smaller ones, has a CompuServe node.

In addition to accessing CompuServe and all it has to offer, you can do the following:

- Send and receive Internet, MCI, and MHS mail.

- Send postal letters (which later are printed at certain CompuServe locations and mailed as regular US postal mail).

- Send faxes.

- Access Internet World Wide Web pages, Usenet news and mail groups, and much more

CompuServe provides many different services. Some of these services cost a little extra.

Getting Started on CompuServe

You can open a CompuServe account in a number of ways, as follows:

- Contact a friend who already has a CompuServe account—your friend will receive free hours online for referring you, and you will also receive a usage credit for signing up.

- Call CompuServe Information Service at (800) 848-8990 or (614) 529-6887.

- Browse your local computer software store for a box that says "CompuServe" on the side. It contains all the information and software you need to go online and get started immediately.

- Look for free CompuServe disks in your favorite computer and general-interest magazines.

NOTE *As soon as you get a CompuServe account, go to the Practice area (**GO PRACTICE**) to practice posting and reading messages. This forum is free of connect time charges, so that you do not have to pay to learn. You can also find some useful information in the libraries there (libraries are discussed later in this appendix).*

Setting Up Your Computer

All you need to use CompuServe is a modem attached to your computer and your telephone. If you do not already have a CompuServe access program, you will also need some communications software, which you can find in any computer retail store or catalog. That's it!

Talking to Microsoft on CompuServe

If you have other Microsoft programs, you'll be happy to know that there are forums on CompuServe devoted to Microsoft products, many of which are monitored by Microsoft employees. To get to the top-level menu of all the Microsoft-specific services on CompuServe, use CompuServe's GO command and use **MICROSOFT** as the destination.

Three main areas in the Microsoft forum provide the support you need for getting help with Excel. These areas are discussed in the next three sections.

Accessing the Excel Forum

Each forum on CompuServe is divided into several sections to better categorize questions and answers and the conversations that occur. At the time this book was written, the Excel forum sections were set up as shown in Figure A.6.

NOTE *To go directly to the Excel forum on CompuServe, use the GO command and MSEXCEL as the destination.*

You can see that the sections are oriented towards answering different categories of questions. Find the category that fits your problem or question, and post a message there. In case you're wondering, the numbers to the right of the message sections indicate the number of topics, or *message threads* (conversations) on the message board, followed by the total number of messages in that section.

Figure A.6

The Microsoft Excel
Forum Message Sections

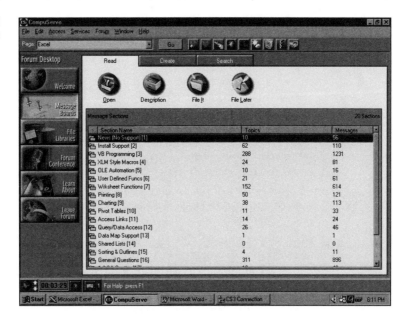

Be sure to check the section you want to view or post a message to
before you post your message, simply to save the sysop (system operator, or
overseer of the forum) some time and to help you get a speedier reply.

If you need to post a question on the message board, keep the following
guidelines in mind:

- **Be polite.** Even if you are frustrated, keep your temper in check. That
  old adage "You can catch more flies with honey than with vinegar"
  applies just as much on CompuServe as it does anywhere else. People
  are more willing to be helpful if you are courteous.

- **Once is enough.** Do not post the same message more than once on a
  forum. If your message is in the wrong place, the sysop will move it to
  the correct message section or let you know where you might post the
  message for a better response. Remember that people do not like to pay
  to download or read the same message more than once.

- **Be concise.** Provide all the pertinent information, but do not wander
  from the point too much. For instance, including such items as "I stayed
  up for 82 hours straight trying to solve this problem" does not help in
  providing people with the information they need to answer your question. You should include the following information in your message:

  - The version of Excel you are using.

- Your operating system (DOS, OS/2, and so on) and version number.

- Your hardware manufacturer and model.

- The keystrokes that you used just prior to having a problem (if applicable). Try to reproduce the problem before you report it.

- If you receive an error message, write down the *exact* wording so that you can include it in your message.

Most forums try to provide answers within 24 hours. Some questions are answered in a matter of an hour or two, and most are answered within the targeted 24-hour period. Do not despair, however, if your question is not answered immediately.

In addition to the sysops, a lot of knowledgeable people tend to "hang out" on the forums (including many of the people involved in writing and producing this book). If your question is answered by someone other than a Microsoft employee, chances are fairly high that the person is well-informed. Very rarely will you receive incorrect answers or bad advice in these particular areas of CompuServe. Because the messages are visible to anyone with a CompuServe account, other people will often correct posted information that they know is wrong.

NOTE *One of the things that makes a support forum on CompuServe so viable is that advice to one person can be read by all people who choose to read the messages. If you pay attention to what other people are asking, you might not need to post your own question, because it might have already been asked and answered. You might also be able to avoid some pitfalls or mistakes by reading what others are doing.*

Using the Microsoft Knowledge Base

You might not even need to post a question on Microsoft's Excel forum if you utilize Microsoft's Knowledge Base, which you can also access over CompuServe. The Knowledge Base is a special database that formerly was available only to Microsoft Technical Support personnel—the people you talk to when you call Microsoft Support. Now you can use it in your own home or office at no cost over and above the regular CompuServe charges.

To get to the Microsoft Knowledge Base on CompuServe, simply use the GO command with MSKB as the destination, or select it from the Microsoft main menu (**GO MICROSOFT**).

TIP *You can also access the Excel Knowledge Base on the Internet by choosing Online Support on Excel's Help menu, which takes you to the main Excel support page on the Web, and then clicking the Knowledge Base button.*

Finding Other Files

CompuServe is rich with all types of resources, including many shareware programs, add-ons, and files. (*Shareware* is try-it-before-you-buy-it software—Excel is *not* shareware, although many of the tools available for download from CIS are.)

CompuServe's Windows File Finder is the central place to go to find out where all the Excel shareware files might be found. Type **GO WINFF** to get there, and start with a keyword search of "EXCEL." You'll need to have additional selection criteria in mind, because so many files related to Excel exist. As of the date of this book, a keyword search for EXCEL in Filefinder found 899 files that had the word "Excel" as a keyword.

Again, this area of CompuServe cannot be auto-navigated, so be sure to have some idea of what you are looking for before you go there.

Dealing with Crashes

If Excel is "crashing"—the program ends abruptly or Windows reports an error message—there are a couple of things you should try before calling for help. Sometimes Excel workbooks get corrupted, such that the information in the file isn't the same as what Excel wrote to the file. Files can sometimes become damaged on diskettes, when sent over networks or modem lines, or even by being stored on a defective area of your hard disk. It's not common, but it can happen to files in any program.

If Excel is terminating abruptly when you open a particular workbook or try some action on a particular workbook, first try duplicating the problem in a fresh workbook. Many times you'll find that the problem disappears in a new workbook. If this is the case, the old one is probably corrupted and should be replaced. Also, if Excel terminates abruptly, try restarting Windows before deciding that the Excel workbook is bad: the problem could be caused by something else wrong in Windows' memory, perhaps even caused by another program you recently used.

When you find an Excel workbook that's gone bad for some reason, you might be able to copy and paste your data into a new workbook. This seems to work about half of the time. If this doesn't work, try copying different ranges from the bad workbook to a new one; the problem may only be in one area of the workbook. Of course, you should have backups of your system, so you might be able to restore an earlier, undamaged version of the workbook from before the time that you experienced the problem.

Another trick that sometimes works to recover data from bad workbooks is saving the worksheets out to a different file format, and then reopening them. For instance, you might try saving your worksheets into Lotus 1-2-3 WK1 format and then reopening the WK1 files. You'll lose your formatting, but you might be able to recover your data this way. Also, if your data has no formulas or other special worksheet features within it, try exporting to CSV (Comma-Separated Value) format and then reloading the data into a fresh workbook.

With a little patience, and some trial and error, you can often recover data from workbooks-gone-bad.

Calling Microsoft

If you still have not found the answer to your question in the Microsoft Excel help system, Office Assistant, manual, or this book, and you cannot find what you are looking for on the Web or on CompuServe (which is very unlikely), you should call Microsoft for support.

NOTE *Before you call Microsoft, take a look at the Common Questions in the help files, as well as the README file that was installed with Excel. You might be able to save yourself some time and money by finding the answers you need there.*

As when composing CompuServe help requests, make sure you have the following information handy before you call Microsoft support:

- The version of Excel you are using, along with your serial number, which you can find in the Excel box or by accessing About Microsoft Excel from the Help menu.

- Your operating system and version number.

- Your hardware manufacturer and model.

- The keystrokes you used just prior to having a problem (if applicable). Try to reproduce the problem before you report it.

- If you receive an error message, write down the exact wording so that you can include it in your message.

Microsoft has two calling plans. Each one costs a lot more money and takes more time than any of the options listed previously.

Accessing Free Support

Between the hours of 6:00 a.m. and 6:00 p.m. Pacific time, Microsoft has a free support line available at (206) 635-7070—there's no charge for the service, but unless you live in the Redmond, Wash. area, you will have to pay long-distance phone charges. Because this number offers free support, you should expect to spend a fair amount of time on hold. You'll hear status messages regarding the average time spent waiting, so you can judge whether to stay on the line or try again later.

Accessing Paid Support

Microsoft offers "priority access" support 24 hours a day, seven days a week, excluding holidays. The numbers vary depending on the payment plan you choose. Here are the numbers:

- (900) 555-2000. The cost is $2 per minute ($25 maximum), and the charges will appear on your telephone bill.

- (800) 936-5700. The charge is $25 per "incident" and can be billed to your VISA, MasterCard, or American Express.

An "incident" means a specific problem or question. If it cannot be taken care of with one telephone call, no additional fee will be charged for additional calls until the problem is resolved.

NOTE *If you want to tell Microsoft what you would like to see in the next version of Excel, then you need to call (206) 936-WISH.*

Using Other Telephone Support

Microsoft offers telephone support to people with special needs. If you have hearing difficulties, you can call Microsoft's text telephone (TT/TDD) at (206) 635-4948 between 6:00 a.m. and 6:00 p.m. Pacific time, Monday through Friday (excluding holidays).

To request support documents via fax, and to receive recorded answers to commonly asked questions, you can dial Microsoft's FastTips telephone number at (800) 936-4100, 24 hours a day, seven days a week. You also can receive articles concerning technical subjects (solving installation problems, resolving compatibility problems, and so on) via the FastTips line.

Finding Excel Training

If you are really stumped about all this Excel business, you might want to consider some formal training courses. In addition to local PC stores that offer training, Microsoft has officially sanctioned certain courses and training centers around the United States and elsewhere. Call (800) 636-7544 between 6:30 a.m. and 5:30 p.m. Pacific time to find out about the location nearest you.

■ Closing Advice

As you can see by browsing this appendix, lots of help options are open to you when you are working with Excel. To overcome likely problems, keep the following advice in mind when you are working with any software program:

- **Be patient.** Expect to take some time to look through this book, the help files in the Excel program, and the manuals. Excel is a large, complex program, and it might take some time and experimentation to find the right answers.

- **Take frequent breaks.** It does not matter whether you walk your kids or pet your dog, but make sure to take frequent breaks. You will be better off in the long run.

- **Take small steps.** Try one thing at a time—do not make lots of changes all at the same time. Lots of changes can cause confusion, and can make a mess even worse. Overdoing it also makes it harder to retrace your steps if you have a crash or get an error message.

- **Look out for bugs.** Programmers are human, and humans do make mistakes. Although Excel is exceptionally clean compared to many software programs, you might run into an occasional problem that is rooted in the program itself. Again, patience is the key here. If you think you have found a software bug, it is very important that you write down all the information concerning the bug and report it to Microsoft. Often they have fixes for those bugs that have already been reported, and can send the fix to you or tell you how to download it.

- **Perform regular backups of your data to protect against a variety of possible mishaps.** Computers can and do break, and sometimes lose data. Also, you might make a mistake and save your workbook not realizing the mistake you made. The ability to restore your data and files from an earlier version protects you against loss, and provides you with a safety net.

- **Have fun!** Remember, the future of Western civilization is not at stake here. Maintain your perspective.

■ Appendix B

■ Keyboard Shortcuts

This appendix contains a number of useful keyboard shortcuts. Learning these key commands can make you more productive with Excel. Use the following tables as a handy reference guide.

Tables B.1 through B.3 list the keys you will use to enter and edit data. These key commands make it easier to navigate your documents, access the Clipboard, and control calculations in your documents. You'll use some shortcuts more often than others.

Table B.1

Entering Data

KEY OR KEY COMBINATION	ACTION
F2	Edits the current cell
Enter	Completes an action
Esc	Cancels an act
F4	Repeats the last act (Redo)
Ctrl+Z	Undoes the last act (Undo)
Ctrl+Shift++ (plus sign)	Inserts new blank cells
Ctrl+- (hyphen)	Deletes the selected object or cells
Del	Clears the selected area of formulas and data; when editing a cell, deletes the character to the right of the current cursor position
Ctrl+X	Cuts the selection
Ctrl+C	Copies the selection
Ctrl+V	Pastes to the selection
Backspace	Edits the formula after clearing the cell entry, or backspaces over a character; when editing a cell, erases the previous character
Shift+F2	Edits a cell comment
F3	Pastes a name into a formula
Shift+F3	Activates the Paste Function dialog box

Table B.1 (Continued)

Entering Data

KEY OR KEY COMBINATION	ACTION
Ctrl+F3	Defines a name
Ctrl+Shift+F3	Creates names from cell text
F9 or Ctrl+= (equal sign)	Calculates all documents in all open workbooks; if you highlight a section, calculates only that section
Shift+F9	Calculates the active document
Alt+=	Inserts the AutoSum formula
Ctrl+; (semicolon)	Enters the date
Ctrl+Shift+: (colon)	Enters the time
Ctrl+D	Fills down
Ctrl+R	Fills right
Enter	Moves down through a selection
Shift+Enter	Moves up through a selection
Tab	Moves right through a selection
Shift+Tab	Moves left through a selection
Ctrl+Shift+A	Completes the punctuation for you when you first type a valid function name into a formula
Alt+Down arrow	Activates the AutoComplete list

Table B.2

Editing Data

KEY OR KEY COMBINATION	ACTION
Ctrl+X	Cuts the selection to the Clipboard
Ctrl+C	Copies the selection to the Clipboard
Ctrl+V	Pastes the selection from the Clipboard
Del	Clears the selection of formulas and data
Ctrl+Shift++	Inserts blank cells
Ctrl+-	Deletes the selected calls
Ctrl+Z	Undoes the last act

Table B.3

Working in Cell Entries

KEY OR KEY COMBINATION	ACTION
=	Starts a formula
Alt+Enter	Inserts a carriage return
Arrow keys	Moves one character up, down, left, or right
Backspace	Deletes the character to the left of the insertion point, or deletes the selection
Ctrl+' (apostrophe)	Copies the formula from the cell above the active cell into the current cell
Ctrl+' (single quote)	Alternates between displaying results or formulas in cells
Ctrl+A	Displays the Function Wizard, if a valid function name is typed in a cell
Ctrl+Alt+Tab	Inserts a tab
Ctrl+Delete	Cuts text to the end of the line
Ctrl+Enter	Fills a selection of cells with the current entry: Select the cells, type the information, then press Ctrl+Enter
Ctrl+Shift+"	Copies the value from the cell above the active cell into the current cell
Ctrl+Shift+:	Inserts the time
Ctrl+Shift+Enter	Enters the formula as an array formula
Del	Deletes the character to the right of the cursor, or deletes the entire selection
Enter	Completes a cell entry
Esc	Cancels an entry
F2	Edits cell entry
F4	Toggles current reference between absolute and relative references
Home	Moves to the start of a line
Shift+Tab	Stores the cell entry and moves to the previous cell in the row or range
Tab	Stores the cell entry and moves to the next cell in the row or range

The workbook metaphor in Excel creates the need for key shortcuts you can use to move between your workbook documents. Table B.4 shows the keys that accomplish these moves, as well as the keys for navigating among and within open Excel windows.

Table B.4

Moving In and Between Documents

KEY OR KEY COMBINATION	ACTION
Alt+PgDn	Moves right one screen
Alt+PgUp	Moves left one screen
Arrow key	Moves one cell in the direction of the arrow key pressed
Ctrl+6	Toggles between hiding objects, displaying objects, and displaying placeholders for graphic objects
Ctrl+7	Toggles the Standard toolbar
Ctrl+A	Selects the entire worksheet
Ctrl+Down arrow	Moves down to the edge of any filled cells or to end of document
Ctrl+End	Moves to the lower-right corner of the worksheet
Ctrl+Home	Moves to cell A1
Ctrl+Left arrow	Moves left to the edge of any filled cells
Ctrl+PgDn	Moves to the next sheet in the workbook
Ctrl+PgUp	Moves to the previous sheet in the workbook
Ctrl+Right arrow	Moves right to the edge of any filled cells, or by one screen width
Ctrl+Shift+* (asterisk)	Selects the current region (contiguous filled cells)
Ctrl+Shift+Arrow key	Extends the selection to the edge of any contiguous filled cells in the direction of the arrow key pressed
Ctrl+Shift+End	Extends the selection to the lower-right corner of the worksheet
Ctrl+Shift+Home	Extends the selection to the beginning of the worksheet
Ctrl+Shift+Spacebar	With an object selected, selects all objects on a sheet
Ctrl+Spacebar	Selects the entire column or all columns for the current selection
Ctrl+Up arrow	Moves up to the edge of the current data region
Home	Moves to the beginning of the row (Column A)

**Table B.4
(Continued)**

Moving In and Between
Documents

KEY OR KEY COMBINATION	ACTION
PgDn	Moves down one screen
PgUp	Moves up one screen
Scroll Lock	Turns scroll lock on or off
Shift+Arrow key	Extends the selection by one cell in the direction of the arrow key pressed
Shift+Backspace	Collapses the selection to the active cell
Shift+Home	Extends selection to the beginning of the row
Shift+End	Extends selection to the end of the row
Shift+PgDn	Extends the selection down one screen
Shift+PgUp	Extends the selection up one screen
Shift+Spacebar	Selects the entire row
Tab	Moves among the unlocked cells in a protected worksheet

Excel contains a special shortcut-key mode called End mode, which you can enter by pressing the End key. When End mode is active, the END indicator appears on the right side of the status bar. Use the keys listed in Table B.5 to jump around your document in ways that you cannot when using other shortcut keys.

Table B.5

End Mode Keys

KEY OR KEY COMBINATION	ACTION
End	Turns End mode on or off
End,Arrow key	Moves by one block of data within a row or column
End,Enter	Moves to the last filled cell in the current row
End,Home	Moves to the lower right corner of the worksheet
End,Shift+Arrow key	Extends the selection to the end of the data block in the direction of the arrow
End,Shift+Enter	Extends the selection to the last cell in the current row
End,Shift+Home	Extends the selection to the lower-right corner of the worksheet

Similar to End mode, Excel also allows you to enter a different keyboard mode when you activate the Scroll Lock key. To use any of the keys in Table B.6, make sure Scroll Lock is on.

KEY OR KEY COMBINATION	ACTION
End	Moves to the lower-right cell in the window
Home	Moves to the upper-left cell in the window
Left or right arrow	Scrolls the screen left or right by one column
Shift+End	Extends the selection to the lower-right cell in the window
Shift+Home	Extends the selection to the upper-left cell in the window
Up or down arrow	Scrolls the screen up or down by one row

Primarily used for data entry, the keys listed in Table B.7 show you how to move around a data-entry area—any series of cells that you have selected before entering data.

KEY OR KEY COMBINATION	ACTION
Enter	Moves from top to bottom within the selection
Shift+Enter	Moves from bottom to top within the selection
Tab	Moves from left to right within the selection; if at far right in selection, wraps to left side of next row
Shift+Tab	Moves from right to left within the selection or to the far right of the previous row
Ctrl+. (period)	Moves clockwise to the next corner of the selection

The shortcut keys listed in Table B.8 do not really fall into any single category, but instead are miscellaneous Excel key shortcuts that you will rarely use. When you do need them, however, they can really come in handy. Of particular interest are the shortcuts that use the left and right brackets ([or]). These keys select cells that contribute to the active cell or that rely on the data in the active cell.

Table B.8

Special Cells

KEY OR KEY COMBINATION	ACTION
Ctrl+Shift+? (question mark)	Selects all cells that contain comments
Ctrl+Shift+*	Selects a range of filled cells around the active cell
Ctrl+/ (forward slash)	Selects the entire array, if any, to which the active cell belongs
Ctrl+[(left bracket)	Selects all cells that are referred to by the formula in the selected cell
Ctrl+Shift+{ (left brace)	Selects all cells directly or indirectly referred to by cells in the selection
Ctrl+] (right bracket)	Selects all cells whose formulas refer to the active cell
Ctrl+Shift+} (right brace)	Selects all cells that directly or indirectly refer to the active cell
Ctrl+\ (backward slash)	Selects cells with contents that are different from the selected cell in current column
Ctrl+Shift+I (vertical bar)	Selects cells with contents that are different from the selected cell in each column
Alt+;	Selects all visible cells in the current selection

The shortcuts listed in Table B.9 are not Excel shortcut keys, but are Windows shortcuts that you might also find helpful when working in Excel.

Table B.9

Switching Windows

KEY OR KEY COMBINATION	ACTION
Alt+Esc	Moves to next application
Alt+Shift+Esc	Moves to previous application
Alt+Tab	Shows the next Windows application
Alt+Shift+Tab	Shows the previous Windows application
Ctrl+Esc	Activates the Windows Task List
Ctrl+F4	Closes document
Ctrl+F5	Restores window size

KEY OR KEY COMBINATION	ACTION
Ctrl+F6	Moves to next window
Ctrl+Shift+F6	Moves to previous window
Ctrl+F7	Move window command
Ctrl+F8	Size window command
Ctrl+F9	Minimizes window
Ctrl+F10	Maximizes window

Excel power users quickly learn that using the mouse actually slows them down. Having to move your hands away from the keyboard is an impediment to speed. If you are trying to use your mouse as little as possible, use the keys in Table B.10 instead to navigate Excel (or Windows) dialog boxes.

KEY OR KEY COMBINATION	ACTION
Tab	Moves to the next section in the dialog box
Shift+Tab	Moves to the previous section in the dialog box
Arrow key	Moves within the section of the dialog box (radio buttons, list boxes)
Spacebar	Selects the active button
Any letter key	Moves to the item beginning with that letter in an active list box
Alt+any letter key	Selects the item with that underlined letter (hot keys)
Enter	Chooses the default command button (it will be surrounded with a thick black line)
Esc	Cancels the dialog box

Most people spend quite a bit of time formatting their worksheets. The keys in Table B.11 are useful for performing a variety of quick formatting tasks.

Table B.11

Formatting Data

KEY OR KEY COMBINATION	ACTION
Alt+' (apostrophe)	Activates the Style dialog box
Ctrl+Shift+~ (tilde)	Applies the General number format
Ctrl+Shift+$ (dollar sign)	Applies the currency format with two decimal places
Ctrl+Shift+% (percent sign)	Applies the percentage format
Ctrl+Shift+^ (carat)	Applies the exponential number format
Ctrl+Shift+# (pound sign)	Applies the standard date format
Ctrl+Shift+@ (at sign)	Applies the standard time format
Ctrl+Shift+& (ampersand)	Applies the outline border
Ctrl+Shift+_ (underscore)	Removes all borders
Ctrl+B	Toggles bold
Ctrl+I	Toggles italic
Ctrl+U	Toggles underline
Ctrl+5	Toggles strikethrough
Ctrl+9	Hides rows
Ctrl+Shift+((open parenthesis)	Unhides rows
Ctrl+0 (zero)	Hides columns
Ctrl+Shift+) (close parenthesis)	Unhides columns

If you are using the Excel outlining features, you can rely on the shortcuts in Table B.12 to help you quickly promote and unhide selected outline groups.

Table B.12

Outlining

KEY OR KEY COMBINATION	ACTION
Alt+Shift+Left Arrow	Ungroups a row or a column
Alt+Shift+Right Arrow	Groups a row or a column
Ctrl+8	Displays or hides the outline symbols

Outlining

KEY OR KEY COMBINATION	ACTION
Ctrl+9	Hides selected rows
Ctrl+Shift+(	Unhides selected rows
Ctrl+0 (zero)	Hides selected columns
Ctrl+Shift+)	Unhides selected columns

Table B.13 lists keys you use to work with AutoFilter in your database files.

Table B.13

Shortcut Keys for AutoFilter

KEY OR KEY COMBINATION	ACTION
Alt+Down arrow	Displays list for selected column label
Alt+Up arrow	Closes list for current column
Up arrow	Chooses previous item in list
Down arrow	Chooses next item in list
Home	Selects first item in list
End	Selects last item in list
Enter	Filters the list using selected item

Table B.14 lists the keys you will use when working with the PivotTable Wizard.

Table B.14

Shortcut Keys for PivotTable Wizard

KEY OR KEY COMBINATION	ACTION
Alt+P	Moves selected field to page area
Alt+R	Moves selected field to row area
Alt+C	Moves selected field to column area
Alt+D	Moves selected field to data area
Alt+L	Shows PivotTable field dialog box
Alt+Down arrow	Displays page field list

Table B.14 (Continued)

Shortcut Keys for PivotTable Wizard

KEY OR KEY COMBINATION	ACTION
Alt+Up arrow	Closes page field list
Alt+Shift+Right arrow	Groups selected PivotTable items
Alt+Shift+Left arrow	Ungroups selected PivotTable items

Table B.15 lists keys you can use to control printing your selection and to navigate the Print Preview function.

Table B.15

Printing and Print Previewing

KEY OR KEY COMBINATION	ACTION
Ctrl+P	Activates the Print dialog box
Arrow keys	Moves around page when zoomed in
Up or down arrow	Moves by one page when zoomed out
PgUp, PgDn	Moves by one page when zoomed out

Sometimes you might have trouble selecting certain chart items. The item you want might be very small or too close to another chart item. When this problem arises, switch to the keys in Table B.16 for assistance.

Table B.16

Selecting Chart Items

KEY OR KEY COMBINATION	ACTION
Down arrow	Selects the previous group of items
Up arrow	Selects the next group of items
Right arrow	Selects the next item within the group
Left arrow	Selects the previous item within the group

Most Windows users will already be familiar with the keystrokes used to speed up working with menus. Take a quick look at Table B.17, however, to make sure that you are making full use of the shortcut keys available for navigating menus.

Table B.17

KEY OR KEY COMBINATION	ACTION
Alt or F10	Activates the menu bar
Shift+F10	Activates the shortcut menu
Alt+Backspace or Ctrl+Z	Undoes the last command
F4	Repeats the last command
Esc or Ctrl+. (period)	Cancels the menu
Spacebar	Displays Control menu
Letter key	Selects the menu or option that contains the underlined letter
Left or right arrow	Selects the menu to the left or right
Down or up arrow	Selects the next or previous command on the menu
Enter	Chooses the selected command
Down or up arrow	Selects the next or previous command on the menu
Left or right arrow	Toggles selection between main menu and submenu

Use the shortcut keys in Table B.18 to access the most frequently used items in the Excel File menu.

Table B.18

KEY OR KEY COMBINATION	ACTION
Ctrl+N	New workbook
Ctrl+O	Open
Ctrl+S	Save
F12	Save As
Ctrl+P	Print
Alt+F4	Closes Excel

Use the shortcut keys in Table B.19 to access the most frequently used items in the Excel Edit menu.

Table B.19

Edit Menu Command Keys

KEY OR KEY COMBINATION	ACTION
Ctrl+Z	Undo
F4	Repeat
Ctrl+X	Cut
Ctrl+C	Copy
Ctrl+V	Paste
Ctrl+D	Fill Down
Ctrl+R	Fill Right
Delete	Clear Contents
Ctrl+-	Deletes the selected cells
Ctrl+F	Displays the Find dialog box
Ctrl+H	Displays the Replace dialog box
Ctrl+Shift+F	Find Next
Ctrl+Shift+E	Find Previous
F5	Go To

Use the keys shown in Table B.20 to quickly insert objects into your workbooks.

Table B.20

Insert Commands

KEY OR KEY COMBINATION	ACTION
Ctrl+Shift++	Activates Insert dialog box
Shift+F11	Inserts new worksheet
F11	Inserts new chart sheet
Ctrl+F11	Inserts new Excel 4.0 macro sheet
Ctrl+F3	Activates the Define Name dialog box
F3	Activates the Paste Name dialog box
Shift+Ctrl+F3	Activates the Create Names dialog box

Use the shortcuts in Table B.21 to access the most commonly used items in the Excel Format menu.

Table B.21

Format Menu Commands

KEY OR KEY COMBINATION	ACTION
Ctrl+1	Format Cells tabbed dialog box
Ctrl+9	Hide rows
Ctrl+Shift+(	Unhide rows
Ctrl+0 (zero)	Hide columns
Ctrl+Shift+)	Unhide columns
Alt+' (apostrophe)	Activates the Style dialog box

Although many of the keys listed in Table B.22 are also listed in other sections of this appendix, this table contains all the function-key shortcuts for easy reference.

Table B.22

Function Keys

KEY OR KEY COMBINATION	ACTION
F1	Help
Shift+F1	Help for current function
F2	Activates the formula bar
Shift+F2	Edit Note
Ctrl+F2	Info window
F3	Paste Name dialog box
Shift+F3	Function Wizard
Ctrl+F3	Define Name command
Ctrl+Shift+F3	Create command
F4	Toggles between relative and absolute references
Ctrl+F4	Closes the window
Alt+F4	Closes Excel

**Table B.22
(Continued)**

Function Keys

KEY OR KEY COMBINATION	ACTION
F5	Go To command
Ctrl+F5	Restores window size
F6	Next pane
Shift+F6	Previous pane
Ctrl+F6	Next window
Ctrl+Shift+F6	Previous window
F7	Checks spelling
Ctrl+F7	Move command
F8	Toggles Extend Mode
Shift+F8	Toggles Add mode
Ctrl+F8	Size command
F9	Calculates all
Shift+F9	Calculates active sheet
Ctrl+F9	Minimizes the workbook
F10	Activates the menu bar
Shift+F10	Activates the shortcut menu
Ctrl+F10	Maximizes the workbook
F11	Inserts new chart sheet
Shift+F11	Inserts new worksheet
Ctrl+F11	Inserts new Excel 4.0 macro sheet
F12	Save As command
Shift+F12	Save command
Ctrl+F12	Open command
Ctrl+Shift+F12	Print command

■ Index

Note: Numbers in italic denote figures or tables.

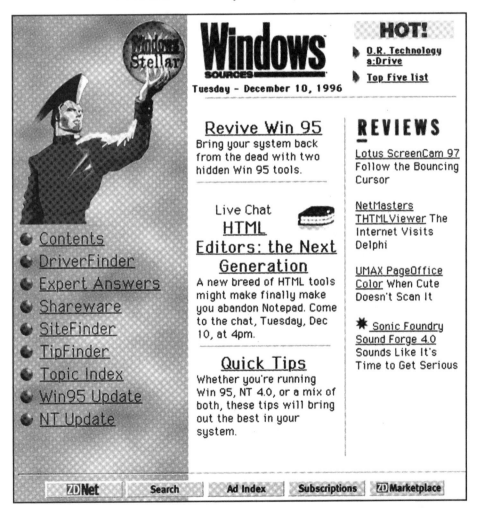